# Stage Design

# Stage

Donald Oenslager

A Studio Book

# Design

## Four Centuries of Scenic Invention

Illustrated with Drawings for
the Theatre from his Collection

The Viking Press     New York

Text and black-and-white illustrations Copyright © 1975 by
The Viking Press, Inc.
Color insert Copyright 1975 in all countries of the International
Copyright Union by The Viking Press, Inc.
All rights reserved
First published in 1975 by The Viking Press, Inc.
625 Madison Avenue, New York, N.Y. 10022
Published simultaneously in Canada by
The Macmillan Company of Canada Limited
SBN  670-66679-3
Library of Congress catalog card number: 74-6999
Color insert printed in Japan
Text and black-and-white illustrations printed in U.S.A.

# Contents

Preface 8

The Designer's Sketch 11

The Heritage of the Renaissance Theatre 13

The Greek Theatre 13  The Medieval Theatre 20
The Roman Theatre 17  The Renaissance Theatre 23

## Designers in the Theatre

Renaissance 27

Aristotile da Sangallo 28  Bartolomeo Neroni 32
Jan Vredeman de Vries 30  Giulio Parigi 36
Sebastiano Serlio 30

# Baroque and Rococo 42

| | | | |
|---|---|---|---|
| Giacomo Torelli | 43 | Vincenzo Re | 81 |
| Ferdiando Tacca | 46 | Giovanni Niccolò Servandoni | 84 |
| Cosimo Lotti | 47 | Charles Michel-Ange Challe | 86 |
| Ludovico Burnacini | 50 | Jacques de Lajoue | 88 |
| Tomaso Francini | 52 | Giuseppe Valeriani | 89 |
| Jean I Berain | 52 | Bernardo Belotto | 91 |
| Andrea Pozzo | 54 | The Quaglio Family | 92 |
| The Bibiena Family | 57 | The Galliari Family | 96 |
| Pietro Righini | 72 | Francesco Orlandi | 105 |
| Filippo Juvara | 76 | Carl Schutz | 107 |
| Jacopo Fabris | 78 | Jean George Köpp | 110 |
| Luigi Vanvitelli | 79 | | |

# Neoclassicism to Realism 111

| | | | |
|---|---|---|---|
| Pio Panfili | 112 | Percier and Fontaine | 156 |
| Pietro de Gaspari | 112 | Jean-Jacques Lequeu | 158 |
| Pietro Gonzaga | 113 | Pierre-Luc-Charles Cicéri | 158 |
| Francesco Chiaruttini | 116 | William Clarkson Stanfield | 160 |
| Domenico Fossati | 116 | Simon Quaglio | 160 |
| Bartolomeo da Verona | 117 | Angelo Quaglio II | 162 |
| Paolo Landriani | 121 | Zarra and Laloue | 167 |
| Lorenzo Sacchetti | 124 | H. Willbrandt | 167 |
| Josef Platzer and the Austrian School | 130 | Andreas Leonhard Roller | 168 |
| Antonio Basoli | 140 | Unknown American Artist, Nineteenth Century | 169 |
| Unknown English Artist, Eighteenth Century | 146 | Joseph Clare | 170 |
| Giuseppe Borsato | 147 | Carlo Ferrario | 173 |
| Giovanni Perego | 148 | Jean-Baptiste Lavastre | 176 |
| Alessandro Sanquirico | 149 | Auguste-Alfred Rubé | 178 |
| Giorgio Fuentes | 152 | Carpezat | 179 |
| Friedrich Beuther | 153 | Max Brückner | 180 |
| Karl Friedrich Schinkel | 155 | | |

# Modern 183

| | | | |
|---|---|---|---|
| Adolphe Appia | 184 | Léon Bakst | 196 |
| Edward Gordon Craig | 187 | Mstislav Doboujinsky | 198 |
| M. A. Schiskov | 191 | Serge Soudeikine | 200 |
| Konstantin Korovine | 192 | Natalia Gontcharova | 201 |
| Alexandre Benois | 193 | Aleksandra Exter | 202 |

Mihail Fedorovitch Andreenko     204
Nikolai Akimov                    208
N. N. Zolotaryov                  210
Andrej Majewski                   211
André Delfau                      212
Karl Walser                       214
Emil Orlik                        215
Alfred Roller                     216
Ernst Stern                       218
Ludwig Sievert                    220
Helmut Jürgens                    222
Ansel Cook                        224
Claude Bragdon                    224
Thomas G. Moses                   225

Erté (Romain de Tirtoff)          226
Joseph Urban                      228
Lee Simonson                      229
Norman Bel Geddes                 232
Robert Edmond Jones               234
Eugene Berman                     236
Pavel Tchelitchew                 238
Rex Whistler                      240
John Piper                        244
Jo Mielziner                      244
Boris Aronson                     248
Donald Oenslager                  249
Oliver Smith                      252
Ming Cho Lee                      254

Color Plates      255

Bibliography      291

Index      297

# Preface

This book is the result of a large part of a lifetime devoted to collecting and collating designs for the theatre. The collection reflects the variety and wealth of theatrical art produced by artists and architects of the western world during the past four hundred years. Some of the drawings are rough sketches or personal recordings of ideas for later use; some are executed with the detailed precision of architectural renderings. Many are working drawings showing alternate schemes for the same scene, intended for use by scene builders and painters, while others were designed for reproduction by engraving in published collections of a designer's oeuvre, as libretto illustrations, or as decorations for commemorative volumes of royal performances. Whatever their purpose, however, all were intended to be framed only by the proscenium, devised for a particular occasion—the production of a play, opera, or ballet. Each drawing, from those of Aristotile da Sangallo to the ones by contemporary working designers, records the germinal intention of an individual artist for a finished stage design. Beyond the varieties in style and the distances in time, each work reveals its creator's deep love of the world of the theatre and arouses our nostalgic and aesthetic curiosity for that mysterious, ever-fascinating world.

I have selected for illustration drawings from my collection that I hope will please the eye of the amateur, intrigue the imagination of the artist, and appeal to the inquiring mind of the theatre specialist or historian. Some of my attributions and hypotheses, tentatively set forth in the text and captions, may well be reconsidered in the light of future research, but my primary intention will, I hope, remain valid and valuable: to present in one volume a chronological narrative that mirrors the changing tastes and theatrical reforms of the stage from the Renaissance through the baroque and rococo eras, the neoclassic and romantic periods, to the revolutionary theatre of the twentieth century. In terms of draftsmanship, some of the designs are obviously the work of routine journeymen; others display incomparable peaks of technical scenic skill, while a few of the drawings are indeed works of art of the highest order. Together, as a collection, they form the branches of a glamorous family tree—four centuries of scenic invention.

I myself am a practicing designer, an artist who has always possessed a passionate enthusiasm to discover the language and to explore the ever-changing directions of my ancestral peers in the visual theatre—particularly those who have always been in revolt against the status quo, cracking the mold of tradition to establish new criteria of taste on ground they believed "firm as the firmament of heaven." No collection, even the world's most prestigious, is the sine qua non—the complete and perfect collection of any single area of human endeavor. The giants' wall of treasure in Wagner's *Das Rheingold* contains the fatal chink which, when filled, brings on the destruction of the treasure, and the process of collecting begins anew. It is the chinks, those things not present, those minuses and pluses of human choice, that give every collection its identity and personality.

The desire to accumulate is inherent in most of us. In my youth I was taken with an uncontrollable desire to horde anything and everything in sight. At some point along my way toward a problematic career in stage design, I came to recognize the validity of collecting drawings, prints, and illustrated books associated with the visual theatre. My first acquisition was a slightly torn Bibiena drawing which I found in a Munich print shop in 1923 during my *wanderjahr* in Europe following my graduation from Harvard. It cost all of sixty cents, and on the back of the drawing I discovered two eighteenth-century inscriptions which established it as an authentic Ferdinando Bibiena (see page 57). A few days later I chanced upon another treasure, also a bargain, a presentation copy of *Le Combat à la Barriére* produced in Nancy in 1637, complete with all the splendid plates of Jacques Callot. My collection had begun. Since those days, designing and collecting have gone hand in hand—work and pleasure supplementing and enriching one another.

I have always been grateful to those great teachers at Harvard, Paul Sachs, Denman Ross, Chandler R. Post, and George Pierce Baker, whose inspiration gave me direction in the theatre. As an undergraduate, I was thankful to Arthur Pope, who permitted me to conduct my own research course in the Fine Arts Department on the evolution of theatrical art from Athens to New York. While I was engaged in my modest labors, a generation of European researchers was already investigating and assimilating at first hand the wealth of theatrical source material they discovered in the libraries and museums of Europe. In England were Allardyce Nicoll, with his all-seeing eye, and Gordon Craig, with his artist's vision; in Germany, Carl Niessen, Franz Rapp, Rudolf Berliner, and Richard Bernheimer; Agne Beijer in Sweden; Corrado Ricci, Valerio Mariani, and Giulio Ferrario in Italy; and in Austria, Josef Gregor and Heinz Kindermann. And under Silvio d'Amico in Rome's Palazzo Venezia, a scholarly staff assembled for ten years theatrical material from all over the world which would eventually become the monumental ten-volume *Enciclopedia dello Spettacolo*, whose first volume would appear in 1954. To that generation of distinguished theatre historians, I acknowledge the deepest gratitude.

Over many years on my travels in Europe, I have visited many theatre collections in libraries and museums. I deeply appreciate their directors' and curators' generosity and enthusiasm in showing me their treasures and sharing their experience and knowledge—in Sweden, Agne Beijer of the Drottningholm Theatre Museum and Per Bjurström of the Royal Gallery in Stockholm; Josef Gregor of the Theatre Collection of the National Library of Vienna; Günter Schöne of the Theatre Museum in Munich and Helmut Grosse of the Theatre Institute in Cologne; Mercedes Viale Ferrero of the Museo Civico in Turin and Maria Teresa Muraro of the Cini Foundation in Venice; also, Carlo Enrico Rava of the Scala Museum and, in Rome, Elena Povoledo, and Enrico Mancini in Naples; André Veinstein of the Bibliotèque de l'Arsenal in Paris; in London, George Nash of the Victoria and Albert Theatre Collection and John Harris of the Royal Institute of Architects; in Russia, the staffs of the State Theatre Museum of Leningrad and of the Bakhrushin Theatre Museum in Moscow. To name them all would be impossible, but I am profoundly grateful to them all.

Over the years, as a faculty member of the Yale School of Drama, I have enjoyed the opportunity of learning from my friends and colleagues as well as from many of my former students who went on to establish their own centers of theatrical research in universities throughout the country. At Harvard, three distinguished old friends —Agnes Mongan, former director of the Fogg Art Museum, William Bond, librarian of the Houghton Library, and Philip Hofer, Curator Emeritus of the Department of Prints and Graphic Arts—have been ever mindful of my interests, and their generous cooperation has never failed me. Nor has the unerring eye of E. Haverkamp Begemann of the Yale Art Gallery. I am also grateful to Diane Kelder, Curator of Drawings at the Finch College Gallery, and to Richard Wunder, former Curator of Drawings at the Cooper Union Museum. The latter, with his perceptive eye, generously helped me with the attribution and cataloguing of many drawings. Felice Stampfle, Curator of Drawings and Prints at the Morgan Library, has tested her memory and always responded generously to my many questions. John McKendry, Curator of Prints, and Jacob Bean, Curator of Drawings, at the Metropolitan Museum of Art, have both been most helpful in making original material available to me. Finally, I am most grateful to A. Hyatt Mayor, Curator Emeritus of Prints at the Metropolitan Museum, who over all the years has shared with me his knowledge and taste for drawings and his enthusiasm for the theatre. As an artist and collector of drawings in a very special field, I owe much of my understanding of quality in drawings to these discriminating collectors and scholarly experts.

In the Library Museum of Lincoln Center, my thanks to Thor Wood, Chief of the Performing Arts Research Center; to Paul Myers, who succeeded my friend George Freedley as Chief of the Theatre Collection; to Genevieve Oswald, Curator of the Dance Collection, and to Frank Campbell, Chief of the Music Collection. Each of these distinguished experts, and also their knowing staffs, I gratefully applaud for their abiding patience with my never-ending requests for books and reference material. I also offer my thanks to Melvyn Parks, Curator of the

Theatre Collection of the Museum of the City of New York, and to his staff, for their cooperative assistance. I should like to express my particular gratitude to Helen Willard and her successor, Jeanne T. Newlin, Curator of the Harvard Theatre Collection, and to Mary Grahn, former Librarian of the Theatre Collection at Yale. And in preparation of this manuscript, my secretary, Suzanne Martiny, who typed and retyped with great patience and forbearance, I owe a special debt of gratitude.

My collection now contains some twenty-five hundred drawings, many of them included in designers' sketchbooks. It is essentially a working collection, and a major portion of the works come from the collections of artists and scene designers—principally the Scholz collection, which includes the Piancastelli-Brandegee and Mayr-Fajt holdings, the Fatio collection, and the Benois collection. I have indicated in the captions, where appropriate, the collection or collections to which each drawing formerly belonged.

In 1951 I learned through the grapevine that Janos Scholz, musician and collector, proposed to sell his extensive collection of theatrical drawings at auction. At the time, no private collectors or museums seemed inclined to acquire this unique body of material; for obviously sentimental reasons I felt that the collection should not be dispersed, and since sentiment is always stronger than discretion, I acquired the drawings and they became the backbone of my own collection. Scholz, a valued friend and connoisseur who continues to share with me his enthusiastic interest in the field, obtained many of his drawings from Cavaliere Giovanni Piancastelli (1845–1926) of Rome, a practicing architect, painter, and curator of the Borghese collection prior to its sale by the family to the Italian government. Piancastelli discovered many portfolios of drawings in the studios of a number of Roman and Bolognese artists, with whose descendants he was acquainted, and by 1901, when he began to dispose of his collection, he had amassed over fifteen thousand drawings. The bulk of the collection went to the Cooper Union Museum for the Decorative Arts, to Mrs. Edward Brandegee of Brookline, Massachusetts, to Professor Certani of Bologna (whose collection is now in the Cini Foundation in Venice). A certain number of the drawings in the Brandegee collection were acquired by János Scholz. Another major portion of the Scholz collection was acquired from Marianne Fajt of Eisenstadt in Austria, who had inherited her remarkable holdings from an ancestor, Michael Mayr, who had been the stage designer for the Esterhazy Princes. Although Mayr had not been a distinguished designer himself, he was active in the theatrical world of Austria and Hungary and avidly accumulated sketches by the important designers of the Napoleonic era practicing in Vienna. Some of the designers were Italian and had brought with them from Italy portfolios of sketches handed down to them by their masters—members of the Bibiena and Galliari families, Giovanni Niccolò Servandoni, and Domenico Fossati.

Edmond Fatio was an architect of Geneva, a man of great taste who devoted his life to assembling a remarkable group of European drawings in the decorative arts, architecture, and stage design. In 1959 when his collection came to auction, a small group of dealers managed to bid the prices up beyond all reason to four times the anticipated estimates; as a consequence, prices of drawings in the field of the decorative arts in both Europe and America have remained very high.

In 1963 I acquired from Alexander Benois's daughter the collection of designs formed by her father, the distinguished Russian stage designer (1870–1960). Benois, who had been a collaborator with Diaghilev in the organization and artistic direction of the Ballets Russes, owned works not only by Russian artists but also by French and Italian designers who had been summoned to Russia in the eighteenth and nineteenth centuries to decorate the stages of the Imperial Theatre in Saint Petersburg.

I have found that handling the actual drawings of great masters of scenic design has served as a stimulating aid in teaching young designers the traditions and disciplines of their craft. As my collection is made up of the work of many artists, so I believe that it belongs properly to all artists of the theatre. It belongs also to those scholars who keep in order the theatre's past, and not least, to that larger audience, those aficionados who share a real affection and enthusiasm for the art of the theatre of the past and present.

# The Designer's Sketch

Fifteen generations of artists are responsible for the changing contours of the theatrical art presented in this book. Each artist's designs influenced the world of the theatre in which he lived and labored, even as they established the measure of his individual talent and the criteria of his success.

From the Renaissance down to this century, scene design has been closely related to architecture and painting. Under the liberal system of royal patronage, architects and painters were also scene designers, engineers, and decorators. Their talent and understanding of mutual problems enabled them to assimilate the conventions of one art and translate those conventions into new and stimulating stylistic developments in allied arts. With equal facility, architects and painters designed villas and gardens, chapels and reception halls, catafalques and parades, masquerades, plays, and operas. Regardless of burdensome commitments, the Bibienas, Juvara, Berain, and Urban always found time and pleasure in tackling new problems with fresh ideas. With their training and inner resources and their facility in draftsmanship, they could swiftly record their thoughts on paper.

Today, as then, the theatrical designer is called upon to fashion scenes and costumes for spectacle, opera, musical, ballet, and all the ranges of comedy and tragedy. Each category is a very special form of theatre, and each requires on the part of the designer a capacity to work in an infinite variety of styles ranging from traditional realism to the most avant-garde fashion in the visual arts. To establish a theatrical atmosphere congenial to the production's character, the designer must first set the direction of his style and then proceed to sail into the breeze of his own intuition.

Engaged in diverse forms of theatre, the scene designer employs for his sketches an extensive repertory of graphic techniques and combinations of mediums—pencil, conté crayon and lithographic crayon, pastel, pen and ink, watercolor, gouache, oil, and collages of many materials. The designer's concept of a production determines his choice of medium so that his characterization pervades the sketch for a scene.

All through this book hints of today's style are detected amidst the theatrical traditions of the past. Echoes of the past re-echo in the changing traditions of the present imperative. "The past is for us," Emerson believed, "but the sole terms in which it can become ours are in subordination to the present. Only an inventor knows how to borrow, and every man is, or should be, an inventor." The best theatre has ever been the work of inventors, and the scene designer at his best is an "inventor" who knows just what to borrow. He is a traditionalist, too, but only in the sense that architect Philip Johnson calls himself a traditionalist: "I like to be buttoned onto tradition. The thing is to improve it; twist it and mold it; to make something new of it; not to deny it. The riches of history can be plucked at any point."

The theatre is one of the most adaptable and flexible of the arts. While it may from time to time feed on the past, it has always lived in the present. It belongs to today—*not* to the ages. The scene designer accepts this insubstantial world and is pleased to work within his own theatrical framework. His sketch for a scene is not intended to be a preliminary study for a permanent work of art like a sculptured relief or a wall decoration or a building. A sketch for a scene is as short-lived as the life of the theatre it supports. If it survives, it survives as brief evidence or as a personal memento of a significant occasion in the theatre. Few designers are good house-keepers. Most are not preservationists, and so their sketches tend to disappear. Unfortunately for theatre historians, a theatre drawing rarely boasts of the artist's signature or the date or name of the production for which it was designed.

A sketch for a scene is contrived to emphasize and enhance the peculiar characteristics of that scene. It is conceived as an appropriate background for the performers and is planned to project the action of a dramatic situation. Robert Edmond Jones believed the setting should contain "the promise of a completion, a promise which the actor later fulfills. It is charged with a sense of expectancy. It waits for the actor, and not until the actor has made his entrance does it become an organic whole." Alone on the stage, without the animus of the actor, the setting remains as lifeless as a still life.

The stage designer's sketch has always had its very own raison d'être. It is intended for theatre workers. It presents his visual intentions and explains his ideas to author, director, and performers. It serves as a guideline for those who actually construct the scene: builders, painters, craftsmen, electricians, technicians. Sometimes it is coded with data and overlaid with measurements and indications of floor plan, and as often as not it is thumbed and spattered with scene paint. His sketch is rarely acquired for permanent installation in museums, despite the fact that many designers in the theatre—Antonio Bibiena, Filippo Juvara, Léon Bakst, and Gordon Craig among them—have been supreme draftsmen. Perhaps because of the very immediacy of their intentions, designers' sketches, when they do survive, seem doomed to an afterlife on library shelves or to languish in museum vaults whence they are occasionally exhumed for special exhibitions. The sketches survive only as fragmentary records of the ephemeral life of the make-believe world of the theatre—enchanting infidelities which illuminate the fog of memories past.

# The Heritage of the Renaissance Theatre

The origins of our theatre conventions and traditions are found in the theatre of the Renaissance in Italy. Since that theatre is our heritage, we must understand its aims and intentions and its background. The men who contributed most positively to the evolution of the Renaissance theatre were possessed with an insatiable curiosity about the theatre of Greece and Rome. They could only move forward in search of a new theatre by vaulting in a clean parabolic arch back over their Gothic heritage of Christian dogma to drink deeply from the Hyperion Springs and thus recover their classical heritage. The Renaissance way of life embraced the past. For the Greeks, the past was darkness. Their way of life was enjoyment in the present, living from day to day under the light of life-giving Helios. For them "the sun stood still, and the moon stayed." The artists and poets who fashioned the Renaissance theatre were energized with the animating force of classicism. This force became the lodestar which set the course of the performing arts for generations to come.

## The Greek Theatre

The Greek theatre was like a bulb with its roots deep in the underground of magic and ritual. Overnight it burst miraculously into the full-blown flower of classic drama, with the priests of Dionysus presiding in the front row encircling his altar centered in the orchestra. Aeschylus, Sophocles, and Euripides evolved in the theatre of Dionysus at Athens a wholly new ceremonial procedure to honor the god, a new concept of theatre for all the Hellenic world to share in. Actors, no longer in the guise of satyrs, now performed in democratic mysteries acting out time-honored tales of familiar gods and giants, legendary heroes and warriors, Centaurs and Oceanides, Furies and Bacchantes. That sudden flowering of dramatic genius in fifth-century B.C. Athens has left the imprint of classic authority on the continuous course of theatre for twenty-five hundred years. Only a few chapters in the theatre's long history ever matched the earth-shaking impact of what happened in the theatre of Dionysus.

In diverse times and places, other potent dramatic forms of ritual and magic have emerged, but they left behind no significant drama—only shells of buildings with even the echo of performance long silenced and only hints of dramatic ceremonies recorded on time-honored walls. In Egypt, a spacious temple complex housed massive religious ceremonials (the pharaoh was deified in his lifetime). In India, a dance hall for ritual adorned every Hindu temple enclosure. In Persepolis, a stepped acropolis with columned halls of audacious scale was erected by Darius and Xerxes to accommodate stage ceremonials. Outside Peking, marble terraces encircle the Temple of Heaven that mystically supports the celestial cosmos; within the temple, the emperor annually officiated over China's revered New Year's celebration. In Greece, elite sanctuaries were associated with the worship of the gods: Apollo in Delphi, Athena on the Acropolis, Zeus in Olympia. Their prescribed order of service included religious processions and dancing in temple ritual, but ritual far too exacting and lofty to beget anything like earthborn drama. All these structures of faith were dedicated to the civilized worship of godhead, not to the enactment of drama.

In the bloodstream of the ancient world existed a lesser, more personal hierarchy of gods popularly worshiped throughout the Levant. Osiris, Attis, Hyacinth, and Dionysus were potent gods of vegetation or fertility. The legend of Dionysus, like the grander legends of his more lordly father, Zeus, is true story theatre. Great Zeus, wishing himself a serpent, visited Persephone one night in "the sightless realm where darkness is awake upon the dark and Persephone is but a voice" in her dark Eleusian cleft. Dionysus was their shining offspring. In a youthful escapade, Dionysus mounted Zeus's throne and hurled his father's avenging thunderbolts down to the earth amidst the Titans. The angry Titans in vengeance laid hold of the manly youth, cut him up in little pieces, and scattered them all over the earth. Miraculously, Lord Dionysus rose from the dead. Before long, in many valleys of Greece, the sacrificial rite of his death and resurrection was annually performed. The Greek word for "rite" means "a thing done." In worshipful honor of Lord Dionysus, the performance of this rite included elements of music (rhythm) and dance (movement). His rural shrines were modest and found in remote valleys close by dancing places like the threshing floors found throughout Greece today.

Dionysus was the popular god of wine, drama, and the afterlife. The Greeks referred to him as "well-fruited," "teeming," "bursting"; his manifestation was the grape or the ivy; his image, a stump or a crude phallic post erected in vineyard or olive grove. The sacrificial goat offered on his altar-tomb was the origin of the crude, phallic regalia of the satyr chorus pictured on so many Attic urns. Out of dark time, the Greek word *tragoi*, meaning goat, was wed to *odia*, meaning song, in a ritual of goat-song, and under the prismatic light of the Hellenic world, this ritual became *tragedy*.

Out of that wine-red satyr play of the re-creation of life enacted by a frenzied chorus of Dionysians and their chorus leader, a respondent came forward from the chorus at a crucial moment to address his leader in iambic verse. At that point, with two characters in conflict, drama was born. A "happening" derived from well-remembered legends of Hellas could be written down and acted out. This is how drama came to Greece.

In Athens around 500 B.C., sculpture was shedding its archaic origins; the Doric temple was growing out of its wooden case; Thespis had introduced his troupe of "thespians" to convert crude ritual into structured drama. The stage was set. The peace that followed the Athenian naval victory over the Persians at Salamis in 480 B.C. provided that breathless pause under the leadership of Pericles in which a small, rock-ribbed country no larger than Maine envisioned what Edith Hamilton has called "the ideal of form attained through intellect plus spirit" and thereby founded a civilization that ever since has been the fact of life for western man.

Unlikely, but legend has it that on that day of victory, the position of three stars augured well for the theatre's horoscope. Aeschylus served in the heavy armed infantry, Sophocles participated in the youths' chorus of victory, and Euripides came into the world! Together this triumvirate found not, but created theatre—the classic theatre of the western world. Of course, the Greeks had no word for "classic." Nothing like it had existed before —nor, strangely, was "classic" a part of the Renaissance artist's or scholar's vocabulary. "Classic" in our sense did not appear until Addison used it in *The Spectator* in 1701.

The Greeks were unaware that they were cultivating a classic style. They had assimilated very little from their ancient Aegean culture or from Egypt or Assyria. During that lusty period of relative peace, rumblings of a new order were discernible in the tavernas, the law courts, the academies, and among groups in the agora. The Greeks were an excitable, voluble people who argued incessantly. Clearly the Athenians were fomenting a spiritual and intellectual revolution but with no entrenched "establishment" to revolt against. Like all revolutionaries, they buttressed their cause with a brand-new set of advanced precepts and modern dimensions for literature, the arts, science, and philosophy. The victory of those modernists was inevitable. Overnight the regime of classicism was a *fait accompli* and demanded a totally new way of thinking, a new language of expression, and a new set of standards and systems exemplifying the new ideals of truth to nature. It found freedom of expression in motifs as modest as the honeysuckle, the egg and dart, and the Greek fret; in bold experiments in color and the new uses of stone, terra-cotta, bronze, gold, and glass; in Polyclitus' and Scopas' canons of the perfect proportion of the human body; in the stylized organization of the Doric and Ionic orders; in the tempered sophistication of costume that clothed the body and spirit moving proudly among those columned orders.

What were the implications of classicism? The assertive forces of Hellenism were imbued with the humanist point of view that affirmed Man to be the measure of all things. His talent embraced his achievements, and his achievements bore his signature. A kylix depicting scenes of Theseus and the Minotaur could only have been painted in the free style with such linear logic by a great master, and he simply recorded the fact "painted by me, The Kodios painter." The architectural sculpture invented by Phidias bore no signature, but he was the acknowledged sculptor of the gods. The philosophy of the Republic could have been envisioned only by Plato, never by a group of politicians. The Long Wall and ordered plan of the Piraeus were not the vision of the Athenian state but of Themistocles, victor of Salamis. From the haunting epic of Agamemnon, Sophocles and Euripides each created his tragic masterpiece, and each called it *Electra*.

Such giants played notable roles in the humanist order of Athenian life. They were the aristocrats of their democratic state. They enjoyed personal acclaim and prestige among the Popular Assembly. They participated in the research of philosophers, scientists, and mathematicians in Plato's Academy, mingled with the poets in Aristotle's Lyceum, and discoursed with vocal virtuosity in Isocrates' School of Rhetoric and Speech.

The Athenian humanist was like a good watch. He kept excellent time within himself. Through awareness of his inward organization, he impressed on his work his concept of ideal form. "The aim of art," wrote Aristotle, "is to represent not the outward appearance of things, but their inward significance . . ." With the Greeks this "inward significance" was as natural as breathing. This effortless breath of life pervaded all they touched or gave thought to. Their balance of intellect and spirit achieved symmetry, unity, and harmony, leaving no room for internal discord or confusion.

The Parthenon of Iktinos, surviving the plunder of time, lives on serene in its subtle balance of the perpendicular and the horizontal, yet organic and mathematical in the precise organization of its individual parts. The Doric order was a codification of architectonic principles. The sculptor Myron wrought his calm *Discobolos* from the fury of molten bronze. The athlete's inward strength controls his outward movement, arrested at the crucial moment before discharging the discus. Youth remains poised forever on a point of action. In *Oedipus Rex*, Sophocles ennobled the character of Oedipus with such large-scale, vital dialogue, balanced with such structured choral splendor, that the play's grandeur and beauty remain immune to time. Winckelmann, the "first scientific archaeologist," understood why. "Beauty with the ancients," he asserted, "was the tongue on the balance of expression."

The Greeks patterned their days according to the dawning conventions of their self-made world. Twenty-five hundred years is a difficult generation gap between their way of life and ours. A few fragments of their world survive in modern, noisy Athens to remind us of their vanished civilization. Other fragments are treasured in libraries and museums all over the world. These fragments are the core of our classical heritage—the substantive force which in times of aesthetic turbulence has exerted a leavening influence and served as a counterpoise to the innovative forward thrust of the arts and letters of the western world.

We have fragmentary knowledge of the Greek theatre of the fifth century B.C. Only a few stones among the confusing ruins of the late Roman Theatre of Dionysus mark the original site of the orchestra where the great dramatists' victories were acclaimed. Outside of Athens, archaeological remains of later Hellenistic theatres are scattered throughout the Aegean world. As to the dramas, only seven plays each of Aeschylus and Sophocles survive and seventeen attest to the popularity of Euripides. Scant accounts—references in literature, and pictorial records from vases and the minor arts—provide us with hints and clues of the Greek theatre in action and attest to the prestigious influence which that theatre exerted on the hearts and minds of the citizens of Greece.

In the structured society of that ideal state, the theatre flourished under the aegis of the state. Pericles made the theatre of Dionysus free to all. The theatre belonged to the people. During the winter months, the entire Attic state looked forward to the popular spring festival in Athens. Plans for the contests in the Theatre of Dionysus were in the hands of the state's highest official—the *archon eponymus*. Dramatists were completing tragedies, satyr plays, and comedies which they would submit to the *archon*, who selected the plays for the competition. He also appointed the *choregi*—sixteen to eighteen directors, wealthy Athenians who provided funds to finance the productions of contesting dramatists. A playwright with a generous *choregus* enjoyed a definite advantage. The *archon* assigned to each *choregus* the actors and musicians for his tetralogy. All were amateurs, participating in plays as part of a religious event honoring Dionysus. Elaborate costumes and masks and scenic paraphernalia were fashioned by the best talent in Athens. Finally, and most important, the judges of the contests were impartially appointed by the state.

Anticipation ran high. Crowds from all over Attica converged on Athens for the great Dionysia. This was the city's most popular Dionysiac festival and lasted for three days in early April. The city was at its best. The sun shone in a cerulean sky. A spirited, rowdy throng spent a good part of those spring days cupped on the steep south slope of the Acropolis. Bread and cheese, olives, and jars of resinated wine took care of the inner man and contributed to the holiday air of the occasion. Seventeen thousand spectators occupied concentric tiers of seats extending three quarters around the circular orchestra. The remaining steep slope provided rugged standing room for the gallery gods who, at a new play, freely gave vent to their emotions. All eyes looked down, absorbing all that took place on the orchestral floor of hard-packed earth, ever mindful that both Aeschylus and Euripides had been forced into exile from Athens for the unpopularity of their religious and political views which they had injected into the theatre. In another mood during a performance of a comedy of Aristophanes, the audience cheered for Socrates to stand up and show how lifelike was the mask of an actor playing the role of Socrates.

Little could distract the eye in the early Greek theatre. Facing the audience and tangent to the orchestra was a long, one-story stage building with a large central door. Behind was the sacred precinct of Dionysus with his small temple housing the gold and ivory cult image of the god sculptured by Alkamenes. Beyond, Athens was to the left, and to the right stretched the open countryside of Attica. That was it.

As the pattern of dramaturgy became fixed, ways and means of presenting the plays became accepted conventions of theatre practice. The separation between stage house and the auditorium provided side entrances (*parados*) into the orchestra circle. The stage house later became two stories high, and at either side two wings (*paraskenia*) projected toward the auditorium. These were connected by a one-story colonnade (*proskenion*) in front of the stage house with its central double door and two side doors. The colonnade supported the upper stage, which had no direct access to the orchestra below. The Greek theatre was never a planned architectural structure. It was a flexible space stage which readily satisfied the needs of the dramatists and became the prototype for most Hellenistic theatres throughout Greece and her colonies.

The stage house was equipped with mechanical and scenic devices geared to the new production needs of tragedy and comedy. These contraptions of the Greeks may seem primitive to the modern technician. Even so, they are the source, the beginning of much of our technical practice today.

The requirements of the comedies and tragedies are the most reliable sources of information on Greek scenery and machinery. Ancient references were almost always vague. Vitruvius, a Roman military engineer and architect writing in the time of Augustus, gave his account of the Greek stage in his invaluable treatise *De Architectura*. Julius Pollux, a second-century Greek lexicographer, in his dictionary the *Onomastikon*, discussed scenery, machinery, and stage costumes. Vitruvius wrote three hundred years and Pollux five hundred years after the late-Hellenistic theatre began to decline. Were they not writing of the Greek theatre from hearsay? How much did their writings relate this hearsay to the techniques of their contemporary Roman theatre? Vitruvius describes how "Agatharcus in Athens, when Aeschylus was bringing out a tragedy, painted a scene, and left a commentary about it. This led Democritus and Anaxagoras to write on the same subject, showing how, given a center in a definite place, the lines should naturally correspond with due regard to the point of sight and the divergence of the visual rays, so that by this deception, a faithful representation of the appearance of the buildings might be given in painted scenery, and so that, though all is drawn on a vertical flat façade, some parts may seem to be withdrawing into the background, and others to be standing out in front."

The Greeks understood well the principles of perspective and put them into practice. Drawings from contemporary vase paintings and frescoes, particularly those recently discovered in a necropolis outside Paestum, indicate the depth and sense of space achieved with perspective in the early fifth century B.C. Aeschylus might well have turned for help with his scenery to illustrious Agatharcus, whom Socrates' friend Alcibiades had already commissioned to decorate the walls of his house. Agatharcus probably painted for Aeschylus an unconventional stage scene with architecture drawn in perspective, for shortly thereafter, *skenographia* (scene painting) became the technical term for any art work executed in perspective.

Was the scene painted on the face of the stage house or on temporary panels? Vitruvius and Pollux both speak of a scenic device called the *periaktoi* employed at either end of the stage house. This was a tall, triangular, revolving prism which was turned to expose its tragic, comic, or satyric side to indicate the type of play being presented. In several Hellenistic theatres, sockets in stones that supported poles for the revolving *periaktoi* have been found. The *proskenion* colonnades of a number of theatres indicate that movable panels were fastened between the columns to form a scenic frieze. But for a huge audience, how underscale and unimportant both *periaktoi* and scenic panels must have appeared as backgrounds for Antigone or Agamemnon attired in voluminous theatrical costumes and wearing massive masks for the projection of voice and heightened emotional expression. Furthermore, most Greek theatres occupied splendid sites. For a Greek audience, could any scenic illusion of temple or palace compete aesthetically with a real panoramic backdrop of Arcady? Even though Aristotle credited Sophocles with inventing the art of "scene painting," this art as we understand it would intrude on the simple visual impact of the formal Greek space stage. Is this relationship between scene painting and space not un-Greek in its lack of harmony and order, which are the very core of Greek drama? Who can say? Perhaps for the Greeks it came to be accepted as a theatre convention like a realistic scene framed within our proscenium.

The *ekkyklema* was the forefather of the modern wagon stage. This was a small platform, square or semicircular, that was rolled out or revolved through the central double doors of the stage house. Pollux refers to it as "the out-wheeling machine," and returning, "the in-wheeling machine." It revealed *tableaux vivants* of scenes occurring off stage, such as Clytemnestra distraught over the slain bodies of Agamemnon and Cassandra or the suicide body of Phaedra. Euripides frequently employed this device in his tragedies, and Aristophanes parodied the use of it in his comedies. In *The Acharnians*, Dicaeopolis goes to Euripides' house to borrow a tragic costume. The latter is very busy working on a new play, so he has himself wheeled out and supplies the costume.

The "flying machine," or "deus ex machina," was another much-used stage mechanism. It was literally a crane operated from above the second floor of one of the *paraskenia*. Dramatists frequently required aerial communication with the stage. An actor could be swung out through the central double door of the upper stage and lowered to the orchestra floor below. At the end of Euripides' play, Medea disappears, with her children she has murdered, via this creaking "hoisting machine." In the *Clouds*, Aristophanes has Socrates suspended in a basket studying astronomy and gazing down on the gods from his own heavenly space. In the *Peace*, Trygaeus, mounted on a beetle's back, is wafted up to the very doors of Zeus. This is a giddy parody of the hero's ascent on Pegasus in Euripides' *Belerophon*. The actor calls to the machinist not to tangle the ropes for fear he might be seasick!

The Greek theatre has always remained for the Renaissance and for subsequent generations a strange interlude isolated in time and baffling with its illusive stage conventions. More strange, the Greeks had no word for theatre, except with specific reference to the auditorium where the "sight-seers" sat and could see the actors "stepping out before the theatre crowd" onto the orchestra circle from the stage house. But most strange, the dramatic poets scarcely ever referred to the stage house for which they wrote their plays; probably to them it was a mere utilitarian structure that had always stood there and was taken for granted like the temple of Dionysus behind it. But what we *can* hold in our hands and treasure is the lodestone we have inherited from the Greek dramatists. Today their plays remain just as inspired, just as passionate in their humanity, and just as green as ever they were in Athens.

We readily accept our conventions in presenting classic theatre within our proscenium. We are deeply moved by Lord Olivier in *Oedipus Rex* and Dame Judith Anderson in *Medea*. But Sophocles and Euripides would shake their heads in puzzlement over our Broadway and Off-Broadway theatre conventions, just as the conventions of the theatre of Dionysus for which they wrote their plays remain equally puzzling to us. Our theatre is the richer for our constant affirmation of their timeless inspiration.

# The Roman Theatre

Many city dwellers of the twentieth century would feel far more at home in the confusion of ancient Rome than in the order of Athens. From the time of Romulus and Remus, Rome never had an integrated plan for urban development. The city of the Republic swarmed over the seven hills and became a congested ghetto within its protecting walls. The emperors never chose to impose an urban plan on the cluttered imperial city. The Tiber was the main artery of traffic. Ground traffic, through a maze of open passages and congested lanes, was intolerable. Rome was a colossal small town with no zoning laws to control the expansion of its vast public works. Consequently it boasted no West End, no Broadway, no Ginza. Theatres and amphitheatres, like temples and forums and baths, were scattered all over town. This disregard for urban planning is perplexing, for Roman architects were engineers who excelled in organization.

If traffic remained an insoluble problem in the Eternal City, the unfettered Builders of the Empire projected grandiose schemes for the advancement of world traffic. Bred on the old Republican concept of discipline and obedience to rule, the Romans by and large were to become preeminently men of war. To survive they were aware they must "conquer or be conquered." The imperial legions chose to conquer. They dramatically planted the Roman *fasces* on the outermost borders of their world. Behind the legions via modern highways and bridges marched "big business" developing new commerce and riches. Culture and theatre marched alongside too. But the true strength of Rome's expanding empire was inherent in and upheld by the force of her abiding Law of Nations. Among all her civilizing institutions, her code of equal justice for men everywhere within the boundaries of the Empire was Rome's most majestic achievement.

Before the Roman conquest of Greece, it was manifest that Rome was succumbing to the civilizing spell of Hellenism. Even in Carthage, Baie, and Tarentum the Romans were living like the Greeks. Their education was supervised by imported Greek intellectuals. Retaining only their domestic gods of the hearth, the Romans equated their pantheon of gods with those of the Greeks. The same temple serviced Athena and Minerva, or Zeus and Jupiter, or Aphrodite and Venus.

The poets and writers of Rome's silver and golden ages were the foster children of the school of Athens. Cicero and Horace were trained in the Greek tradition. The newest comedy adaptations by Plautus and Terence were zealously applauded. Art treasures plundered from Greece fetched soaring prices. Cicero paid dearly for Greek objects of the highest quality. For those less privileged there was a flourishing trade in Roman copies. Contemporary paintings and sculptures copied after the *Laocoön* and the Farnese Bull were created for the Roman market by those hungry Greeklings inhabiting the Eastern Mediterranean.

A peer among artists was the engineer. All Roman architects combined skillful planning with engineering genius. They conceived their works on a magnificent scale—forums, temples, basilicas, baths, palaces, aqueducts, and of course theatres. All of these were innovative forms of architecture. Erected in the name of the emperor, they accommodated the new needs and the population growth of a new society. In developing the arch and dome, they invented their own methods of construction in concrete and brick, rearing vaults and domes to span vast spaces. The Greek orders were superimposed one on another and used as decoration to conceal and adorn the superbly engineered surfaces of the new architecture. They believed in the formula that one column on top of another was twice as good as one. The Romans' love of overdecoration and "illusionism" in sculpture and painting reflected the pretentious grandeur and decadent taste that emanated from the Capitoline Hill.

Just what kind of entertainment did a single entrance ticket provide in that plush theatre built by Pompey? All Roman theatre, unlike "all Gaul," was divided into two parts: the popular entertainments associated with Plautus and Terence of the Republic, and the later "spectaculars" associated with the big imperial theatres and amphitheatres known to all Roman travelers from the Atlantic seaboard to the docks of the Euphrates. Except for tedious literary adaptations of Greek tragedy and ribald improvised farces, very little Latin theatre flourished between these two minor and major leagues of entertainment. The tradition of the troupers' theatre had long existed among the Greek colonies in Sicily and southern Italy. The winds of popularity bore them northward to Rome. Those grotesque comics Maccus, Pappus, and Dossenus were the very ancestors of Pulcinella, Pantalone, and Il Dottore of the ubiquitous commedia dell'arte troupes of Italy, whose spontaneity and style would cast their spell on Shakespeare, Molière, and Goldoni and captivate the courts and market places of Europe until the nineteenth century.

In Rome, the troupers' improvised platform stages were set up in a forum, before a temple, or in a circus. Before long, temporary wooden theatres were erected for theatrical performances designated for official holidays. But whatever originality that indigenous Latin theatre sparked, the audience of the Republic succumbed to the new "Greek" influence. Plautus' witty plays are free translations from the New Comedy of Greek Manners. One critic of declining Athens rhetorically quizzed the leading playwright of the New Comedy: "Oh Menander, Oh Life, which is the plagiarist?" Plautus held Menander's mirror up to the daily life of Republican Rome. Terence also was Roman and Greek, polished and stylish; he might belong to any place and time. "I am a human being," he said, "and think all human affairs my concern." Little wonder the works of Plautus and Terence delighted the humanists of the Renaissance. To the conservative eyes of Cato, the Censor, the rising tide of Hellenism threatened to destroy the ancient Republican austerity. Cato exhorted the Senate to oppose the intrusion of the new Hellenic influence. He objected to the construction of a permanent theatre building and also urged the Senate to prohibit the Romans from attending any entertainment derived from the Greek. His was the Elder's stentorian voice scarcely heard by the younger Greco-Roman cultural entente.

Admission to the Roman theatre of the Republic had always been open to all—citizens and slaves, soldiers and courtesans, old and young. For an audience, going to the theatre was like sitting on the sidelines of a crowded forum watching the frenetic world of Rome pass by. The only setting Plautus and Terence really required for the action of their characters was a public place containing a number of doors for convenience's sake. This door-to-door arrangement served just as well for most adaptations of tragedy.

Fourteen years after Terence's death, a wooden theatre closer in plan to the Hellenistic theatre, and similar to those found in Segesta and Pompeii, was erected in Rome in 145 B.C. Stage and auditorium were joined together. The Hellenistic *proskenion* with three doors became the Roman front stage (*scaenae frons*). In 99 B.C., Pliny reported that the architectural painting on one theatre's *scaenae frons* was so realistic that birds tried to alight on the roofs! The stage background continued to display more lavish use of painting and increasing relief work. In 58 B.C., as a generous gesture to Rome, Pliny recounts how the aedile Aemelius Scaurus, charged with supervising state entertainment, built a dazzling wooden theatre to end all wooden theatres; it was purported to hold eighty thousand spectators! The *scaenae frons* contained three hundred and sixty columns and rose three stories high. The first story was marble, the second was glass, and the third, gilded wood. The structure was adorned with three thousand statues. Pliny also informs us that in 53 B.C. Scribonius Scribo, as a gesture of Roman paternal piety on the occasion of his father's memorial service honoring his recent death, caused two wooden theatres to be erected back to back. On the conclusion of the first half of the program of festivities, both theatres, to the delight of all those in mourning, revolved and formed an amphitheatre to accommodate the second half of the more spectacular proceedings—O Death, where was thy sting on that occasion?

Pompey, after his return from the Mithridatic campaign, built the first stone theatre in Rome's Campus Martius just three years after the great wooden Scaurus theatre had opened. Seventeen thousand spectators could admire the theatre's extravagant *scaenae frons* composed of one hundred and fifty columns of polychrome marble, porphyry, and serpentine. Four times this theatre was rebuilt after destruction by fire. Today concealed beneath the rubble of centuries, the subterranean vaults of Pompey's noble theatre echo with the gaiety of an excellent Ristorante Romano. In 13 B.C., Cornelius Balbus built Rome's second stone theatre. Little or nothing survives of that imposing structure. In 11 B.C., a third stone theatre was finally opened for the delectation of Rome's drama aficionados. It had been begun by Julius Caesar and was completed by the Emperor Augustus, who dedicated it to the memory of his nephew and son-in-law Marcellus. Much of the exterior of this monumental theatre of Marcellus stands today. Measured drawings of the theatre, possibly made by Peruzzi, were first published by Serlio in 1540. We know the theatre's plan, for it is clearly incised in the ancient marble Forma Urbis Severiana.

The Roman architect-engineer Marcus Vitruvius Pollio knew these three permanent theatres well. His celebrated treatise in ten books, *De Architectura*, was dedicated to the Emperor Augustus. It includes precise descriptions of the Greek and Roman theatres, which have been of great assistance to theatre historians and architects. Vitruvius established the rules for planning and constructing a typical Roman theatre, and he proposed the theatre of Marcellus as a model for future use throughout the Empire. *De Architectura* was to become the bible and source book of the classical theatre for architects of the Renaissance.

The theatre of Marcellus was a model Roman theatre. Unlike the separate stage house and hillside auditorium of the Greek theatre, the Roman theatre had a coordinated plan. Stage and auditorium were united in a single organic structure. The shape of the auditorium (*cavea*) was semicircular, extending around the orchestra space in a series of wedge-shaped tiers surmounted by a colonnade. The open-air auditorium frequently had a linen canopy (*velarium*) stretched overhead to protect spectators from rain and sun. A Pompeian theatre "poster" once boasted the use of a cooling system of artificial showers. The stage (*pulpitum*) was raised four or five feet above the orchestra. The stage was flat and, though relatively shallow, extended the full width of the auditorium. The back wall of the stage had a large center door and two side doors. Each side wall right and left also had an entrance. The lofty *scaenae frons* rose two or three stories, and its superimposed orders of architecture were frequently repeated on the exterior wall of the auditorium. The *scaenae frons* had the lavish aspect of a triumphal arch. It was protected by a sloping coffered ceiling covering the entire stage. This ceiling also served as an acoustical aid.

Occasional references are made to the Romans' use of stage machinery. This included the three-sided *periaktoi* of the Greek theatre and also a rolling platform (*scena ductilis*) similar to the *ekkyklema*. But how could a few mobile scenic elements have held their own against the awesome permanent architecture of the *scaenae frons*? The forward areas of a few Roman stage floors contain a long deep trough which to some suggests

19

a space to accommodate a descending theatre curtain. But what eye-filling scenery might a descending curtain have concealed or revealed to a Roman audience? It would only resemble a crystal chandelier under summer wraps. How could a Roman impresario cover a costly permanent architectural *scaenae frons* with any kind of temporary or appropriate scenery? Neither plays nor spectacles nor Roman audiences tell us. It is more likely that those troughs housed acoustical apparatus.

A Roman company manager's map of the empire might have been dotted with many stars indicating the names and locations of provincial towns where his touring troupe could perform. They would extend from Canterbury in England, to Orange in France, to Cordova in Spain, along the coast of Africa to Dugga, and from Leptis Magna in Libya to Aspendos in Asia Minor. Theatres and amphitheatres occupied strategic sites in the heart of every provincial center. All were cultural oases in the far-flung provinces of the Empire. Even the revered theatre of Dionysus in Athens was finally "Romanized" by Nero in A.D. 60. Henceforth the Greek god of drama was required to share honors with the imperial god of cultural affairs.

What performing arts were presented in these omnipresent pleasure domes dedicated to the Muses? What kind of entertainment satisfied the mixed populaces of Anglia, Gallia, Cappadocia, and of course Urbs Orbis herself? The Romans hungered for sensational amusement of all kinds—live shows, dumb shows, shows of blood and thunder. By the middle of the fourth century A.D., in one year 101 festival days out of 175 were given over to theatrical shows. Typical festivals were the Ludi Romani in honor of Jupiter Capitolinus, the Ludi Plebeii of and for the people, the Ludi Floriales devoted to Flora, and the Ludi Funebris honoring the dead. After the first years of Empire, scenes from comedy and tragedy became eclipsed by variety and burlesque, jugglers and acrobats, degenerate mimes, erotic pantomimes with female performers, chorus and music "doing" Leda and the Swan, Venus and Adonis, or Nero himself enacting a lurid version of the Judgment of Paris. Those mammoth ruins of theatre and amphitheatre, of stadium and *naumachia*, are sobering reminders of the later Latins' passion for spectacle: triumphal displays of foreign booty, subject slaves' gladiatorial combats and wild-animal baiting, sports, races, and aquatic pageants.

The performing arts today suffer also from a lack of vision and direction on the part of the impresario and spectator. The theatre has forgotten its audience, and the audience has forgotten its theatre. We have ready-made comedies and all sorts of live entertainment for "ladies and gentlemen over twenty-one." For the theatre of five thousand and more, our civic arenas are bursting with dazzling attractions—the Lippizaner horses from Vienna, the circus (since Rome the greatest show on earth), rodeos, dance festivals, ice shows, football, and baseball. As long as they lasted, our movie palaces also dispensed mass entertainment in the grand manner. A long time ago, Wolcott Gibbs in *The New Yorker* recalled critic George Jean Nathan celebrating the opening of the Paramount theatre in Times Square:

> Mr. Nathan went on at some length, and in a tone that could easily be confused with reverence, about the singular majesty of the trappings of the building: the great chandeliers outwinking the stars; the acres of canvas that had gone into paintings, and the unthinkable weight of marble and statuary; the fifty-piece orchestra that, propelled by some prodigy of hydraulics, rose shimmering out of Hell to furnish angel music; the stairways that reached up to no conceivable destination less appalling than the gates of Heaven; the usherettes walking in beauty; the lovely grottoes underground where one might, though with enormous temerity, wash one's hands; the cathedral hush that, like incense, like a benediction, hung over all those wondrous things. And then, in a tone that even for him might be esteemed sombre, the curtain, itself a hymn to splendor, went up on a picture of a cowboy kissing a horse.

Any citizen of Imperial Rome in the Paramount that evening would have felt back home in the theatre of Marcellus. He would also be "with it" in much of today's multimedia off-off-Broadway entertainment. In our contemporary theatre, we can also look back and admit to understanding much of the Roman theatre of eighteen hundred years ago because indeed it is "with us" today.

# The Medieval Theatre

The conversion of Constantine in A.D. 313 confirmed the triumph of Christianity over the classical civilization of Greece and Rome. For the next twelve hundred years, the culture of Europe would be dominated by the Catholic Church.

After the first headstrong years of mass conversion, pagan temples and basilicas were consecrated to early Christian worship. Bronze images were melted down and marble sculpture was defaced or condemned to the lime kiln. Ancient theatres and amphitheatres became quarries for builders of the new faith. With Christian zeal, mighty imperial monuments were pulled down and their columns and wealth of marble detail hauled away to enrich the new Byzantine architecture. At length, the ravaged centers of classical culture were absorbed by the receiving earth and lay half-buried beneath nature's romantic pall of vegetation.

Here and there throughout Christendom, the classical tradition was nourished beneath the robes of office of Jesuit or Benedictine. In cathedral and abbey a few precious works of classical antiquity were bent to Christian use and escaped destruction. Ancient manuscripts of Greek and Roman authors were treasured and lovingly transcribed by nameless scholars in monastic libraries such as Monte Cassino and Saint Gall.

The classical theatre could not possibly be converted to the doctrines of the early Christian Fathers. While all of Rome's theatres remained open during the transition of the Christian takeover, popular entertainment was soon suppressed and man's instinct for drama was driven underground for centuries. A few farces escaped the purging fires. Only the morality play, promoting the triumph of good over evil, was acknowledged as worthy, even though it was as interminable and static as the French *roman* and *fabliau.*

For twelve hundred years, the Catholic Church nourished its changing theatre to suit its growing needs. All over Europe, Christian theatre was harnessed to the propagation of the faith. Ways and means of presenting this international school of religious drama varied according to nationalistic tastes and regional characteristics. In the beginning there was no Christian theatre—only the ritual and celebration of the Mass at the high altar, a symbol of the table of the Last Supper.

The trope was an awesome dramatic seed which was planted within the introit of the Mass. The tenth-century Easter trope from Saint Gall was one of the earliest—only two lines in Latin verse.

Int.—*Quem quaeritis in Sepulcro, O Cristicolae?*
Resp.—*Jesum-Nazarenum crucifixum, O Celicolae.*

(Interrogator: Whom do you seek in the tomb, O servants of Christ?
Respondent: Jesus of Nazareth crucified, O servants of Heaven.)

Before long, this trope grew into a scene played around the tomb, as represented by the high altar. Sometime later, this scene was extracted from the Mass, expanded, and performed independently as a liturgical drama. With the addition of related sequential scenes and properties, this form of drama, no longer in Latin but in the vernacular, expanded into the mystery play.

Ultimately, these modest plays flowered into extraordinary cyclical plays derived from scenes and episodes that stretched from the Creation all the way to the Second Coming and derived from both the Old and the New Testaments. Their characters were the principals of the Church Militant and Triumphant, the evangelists, the Apostles, and the army of Christian martyrs. The cyclical plays became large-scale panoramas of the Christian faith. The miracle plays as language were not literature. The words were least important. Most of the scripts were anonymous. Their appeal was to the eye and to the heart. The miracle play was a community enterprise which enthralled the humblest surf or overlord, priest or bishop. Every citizen participated either as spectator or performer. In a real sense it was the first community theatre. The production rolled on interminably, sometimes playing for days and weeks on end. By the close of the Middle Ages, and with the curtain about to rise on the Renaissance, the great cyclical plays had outgrown their religious intentions. Overburdened with barnacles of realism, fraught with sound and fury, and also for lack of spiritual conviction, these monster shows finally succumbed, just like the mastodon on his Pleistocene stage whose future was a dead end.

The development of the Christian theatre was as complex and inevitable in its unfolding as *Pilgrim's Progress.* The stage evolved with the drama it accommodated. The area of the high altar provided the perfect space stage so meaningful for that early trope of the three Marys at the tomb. As the number of scenes increased, the stages for their action spilled out of the choir into the nave. At that time, the clergy presented their simple dramas on raised decorated scaffolds, erected temporarily between the piers of the nave arcades to intimately surround the worshipers. The Christian Fathers were not slow to grasp the social and religious impact of Christian drama on their congregation. In the all-seeing eye of the Church, the plays provided people of all ages with a living education in the way of Christian life and faith. Here was a noble concept of educational theatre that worked.

One day the great west doors of the cathedral opened wide out onto the cathedral square. The plays' scaffolds, cramped with their vivid paraphernalia, moved out and took up improved positions along the front of the cathedral, whose Gothic façade was generally in some stage of construction by the townsmen for the glory of their God. The façade gave the proper ambiance to the performance, with the congregation transformed from worshipers into an unsophisticated audience in their own cathedral square. The cathedral was the focal point of every town and played both a spiritual and secular role in the community. First and foremost, it was the House of the Lord on earth—inspiring, ascendant, full of beauty and mystery and holy wonderment. In its secular capacity, it was called upon to serve as fortress, school, hospital, meeting place, and theatre. As a theatre, it combined gloriously the spiritual and secular needs of the entire community.

After the theatre emerged from the Church, the authority and responsibility for presenting the miracle plays was gradually transferred from the religious orders to the laity, vested either with a literary society or with guilds of workmen and craftsmen whose members represented the civic core of the medieval town. Each guild assumed responsibility for financing and producing episodes appropriate to its particular trade: Jonah for the fishermen, the Wise Men and the Nativity for the goldsmiths, and so forth. In the fourteenth century, released from the jurisdiction of the Church, the presentation of religious drama altered rapidly. Methods of presentation varied according to the countries and the seasons of the Church calendar. In England, the miracle plays were performed on pageant wagons; in France, the *mystère* on a long raised stage; in Germany, the *Mysterienspiel* generally on platforms; in Spain, the *Auto Sacramental* on rolling floats; and in Italy, the *sacre rappresentazione* on raised or wagon stages.

The production of religious plays expanded in the direction of naturalism. According to local conditions, they were performed in the market square, along the streets, occasionally in an old Roman amphitheatre, or even in a great hall as at Mons and Valenciennes, or in Paris in the Hôtel de Bourgogne under the license of a guild of amateur actors called the Confraternité de la Passion.

An international style of scenic investiture was recognized all over Europe. Each station could serve the action of many scenes. The earliest was called in Latin the *locus* or *sedes*, later a house or booth, *étal* or *mansion*. These were conveniently arranged side by side in a "polyscenic pattern" often sandwiched between Paradise at one side and Hellmouth at the other. The number of houses varied. The *sacre rappresentazione* of San Giovanni, presented in Florence in 1454, required twenty-two *edifizi* or houses.

Many contemporary drawings and plans from manuscripts and prompt books disclose detailed and varied scenic arrangements for the plays. A page of Jean Fouquet's *Très Riches Heures* (1425) provides a lively view of the *Mystère de Sainte Appolonia* with the director rehearsing the gory martyrdom of the unhappy saint before six busy scaffolds in the background. The frontispiece of the Valenciennes Manuscript of the *Mystère de la Passion* (1547) illustrates a permanent arrangement of three mansions lined up between Heaven on the left and Hellmouth on the right. In the back are city walls with gates to Jerusalem and Nazareth. The lake of Tiberius with one boat is on the right. Dozens of descriptive miniatures follow, clearly indicating the dramatic use of this simultaneous scene and providing a vivid slow-motion-picture account of the entire *mystère* in action. A primitive sketch of a German play of Saint Laurence shows a trestle stage set up in a Cologne square in 1581. This homemade stage was built under the shelter of several trees. Very prominent is the ominous grill on which the docile martyr will play his violent last scene. A backcloth is painted with gates and roads that lead off to the country. A Lucerne Easter play (1531) provides a busy ground plan with all the mansions disposed around the perimeter of the main square with standing room reserved for all the craning spectators in the center of the square.

Professor Gustave Cohen uncovered the remarkable prompt copy of the *Mystère de la Passion* as it was presented in Mons in 1501. This manuscript is an eyewitness backstage account of the organization and production of a great cycle containing 34,576 lines requiring 317 actors and forty-eight days of rehearsal. Minute expense accounts note every detail of this lavish naturalistic production that rolled on twice daily at four a.m. and four p.m. for days to its final conclusion. A large tank of water sunk in the stage was stocked with an assortment of fish and birds. A menagerie provided animals for many scenes. It was emptied for the Nativity and Noah's Ark and for the Creation too. For the latter there was real grass and flowers and trees in fruit. Trap doors, mechanical stage devices, and cloud machines were required to create the harrowing of Hell, the Ascension, and the Transfiguration, supplemented by fireworks, firelight, and starlight.

Every year in Mons, all this lavish realism brought the old recorded scenes dramatically back to life. For performers and spectators, the passion play was a total religious experience. Three hundred and seventeen friends and relatives lost their identity in assuming the roles of as many biblical characters. The audience was entranced with its intoxicating proximity to Eden or Hell and was emotionally transported to Jerusalem and the immediacy of those final days of Christ's Passion. "By the truth you shall know him." The ever-constant power of truth in reality was cogently set forth by Lee Simonson. "Realism and reality—in this case the reality of a religious truth—are not contradictory terms. The spiritual values of a passion play, like those of any other play, were created by the mind of its audience. And the performance, despite any amount of naturalistic detail, provided as violent a purgation by pity and terror as a classic tragedy could have given its hearers."

Those tragedies of the Greek dramatists presented in honor of Dionysus had the power to elevate the Athenians in their theatre with the same animating spirit that the spectacular theatre conceived for the glory of God later did for the citizens of Mons. Here is the confirmation that in all times for mankind "things of the spirit are created by the spirit."

# The Renaissance Theatre

An ancient tree stump sending forth a new green branch had long symbolized, according to Christian iconography, the Old Dispensation and the New. To the neo-Platonists and to the humanist theologians of the Renaissance, it also symbolized the revival of classical learning.

After twelve hundred years of feudalism and the domination of Catholicism, the New Dispensation heralded a new era of intellectual and artistic liberation born aloft on the wings of *il dolce stil nuovo*. The advent of the Renaissance was inevitable with the growth of a leisure class, the emergence of great houses of bankers and patrons, and the social and political maneuvering of powerful families. In Rome, the Orsini and Massimo clans were entrenched, the latter even claiming descent from the ancient Maximi recognized as early saviors of Republican Rome. Occupying the ancient Castello of Milan were the aggressive Sforzas, and in Florence, the house of de' Medici was founded by the pater familiae, Cosimo I. The noble families of Mantua and Ferrara were the Gonzagas and the d'Estes. Ercole I made Ferrara a model of cultivated taste and learning. The city was laid out on a grid with the ducal castello appropriately focused within the total plan. Ferrara took pride in her university boasting a distinguished faculty of some forty-five professors. Among them, and also attached to the d'Este court, were scholars and poets—Guarini, Pico della Mirandola, Bembo, Ariosto, and Castiglione. Outside the walls of Ferrara was Ercole's country retreat, the Palazzo Schiffanoia with a great festival hall and a *wunderkammer* and even an amusing small-scale wing to house the dwarfs attached to his court. The palazzo was set amidst a park with a model farm, a zoo, and buildings devoted to the practice of the arts and crafts. Ercole attracted a brilliant array of artists-in-residence to exercise their talents in the adornment of his court: Bramante, Leonardo, Mantegna, Jacopo Bellini, Cossa, and Piero della Francesca.

The members of those enlightened Italian enclaves of culture and learning believed that whatever was infused with the wisdom of the Greeks and Romans, whatever was wrought by their hands, was worthy of collecting and assimilating. Those ardent humanists of the Renaissance basked under the new-found "light of life-giving Helios," and as a result of this radiant process of transmission their renascent Italian civilization, like that of Greece, combined spirit and intellect without moral restraint. As Phidias had been ostracized from Athens for his audacity in representing the likeness of his friend Pericles on the shield of Athena enshrined in the Parthenon, so in Florence, Filippino Lippi offended the Church because he was pleased to paint the likeness of his mistress as the loveliest of virgins on the altar painting of one of the city's major churches.

There were many causes for the resurgence of paganism in the Renaissance of Italy. On all sides, from the Apennines to Naples, voices were rising from the past, speaking to the humanists in a language they understood, inciting them to revive the classic world that had been sleeping for centuries beneath the pall of the Dark Ages. The recoveries of the *Marble Faun* and the *Poetics* of Aristotle were hailed by the humanists with ecstatic furor not equaled by the Metropolitan Museum's acquisition of Rembrandt's *Aristotle Contemplating the Bust of Homer*.

Ancient classical sites were excavated and surrendered their treasures of sculpture, painting, and the decorative arts. Bramante and Alberti, Peruzzi, Serlio, and Palladio carried out expeditions to measure and sketch countless ancient structures. They codified their work and collated their findings with Vitruvius' seminal book

*De Architectura,* first published in Italy in 1486. During the next hundred years it would appear in thirty editions and five languages. This monumental work exerted a strong and lasting influence on all the architects and builders of the Renaissance. Vitruvius would be pleased to know that in Rome was formed a Classical Society whose members devoted themselves exclusively to the study and interpretation of his work.

In many Italian cities, scholars and humanists founded societies for translating and reading ancient Greek and Latin, and for the research and cultivation of the classical arts and letters. In Vicenza there was the Olympic Academy, for whom Andrea Palladio, a founding member, logically designed the Teatro Olimpico in the Roman theatre tradition. In Florence, the Platonic Academy was founded under the auspices of Cosimo de' Medici. The neo-Platonists were a cult of artists and savants who attempted to reconcile Christianity with the religion and myths of ancient Greece. Moses and Homer were identified together. With great splendor, Michelangelo portrayed *The Holy Family,* with Mary and Joseph resembling the archetypes of Hera and Zeus in front of a terrace occupied by a band of youthful nude Dionysian revelers. The cult found it difficult to equate Parnassus and Heaven, except in the theatre, where cloud machines could serve both parties quite satisfactorily. In Rome there was the Roman Academy founded in 1487 by humanist Pomponius Laetus. Members assumed Roman names, spoke Latin, and on occasion retreated to the Alban Hills, where they lived together on a farm in the manner of Pliny and Varro.

The printing press, imported to Italy from Germany in 1465, became the instrument, the quattrocento computer, for releasing the stored-up knowledge of philosophy, history, poetry, drama, and literature of classical antiquity. Humanists, scholars, and printers, with artists as illustrators, conspired to disseminate this world of wisdom heretofore preserved in illuminated incunabula and manuscripts held by a few exclusive keepers such as the banker-collector Cosimo de' Medici or the Benedictine abbot of Monte Cassino. Within twenty-five years appeared a sequence of notable first editions. Among them were Plato, Aristotle, Vitruvius, Plautus and Terence, Sophocles and Euripides. Hot off the primitive press, these great books dramatically created new institutions for man—the book shop as well as the private library. Vitruvius became available to architects, the comedies and tragedies of Greece and Rome provided entertainment for the academies and the ducal courts. The intellectual might of the classical world was at last accessible. The windows were open wide for all to see and hear. "The essence of humanism," Walter Pater asserted, "is the belief that nothing which has ever interested living men and women can wholly lose its vitality—no language they have spoken, nor oracle beside which they have ever been passionate, or expended time and zeal."

In the courts of the Renaissance, diversion and entertainment were woven closely into the design of daily court life. Occasions arose for more splendid celebration—the birth of an heir, marriage festivities or obsequies, an official visitor from another state, or high religious feast days. Their arrangements required careful planning, for the formal program might continue for more than a few days, with the court and guests participating full tilt in races and games, tourneys and equestrian ballets, processions and triumphal entries, water festivals, music, and dance.

Theatre could not hold its own weight as a counterbalance to all this festive diversion. There had been no valid tradition of secular theatre at the close of the Middle Ages on which to build a changing theatre relevant to the spirited new audience of the quattrocento. A new formula of theatre had to be discovered. Since the art of the new theatre was shepherded by poets and humanists, it was logical that they first take a long look backward to Rome and Athens. In the courts of northern Italy, Latin comedies and, later, Greek tragedies were at first recited and soon given erudite revivals in Latin. In 1486, *The Menaechmi* was performed in the cortile of the d'Este castello against a thousand-ducat production that featured a large boat. Before long, weather conditions and the intrusion of more sumptuous scenic innovations would necessitate moving theatre indoors forever. In the *sala festeggiante,* unity of place and limited space for new stage techniques would make the use of perspective essential and a proscenium separation necessary. In 1502, again in Ferrara, five days of Latin comedies were presented as part of the festivities of Lucrezia and Alfonso d'Este against contemporary decorations devised by Leonardo and Bramante. A century of classic revivals culminated in 1585 with the performance of Sophocles' *Oedipus Tyrannus* which opened Palladio's noble Teatro Olimpico in Vicenza.

Save for Machiavelli's hilarious and baudy *Mandragola,* very little significant original dramatic literature was produced in the Renaissance. Every city produced dramatists who drew on Plautus and Terence and continued to turn out frigid literary dramas for the governing intelligentsia. The poets Tasso, Guarini, Ariosto, and

Cardinal Bibbiena sought to build new comedies on ancient foundations by welding classic characters to their modern literary purpose. Ariosto's *Cassaria* met with great success in Ferrara in 1508. The scenery was enthusiastically applauded. Bernardino Prosperi described it in a letter to the former Isabella d'Este: "But what has been the best in all these festivities and representations has been the scenery in which they have been played, which Master Pelegrino, the Duke's painter, has made. It has been a view in perspective of a town with houses, churches, belfries and gardens, such that one could never tire of looking at it, because of the different things that were there, all most cleverly designed and executed. I suppose that this will not be destroyed, but that they will preserve it to use on other occasions." In 1513, Cardinal Bibbiena completed his *Calandria* in the "vulgar" Italian tongue. Though derived from Plautus' *Menaechmi*, the comedy was spiced up by using male and female twins. It "was presented in a truly magnificent style" under the supervision of "the perfect courtier," Baldassare Castiglione, in the Duke of Urbino's great hall. Girolamo Genga designed walled ramparts of a city to house the spectators, and, as a contemporary eyewitness reported, his "scene was laid in a very fine city with streets, palaces, churches and towers, all in relief and looking as if they were real, the effect being completed by admirable paintings in scientific perspective." The cardinal's comedy was performed five years later before Leo X in the Vatican with the design for the street scene entrusted to Baldassare Peruzzi, who was most skilled in the sorcery of perspective. On the death of Bramante, Leo X appointed young Raphael for the construction of Saint Peter's, for the papal excavations conducted in and around Rome, and also for the back-breaking supervision of the festivities of the papal court. In 1518, he installed according to Vitruvian precepts a classical theatre in the Pope's Castel Sant' Angelo for a single performance of Ariosto's *Suppositi*. A street scene with houses aligned in perfect perspective under a Raphaelesque sky evoked the admiration of His Holiness. Young Raphael could do no wrong.

The Renaissance poets, when not sharing Thalia with Plautus and Terence, turned their talents to cultivating the pastoral. This was a solemn, courtly form of nondirectional cinematic drama employing the loose structure of the *sacre rappresentazione* on which they superimposed classical and profane themes. An early experiment in this highly rhetorical genre of drama was Politian's *Favola d'Orfeo*, written in the vernacular and produced for the first time as a novelty in Mantua in 1471. Later, Tasso with *Aminta*, and Guarini with *Pastor Fido*, transformed this popular formula into an epic "spectacular." The setting was always the never-never land of Arcadia right out of Serlio's umbrageous satyric scene and inhabited by nymphs and satyrs, shepherds and rustics and enchanters.

In Florence at the close of the sixteenth century there was an avant-garde group of nobles, poets, and musicians who dubbed themselves the Camerata. Their amateur interest was in the visual and performing arts of the time and in establishing an organic union of music and drama. In searching for the "element of dramatic musical speech," they happened upon the formula of opera. In 1597–1598, Jacopo Peri, a composer member of the Camerata, took a short pastoral about Daphne and Apollo under the laurels and miraculously succeeded in wrapping their affair up in sheets of music. With this rudimentary musical play, opera, the *enfant terrible* of the performing arts, was born. Several years later, Peri converted the popular myth of Orfeo into lyric theatre. *Mirabile dictu*, only seven years later, Monteverdi, organist of San Marco in Venice, employing the same deathless tale of Orfeo, composed an avant-garde score of such dramatic power and magnitude that his opera continues to captivate modern audiences with the same splendor that shone forth at its premiere performance in Mantua in 1607. Only thirty years after the opening performance of Monteverdi's lyric masterpiece, the first public opera house, the Teatro San Cassiano, boasting three horseshoe galleries divided into boxes and built by public subscription, opened wide its doors to a popular audience in Venice. The theatre, both as an aristocratic and a public institution, was marching forward.

These two hundred explosive years of theatre, torn between adulation for the past of Greece and Rome and establishing new guidelines for the future, constitute our Renaissance theatre heritage. This heritage is the cornerstone for all that would happen later in the theatre of the western world.

# Designers in the Theatre

# Renaissance

During the quattrocento, the opportunities of perspective in achieving the illusion of reality in painting were fully explored by Giovanni Bellini, Mantegna, Botticelli, Perugino, and notably Luciano da Laurana and Piero della Francesca. The secular theatre, still laboring under the traditional techniques of the *sacre rappresentazione*, was slow to respond to this visual stimulus. But with the revival of classical drama in the following century, a universal concern was shown for setting the stage. In 1486, a contemporary reference was made to "the painted scenes—the first in our time" for a performance of *The Menaechmi* in Ferrara. The great halls in the palaces of Milan, Ferrara, Mantua, Urbino, and Florence became the testing grounds for experiments by artists and architects in achieving illusionistic effects of space and distance. A close relation between stage and hall was considered essential. Occasionally the entire hall was transformed into a town embracing a stage scene made up of three-dimensional painted scenery. Fanciful views in true perspective of Ferrara, Rome, and Florence were eye-filling. Vasari occasionally designed scenes for plays and frequently recorded in *The Lives of the Painters* his enthusiasm for the fashionable vogue of the neo-Vitruvian scene. A few artists and architects displayed special aptitude for devising scenery, machines, and lighting, and some collaborated with poets and musicians on new forms of plays with ballet and musical intermezzi for court entertainment.

(1) Sangallo, Aristotile da, 1481–1551 (attributed)
Italy, Florence
*Scena Urba*, c. 1535
Pen and bister washes on tan paper, 196 x 333 mm.

### *Aristotile da Sangallo*

Aristotile da Sangallo was both a painter and architect and one of the first scenographers of the Renaissance. His earliest scenic work was for the wedding festivities of Lorenzo de' Medici in 1518. A few years later, he provided the street scenes for Machiavelli's two ribald comedies *La Mandragola* (1520) and *La Cliza* (1526), which were performed in the homes of two Florentine patrons. Sangallo might have derived these indoor perspective scenes from the Via Larga and the Via Maggio, which by long Florentine custom had served as actual street scenes for splendid entries and carnival shows.

In 1539, many Florentine artists were engaged on the festivities for the nuptials of Cosimo I and Eleonora of Toledo. Sangallo designed a *prospettiva* for Antonio Landi's comedy *Il Commodo* set up in the second courtyard of the Palazzo de' Medici. The scene presented a view of Pisa with bizarre and capricious façades of palaces dominated by the leaning tower and the baptistry and illuminated by a sun that rose and set during the comedy. Cosimo was so pleased with Sangallo's artful achievement of unity of place and time that he was entrusted with the stage decorations for the city's carnival comedies for succeeding years.

Sangallo worked in Rome between 1543 and 1547 in the private theatres of Roberto Strozzi, of Cardinal Alessandro Farnese in the Palazzo Cancellaria, and of Pierluigi Farnese in Castro. In the latter's theatre, he introduced the revolving *periaktoi* of the classical theatre to achieve a rapid change of scene. This device is illustrated in Vignola's *Le Due Regole della Prospettiva*, published after his death in 1583 by Egnazio Danti. Danti states that this system of revolving prisms for changing scenes had been used for the first time by Sangallo in the theatre of Castro. Sangallo admired Vitruvius. He made perspective sketches for the tragic and comic scenes along the margin of his own copy of Vitruvius' treatise on the Roman theatre. Sangallo, with all his experience in the theatre, contemplated writing a book on trends of scenography, but unfortunately his time and interest ran out, leaving the field to his contemporary Sebastiano Serlio.

*Illustration 1.* For what play was this scene intended? Was the scene designed by Aristotile da Sangallo himself or by the exploring hand of a contemporary? Who can say? The design is the important thing, for certainly it suggests the proliferation of the city scene (*scena urba*) of Sangallo's more advanced thinking. There is the elaborate double-triple arrangement of steps connecting the stage and auditorium. The walls of the latter probably continued the painting of the front houses of the scene. Those four lines clearly drawn on the floor parallel to the front of the stage cannot be without meaning. They might indicate grooves to guide concealing scenic panels to roll on stage for *intermezzi*. Or they might indicate tracks in which to roll the Florentine house wings on and off stage to effect a change of scene.

The artist is experimenting with space and introduces three *perspettive* within a single scene. One recalls that three *perspettive* appear through the three doors of the Vitruvian *scaenae frons* illustrated in the 1556 edition of Vitruvius published by the noted humanist Daniele di Barbaro with woodcuts designed by Andrea Palladio. Place before the rear of this scene of Sangallo the stage façade of Palladio's Teatro Olimpico with its three openings, and there is the prototype of Scamozzi's three "revolutionary" *perspettive* which he would later introduce behind Palladio's *scaenae frons*. Aristotile da Sangallo, as a practicing scenographer, learned that, as

Leonardo said, "perspective could not function without architecture nor architecture without perspective."

Agne Beijer, in his study of an early sixteenth-century Roman scenic design in the National Museum of Stockholm, presents material on early Italian perspective scenes which relates to the characteristics of this design.

*Illustration 2.* The drawing shows two examples of the one-point perspective street scene which was the early scenic formula of the Renaissance theatre.

The attribution to Sallustio Peruzzi, son of the famous architect of the High Renaissance, is based on a similarity in style between these two drawings and another attributed to Peruzzi in the Uffizi.

(2) Peruzzi, Sallustio, d. 1573 (attributed)
Italy, Florence
Two Designs for Street Scenes, 1560–1570
Pen and brown ink with gray ink wash on white paper, 215 x 140 mm.
On the verso is a pen and brown ink drawing of two hermit saints with a bird—possibly a copy of an engraving after Parmigianino.

### Jan Vredeman de Vries

Jan Vredeman de Vries was a Dutch painter, decorator, and engraver of architecture, ornament, and perspective. He studied painting in Antwerp and Maline and received many commissions in cities of the Low Countries and Germany.

In Flanders in the early sixteenth century, the universities and courts and expanding commercial cities such as Louvain and Antwerp became influential centers for the dissemination of Italian humanism. Latin and Greek classics became familiar to a large public through translations edited by northern scholars and artists. Pieter Coecke van Alst (1502–1550), painter and architect, made the first translation of Vitruvius (1537) and Serlio (1539) in Antwerp and Brussels.

Jan Vredeman de Vries was called "the Flemish Vitruvius" because he was so influential in furthering the architectural ideas of the High Renaissance in northern Europe. His *Architectura*, published in 1563, was a mannerist patternbook of Flemish architecture overlaid with classical and Renaissance motifs. This work exerted a strong influence on English building, and also on the architecture of northern Europe beyond the mid-seventeenth century. His book *Artis Perspectivae*, first published in Antwerp in 1568, included all the formulas and latest thinking on perspective in Italy. Two more books of de Vries were published in 1604 and 1605 in The Hague and Leyden. These works, with his arresting engravings, popularized Renaissance architecture in several series of engravings which illustrated stage perspective, interiors, palace and garden architecture.

*Illustration 3*. The drawing, like so many of Jan Vredeman de Vries' engravings, has all the appearance of a stage decoration. An Italian Renaissance street scene in perspective terminates in classical ruins.

The only record of de Vries' activity in the theatre was in connection with the greatest imperial fete of the sixteenth century—the triumphal entry of Philip II of Spain into Antwerp in 1549. These festivities marked the recognition of the son of Charles V as hereditary ruler of the Low Countries. Delegations of artists from Spain, Germany, England, Florence, and Genoa provided the decorations. De Vries, only twenty-two years old, is said to have worked on many of the Renaissance architectural features of triumphal arches and theatres for *tableaux vivants*. These are splendidly illustrated in one of the earliest Renaissance festival books, *Spectaculorum . . . ,* which Cornelius Grapheus, the Secretary of Antwerp, had published in Latin, French, and Flemish as a pictorial record of this international occasion.

### Sebastiano Serlio

Sebastiano Serlio learned to draw and paint from his journeyman father, and though he spent forty years painting frescoes in churches, palaces, and public buildings, optics, the science of perspective, and measuring ancient buildings with drawing instruments were his deep interests. One day in 1525, at the age of fifty, Serlio awoke and, discarding his paints and brushes, adopted the plumbline and measure as his new tools, and left Bologna for Rome.

When he arrived, Bramante, Raphael, Michelangelo, and Baldassare Peruzzi were the archangels of painting and architecture. At once he fell under the spell of Peruzzi, and though it seems doubtful that Serlio at fifty, four years older than Peruzzi, was actually an apprentice, he regarded Peruzzi "his most intelligent preceptor—of whom I am the humble disciple and the heir of a minute particle of his knowledge." Peruzzi was a creative Renaissance genius who found time to analyze the classical orders, investigate perspective, write a commentary on the ten books of Vitruvius, and carry out excavations of antiquities in Rome for the Pope.

While Serlio absorbed what Peruzzi had to teach, he led a precarious existence. A few minor architectural commissions in Venice came his way, he devised a wooden theatre in the courtyard of the Porta Palace in Vicenza, and he made an expedition to the Dalmatian coast to measure Roman monuments, notably the amphitheatre at Pola. But most important, he was preparing his monumental commentary on architecture to appear separately in seven books, beginning in 1537, the year Peruzzi died. Peruzzi's legacy to his elder apprentice was a collection of his manuscripts and drawings which would become incorporated in Serlio's architectural project. In order to get support for his major opus, Serlio dispatched a copy of Book IV to François I, Europe's most liberal patron. In 1541, the king responded and summoned Serlio to Paris to join a group of Italian artists, among them Il Rosso, Primaticcio, and Cellini, whose civilizing art added luster and polish to his northern court. Serlio was engaged to design a wing of the Louvre and of the chateau at Fontainebleau, though he continued work with his books on architecture. When François I died, the foreign artists in residence fell out of royal favor and Philibert de l'Orme supplanted Serlio. Rheumatic and destitute, he found sanctuary with the Italian Cardinal of Ferrara in Lyon, and by working on minor projects, he saw Books V and VI published. Book VII he sold to Strada the antiquarian and it was ultimately published twenty years later in Augsburg. Still hoping for reemployment, he returned to Fontainebleau and died in 1554. Serlio was an academician and a theorist; a "collector and a disseminator," as Lionello Venturi called him. Above all, he was a dedicated architectural historian who "transcribed the images of the past for the glory of the future." Serlio had gone far for one born an old man.

Book II, published when Serlio was seventy, and devoted to general problems of perspective, was of the greatest influence. At the end of the book, Serlio gives special attention to the planning of theatres and to the design and making of stage scenery; this was the first account of accepted Renaissance theatre practice in the first half of the sixteenth century in Italy. It would exert an enormous influence on the subsequent development of the theatre of Europe and remains today a seminal document of Renaissance theatre practice.

(3) de Vries, Jan Vredeman, 1527–1604
(attributed)
Holland (active in Antwerp, The Hague,
Leyden, and Germany)
Street Scene, c. 1580
Sepia pen with brown wash, 228 x 162 mm.

Where did Serlio acquire his knowledge of the Renaissance theatre? The temporary wooden theatre he built at Vicenza seemed to be his only practical experience in the theatre. In seventy years, however, Serlio must have seen much theatrical entertainment and, like all architects and painters of the Renaissance, he was interested in everything he saw. The modern theatres and scenes based on classical precepts so intrigued him that he could easily turn out a treatise on technical matters of the theatre and the craft of scenography with the authority of an academician.

*Illustration 4.* The tattered sketch for the *scena comica* is an accurate representation of Serlio's woodcut of 1545, which he describes in detail: "The first scene, the Comic Scene, shall represent the dwellings of private persons such as citizens, lawyers, merchants, parasites and other like men. The house of the Procuress (Rufiana) must not be lacking, nor must the scene be without a tavern. A Church is also very necessary. The method of setting these buildings in position I have already given and I now discuss the details of their construction. In a small engraving I can do no more than suggest some details certain to please, such as an open portico with arches in the modern style that lead to another house.

"The balconies are well adapted to perspective; so are the cornices whose ends project from the corners of the building, cleverly intermingled with others that are merely painted, which produce an excellent effect. Those houses too, which have a heavily projecting upper story, are of great use; you may see one in the Hostelry of the Moon. One must take especial care to remember to place the

(4) Serlio, Sebastiano, 1475–1554 (copy after)
Italy, Bologna (active also in Rome)
The Comic Scene, c. 1550 (See also color plate 1)
Red chalk and gray ink wash on white paper, 260 x
190 mm.
Inscribed in cartouche at top: "*Scena Comica*"

### Bartolomeo Neroni

In 1560, Cosimo I de' Medici, Grand Duke of Tuscany, made a state visit to Siena. One of the events of the series of festivities given in his honor was a performance of Alessandro Piccolomini's play *L'Ortensio* presented in the learned Accademia degli Intronati. The design for the play was entrusted to Bartolomeo Neroni ("Il Riccio"), a Sienese painter who had studied with Il Sodoma and painted decorations for many of Siena's churches.

The stage and hall of the Renaissance theatre were traditionally united by flights of steps, but in this Sienese design the stage scene becomes permanently divorced from the architecture of the auditorium by Neroni's impressive proscenium arch. The arch is adorned with the Muses of Comedy and Poetry seated above two standing figures representing Prologues. Overhead a massive cornice supports a valance and a rich cartouche reserved for the Medici crest. Neroni's elaborate Renaissance picture frame must have related to the decoration of the hall of the Accademia. It bore no relation to the perspective scene or to the actors on the stage in front of the scene. It made possible highly desirable working areas offstage right and left and also overhead. It provided for a theatre curtain which would further alienate the stage from the hall. In 1560 this proscenium was a very novel and fateful idea which would soon take over and become a fixed convention—a convention which the theatre has lived with for four hundred years.

*Illustration 5.* Bartolomeo Neroni's design reveals a Sienese *strada nobile* lined with palaces and stately buildings including the Gothic façade of the Duomo in the distance. When this setting first appeared on the stage, it must have had some unusual significance and made a lasting impression on the spectators, for twenty-nine years later a chiaroscuro woodcut by Bolsi was published by Andreani to record the scene.

A crayon and ink copy of this setting without the proscenium is in the Theatre Collection of the National Museum in Stockholm. Girolamo da Bolsena made a chiaroscuro woodcut of the drawing which was published by Andrea Andreani in 1589. This woodcut is in the print collections of the Metropolitan Museum and the Victoria and Albert Museum.

*Illustration 6.* The more sophisticated sixteenth-century modernists steered clear of the "unrealism" of the formal classical stage such as that of the Teatro Olimpico. Their development of the use of the *periaktoi* made shifting scenes possible and thus encouraged more elaborate productions. The Vitruvian tradition of tragic, comic, and

smaller houses in the foreground, in order that the others which are behind may be visible, as for instance, the house of the Procuress whose sign, the three hooks, may be seen in the illustration. The superior height of the houses further back gives the appearance of grandeur and better completes the scene, which would not be the case if each house were lower than the one in front.

"Although the things here designed have their shadows painted on one side, still they show to better advantage when they are illuminated from the middle of the stage; therefore let the strongest lights hang high up above the center of the stage. Those roundels or squares that appear throughout the scene are all transparent lights of various colors. It will be well to put lights behind the windows which are facing, whether they be of glass, of paper or of painted linen. But were I to give you all the hints I could about these things, I should be held to be tedious. Therefore I will leave them for the invention of those who wish to exercise their intelligence."

The cartouche is a later addition. Stylistically, it is out of character with the drawing. The watermark, a seven-petaled flower, indicates a sixteenth-century Lombard or Venetian origin for the paper.

satyric scenes succeeded in converting the entire stage into a realistic realm of make-believe. The cinquecento designers of street scenes recognized the pictorial possibilities of a modern city. They gave their buildings an ordered "real" look. But in stark contrast, their streets are empty and the buildings seem silent and uninhabited, with that sleepy air of loneliness one finds in Edward Hopper's cityscapes. They look as though they were waiting for the doors to be unlocked and the play to begin. Where are the actors?

This is probably a north Italian drawing. The architecture, carefully rendered in red crayon, suggests Ferrara. A modest proscenium is indicated on the left side of the sketch. This frames two sets of wings that conform with the perspective painting of the rear drop. The setting was admirably designed in accordance with Vignola's principles of stage perspective. Vignola was one of the greatest Roman architects and architectural writers of the cinquecento. The *Due Regole della Prospettiva Pratica* was among his papers at the time of his death, which Egnazio Danti, mathematician, cosmographer, and archi-

tect, edited with his commentary in 1583. It remained a basic text on perspective well into the seventeenth century. On page 34 are Vignola's two diagramatic woodcuts that illustrate "the method of designing the perspective of the scene so that that which is painted on the back wall accords with that painted on the real houses on the stage," and also his method of shifting scenes by means of five *periaktoi*. Vignola's woodcuts are the basis of this north Italian artist's scene design, and the scene design exemplifies Vignola's system of scenography.

*Illustration 7*. By the seventeenth century, Serlio's basic rustic exterior was subjected to undreamed-of modifications. The possibilities of changing scenes by rotating prisms or sliding wings in slots on the stage floor gave the designer far greater flexibility and opened up new avenues of eye-filling scenic transformations.

This *scena maritima* with soaring cliffs bordering a stage-wide river is a common seventeenth-century design. The wings of cliffs and trees are deliberately out of scale with the miniature villas and castles that adorn them. The

(5) Neroni, Bartolomeo (called "Il Riccio"), c. 1500–1571 (attributed)
Italy, Siena
A Street in Siena behind a Proscenium Arch, 1560
Pen and bister ink with ink wash on white paper, 279 x 380 mm.
Collections: Flury-Herard, Paris; Alexandre Benois

stage floor is a watery plain of painted ground rows receding toward the horizon.

Many variations of this stock scene appear frequently in illustrated seventeenth-century festival books. It was used in Obizzi's *L'Ermiona* presented in Padua in 1636. Neptune and Venus are in a car drawn by swans, and Egeus appears on horseback calmly riding the waves. *Fedra Incoronata* was presented in the Munich Opera House in 1662 with settings by Francesco Santurini. One setting depicts six pairs of rock wings surrounding a bay, divided horizontally by the water's surface to reveal, below, Neptune's aqueous throne hall in a grotto, and above, an oarsman steering his barque over the water. In the very rare copy of Obizzi's *L'Amor Riformato*, presented in Ferrara in 1671, six out of eleven illustrations represent a *scena maritima*, each depicting a boat, an island, or a conch shell floating on the waves, or a band of gods and heroes emerging from a submarine garden.

A similar scene appears in Aureli's *Il Favore degli Dei*, presented in the great theatre of Parma in 1690. In this

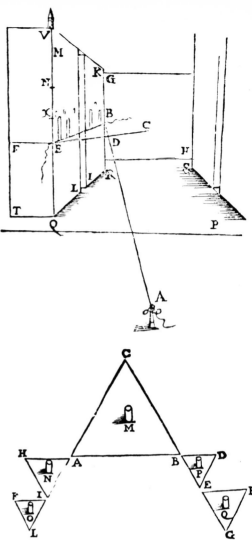

(6) Unknown artist, sixteenth century
    Italy
    A Street Scene, c. 1590
    Red crayon, 280 x 377 mm.

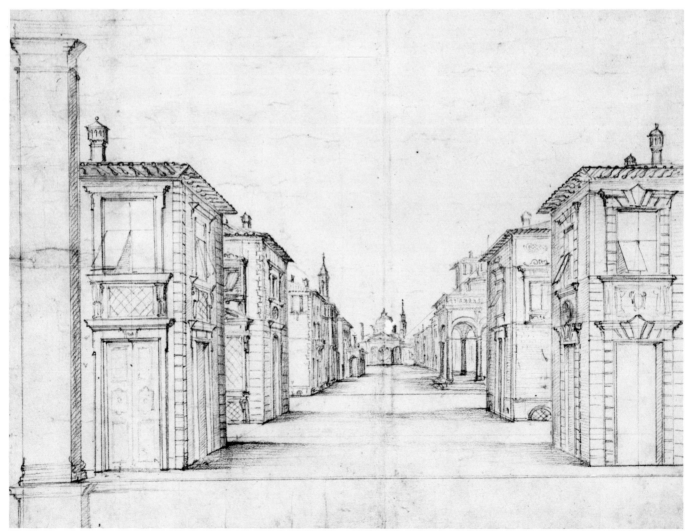

(7) Unknown artist, seventeenth century
Italy
Cliffs with River Between, c. 1620
Pen and bister with gray wash, 230 x 313 mm.

design, Ferdinando Bibiena introduced Juno, born by a sea monster, arriving on a desert island encircled by the inevitable rocky cliffs.

There were infinite variations on the theme of the *scena maritima*, which was one of a dozen prescribed locales in baroque scenography; some others were the royal atrium, the public place, the military encampment, the prison, and the *aula sepolcrale* or the lower world. The limited scenic repertory of the baroque opera house was defined by the standard scenic requirements of the opera librettist. However, the designer's ingenious modifications within the framework of this limited repertory proved inexhaustible.

*Illustration 8*. This terrifying scene with a volcano in eruption might have employed the same high cliffs of the preceding drawing. The volcano, however, is the important feature and dominates the scene. Italian audiences have always thrilled to the sight of Etna or Vesuvius performing in their laps, belching fire and smoke, and rocketing ash with a deafening din. The same audience would have fled in terror from the real thing, but, on the stage,

one rarely saw the real thing, except when a theatre caught fire and burned to the ground under the fiery collaboration of Vulcan and the designer. That happened to many an old theatre. This early design is tne forerunner of a long line of visual violence on the Italian stage.

*Illustration 9*. This Arcadian setting for an unknown pastoral play recalls John Addington Symonds' definition of the central motif of *Pastor Fido* as "the contrast between the actual world of ambition, treachery, and sordid strife, and the ideal world of pleasure, loyalty, and tranquil ease."

The artist tried to create order out of many unrelated elements by aligning his wings in perspective on the stage floor. Thus he incorporated many locales in one scene—a rustic house, a rocky forest, a waterfall, a fence with garden gate, a *tempietta*, and, atop the opposite precipice, a villa. The composite scene debouched into an open landscape with a fortified hilltown above a river receding in the distance, quite reminiscent of those charming views seen through the windows of Renaissance paintings.

Like the simultaneous scene required by the Italian

religious play, this composite scene served the fluid action of pastoral plays such as Tasso's *Aminta* and Guarini's *Pastor Fido*. These plays were translated and imitated everywhere. In Paris a few years later, with the same theatrical intention, two French designers, Mahelot and Laurent, devised practical, though more primitive sketches of simultaneous scenes for the plays of Hardy and Rotrou for the stage of the two-hundred-year-old Hôtel de Bourgogne. At the same time, across the channel in London, Shakespeare's multi-scened plays were being performed on the bare stage of the Globe without benefit of one wing of scenery.

This drawing was acquired with Illustration 8. It appears to be by the same hand, though this drawing bears indication of later washes.

### *Giulio Parigi*

In Florence by the close of the cinquecento, plays were interspersed with many *intermezzi* or interludes combining instrumental music, song, dance, and scenery. Because of its dramatic attraction, the *intermezzo* of the Inferno was invariably included in every court entertainment of the seventeenth century. The Inferno served as a violent intrusion, a dramatic contrast to the pacific or celestial scenes that preceded or followed it. The setting for the Inferno was a High-Renaissance interpretation of the oldest and most popular stage scene in the western theatre. Appropriately, it combined Hades, which was the lower world of the ancients, with the Hellmouth of Christian drama.

Dante conceived his Inferno as a conical void descending to the very core of the earth. The Renaissance scene designers conceived the realm of Pluto and Lucifer as a rockbound, flaming habitation of winged dragons, loathsome harpies, demons, and Furies brandishing sulphurous torches. Of such grotesquerie are the macabre sights in Hieronymus Bosch's *Last Judgment* and *Garden of Pleasures*, the fantasy in Breughel's *Seven Vices*, Callot's *Temptation of Saint Anthony*, and *The Inferno* of William Blake. The Inferno was always an awesome sight for the ducal spectators, with Mars or Hercules, Paris or Circe, and their chorus of attendants descending into the lower regions.

These elaborate productions tested the talent and engineering skill of several generations of Florentine scenic designers. Bernardo Buontalenti, appropriately called *delle Girandole* ("of the fireworks"), was in the service of the Medici for nearly sixty years, designing everything from villas to fortresses. For the grand-ducal festivities he designed scenery, invented machinery and fireworks, and

(8) Unknown artist, seventeenth century
Italy
Landscape with Volcano in Eruption, c. 1620
(See also color plate 2)
Pen and bister with watercolor, 260 x 350 mm.
Collection: Alexandre Benois

OVERLEAF

(9) Unknown artist, seventeenth century
Italy
Landscape with Rustic Houses and Waterfall, c. 1620
(See also color plate 4)
Pen and bister with watercolor, 270 x 351 mm.
Collection: Alexandre Benois

(10) Parigi, Giulio, 1590–1636
Italy, Florence
Inferno with Hellmouth, c. 1625
Pen and bister ink with gray ink wash, 320 x 480 mm.
Collections: Wilhelm Alexander Freud, Berlin
(Lugt 954) ; Smith College Museum of Art

arranged pageants and processions. He was a typical man of the Renaissance. His pupil Giulio Parigi carried on his work, and later, Giulio's son Alfonso succeeded his father. Fortunately, many of their scenes have been brilliantly recorded in the illustrations of *libretti* engraved by Agostino Carracci, Cantagallina, Stefano della Bella, and Jacques Callot. Souvenir festival books memorializing the splendid occasions of other courts of Italy reveal that many other talented designers such as Tacca, Guitti, and Santurini also surpassed themselves in their designs for the *intermezzi* and especially for the Inferno scene. They invented endless variations on the theme.

*Illustration 10*. The rocky clefts of this design scarcely contained the toothsome Hellmouth with lolling eyes and flattened nostrils. On the cue for all hell to break loose, the cavernous throat literally belched fire by means of stagehands suddenly igniting dozens of balls of cotton impregnated with *aqua vitae*.

Few drawings of Giulio Parigi have survived. This detailed drawing has the precision and mannerisms asso-

ciated with Parigi's style as reflected in contemporary engravings of his work.

*Illustration 11*. These drawings (see page 40) might have been for Monteverdi's *Orfeo*, which enjoyed continued success long after its initial production at the Court of Mantua in 1607.

These sketches are working drawings made by an anonymous designer for a scene of Pluto's throne hall. They clearly indicate how the entire setting was to be built and painted. A marginal notation on the left drawing indicates four wings with four backings. These are represented in perspective on the elevation. Above is a profile canopy that hung in the center of the scene over Pluto's throne. The right drawing indicates half of the cut-out backdrop with a suggestion in pen of the rear exterior backdrop. The Serlian style of rusticated architecture is eerily interwoven with demon faces and serpents with grotesque heads. Though there is no indication of stifling smoke or fire, Pluto must have been delighted with his demonic throne hall.

*Illustration 12.* This costume is strikingly like many pictured in Bernardo Buontalenti's designs for the six *intermezzi* of *La Pellegrina* performed in the Uffizi on May 2, 1589, celebrating the nuptials of Grand Duke Ferdinand and Christine of Lorraine. Francis Yates considers these *intermezzi* "a landmark in the history of Court Festival, for with them the new European genre of opera comes to birth."

(11) Unknown artist, seventeenth century
  Italy
  Throne Hall of the Palace of Pluto, 1630–1650
  Pencil, pen, and bister wash; right: 265 x 210 mm.;
  below: 280 x 165 mm.

*Illustration 13.* In 1613, Inigo Jones journeyed to Italy in the train of Thomas, Earl of Arundel. There is no evidence that while in Florence he actually witnessed any *intermezzi* designed by Parigi or Buontalenti. However, he must have returned to London armed with engravings of those spectacular scenes they had designed for the Medici festivals. Also, he must have later acquired engravings of their subsequent productions up to 1637, for he borrowed or domesticated practically every one of their designs for the masques he devised for his Stuart patrons at Whitehall.

Inigo Jones may have intended his costume design of an elderly anti-masquer for Sir William Davenant's *Brit-*

(12) Buontalenti, Bernardo, 1536–1608
Italy, Florence
Costume for an Intermezzo, 1589
Pen, brown ink, and wash, 362 x 247 mm.

(13) Jones, Inigo, 1573–1652
England, London
Costume Design for an Old Man, probably 1638
Pen and sepia ink with gray wash, 151 x 91 mm.
Collections: P. Crozat (Lugt 474) ; Reitlinger

*tania Triumphans*, which was presented in the temporary masquing room of Whitehall in 1638. A brief pen sketch of a masquer's headdress also appears on the lower margin of this design. The six entries of the anti-masquers were performed against "a horrid hell"—a scene Jones had copied from the Realm of Pluto which Alfonso Parigi had designed for *La Flora*, a Medici festivity presented in Florence in 1628.

Many costumes for *Brittania Triumphans* are in the collection of the Duke of Devonshire in Chatsworth House and are reproduced in the definitive work on Inigo Jones by Stephen Orgel and Roy Strong, *Inigo Jones: The Theatre of the Stuart Court* (London, 1973).

# Baroque and Rococo

The baroque scenographer was a canny engineer with a touch of genius. He could transform an entire *scène à vista* within a few seconds. He could engulf a palace in clouds or a city in fire or flood. He contrived machines that sent gods and goddesses soaring through space in aerial chariots, accompanied by flying choruses of singing nymphs. A huge figure of Atlas shouldering the globe could turn into an Atlas mountain. He dispatched sea monsters and galleons cleaving through turbulent seas. He set the sun, the moon, and the stars in motion. He could dramatize visually anything and everything short of an act of God. His was theatre at its most theatrical.

Mural painting is the clue to an understanding of the craft of scene painting in the seventeenth and eighteenth centuries. Good scene painting followed the practice of good mural painting. There is a fresco by Ferdinando Bibiena on the barrel vault of the nave of San Agostino in Fano, which was executed with the same painting technique and theatrical projection employed in painting scenery, as was Pozzo's ceiling of San Ignazio in Rome, and Colonna's and Mitelli's miraculous architectural *trompe l'oeil* on the walls of the Sala degli Argenti in the Pitti Palace in Florence. The same telling brushwork was applied alike to plaster wall and canvas scene.

Scenery was painted in light and shade by the scene painters from the sketch of the scenographer. The scenographers relied heavily on the scene painters' skill and ingenuity, for the scene painters were a superior breed of craftsmen. With their traditional training and knowledge of architectural decoration, they were adept at taking the designers' small sketches, with generally no indication of scale, and translating and expanding them into the full scale of the actual scene on the stage of the opera house.

The colors of most baroque architectural decoration were generally muted. For good but different reasons, scenographers preferred the same low-keyed, limited palette in the execution of their scenes. The light from candle and oil, which provided general stage illumination, was yellow and smoky. This light played unfortunate tricks with clear warm and cool tempera colors. If you place the original color sketch by Ferdinando Bibiena shown in Illustration 29 under warm candlelight, it loses its color intensity and approaches a color-value drawing. Similarly, in the eighteenth-century theatre, the unfortunate effect of stage lighting on true color forced the scenic artist to adopt the convention of painting scenery in color value to achieve the most naturalistic effect. Light and shadow were painted in neutral tones and their color values exaggerated. By so doing, scenery held its own under stage illumination.

(14) Torelli, Giacomo, 1604–1678
Italy, Venice (active in Paris)
A Royal Entry in a Classical Court, 1655–1660
Pen and gray wash on gray paper, 285 x 340 mm.

### Giacomo Torelli

Giacomo Torelli was the scion of a prominent family of Fano. Independent, wealthy, and headstrong, he was determined to have a career in the performing arts. In neighboring Ferrara he fell under the influence of the talented designer Francesco Guitti, and of the theatre architect-engineer Gianbattista Aleotti, who had designed the Teatro Farnese and its stage machinery in Parma in 1618. Later Torelli worked as an apprentice in the Teatro del Sole in Pesaro, where Nicolo Sabbatini was the designer and machinist. Sabbatini's seminal treatise, *Pratica*

*di Fabricar Scene e Macchine ne' Teatri*, published in Pesaro in 1638, describes and illustrates the scenic practices of the late-sixteenth- and early-seventeenth-century theatre in Italy. It was this theatrical training in Pesaro that sent Torelli in 1640 to Venice, the acknowledged opera center of Europe where every quarter boasted a theatre.

Torelli, with his ambition and drive, quickly made a place for himself in the new Teatro Novissimo as machinist and designer. The theatre opened the following season with *La Finta Pazza*, and his five scenes with machines were a smashing success. For each of three succeeding seasons he mounted a new spectacular opera. The printed libretti of two of these operas contain engravings of his designs which reveal he was exploring new ways of using stage space and perspective. His designs were consciously composed for the proscenium frame. Torelli's pictorial concern for the picture frame increased the separation of stage and auditorium for all time.

On the stage of the Novissimo, Torelli could develop his technical ideas for stage machinery. He improved on Sabbatini's cloud machines, flying devices, and lighting control. He invented a new system for shifting scenery which would serve most of the stages of Europe through the eighteenth century. This centralized system utilized eight sets of carriages rolling in tracks below the stage. These carriages supported frames in slots of the stage floor, and painted wings were attached to the frames. All the carriages were controlled below stage by a single drum so counterweighted that one stagehand turning a windlass could shift all sixteen wings in orderly unison. These swift *à vista* changes of scene achieved the fluidity and visual animation essential to baroque opera. Exterior scenes could meld into interiors complete with ceilings. Heaven could flow into Hell, and Hell in turn could be lost in clouds. Mechanical expertise made the professional designer an essential collaborator with the librettist and composer of the new baroque opera.

In 1645, the widowed Queen Anne of France requested the Duke of Parma to send his stage designer, choreographer, and some players to join her favorite Italian troupe playing in Paris. The Duke obliged with the choreographer and the actors, but, believing the French court should have the best of Italian designers, he recommended Torelli. Hoping to repeat his initial success in Venice, Torelli chose *La Finta Pazza* for his opening opera in the renovated Théâtre du Petit Bourbon. To please the French, he set the harbor of Skyros for Act I on the banks of the Seine with a view of the Pont Neuf, Sainte Chapelle, and the distant towers of Notre Dame. The opera was a *succès fou* and it launched Torelli's career in Paris.

*Orphée*, a tragicomedy by Buti with music by Rossi, was Torelli's next major production, presented in 1647 on the new stage of the Palais Royal (formerly Richelieu's theatre). Charles Errard, *peintre et architecte ordinaire du Roi*, assisted by Noel Coypel and Gilbert de Sève, was engaged to design the settings for *Orphée* under the surveillance of Torelli. Per Bjurström writes, "Most likely Torelli was responsible for the machinery while the French artists looked after the scenery. This would have been in keeping with what we know of Mazarin's efforts to suit the new art to French taste."

The marvels of Torelli's machinery and his lavish scenic inventions were unknown to the theatre of France and were acclaimed enthusiastically. But the heralded *Orphée*, which lasted six hours, was too Italian and had only six performances. The Queen and Mazarin, clearly interested in a new form of musical creation more congenial to the French taste, commissioned Corneille in 1650 to write a new libretto. With a French eye to economy, Mazarin persuaded the great Corneille to write his text around the old *Orphée* scenery stored in a warehouse, and the result was the tragedy of *Andromède*. There was a prologue and one setting for each act of the play, but something was missing. Corneille confessed in the printed preface of the play, "*Cette pièce n'est que pour les yeux.*"

In 1659, the architect and designer Gaspare Vigarani was imported from Modena to build a great new theatre in the Tuileries that would surpass in grandeur every other theatre in Europe. Vigarani schemed jealously against any competition from Torelli, who, after all, was the principal court designer. Mazarin continued to support Torelli, but his career in the French theatre was drawing to a close and he found himself excluded from any plans for the king's sumptuous wedding festivities. In 1661, Mazarin died, and in the same year, Louis XIV's powerful minister Fouquet was the host of an extravagant fête in honor of the king, featuring the première of Molière's *Les Fâcheux*, designed by Torelli. The king at eighteen was envious and angry at this ostentatious display, and Fouquet was deprived of his estate and imprisoned for life. For his participation in this event, Torelli became persona non grata in the French court.

After sixteen years in France, Torelli returned to Italy and resumed his patrician role as a leading citizen of Fano. He started life in the theatre all over again with a new theatre aptly called the Teatro della Fortuna. His final production was his own memorial—a theatrical sarcophagus in the church of San Pietro in Valle.

*Illustration 14.* Giacomo Torelli must have supervised the designs for many *fêtes de la Cour* during the early years of Louis XIV's reign. This design for "A Royal Entry" was probably made for one of those splendid occasions, since it cannot be attributed to a particular opera or ballet. It is a Roman Triumph set in a Franco-Italian Doric atrium. The youthful Sun King as Emperor of the Romans, his robes embroidered with *fleurs-de-lys*, sits majestically in his baroque festival car drawn by two docile lions. In the background, a Roman sacrifice is made to the sound of classic music. The king is surrounded by members of his court, all participating in his triumphal procession. The atrium's balconies and other points of vantage are filled with spectators in contemporary dress admiring the childlike pleasures of their young king.

*Illustrations 15 & 16.* The drawing in illus. 15 was probably made by Charles Errard (or Coypel or de Sève) for one of the original scenes for *Orphée* since the French artists were credited with the designs for the scenes and Torelli with the overall supervision of the production and the machines. Unfortunately, no engravings illustrate the *Orphée* libretto. However, this design does suit the description of the opening scene of *Orphée*'s third act—a wild, deserted landscape, with a cave in the rear like a rocky *allée* leading back to a patch of sea and sky. It also

(15) Errard, Charles, 1606–1689 (attributed)
France, Paris
A Deserted Landscape with Open Cave, 1647
(See also color plate 3)
Pen and black ink with opaque watercolor,
309 x 420 mm.
Collection: Léon Bakst

(16) Errard, Charles (attributed)
Prologue for *Andromède* by Pierre Corneille
Engraving by F. Chauveau
Paris, 1650

most certainly suited the Prologue of *Andromède*, for it is almost identical with Chauveau's engraving (Illus. 16) for the Prologue in the first illustrated edition of Corneille's *Andromède, Tragedie Représentée avec Les Machines sur le Théâtre Royal de Bourbon* published in 1650.

### Ferdinando Tacca

Ferdinando Tacca's father, Pietro, was a sculptor attached to the Medici court where Ferdinando was early exposed to the scenic traditions of Buontalenti. He became a follower of the Parigis, father and son, and was soon collaborating with the latter on many Medici festivals. When Alfonso Parigi died in 1656, Tacca succeeded him as court scenographer and architect.

The Accademia degli Immobili was an artistic group of Florentine noblemen—amateurs who enjoyed acting, dancing, and presenting plays and music. As their ambitions increased, they outgrew their cramped hall and their small audience. In 1652, with financial support from their

patron, Cardinal Gian Carlo de' Medici, the members turned to Tacca and commissioned him to design an innovative and comfortable theatre on the Via Pergola. Tacca introduced into their theatre the appropriate atmosphere of a *sala all'Italia*. He also organized the different areas of the theatre into a functional unified plan. The horseshoe hall had a spacious arrangement of boxes with good sightlines. The stage, equipped with the latest mechanics, was ten wings deep, and the rear shutters revealed an inner stage with additional wings. The theatre took five years to complete before the Florentines could attend and proudly applaud their Immobili seasons of *melodrammi giocosi* and opera, just as today the Florentines applaud the performers in the Teatro della Pergola, which occupies the original site of Tacca's Teatro Immobili.

Having planned the *apparata* for the stage of the Immobili, Tacca was not slow to show off the stage's spectacular resources. Engravings for the scenes for Moniglia's libretti of two major Medici operas, the *Hiper-*

*mestra* of 1658 and the *Ercole Amante* of 1661, make it clear that the Immobili stage was something to conjure with.

*Illustration 17.* This study by Ferdinando Tacca cannot be assigned to any specific opera for the Immobili. It is a design for a *cortile regio* of Jupiter and recalls several similar *cortiles* he had designed for the two operas already mentioned. The six nonillusionistic columns surmounted by Jovian eagles are designed with the vanishing point resting right on the stage floor. The architectural sobriety reflects Tacca's restrained style, which lacks the exuberance of Burnacini and the pictorial alchemy of Torelli. On all sides, scallops of linear clouds suggest that a typical prologue set in heaven has just disappeared, disclosing this symmetry of columns pointing to the pavilion of Jupiter in the rear court. Tacca's designs are typical of the restrained Florentine baroque tradition that flowered under the auspices of the House of Medici.

The attribution of this drawing to Ferdinando Tacca was made by Corrado Ricci.

## Cosimo Lotti

Cosimo Lotti was a Florentine, trained in the workshop of the fresco painter Bernardino Poccetti. He early displayed a special talent for mechanical contrivances and hydraulics, and when he entered the service of Cosimo II he became engaged in the execution of the Duke's gardens, fountains, and villas. Working with Bernardo Buontalenti, the senior court designer of the Medici, Lotti invented certain hydraulic devices used to activate the fountains and to create surprise effects and scenic decorations in the Boboli Gardens behind the Pitti Palace. Lotti, as a theatrical friend of Cicognini, the prolific Florentine playwright, designed perspective scenes and machines for some of his entertainments.

In 1618, on the recommendation of Giulio Parigi, Lotti was borrowed from the court of Cosimo II to serve as engineer in the hedonistic court of Philip IV in Madrid. Regardless of foreign military and political intrusions during his reign, the king made his court the center of Spain's golden age of art, science, and literature. Lope de Vega and Calderon were favored stars of his realm, and

(17) Tacca, Ferdinando, 1619–1686 (attributed)
Italy, Florence
Royal Court Enclosed in Clouds (Left Half), c. 1670
Pen and bister and gray wash, 250 x 210 mm.
Collections: Sir Robert Witt, Lewis, Bishop, Philpotts

(18) Lotti, Cosimo, d. 1650
Italy, Florence (active also in Madrid)
Apollo Enthroned, 1641
Pen and ink with gray wash, 292 x 351 mm.
Inscribed lower left corner: "C.L. 1641"
Collection: G. P. Baker

(19–21) Unknown artist, seventeenth century
Italy, Bologna
Public Square, Sculpture Rotunda, and Title Page
from an Album of 238 Architectural and
Theatrical Drawings, c. 1665
Sepia pen and wash, 290 x 212 mm.
Collection: Anatole Demidoff, Prince of Donato

he was also the patron of Zurbarán, Murillo, and Veláz-quez. Velázquez was the king's faithful friend who, as inspector of works in the palace, must have enjoyed close cooperation with Lotti.

Lotti introduced elaborate hydraulics to provide Italianate water displays for the royal gardens of Aranjuéz, Zarzuelo, and Buen Retiro, but he soon assumed many responsibilities beyond his role of engineer. He devised scenes and machines and lavish pageant wagons for royal festivities, and in the square before the royal palace in Madrid, he erected a portable theatre complete with technical facilities to provide perspective scene changes *à vista*. The theatre was so arranged that the sovereigns could follow the performance from the privacy of their apartments. In 1629, a new royal theatre, complete with Lotti's latest mechanical equipment, was opened with Lope de Vega's *La Selva sin Amor*. Lope de Vega, in his introduction to the play, elegized Lotti's scenic inventions. The curtain rose on a wide sea before a harbor surrounding a large city. Ships responded to salutes fired from the castles, and fish could be seen in the movement of the waves. The sea actually rolled with such motion that some spectators went away ill! All was illuminated with more than three hundred concealed lights which provided the illusion of daylight. At length, the waters of the sea subsided and were transformed into the wooded valley of Manzanarre. During the following decade, many productions of Lope de Vega's new plays were designed by Lotti.

Cosimo Lotti introduced into Spain the Italian baroque methods of scenography, and the Spaniards applauded his efforts. Primarily an engineer, his theatrical machines no doubt influenced the design of his scenery. The scenic traditions he established in Spain continued down through the nineteenth century.

*Illustration 18.* The *Enciclopedia dello Spettacolo* states that Cosimo Lotti was the author of a "projected book" with illustrations and notes on the use of theatrical machines and their construction. This drawing, dated 1641, represents Apollo enthroned on a dais, descending among clouds into a baroque chamber. The drawing suggests an illustration rather than a scene for an opera. With obvious emphasis on the cloud machine, the design may have been made by Lotti for his unpublished volume on theatrical machinery.

*Illustrations 19–21.* The first group of 141 drawings in the album include a number of sketches for theatrical scenes. However, the majority of the drawings are of architectural subjects—interiors and gardens, altars and shrines for churches, *trompes l'oeil* for murals and ceiling decorations. Two sheets are studies of Vignola's dome of the Church of the Gesù in Rome.

The second group of 97 drawings are all designs for stage scenes except the first sketch, which is a dual study for a flamboyant title page. This may have been intended for a separate volume to contain a selection of these designs for the theatre.

Most of the drawings in the album are of high quality, executed with a sure and sensitive feeling for line and mass. There are interior and exterior scenes and scenic fantasies flaunting insubstantial stairways. Many of the designs are four wings deep, their classical columns leading back to a principal vanishing point through a cross-arcade; beyond, right and left, appear two- and three-point perspective vistas. Only one set suggests a recognizable locale, a public square whose battlements were undoubtedly inspired by the Palazzo di Re Enzo in Bologna.

Who was this theatre artist with such an individual style? A definite attribution is difficult. When the album was in the collection of the Palazzo San Donato, the drawings were erroneously ascribed to Giacomo Torelli. Several scholars support the opinion that the drawings are by Giuseppe Maria Mitelli (1609–1660), son of the Bolognese painter and scenographer Agostino Mitelli, though there is no record that Giuseppe ever worked in the theatre. So for the present these drawings remain orphans of anonymity, unable to reveal the name of the hand that made them.

Several of the drawings are stamped with a GM monogram. The spandrel of drawing number 74 contains the initials GM in an architectural escutcheon with the date 1666. The drawings are in two series, the first numbered 1–141, the second numbered 1–97. The older numeration is in ink on the verso; the later, in crayon on the recto.

### Ludovico Burnacini

In 1651, Ludovico Burnacini's father, Giovanni, was lured from Venice to Vienna by Emperor Leopold I as court architect and engineer. His designs for the stage of Teatro SS. Giovanni e Paolo had been highly esteemed—*meraviglioso*, the Venetians called it. In the Venetian theatre, Giovanni had been a colleague of Giacomo Torelli, who had gone to Paris in 1645 at Mazarin's invitation. Initiated in the ways of the theatre by his father, Ludovico Burnacini was destined to serve the Habsburg court of Leopold I for over forty years as theatrical engineer. This position provided him with unlimited resources and opportunities to concentrate his talent on diverse court festivities within the Hofburg of Vienna, at Schönbrunn and Laxenburg Castles, and the palaces in Neustadt and Prague.

Between 1656 and 1705, Burnacini provided settings and sometimes costumes for nearly four hundred operas,

(22) Burnacini, Ludovico, 1636–1707 (attributed)
Italy, Venice (active in Vienna)
A Formal Garden (Left Half), c. 1680–1700
Sepia pen and gray wash, 170 x 245 mm.
Collections: C. Argentieri, P. G. Vreschi

spectacles, and sacred plays. As his responsibilities at court increased, his designs acquired more finesse, elegance, and fantasy, and his inherited rigidity gave way to his own natural exuberance. His theatrical costume sketches for Persians and Indians, Romans and Turks (the latter defeated at the very gates of Vienna in 1683), for shepherds and gardeners and buffoons, were breathtaking achievements in their union of baroque color and surrealistic fancy.

In 1662, the wedding of Emperor Leopold was glamorous cause for celebration up and down the Danube, and the Habsburg capital was decorated in its baroque best. Vienna's flamboyant opera house equipped with the most advanced stage machinery brought the wedding festivities to a climax with Cesti's new opera *Il Pomo d'Oro*, an impressive affair with twenty-one gigantic scenes. So phenomenal was the success of the gala premiere that the opera, planned for a single occasion, had to be repeated more than a hundred times.

Throughout his distinguished career, Burnacini seemed to seek perfection by trying to reach beyond his own vanishing point, though perspective always controlled his artistic principles and technical innovations.

*Illustration 22.* This drawing for a formal garden setting, though lacking the wings on the right side, shows how perfectly Burnacini handled central perspective. Sometimes, as in this case, he employed wings eight to ten sets deep and at a midway point continued his perspective in two directions. In this design his central perspective recedes into a distant circular garden court. He also used the same system with interior scenes; a spacious front room with a perspective ceiling leads back to an inner room in deeper perspective. Burnacini's scene designs were always formal. This drawing must have been used as a working sketch in the scenic studio; before it was cleaned, there were many tempera spots spattered on the drawing.

*Illustration 23.* This drawing is one of Burnacini's designs for an oratorio, a form of baroque religious theatre greatly admired and supported by Leopold I. In Vienna, oratorios were generally presented either in the Burgkapelle or in the transept of the Hofkapelle, which was a rather small chapel. Burnacini's surviving designs for the baroque Theatrum Sacrum are mostly tall and semicircular overhead to conform with the Hofkapelle's architecture as well as to suit the oratorio's theme. This oratorio, derived from the Book of Genesis, deals with Abraham's sterility and his confrontations with his wife, Sarah, and her maid, Hagar. Several side wings of desolate ruins lead back to the Plain of Mamre in Hebron. An angel descends and appears to Hagar "by a fountain of water in the wilderness." On hearing from the angel that she is with child, in her affliction "she called the name of the Lord that spoke unto her, 'Thou God seest me?'" Overhead, the mandorla of clouds and angels opens and encircles the Lord God and the Sacrament; and Hagar holds comforting dialogue with Him.

(23) Burnacini, Ludovico (attributed)
An Oratorio of Abraham, c. 1670
Pen and gray wash, 325 x 163 mm.

The Hofkapelle still resounds with the heavenly voices of the Vienna Choirboys, a group originally founded by Emperor Maximilian I in 1498. During the seventeenth century, their voices surely soared upward competing with those cloud machines created by Ludovico Burnacini.

Flora Biach-Schiffmann in *Giovanni und Ludovico Burnacini* (Vienna, 1931) lists some fifty oratorios actually published for which Ludovico designed the scenes. This oratorio is not in that list.

### Tomaso Francini

During the seventeenth century, the French kings enriched their northern *mascarades* with entertainment from Italy.

Louis XIII in 1610, at the age of nine and with the obsequies of his murdered father still fresh in his memory, eagerly applauded the *Ballet d'Alcina* unfolding before a series of receding Italianate backdrops. In spite of religious and political conflicts of state, the Duc de Nemours produced a diverting program of Grand Ballets for the court, in which the tireless young king himself always assumed a principal role. These elaborate ballets were generally supervised between 1610 and 1626 by the machinist-decorator Tomaso Francini, with the assistance of his architect brother whom the Regent Marie de' Medici had summoned to the French court from Florence. These *ballets à entrées*, as they came to be called, were presented in a great hall, either La Salle du Petit Bourbon or La Grande Salle du Louvre. The audience occupied bleachers and balconies arranged around three sides of the hall, with the royal family enthroned in the center. The choreographic routine of the *ballet à entrée* required the actors and dancers to perform first on the stage above, and then to descend the ramp to the Salle to continue their dancing. Toward the end of the performance, they would return to the stage and disappear behind the setting.

In 1621, the *Grand Ballet de la Reine représentant le Soleil* was performed in the Salle du Petit Bourbon. After a long lyric Prologue, the ballet was presented in four parts, each representing a season. In the final scene, the Grand Ballet was danced by the twelve hours of the day. Dialogue and dance alternated with chorus and music throughout, and there was little concern for plot. If Cardinal Richelieu, the rising power behind the throne, had watched this ballet, he was possibly dreaming about a plan for his own proscenium theatre in his projected Palais Cardinal, which would open twenty years hence with *Miramé*, produced in the newest classical style.

*Illustration 24.* Francini's sketch, halved by a dotted line, is probably a working design and certainly illustrates the scenic arrangement for the *Grand Ballet de la Reine représentant le Soleil*. The scale of the stage is indicated on the floor. The two interior and exterior wings on the right border a portion of the main dancing floor and provide entrances and exits. A ramp in the Italian style leads up to the stage. The flat rocky pedestal supports the decorative proscenium which frames pink clouds enveloping a large golden sun.

This design seems to fit the action of this particular ballet precisely. The clouds could shift to reveal the four inner scenes of the seasons, and as a grand finale the clouds would transport Queen Anne to her sunny apotheosis.

### Jean I Berain

Jean I Berain was an artist in tune with the vision and in scale with the authority of Louis XIV. Early in his career he had been a brilliant engraver. Later apprenticed to Le Brun, he lent his sure hand to designing furniture and lighting fixtures, fabrics and tapestries, theatres and ballrooms, sedan chairs and poop decks of ships. His designs were an integrated potpourri of bizarre motifs—masks, caryatids, griffins, grotesques, arabesques, baldachinos, and cornices. In 1675, the king appointed him *Graveur et Dessinateur de la Chambre et du Cabinet du Roi*. Vested with this awesome authority, for thirty years he supervised all the court entertainment and administered the *menus-plaisir*.

After a long period of discontent with Italian designers imposing their style on the theatre of France, Berain with his royal badge of authority succeeded in introducing the accepted classical style of Louis XIV into the theatre. This distinct and formal style was achieved under the aegis of Le Grand Monarch through the genius and rapport of Berain, Le Brun, Mansart, and Lenôtre.

Berain, like his royal master who had attended the theatre from his youth, had always delighted in the performing arts. He designed, in collaboration with Molière, Racine, and Lulli, some of the king's fêtes in the park at Versailles. Soon Berain eclipsed Vigarani, the renowned *machiniste-décorateur* whom the king had imported to his court from Italy. When the latter's contract expired in 1680, Lulli engaged Berain to design all the opera and ballet for l'Académie Royale de Musique. This appointment dovetailed perfectly with the responsibilities of his royal post. Henceforth, he would devote even more of his time and talent to the king's pleasures, whose daily life from *levée* to *couchée* was a play in twenty-four acts.

He provided decors for the royal theatre; he designed carousels and *spectacles de la cour*, fêtes and ceremonies, collations and costume balls, fireworks and the illumination of the galleries of the Louvre, as well as *pompes funèbres*. All of these splendid occasions were his responsibility—"Bérinades" they were called. Berain, with the burden of many other duties, could not possibly have created and executed all of these programs and must have had a large atelier. The *Albums des Menus-Plaisirs* in the archives of the Opéra in Paris contain quantities of decor that can be attributed to Berain's students and assistants —Daniel Marot, Jacques Rousseau, and Claude Gillot.

In the theatre, Berain was an inventive *machiniste*. While he relied on Vigarani's and Torelli's efficient Italian system of wings and single-point perspective, he did not choose to project scenic space to its ultimate end. As an *ornamentiste*, Berain invariably displayed a wealth of invention rather than massive detail in his designs for the theatre. He sought to provide the audience with an elegant sense of the marvelous rather than verisimilitude. Here in the theatre at last was the French touch—the cachet of Berain.

(24)  Francini, Tomaso, 1571–1648 (attributed)
Italy, Florence (active in Paris)
Setting for a *Ballet de Cour*, 1621
Pen and brown ink with wash and watercolors, 295 x 210 mm.
Collection: E. Colando, Paris

(25) Berain, Jean I, 1637–1711 (attributed)
France, Paris
Royal Hall with Bridge in Distance, c. 1690
Pen and gray wash on gray paper, 273 x 368 mm.

(26) Berain, Jean I
Costume for a Prince for a *Ballet de Cour*, c. 1670
Pencil and blue and black watercolor, 247 x 165 mm.
Collection: R. Gunter

*Illustration 25*. The Ionic columns of Berain's setting for a royal hall support a stylish array of arches and valances. The colonnades, however, stop short upstage before a flight of steps. The final arch both defines the scenic space of the hall and frames the unusual sight of two spans rising from a central pier supporting a transverse bridge. No hall in any French noble's palace was ever seen to debouch like this one on a beautiful bridge spanning dry water. Everywhere is abundant evidence of the refining hand of the sculptor.

Large collections of Berain's scene and costume designs are in the Archives Nationale and the Bibliothèque d'Opéra in Paris and in the National Museum in Stockholm.

*Illustration 26*. Many of Berain's costume sketches are counterproofs of his original watercolors. These were used as working drawings for the royal theatres. An album of forty-one of these counterproofs in the Oenslager collection was formerly in the possession of Rudolph Valentino.

### Andrea Pozzo

Andrea Pozzo exercised his talents in the most varied forms: church architecture, religious painting and sculpture, theatre decoration, and portraits. As an artist in Venice he became a coadjutor of the Jesuit order, but, as with so many baroque artists, his goal was Rome. With his talent and his willingness to serve, he achieved in Rome an enviable position in the headquarters of the Jesuit hierarchy. As a practicing virtuoso in the arts and a modest writer, Pozzo became a propagator of the Jesuits' lofty precepts in the practice of the arts. During the latter years of his life, Pozzo transferred his drafting board from Rome to Vienna, where he served as resident architect and artist in the court of Leopold I. He designed many stately churches and other noble works for the Hapsburgs, including the pompous catafalque for the emperor in 1705. It is amusing to visualize this genial Jesuit from Venice and Rome and Ludovico Burnacini from Venice as fellow artists in the decorous Hapsburg

court indulging privately in good sacred and profane theatre talk.

In Rome, Pozzo clarified and organized his theories on the visual arts in his monumental two-volume *De Perspectiva Pictorum et Architectorum*. This stimulating work proved to be the long-awaited vehicle for the dissemination of the High baroque outside Italy. The first volume was dedicated with some foresight to Leopold I of Austria and was published in Rome in 1693. The second volume was published in Rome in 1700 and dedicated to Archduke Joseph I. The sections of *De Perspectiva* devoted to the use of perspective and space for scenic illusionism in both religious and secular theatre is the third important treatise on stage scenery following Serlio's and Sabbatini's earlier works. Pozzo was a vigorous proponent of one-point perspective to achieve the ultimate in illusionistic scenery.

As an informed Jesuit, Pozzo witnessed church music and sacred ceremonies merging into the ultimate extension of the *sacre rappresentazione* as a propagandistic form of religious opera-drama. As a practicing designer, he created backgrounds for many of these sacred works. Three of his *apparati* were erected in Rome's Church of the Gesù, and he describes and illustrates them in *De Perspectiva*. The engraving of *Theatrum Sacrum* (Illus. 27) was one of them.

In seeking a fresh design solution for this presentation, Pozzo must have done some soul-searching: "How should I design the Marriage of Cana this year of our Lord, 1685, in the great Church of the Gesù?" He had to inquire into the status of the contemporary Church in a changing Roman society, and how religion affected the ordinary life of people, their daily work and leisure. Could he design this work in the manner of a new opera for the popular theatre? All these exploratory thoughts must have influenced the style of Pozzo's design. From his days in Venice he could recall Veronese's vast composition for the *Marriage at Cana*. However, in hedonistic Rome the scene must grow more vast, with live actors dining midway up a theatrical flight of stairs. What an audacious work he conceived beneath Vignola's dome in the Gesù! Pozzo's own description in *De Perspectiva* sets the church bells ringing:

The machine which I erected in the year 1685 in the Jesuits' Church at Rome for the Devotions of the Forty Hours, had so admirable an effect and so pleasantly deceived the eye that I resolved to gratify the studious not only with a general view, but with the plan and elevation; all was performed with such exactness that the work seemed to consist of solid stones rather than wrought by the painter's hand.

From the plan and section is drawn the perspective of this noble piece of architecture which struck the eye when seen by daylight, but was more especially surprising by candlelight; many of the candles being exposed to sight, and others altogether hidden to illuminate the six different ranges of scenes. In the midst of the great Arch, clouds appeared filled with angels adoring the Blessed Sacrament. Those clouds are here omitted, so that the inner parts might be better seen.

I doubt not but those who have followed me thus far will be so encouraged to prosecute their studies that they may

(28) Pozzo, Andrea
*Theatrum Sacrum* (Left Half), 1685
Pen, brown and gray wash, 412 x 168 mm.
Collections: Mayr, Fajt, Scholz

FIG. LXXI.

(27) Pozzo, Andrea, 1642–1709
Italy, Rome
*Theatrum Sacrum*, 1693
Engraving

design even greater and more noble works than these of mine.

*Illustration 27.* Andrea Pozzo's drawing of a theatre representing the Marriage of Cana in Galilee erected in the Jesuits' Church in Rome, 1685, for the solemnity of exposing the holy sacrament.

This originally appeared as Fig. 71 in *De Perspectiva Pictorum et Architectorum*, published in Rome, 1693. This engraving, reversed, is from the London edition of 1707.

*Illustration 28.* Franz Rapp believed this drawing to be an eighteenth-century copy in the style of Louis XVI of Pozzo's engraving of his *Theatrum Sacrum* of 1685. In spite of differences in architectural detail, János Scholz believes "the pen work and the use of various washes are identical with some of the artist's authenticated drawings." Richard Wunder concurs that "This drawing probably constituted a first study for the more ambitious scheme published by Pozzo."

### The Bibiena Family

There were three notable families of Italian scenographers, the Bibienas, the Quaglios, and the Galliaris, each of whom for a number of generations maintained their traditions and kept their craft within the family circle. These royal families of the scenic art exerted great influence on the standards and changing styles of the visual theatre of Europe for over two hundred years.

In Bologna along the arcaded via San Vitale, a landmark plaque informs the world that number 13 was the home of the illustrious Galli Bibiena dynasty of theatre artists and architects. The paterfamilias of the Galli family originally came from Florence, and in the early years of the seventeenth century became the *podestà* of the Tuscan hill town of Bibbiena. A century earlier, Cardinal Bernardo Dovizi da Bibbiena, whose plays were applauded in all the courts of Italy, had been the first to lend theatrical prestige to this town. Eight members of the Galli family would bring even greater theatrical kudos to Bibbiena.

Giovanni Maria Galli, the *podestà*'s son, began his career as a painter. Traditionally he would have gone to Florence for his training, but his father sent him north to Bologna to the workshop of Francesco Albani. To distinguish himself from another apprentice also named Galli, he added "da Bibiena" (*sic*) to his name. In Bologna, Giovanni Maria Galli da Bibiena, called *Il Fontaniere*, never received much attention for the water and fountains he painted in the works of other artists. He was overshadowed by the brilliant members of the Bolognese baroque school—the Carracci brothers, Domenichino, Guido Reni, and Guercino. Giovanni Maria did, however, before he died, succeed in transmitting his enthusiasm for art and the theatre to his four young sons. All became painters, architects, and scenographers. Ferdinando and Francesco would make the name derived from that modest Tuscan hill town illustrious throughout Italy and Europe.

Bologna became the home base for three generations of Galli Bibiena scenographers. They carried their inherited skills and talents to all the royal courts and public theatres of Europe. Hyatt Mayor gives a vivid glimpse of the entire peripatetic clan, their coattails flying, as they ranged over Europe in scenic service to the great world theatre: "Though most of the family used Vienna for their headquarters and Bologna for their home, their work kept them all wandering." Ferdinando says that during his twenty-eight years of service under the Farnese he made "a great many theatre sets in Parma, not a few in Bologna, some in Venice, Turin, Rome, Naples, Milan, Florence and elsewhere in Italy." His eldest son, Alessandro, was one of the most stationary of the family, but even he traveled until he was about thirty before settling for life in Mannheim. Ferdinando's second son, Giuseppe, accompanied his brothers and his father and then inherited his father's post as theatrical engineer in Vienna after the latter went home to Bologna to have cataracts removed from his eyes. The third son, Antonio, was only twelve when his father went to Vienna, but he accompanied him to Bologna and then spent over twenty years in Austria and nearly thirty years in Italy building more theatres than any one man of his time. The youngest son, Giovanni Maria the younger, went to Prague where "he married a Bohemian girl rich enough to keep him in idleness and elegance." Ferdinando's brother Francesco was the first of the family to work in Vienna, but spent most of his life here and there in Italy. The last and least inventive of the Bibienas was Giuseppe's son Carlo, who is also the hardest to trace because he "traveled as far as his family's fame would carry him, to France, England, the Netherlands, Sweden and Russia."

The Bibienas were journeyman artists in the true sense, implanting their Italian style of scenery on the stages of all the northern capitals of Europe. They were a close-knit family cooperative, sometimes working together and always abetting one another's careers. Their services were everywhere in great demand, and together they established "the Bibiena style" which has survived as a meaningful scenic style to this day. Like members of the Bauhaus, all ardently shared the same aesthetic convictions. They frequently employed a common architectural family style in sketching, sometimes even working together on the same drawing. Their fluency makes individual attributions of their drawings an agonizing pleasure. I suspect with Franz Rapp that eighty percent of all eighteenth-century stage designs are attributed to the Bibiena clan. Mediocre drawings by anonymous scenographers, regardless of school, are ascribed freely to one or another member of the family, proof positive that theirs was a recognized school of scene design.

The reputation of the Bibienas' fleeting scenes has outlasted their more permanent work in stone and brick and fresco. Yet their genius for scenic artifice could not have been so dazzling had they not excelled in architecture, painting, and the decorative arts. As architects they designed theatres for Rome, Verona, Nancy, Dresden, Bayreuth, and a dozen other cities. They planned these lavish opera houses with stages to best serve their operatic scenic requirements.

Sitting today in the margrave's pristine Bayreuth court theatre built in 1748, one can believe that Giuseppe and his son Carlo have just departed with all their tools and brushes by coach for Italy. One regrets not meeting them to congratulate them for rearing this fabulous rococo pleasure house whose overwrought exuberance and theatrical hospitality seem so far removed from the acoustical austerity of most of our new theatres today. This theatre in Bayreuth is one of Giuseppe's scenic fantasies come to life in three-dimensional golden splendor with Apollo and his company of Muses presiding overhead in frescoed glory. The margrave's box almost outshines the extravagance of the proscenium arch. The box's sculptured baldachino supports a cartouche proclaiming in

bold Latin that Giuseppe completed this theatre for Friedrich and Sophia in 1748.

In addition to all their theatres, the Bibienas designed high altars and catafalques, oratories and churches, palaces and gardens, colleges and town halls. They embellished vaults and domes with architectural decorations that appear to defy gravity. Acquaintance with their achievements in these more permanent arts provides a deeper appreciation of their ephemeral work in the theatre.

Eclecticism was at the heart of the Bibienas' unfettered style and voguish mannerisms. They shamelessly assimilated all styles. No holds with the past were barred, and theirs was the right to invade and exploit every architectural system. They distorted the architecture of Greece and Rome to suit their purposes, and when desirable they deformed the classical orders. Yet Giuseppe with the help of his apprentices made a series of brilliant studies of Greek and Roman architecture and monuments, composed in cunning perspective amidst outcroppings of romantic ruins. Though not intended for the theatre, these classical scenes are often charmingly inhabited by baroque actors.

Bologna had once been an important center of Italian Gothic architecture, and the Bibienas, through their interest in defining locale in scenography, were among the first artists to explore and popularize Gothic architecture with their designs of scenes for prisons, crypts, and fortresses. Thus they opened the way for the significant revival of Gothic romanticism in the baroque age. They also avidly explored the Renaissance volumes of Serlio, Vignola, Palladio, and Scamozzi and did not hesitate to incorporate what they found into their own aerial constructions. The classical line and the Gothic arch alike could be made to conform and harmonize with the Bibienas' baroque curve.

Each generation of the Bibienas was schooled in drawing, yet they rarely signed or even initialed their designs. Sometimes several studies were made for the same scene; these designs were often copied by lesser hands, and today these copies repose next to the originals in many European and American collections. Individual Bibiena drawings are by no means easy to identify, even though each artist had his own way with pen and wash and his own recognized variation on the hallmark of the family style.

In eighteenth-century opera, eye appeal outweighed the appeal of sound and was more than half the evening's pleasure. It seems axiomatic that both scenery and costumes should have been entrusted to the supervising eye of one designer, but this was not the case. Theatrical costumes surely matched the splendor of the settings, but except for Burnacini, Berain, and a few other important stage designers, costumes and settings were rarely designed by the guiding hand of one artist. It is thus not surprising that no Bibiena costume designs survive. Only Antonio excelled in figure drawing; for the brothers and the uncles and the cousins, the performers occasionally gracing their sketches were often drawn in by another hand.

(29) Bibiena, Ferdinando Galli, 1657–1743
Italy, Bologna (also active in Spain and Austria)
Palatial Court (Left Half), c. 1725
Pen and brown ink with sienna, blue, orange, and
ivory watercolor, 173 x 173 mm.

On the verso are two contemporary inscriptions in
ink and crayon attributing this drawing to Ferdinando
Bibiena. This was the first theatre drawing that I
acquired, in Munich in 1923.

Many of the operas for which the Bibienas designed the scenes are identified, but the conservative librettists limited their scenes to a dozen stereotype sets for the entire repertory of eighteenth-century opera. Consequently, designers were called upon to play the same scenic tunes over and over. The Bibienas turned out hundreds of drawings for these stereotype royal halls, for-tresses, military camps, and gardens, yet, amazingly, no two are alike.

The Bibienas also filled endless sketchbooks with linear ideas for settings for court festivities and religious ceremonies, fireworks, and natal and mortuary monuments. Some of these sketchbooks survive. Among the most important is one with 452 sketches in the Theatre Collection of the Austrian National Library, from which Franz Hadamowsky has made an illuminating study of the drawings of Ferdinando, Giuseppe, and Antonio. A second album was presented as the work of Ferdinando to the Accademia di San Luca in Rome by Count Francesco Algarotti (1712–1764), friend and biographer of the Bibienas. An album of sketches is in the Theatre Museum of Munich. Four other albums of drawings by various members of the family are in America at Harvard, Wildenstein's, and in my own collection.

In addition to all the drawings, hundreds of engravings and etchings illustrate the Bibienas' volumes on architecture and perspective, opera libretti and festival books, and suites of theatre plans. These carry their individual names and provide the scholar and collector with invaluable clues in ascertaining the personal style and variety of each artist's oeuvre and thus retrieve the Bibienas from their massive cold front of anonymity.

For a century the Bibienas remained an indestructible family institution and exerted a potent influence on the visual theatre of Europe. Their scenic magnificence and architectural fantasy assumed majestic proportions, and the overpowering beauty they achieved came close to engulfing all human values. Their adventurous followers sought to press beyond the Bibiena formula, overloading their architecture with all-too-fanciful detail and creating architectural labyrinths devoid of reality. Each one of the Galli masters from Bibiena possessed the family secret of containing their grandiose scenic fantasies within logical limits. They knew just how far their vision could carry them and just how far their quills could soar. With their combined genius, no wonder they designed their way into history.

*Illustration 29.* Few theatre drawings of the seventeenth and eighteenth centuries possess the range of color found in this design of Ferdinando Bibiena. With certain notable exceptions, European stage designs of this epoch were monochromatic. Pen drawing with brown or gray wash was the traditional mode of representation. Occasionally a pale blue sky appeared, or accents of color to emphasize architectural detail.

*Illustrations 30–32.* The draftsmanship of these three drawings is masterly. The strong lines and reinforcing areas of wash closely resemble the distinct style of Ferdinando reflected in the drawings of the two albums ascribed to him in the Accademia di San Luca, Rome. Their date is placed during the period when Ferdinando was teaching painting and sculpture in Bologna.

In Illustration 31, the artist cut out the large central arch and, pasting another piece of paper behind it, completed his revised drawing. This short-cut procedure was often employed in experimenting with alternate design possibilities. Ferdinando made these designs for his own delight and satisfaction. Spontaneity, freshness, and high imagination were never lacking in his smallest study sketches, which were frequently made for his noblest theatrical decor.

*Illustration 33.* During the carnival of 1694 in Bologna, the Teatro Malvezzi presented a first performance of the opera *La Forza della Virtù*, which inaugurated a new epoch in the history of Italian scenography. In this production the convention of the central perspective street scene, which had been accepted since the performance of Ariosto's *Cassaria* in 1507, was suddenly shattered. Those settings of 1694 were designed by the Bolognese artist Marcantonio Chiarini (1652–1730), a practicing easel painter unconcerned with the ways of scene design, who discarded the traditional stage convention of frontal symmetry and replaced it with an irregular *scena al angola*, or scene at an angle.

Ferdinando Bibiena, Chiarini's more illustrious Bolognese colleague, took over and developed the idea of the revolutionary *scena al angola* and first put it into practice in 1703. In his *L'Architettura Civile* (1711) he described and illustrated how from an irregular plan of a scene he could give an accurate elevation of it on a flat background. Although Ferdinando continued to utilize the old parallel-wing system as in his design in Illustration 29, his scenic innovation, which also required new scene-shifting devices, was triumphantly there to stay. With his new concept of stage space, Ferdinando gave new direction to the visual theatre, which members of his family were quick to seize and exploit. Count Francesco Algarotti (1712–1764), critic and intimate friend of the Bibiena family, applauded their innovative *scene al angola*: "They make the most beautiful effect and a grand feast to the eyes—

(30–32) Bibiena, Ferdinando Galli (attributed)
Three Variations of a Monumental Stair Hall, 1726–1743
Pen and bister ink with bister and gray washes, each drawing 150 x 100 mm.
Collection: Paul Fatio
These three very small *primi pensieri* from the collection of Paul Fatio are similar to another group of small drawings attributed to Ferdinando formerly in the Edmund Fatio collection; all probably came from a common source.

ABOVE

(33) Bibiena, Ferdinando Galli (attributed)
Portico and Staircase, 1700–1710
Pen and bister ink, 255 x 222 mm.
Collection: Randolph Gunter
A detailed study by Ferdinando of the corner portion of this drawing of a *scena al angola* is in the collection of the Ackland Memorial Art Center of the University of North Carolina. The bold handling of perspective in this design is comparable to that found in several etchings of Ferdinando's designs for stage scenes in the *Varie Opere de Prospettiva* issued in Bologna between 1703 and 1708.

OVERLEAF

(34) Bibiena, Francesco Galli, 1659–1739
Italy, Bologna (also active in Austria and France)
A Prison Courtyard, 1710–1730
Pen and bister with gray wash, 247 x 368 mm.
Collections: Mayr, Fajt, Scholz

as do the accidental points in scenes observed from the front, in various oblique directions resulting from the (purposely) complicated plan of the structures." Ferdinando had opened wide a new door on the new art of the theatre.

*Illustration 34.* Francesco created a complicated *scena al angola* for this busy Gothic prison. His entrances and exits lead to open corridors, inviting the audience to spy around corners into his skillful perspectives. He uses perspective like a telescope to bring distant parts into proper focus with the scene. Posturing performers in baroque dress are dwarfed beneath the towering confusion of the Gothic scene, but he places the principal singers, in true operatic style, well downstage over the orchestra pit.

Janos Scholz ascribes the drawing to Francesco and finds it similar in conception and execution to the drawing in Vienna reproduced by Gregor in *Monumenta Scenica.*

*Illustration 35.* Early in 1940, Herbert Bittner, a progressive publisher and dealer, staged an exhibition of "Theatre Decorations" in his gallery in New York. Franz Rapp reported that "Mr. Bittner's exhibition attracted lovers of theatre art and connoisseurs of fine drawings. It also laid the foundation for more than one private American col-

lection concentrating on stage design." Later that year, Bittner published and George Freedley edited *Theatrical Designs from the Baroque through Neo-Classicism, Unpublished Material from American Private Collections* in three handsome portfolios. The seventy-two plates were considered the most important drawings in the exhibition. At that time, specific attributions of drawings to individual Bibienas were freely assigned.

The design of this drawing symbolizes the variety of scholarly judgment that a single Bibiena drawing may elicit. János Scholz, in *Baroque and Romantic Stage Design,* attributed this drawing to Giuseppe. Franz Rapp, reviewing Scholz' book in *The Art Bulletin* in 1951, felt this drawing was "apparently the work of Francesco Bibiena who designed the Opera House of Vienna." Richard Wunder, who prepared the catalogue for an exhibition of drawings from my collection for the Minneapolis Institute of Arts in 1963, agreed that "Rapp is correct in this change of attribution." Diane Kelder, in her catalogue for a Philadelphia exhibition in 1968, compares this drawing with several other works of Francesco and pins her question mark on Francesco. Maria Teresa Muraro and Elena Povoledo, in the catalogue of their splendid Bibiena exhibition in Venice in 1970, believe the drawing is by Francesco's nephew Giuseppe and assert the design reflects the influence of his father, Ferdinando.

(35) Bibiena, Giuseppe Galli, 1696–1757
    Italy, Bologna (active in Germany, Austria, Bohemia, and Poland)
    Rotunda with Radiating Courts Set within a
    Proscenium Arch, c. 1750

Pen and brown ink with wash on brown paper, 498 x 590 mm.
Collections: Piancastelli, Brandegee, Scholz

(36) Bibiena, Giuseppe Galli
*Aula Sepolcrale* Reminiscent of the Colosseum Ruins,
c. 1750
Pen and brown ink with gray washes on tan paper,
409 x 549 mm.
Collections: Mayr, Fajt, Scholz

(37) Bibiena, Giuseppe Galli
Palace Atrium, c. 1750
Pen and brown ink with brown and gray washes,
226 x 320 mm.
Collections: Mayr, Fajt, Scholz

 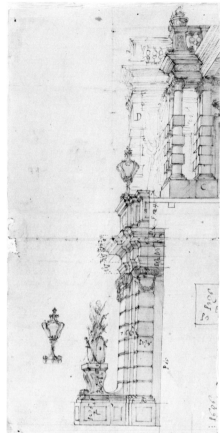 

(38–40)  Bibiena, Giuseppe Galli
Interior–Exterior of a Palatial Auditorium, c. 1750
Pen and sepia wash, 345 x 193 mm.
Collections: The Brera Academy, Gibelli, Baldini,
Wunder
This schematic drawing *(38)*, clearly in the grand
manner of Giuseppe, is from an album of
eighteenth-century drawings once in the possession
of the Brera Academy in Milan. The album was
presented by Luigi Bisi (1814–1886), President
of the Academy, to Giuseppe Gibelli upon his
graduation for excellence in his work. The latter
came to America and engaged in mural

decorations; some he executed for hotels in
Atlantic City. His grandson inherited the album
and eventually disposed of it.

(41)  Bibiena, Antonio Galli, 1700–1774
Italy, Bologna (active in Italy, Austria, Hungary,
Bohemia, and Germany)
Design for a Triumphal Arch (Left Half), 1721
Pencil, pen, and brown ink, 415 x 291 mm.
Inscribed on verso in ink: "1721/disegno del Gran
Antonio Bibiena/Io Maria Ester Galli Bibiena/
Bologna"
Collections: Mayr, Fajt, Scholz

As a scene designer, I have developed my own rapport with the individual characteristics of the Bibienas as
designers, and my own instinct tells me this drawing is by
the hand of Giuseppe.

*Illustration 36.* The Vienna sketchbook contains less
finished but similar drawings which support the attribution of this drawing to Giuseppe Bibiena. This sunny
*capriccio* was probably not intended for a stage scene,
although its style is highly theatrical. Giuseppe and his
assistants made a large group of interesting designs which
combined classical ruins and baroque monuments. A
number of these pseudoclassical *vedute* are included in
Giuseppe's *Architettura e Prospettive* published in Augsburg in 1740–1744. They reflect the increasing interest
during the eighteenth century in classical antiquity.

*Illustration 37.* Corrado Ricci reproduced in *I Bibiena* a
copy of this drawing from the Pogliaghi collection in

Milan, mistakenly ascribing it to Giuseppe's son Carlo.
This drawing by Giuseppe epitomizes the exuberant
though calculated intention of Bolognese *quadratura* art.
Though controlled by perspective, the design falls into a
carefully contrived and subtle composition. Complicated
detail is absorbed in the velvet brown and gray washes.
A luminous harmony pervades this finished design which
his restless son Carlo only rarely achieved.

*Illustrations 38–40.* Aside from the unusual subject of the
drawing *(38)*, the design has additional interest as a cut-
out double overlay and hence provides some insight into
the practical working procedure of the designer. The
working drawing *(39)* with its system of directional code
numbers, initials, and linear explanations is similar to
some of the drawings found in the Bibiena album in
Vienna. This particular scene was a double-decker. An
inner scene was revealed behind the upper-central *tempietto* while the chorus, seated in the upper auditorium,

appeared behind the two curving side façades. On the verso of the undersheet (40) are drawn a lower and upper wing, a series of which most likely framed the central circular design upstage rear. How simply and economically this drawing of Giuseppe explained to the scenic craftsmen in their studio exactly how his design would work out! Builders and painters in our scenic studios today would require a dozen scale drawings.

*Illustration 41.* In 1721, Antonio Bibiena was assisting his father Ferdinando, after his cataract operation, on settings for the Teatro Malvezzi in Bologna before accompanying him back to his imperial post in Vienna. János Scholz points out that this design was intended for a festival of Charles VI commemorating the Hapsburg victory of his grandfather, Leopold I, over the Turks in 1683. This unfinished sketch clearly reveals Antonio's fastidious drawing technique. First he laid out the total design with a hard pencil. With his quill pen he methodically pro-

ceeded to complete one area of the drawing before moving to another. Because he completed all of his figures first, one might assume that Antonio was more interested in them than in the architecture of the triumphal arch framed within the unfinished proscenium. His interest, however, was in leaving his sculptured figures free from architectural intrusion.

*Illustrations 42 & 43.* This eighteenth-century album, bound later in leather, contains 101 drawings of various sizes carefully assembled and mounted on twenty leaves. On the lower-right-hand corner of every leaf appears the notation "C. A°. Bibiena" (Cavalier Antonio Bibiena). On the verso of a few drawings are scraps of writing identical with Antonio's autographed letters. The sketches are related to a group of designs in Vienna which Hadamowsky attributes to Antonio, and also to a number of drawings in the Royal Institute of British Architects ascribed to Antonio.

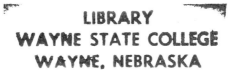

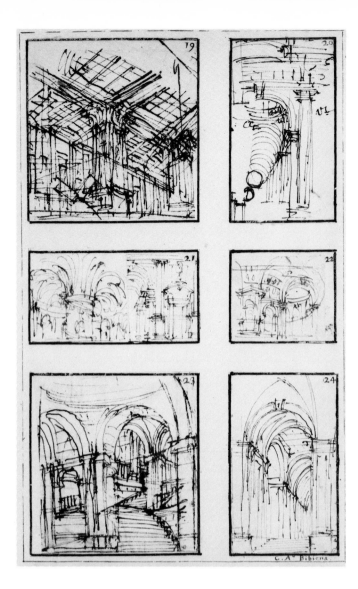

theatre artists who adopted, borrowed, or were influenced by one another's work. The Bibiena family exerted just such a leavening influence. Antonio Bibiena's and Servandoni's and Belotto's period of creative activity covered the same span of years. Which artist produced this particular design first? Whose original design influenced the other and under what circumstances? It is unlikely that this fascinating mystery of the battle encampment will ever be solved. Because of his prestigious authority in the theatre, Antonio's drawing probably came first.

(42 & 43)  Bibiena, Antonio Galli
Album of Drawings
Pencil, pen, and brown ink, 293 x 197 mm.
Collections: H. Hoepli, E. Fatio

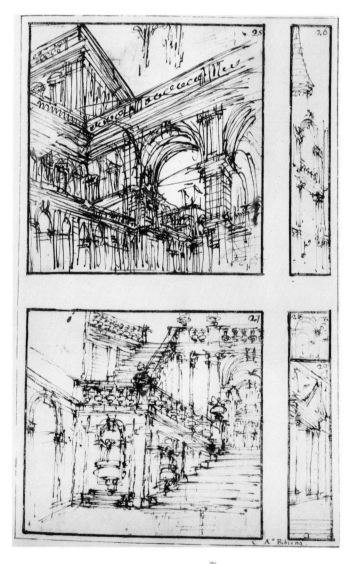

These sketches for stage settings, church decorations, illusionistic ceilings, and architectural details illustrate Antonio's great capacity for architectural decoration. He was probably the most prolific architect of the Bibiena dynasty. He designed or rebuilt some nine theatres. Appropriately, the largest was the handsome Teatro Communale which he designed for his fellow citizens of Bologna.

The drawings in this sketchbook are animated first thoughts. Antonio was thinking with his pen. His sketches are hasty, sure, emotive, and overflowing with ideas. The elegant lines read like calligraphy. His sure penmanship reveals a wealth of accumulated knowledge. The fanciful world of the Italian rococo comes to vibrant life in these brief drawings.

*Illustration 44.* Some years ago in New York, a reproduction of this fluent example of Antonio's impeccable draftsmanship was blown up and used as a backdrop for a New York City Ballet production of *Divertimento No. 15.* The program gave credit for this design to a young American designer who, obviously in desperate need of an eighteenth-century lifesaver, clung to the long arm of Antonio Bibiena (to whom all credit for the design was justly due).

Throughout the eighteenth century, European stage designers constituted an international circle of specialized

(44) Bibiena, Antonio Galli
Royal Canopy in a Military Encampment, 1720–1725
Pen and bister ink with wash, 227 x 365 mm.
Collections: Mayr, Fajt, Scholz
A lively preliminary sketch for this finished drawing
of Antonio Bibiena is in the collection of Mrs. Phyllis
Lambert of Chicago.

(45 & 46) Unknown artist, eighteenth century
Italy
Enclosure of a Royal Encampment
Pen and black ink, two drawings, 195 x 240
mm. each
Collections: Mayr, Fajt, Scholz

*Illustrations 45 & 46.* The Oenslager collection contains a
sketchbook of twenty-two sheets of drawings attributed
by Janos Scholz to Giovanni Servandoni (1695–1766)
and by Richard Bernheimer to Bernardo Belotto (1720–
1780). Two of these sheets contain vigorous pen drawings
of a royal enclosure of a battle tent. They are almost identical in plan and elevation with Antonio's design.

(47) Bibiena, Carlo Galli, 1728–1787
Austria, Vienna (active in Italy, Germany, France,
Netherlands, England, Sweden, and Russia)
Palace Garden with Fountain, 1750–1758
Pen and brown ink with gray wash, 184 x 293 mm.
Collections: Piancastelli, Brandegee, Scholz
This drawing with three others in the Oenslager
Collection is attributed by Scholz to Carlo Bibiena.
They belong to a rather large group of designs

originally in the Piancastelli collection and now
scattered in various museums and private collections
in America.

(48) Bibiena, Carlo Galli
Courts of Delight, 1758–1766
Pen and brush with gray and blue washes, 260 x
205 mm.

*Illustration 47.* The drawings of Carlo, the last of the
phenomenal line of the Bibienas, fall into three distinct
styles. The group of drawings represented here belong to
his first period when he was actively collaborating with
his father, Giuseppe, on designs for operas, royal decorations, and plans for the new opera house in Dresden.
While Carlo's early work reveals his independent talent
and originality, he was strongly influenced by his father's
extravagant baroquerie, his handling of scale, and mastery of architectural space composition.

In his first period, it was apparent that the natural landscape would never be Carlo's forte. In this formal palace
garden design, the manicured trees are carelessly handled
and lack the sophistication of the palace architecture and
the garden terraces of which they should be an integral
part. They are lacking in architectural form and seem
lifeless, a statement that could never be made of his
architecture.

*Illustration 48.* When Carlo was working with his father
during 1750–1756 on scenes for the old Dresden Opera

House, he must have found pleasure in the rococo aban-
don of the new Zwinger Palace nearby, for in his earlier
years, his enthusiasm for the latest trends advanced him
to the front ranks of the rococo vanguard. No surface was
left unadorned with volutes, scrolls, swags, and festoons
of flowers.

Carlo was only twenty-nine when his father died in
1758 and could at last concentrate on his own career. He
envisioned new horizons both for his own way of life and
for his life work and dreamed of visiting foreign lands.
His dream came true, for he became the most peripatetic
of all the Bibienas. During the last thirty years of his life,
he designed scenes for most of the great opera houses of
Europe from Naples to Stockholm, from London to Saint
Petersburg.

This design belongs to Carlo's second period and
exudes a new-found theatrical exuberance. It may have
been commissioned for an opera for the court theatre of
Bayreuth or Brunswick where he was working in 1760.
As a design it is the essence of fantasy—pure theatre—
effervescent, capricious, excessive. Here is scenic archi-

tecture, not built, but embroidered and starched for the modes and manners of a society long since departed this world.

*Illustration 49.* Carlo Bibiena, with his eye to the changing voguish taste of his international set of royal patrons, was one of the first designers of the eighteenth century to essay the neoclassical style in stage settings. This drawing is an example of the artist's third distinct style—the reverse of his rococo enthusiasm and of the baroque tradition of his father.

In this drawing, Carlo's style has become sharply defined and studied, emphasizing the perpendicular and horizontal in abrupt contrast to his earlier curvaceous spontaneity. This monumental palace hall is austere with its Ionic columns framing classical sculptures. There is an absence of excessive ornament. The mood is cool and spacious, elegiac with retreating planes of lessening shade and precise lines receding into the microscopically rendered perspective stair hall. The artist added three inches of paper to the top of his original sheet to accommodate the plane of balustrades essential to the composition of the chiaroscuro foreground. That kind of adjustment which Carlo Bibiena made to improve his design remains the practice of every conscientious scene designer in the theatre today.

### Pietro Righini

Righini's drawings for both architecture and theatrical scenes are rare, and consequently, attribution of his sketches is difficult to establish. His scenic style is mostly determined by prints of his designs found in the libretti of the many operas he designed. His early work in Reggio, Turin, and Milan possesses the freedom of Juvara and the *al-angola* formula of Ferdinando Bibiena. Indeed, Righini

(49) Bibiena, Carlo Galli
Monumental Palace Hall, 1765–1778
Pen and ink with gray and blue washes, 367 x 500 mm.
This drawing was presented to me in 1966 on the
occasion of the opening of the Scott Theatre in
Fort Worth, Texas, which I designed.

succeeded Ferdinando as designer in the Farnese court in Parma in 1757. He held this position for ten years before his assignment to the court of Naples to design the inaugural spectacle of Sarro's opera *Achille in Sciro* for the Teatro San Carlo as part of the wedding festivities of Charles III of Bourbon. He remained in Naples as court designer for three years of prolific activity before finally retiring to Parma.

The scene designs of many contemporary junior artists recall details derived from Righini's seminal Augsburg set of prints, which seem to have established the criteria for contemporary standards of scenic style. In his later designs for the opera houses of Parma and Naples, Righini redefined and expanded his earlier scenographic formula with his graceful adoption of the visual language of the Italian rococo. His later designs exerted even greater influence on the younger generation of Central

(50) Righini, Pietro, 1683–1742
    Italy (active in Reggio, Parma, Milan, Turin, and Naples)
    Atrium of a Palace with Ruins beyond a River (Left Half), c. 1735
    Pencil, pen, and bister ink with ink wash, 208 x 149 mm.
    Inscribed in ink on verso of mount:
    *"Disegno del Sig. Pietro Righini, Parmeggiano— di sua mano propra"*
    Collection: Herbert Bittner

*Atrio nella Reggia*

*Der Eingang in den Königlichen Saal.*

(51) Righini, Pietro
    *Atrio nella Reggia*

Engraving by Martin Engelbrecht, 1735
215 x 284 mm.

(52) Righini, Pietro
Courtyard of a Prison, c. 1735
Sepia pen, 194 x 299 mm.
Inscribed beneath lower margin:
*"Anteriore d'un Seralio di fiere"*
Collections: Brera, Gibelli, Baldini, Wunder

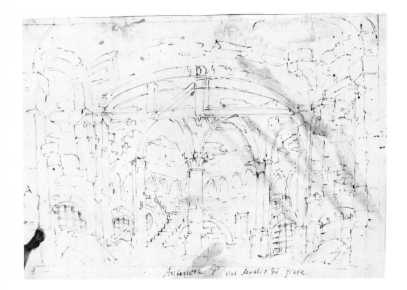

European and Italian theatre artists—notably in Naples, on Francesco Saracino and Vincenzo Re.

Pietro Righini was a man of the theatre accustomed to receiving the plaudits of his royal patrons and his public. But not often is a designer rewarded by praise in verse. Frugoni, poet and inventor of equestrian ballets, with whom Righini had collaborated on several occasions in Parma, was moved to compose two sonnets in praise of Righini's master talents. One was for the decorations he devised for the noble catafalque of Duke Francesco Farnese in Parma; the second was written some years later in homage to Righini for his last triumphant designs for Popora's opera *Trionfo di Camilla* in the Teatro San Carlo in Naples. How regrettable that few of his drawings have survived to record his triumphs and to tell the story of his talent to another generation of designers.

*Illustration 50.* The drawing served for one half of the engraving (printed in reverse, Illus. 51) of the *atrio nella reggia* which was one of the widely recognized set of eight theatrical scenes designed by Pietro Righini entitled *Theatralische Veränderungen Vorgestellt in einer zu Mayland Vorgestellt* and published by Martin Engelbrecht in Augsburg in 1735.

*Illustration 52.* The swift, sensitive drawing by Righini has left in its wake a long and interesting record. It is a preliminary sketch for his prison design for the engraving (printed in reverse and bearing the same title, Illus. 53) that is one of the same set of eight engravings as Illustration 51. These eight arresting designs, intended for the opera house in Milan, exerted considerable influence on younger designers in Italy and subsequent scenography in Europe.

In 1760, the *Dramma per Musica* titled *Talestri, Regina delle Amazzoni* by E.T.P.A. (Maria Antonia Walpurgis, Princess of Bavaria and sister of Frederick the Great) was first performed in the opera house of Nymphenburg. The musical score of *Talestri* was handsomely published in 1765 in Leipzig in the new Breitkopf type, embellished with a medallion portrait of the princess, and seven scene designs engraved by B. Muellers. Four of these designs state that they were made by F. Bibiena. Ferdinando had died seventeen years before *Talestri* was first performed. Furthermore, Ferdinando designed no scenery during his latter years in Bologna because of his failing eyesight. The design for plate number 6 in the score (Illus. 54), with the designation "F. Bibiena fecit," is obviously not by Bibiena but derived from the design of Righini and given the new title *Recinto destinato alla custodia di prigionieri*. Two mincing Amazons

(53) Righini, Pietro
*Anteriore d'un Seraglio di Fiere*, 1735
Engraving by Martin Engelbrecht, 215 x 284 mm.

were added to the scene. A drawing of the same scene with the same title is in the Biblioteca Civica in Cagli and is probably a later copy. How was the designing of this opera credited to the account of the great Ferdinando Bibiena? The princess, perhaps as autocratic and money-pinching as her kingly brother in theatrical matters, probably presented her court designer-technician of Nymphenburg with an assorted lot of engravings of the Bibiena family and other designers, including Righini, and said, "We will adapt these designs to the needs of my Amazzoni," and rubber-stamped them with "F. Bibiena."

Pierre-Luc-Charles Cicéri, 1782–1866 (see Illus. 55), copied this same baroque design of Righini's in Paris for the first act of the drama *Diamants de la Couronne* and called it *Ruines du Palais de l'Inquisition à Madrid, demolé par l'armée française en 1809*. He affixed his own signature to Righini's design.

(54) Bibiena, Ferdinando (attributed)
*Recinto Destinato alla Custodia di Prigionieri*, 1760
Engravings by B. Muellers, 188 x 285 mm.

(55) Cicéri, Pierre-Luc-Charles, 1782–1868
France, Paris (active in New York, Paris, and London)
Ruins of the Palace of the Inquisition—Madrid, 1810–1815
Sepia washes, 197 x 280 mm.
Signed in ink at lower right: "Cicéri"; inscribed in ink along lower margin: *"Ruines du Palais de l'Inquisition à Madrid, demolé par l'armée française en 1809"*; inscribed in pencil below; *"Decor du Acte I de Diamants de la Couronne"*

(56) Conti, Metrodoro (Aretino), first half of nineteenth century
Interior of a Prison
Pen and watercolor, 243 x 319 mm.
Inscribed in lower left corner: "C. M. Inv."; and beneath lower margin: *Interno d'un Serraglio di Fiere*—sheet number "90"

Another nineteenth-century watercolor design (Illus. 56) is also a direct steal from Righini's prison scene. This romantic drawing is by Metrodoro Conti Aretino—a scene designer who traveled about Europe recording those designs for the stage which most appealed to him. Beneath his design number "90" he adapted Righini's title, *Interno d'un Serraglio di fiere*, and substituted his own initials for Righini's name.

One must share with Coleridge the belief that "in today already walks tomorrow." So it was with Righini's prison scene. The timeless process of artists borrowing and adapting from another age continues. The chances are, another designer will undoubtedly put this design of Righini, Bibiena, Cicéri, or Conti to work once more in tomorrow's theatre.

*Illustration 54.* This engraving is one of the designs attributed to Ferdinando Bibiena for Ermalinda Talea's opera *Talestri, Queen of the Amazons*, presented in the opera house of Nymphenburg in 1760. The score was published in 1765 in Leipzig with illustrations of the opera's seven scenes.

*Illustration 56.* This drawing is the reverse of Righini's engraving (Illus. 53). In his travels, Metrodoro Conti might have come across Righini's original drawing and copied it. He emulated the styles of many designers and employed the scenic convention of many periods.

### *Filippo Juvara*

Filippo Juvara was thirty-two when he was summoned from Messina to Rome in 1708 at the request of Cardinal Pietro Ottoboni to install an intimate theatre in the spacious Palazzo Cancellaria. Theatricality was embedded in the very stones of that magnificent Renaissance palace. The great blocks of travertine had been wrenched from the Colosseum, and the courtyard consisted of forty-four granite columns plundered from the Theatre of Pompey. The hedonistic cardinal made his Renaissance palazzo the artistic center for the arts and music of baroque Rome.

(57) Juvara, Filippo, 1676–1736
Italy, Messina (active in Rome and Turin)
Hall in a Palace, 1708–1714
Pen and bister ink with wash, 187 x 247 mm.

(58) Juvara, Filippo
Great Hall with Staircase (Left Half), 1708–1714
Pencil, pen, and sepia ink with wash, 284 x 371 mm.
On the verso, sketches in pencil and ink of a palace wing and a set of ruins in a landscape.
Collections: Piancastelli, Brandegee, Scholz

Here he lavishly presented the dramatic musical works of Scarlatti and Handel with the finest Roman musicians and singers and Juvara as his designer. Scipione Maffei, in his *Osservazione Letterarie*, recorded that "at this theatre, Pellegrino (Maestro di Camera) and Juvara worked in collaboration, and in truth there were never seen more admirable and more ingenious scenery, perspectives and stage effects in such small spaces." (One hundred and twenty-six of Juvara's *Pensieri di scene apparecchie* for the cardinal's *teatrino* are contained in a single volume at the Victoria and Albert Museum.) For six years Juvara was intensely occupied with designing for the theatre in Rome. Along with his involvement in the cardinal's *teatrino*, he was devising scenes for the *teatrino* of Queen Maria Casamira of Poland in her Palazzo Zuccari, and also for the renovated Teatro Capronica.

Both of the drawings for scenic fantasies illustrated here are similar in character to those in the *Pensieri*. Their free curvilinear rhythms reflect the dynamic and elegant style Juvara acquired during his six-year sojourn in Rome. His designs represented the most advanced tendencies of the visual theatre in Europe. All of Juvara's scenic decors of this brief, climactic Roman period have brio and spontaneity—visionary preludes to his later boldly conceived and soundly constructed architectural masterworks, the Superga of Turin and the Stupenigi Palace nearby. His ephemeral designs became the source of

inspiration and the lasting expression of his later brilliant Piedmontese architectural style.

*Illustration 57*. Filippo Juvara's luminous design for a palace hall is divided intentionally into two parts. Each side of the ink center line represents a subtle variation of the refined elegance for the final design of the scene. The right arch is more spacious than the left and frames a stairway. This economical procedure on the part of the designer for presenting two design schemes in a single sketch was common practice with eighteenth-century scenographers.

*Illustration 58*. The right half of Juvara's working sketch contains a brief pencil plan of the setting. The steps up center and left and right are "practical." The center steps seem to descend almost to the footlights. Since they cut the stage floor in half, they would make free movement on the stage impractical. However, the upper-left corner of the drawing contains the silhouette of a proscenium valance hanging far downstage from the scene. Here is an indication that this design was planned for the rear stage area and that Juvara must have intended a series of Solomonic columnar wings (like the extreme left one) to connect this rear area of the scene with the proscenium arch, and thus achieve in depth a full-stage Great Hall with Staircase.

### Jacopo Fabris

If Jacopo Fabris were working in the theatre today, he would be called a designer-technician. An itinerant painter born in Venice, he early showed a talent that was channeled into the theatre and he introduced the Bibienesque traditions of Italian scenography into Germany and Denmark.

We know Fabris first as the court painter of the Margrave of Baden-Durlach in 1719, in which capacity he assumed also the duties of court designer. In 1724 he was working in the opera house in Hamburg, where he invented the scenes for some twenty-five operas within a period of six years. Then for ten years he dropped out of sight. Having married an English woman, Susanna Geoffreys, he may have resided in England and worked in the theatre, although no record of his activity in the English theatre has been found.

In 1740 he reappears occupying the enviable post of court designer of Frederick the Great in Berlin. As a theatre technician, he collaborated with the architect Knobelsdorff first on a temporary theatre in the royal palace before they finally completed the new royal opera house, which was inaugurated in 1742 with a lavish production designed by Fabris of Graun's new opera *Cleopatra and Caesar*. For seven years he devised the scenes for a number of Graun's and Metastasio's classical operas in the Prussian capital.

In 1747, Fabris was appointed resident designer-technician in the court of Christian VI of Denmark. The king was a devotee of the theatre, and he was determined to provide his subjects with the finest continental theatre. Fabris assisted the king's architect, Nicolas Eigtved, in planning the new royal theatre in the Charlottenborg Castle and the Kongens Nytorv Theatre. He was responsible for providing all their scenic requirements, includ-

(59)  Fabris, Jacopo, 1689–1761
Italy, Venice (active in Baden, Hamburg, Berlin, and Copenhagen)
Vulcan's Forge, c. 1760
Pen and sepia ink with gray and brown wash, 300 x 380 mm.
Signed in ink at lower left: "Jacobus Fabris inv. et del."

(60)  Vanvitelli, Luigi, 1700–1773
Italy, Naples (active in Rome)
Royal Hall for *Didone Abbandonata*, 1770
Pen and gray ink with ink wash, 234 x 265 mm.
On the verso is a pencil sketch of a setting similar to this drawing; also a pen and bister sketch of an altar prepared for a Holy Week *Theatrum Sacrum*.
Collection: Edmund Fatio

ing settings for the new comedies of the popular Danish dramatist Ludwig Holberg at the Komedienhaus in Copenhagen.

Fabris took time off from the theatre to indulge in teaching art and perspective. The Royal Library in Copenhagen possesses a manuscript by Fabris in five volumes dealing with geometry, perspective, and architecture. *Instruction in der Theatralischen Architectur und Mechanique* was volume IV, which he completed in 1760, the year before he died. This significant treatise was reproduced with an introduction by Torben Krogh in Copenhagen in 1930 and is a first-hand exposition of eighteenth-century continental practice in theatre architecture and scenic design. The last seven drawings in the manuscript illustrate his factual approach to the art of the theatre. His sketches are precise, workmanlike, practical, and clear, but drawn by the inspired hand of a technician rather than a designer.

*Illustration 59.* The drawing of Vulcan's forge, or better,

seven forges, is very close to the style of Jacopo Fabris' designs that illustrate his informative treatise on theatres and scenery.

### Luigi Vanvitelli

Luigi Vanvitelli was trained as a painter by his father, the Flemish-born Venetian view-painter Gaspar Van Wittel. For many years Van Wittel resided in Rome and was a close friend of Juvara during the years when Juvara was so absorbed in the Roman theatre. Very likely, Vanvitelli studied with Juvara; certainly his interest in the visual theatre must have been sparked by Juvara's infectious enthusiasm. Juvara's influence on Vanvitelli is apparent in the ordered spaciousness of the drawing for a royal hall (Illus. 60).

Vanvitelli enjoyed a long and successful career both as a scenographer and architect in Rome. He designed many imposing palaces and churches, carried forward Michelangelo's program for Santa Maria degli Angeli, and brilliantly redesigned the church and monastery of Sant'

*Coupe sur la Largeur DC du petit Théâtre du Palais de Caserte, qui fait voir la Scène xx*

(61) Unknown artist
France
*Coupe sur la Largeur du Petit Théâtre du Palais de Caserte*, c. 1775
Pen and gray ink with ink wash, 312 x 355 mm.
Present collection: Metropolitan Museum of Art

(62) Re, Vincenzo, d. 1762
Italy, Parma (active in Naples)
Festival Hall Overlooking a Harbor, c. 1750
Pencil, pen, and gray wash, 332 x 450 mm.
Inscribed in ink in lower left margin: "V Re"
Collection: George Home of Paxton

Agostino. His fully developed style represented his transition from baroque to neoclassicism.

In 1751 Charles VI, King of Naples and the Two Sicilies, appointed him court architect, and Vanvitelli returned to Naples, his birthplace. He was commissioned to design the grandiose palace and gardens at Caserta, a project that was under construction for many years.

*Illustration 60.* Illustration 61 shows the boxes and the proscenium of the theatre at Caserta framing a setting for Dido's palace. This drawing is Luigi Vanvitelli's actual scene shown within that proscenium. Downstage left, a blazing pyre is introduced, and beside it Dido is preparing herself for immolation. Mary Myers of the Drawing Department of the Metropolitan Museum, a specialist in Vanvitelli, points out that during the Carnaval of 1770, a Dido opera was performed at Caserta. She believes it must have been for Metastasio's libretto of

*Didone Abbandonata*, which was frequently performed in Naples to the music of various composers. Since the Vanvitelli drawing was significantly incorporated within the proscenium of the French drawing, it may have served for the opening opera performance of the theatre.

Mindful of Juvara and ever emulating his vision, Vanvitelli, in updating *Didone*, audaciously set the scene for the Queen of Carthage's fiery finale within a *sala reggia* whose scale approximated the vast neoclassical arched entrance hall of Caserta. The passage from the reality of that entrance hall to Didone's royal hall in the theatre was artfully bridged by Vanvitelli for His Majesty's audience.

*Illustration 61.* The Metropolitan Museum possesses four handsome eighteenth-century drawings (a plan and three sections) of Vanvitelli's theatre. These drawings were undoubtedly made by a French artist and intended for an

OVERLEAF

(63) Re, Vincenzo
Royal Encampment, c. 1740–1750
Pen and black ink with gray wash, 306 x 467 mm.

unpublished volume on theatre architecture. Vanvitelli's model theatre at Caserta influenced the design of many theatres erected subsequently in other courts of Europe.

### Vincenzo Re

Vincenzo Re was a muralist and engraver, and undoubtedly the most brilliant scene designer of the eighteenth century in southern Italy. He learned his craft working as an assistant to Pietro Righini, who was the official designer to the Bourbon court in Naples. Re's talent was first recognized in the mural decorations he painted for the interior of the new Teatro San Carlo. He also designed the sumptuous decor for *Achille in Sciro*, which inaugurated the San Carlo in 1737. The following year, he succeeded his master Righini as *architetto teatrale* to the court of Charles III. The king's palace, high above the bay of Naples, was famous throughout Europe for the splendor of its festivals and entertainments. Vincenzo Re established the tradition of scenic excellence at the San Carlo, and ever since, this famous opera house has set the highest artistic standards for the lyric theatre throughout the capitals of Europe.

Architect Francesco Mancini, authority on the baroque, classical, and romantic theatre of Naples, in his distinguished monograph on Vincenzo Re, lists some hundred ballets, operas, and *serenatas* for which Re was *"Inventore, direttore e architetto delle scene"* during the first twenty-five years of the Teatro San Carlo. In addition to Re's varied royal assignments, these productions alone are a prodigious achievement and reflect his inexhaustible capacity for scenic invention.

*Illustration 62.* This design for a festival hall overlooking a harbor has not been ascribed to an individual opera. It has all of the rococo exuberance and decorative felicity that Vincenzo Re displayed in his designs for the monumental fête book *Narrazione delle Solenni Reale Feste* of 1747. It is also evidence of the extravagant decor that Re provided for the court presentations of the Teatro San Carlo.

This festival hall or open gallery faces a landing stage with ships arriving in full sail. The gallery is supported by tall colonnades hung with swaggering draperies, and prominently displayed is the portrait of a queen, possibly King Charles' wife, Maria Amalia of Saxony. Contrary to Re's general practice, three posturing performers grace this scene. They provide scale and lend animation to this rococo creation. Might this scenic marvel of Vincenzo Re represent a mythical royal palace on the bay of Naples? On second thought, probably not, for no Neapolitan designer could possibly forget to include omnipresent Vesuvius.

*Illustration 63.* The royal encampment was an important theme in the pictorial literature of seventeenth- and eighteenth-century opera, and the scene was a challenge to every designer. Burnacini and Santurini, Ferdinando and Antonio Bibiena, all designed charming royal encampments. The scenic repertory of the Drottningholm Theatre includes a full-scale eighteenth-century royal camp eight wings deep. Outdoors in the park near the court theatre, the Swedish palace guards were quartered in a large royal battle tent made of copper and painted like scenery. Every nineteenth-century German toy theatre contained, among its stock of gaily colored lithographic sets, a royal encampment, continuing the persistent tradition of this rococo design of Vincenzo Re.

The typical royal encampment consisted of an avenue of elegant canopied tents receding in perspective amidst a pastoral background. The brave valanced tents were topped with onion domes, golden minarets, and pagodas decorated with plumes, flowers, or pennants. They were resplendent, hung in rich brocades and bright silks. Their sumptuous folds were caught up to reveal the glorious accoutrement of battle: shields and helmets, assorted weapons, drums, bugles, and flags.

The principals who commanded the *barocco-rococo* encampments were heroic figures—the Queen of the Amazons, Ajax or Agamemnon, the Horatii, Alexander the Great, Roland or Charlemagne. The opera libretti were conceived as heroic tragedies. Their characters were large scale, ever splendid in defeat or victory, and their battles were fought according to the highest code of royal etiquette. Nobility and honor and chivalry guided the course of battle, and the historical time and place were unimportant. The same encampment scene served Troy, Rome, Constantinople, or Trebizond with equal felicity. The terror that reigned during the Hundred Years' War, the bloody massacre of the Huguenots, Callot's *Miseries of War*, or the miseries of Valley Forge, never appeared on the decorous operatic stage. This black and white wash drawing of Vincenzo Re reflects all the opulence and color of a typical royal encampment. It lacks only the operatic sounds and drama of alarums and excursions.

### Giovanni Niccolò Servandoni

Giovanni Niccolò Servandoni, the son of an Italian coachman, rocketed to stardom in the mid-eighteenth-century theatre of Paris. He was the wonder boy of his age, and the Paris journals asserted he could do no wrong.

Servandoni was first apprenticed in Florence to the painter Giovanni Paolo Pannini, with whose architectural *capriccios* and ruins he was much in tune. Later he moved on to Rome and studied with the architect Giuseppe Rossi. Propelled by his own ambition for success, he moved to Paris in 1724 at the age of twenty-nine in search of wealth, glory, and honor. He found all three on the stage of the Académie Royale de Musique, where he designed scenes for the operas *Pyramus et Thisbe* and *Proserpine.* Within four years he became *premier peintre-decorateur* of the opera, succeeding the Berains, father and son.

Servandoni introduced the *scena al angola* to the French stage. A brilliant, not quite gaudy colorist, he worked in a variety of scenic techniques—illusionistic, romantic, and fantastic. In devising his scene for the Elysian Fields, he revived the landscape style of Claude Lorrain. For a palace scene, his wings were profiled in the latest open-work rococo mode. His backdrop was inspired by a seventeenth-century engraving of a classical garden with painted fountains and strolling courtiers. Servandoni considered anything and everything legitimate in stage design. Between 1728 and 1737, his extravagant decors had transformed the traditional mise-en-scène of the royal opera house, but by 1737 he felt he could go no further and left the opera with a hopeless deficit, turning the stage over to François Boucher.

His prestige rose from one success to another. He obtained a commission to reopen the vast Salle des Machines which Vigarani had built for Louis XIV in the Tuilleries. Here in 1739 he presented for the first time a novel performance of his own invention—*son et lumière.* This was an optical spectacle of *Saint Peter's Cathedral in Rome,* utilizing a diorama with all the elements of sound, light, and motion combined in a unified theatrical experience. This was the first of many annual spectaculars he presented in the Salle des Machines.

Servandoni was also responsible for organizing all the court fêtes for royal occasions, and in 1739 he surpassed himself with decorations for wedding festivities of the Princess Louise-Elizabeth, daughter of Louis XV, and the Infante don Philippe of Spain. The vast illuminated scene included the new wing of the Louvre as backdrop, and embraced the Seine between the pont Neuf and the pont Royal. The shores were bordered with terraces adorned with illuminated urns and obelisks, and an artificial island, with an octagonal transparent music room for a hundred musicians, was anchored amidst a flotilla of pleasure boats. A miraculous pyrotechnical display, for which Servandoni had become famous, brought the evening to a climactic finale.

As a member of the Royal Academy of Painting and Sculpture, he found time to paint and to exhibit his *capriccios* and ruins at the annual Salon. He received many commissions to decorate the fashionable *hôtels particuliers* of dukes and princes.

Servandoni's talents were in demand throughout Europe. In 1742, he collaborated on an opera in Lisbon with Carlo Bibiena, and he frequently visited Brussels to design for the Théâtre de la Monnaie. In 1749 he was in London working in Covent Garden and supervising a fireworks display in St. James's Park in celebration of the new peace. In 1754, Augustus III invited him to the baroque capital of Dresden to design an opera house complete with all the scenic decor. In 1760, he devised festivities for the wedding of the Hapsburg Grand Duke in Vienna, and in 1763 he was engaged by Herzog Karl Eugen for a year in Württemberg at the fabulous salary of fifteen thousand marks, to work on a series of settings for his luxurious opera house. In Württemberg Servandoni collaborated with Colomba, the court's resident Italian designer; Boquet, the costume designer from Paris; Jommelli, the kapellmeister; and Noverre, with his troupe of

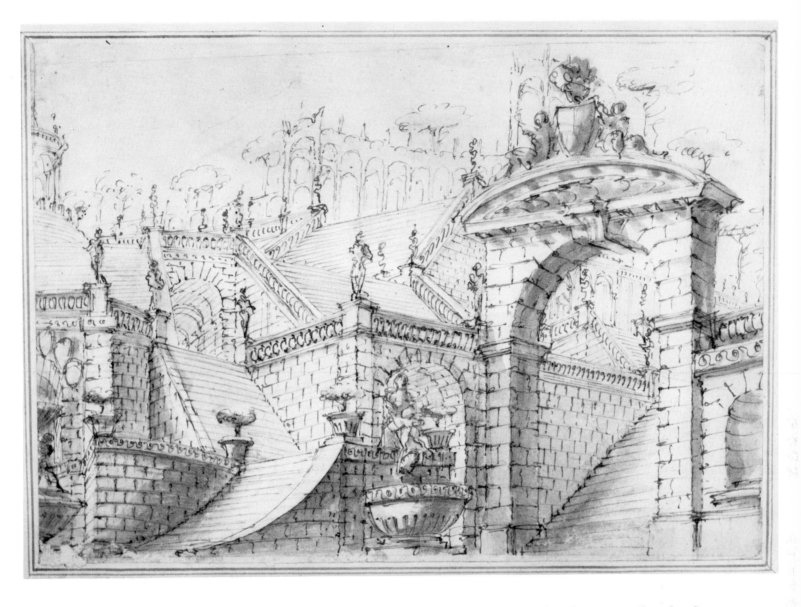

(64) Servandoni, Giovanni Niccolò, 1695–1766 (attributed)
Italy, Florence (active in London, Paris, Lisbon, Dresden, Vienna, and Brussels)
Garden Terraces, c. 1750
Pencil, pen, and brown ink with gray wash, 185 x 275 mm.
Collection: C L O (unrecorded in Lugt)

*Illustration 64.* This restless drawing attributed to Servandoni for a decor of garden terraces has the breadth and height and depth associated with Servandoni's later commodious designs for the theatre. The escalating stairs, like the flights of fancy in Piranesi's *Carceri* series, lead up and up and off attaining ever new heights and vistas—very much like Servandoni's own meteoric career. The design also displays those stations for drama that one discovers in the architectural fantasies of Pannini. Are these scenic flights of Servandoni stairs real, or are they painted scenery? Probably they are half and half. Their scale suggests his later decorations for the Salle des Machines, and also the eye-filling legendary fêtes and theatrical diversions he contrived for the pleasure of his royal master Louis XV.

one hundred dancers. Nearly three hundred artists were employed in the Herzog's theatre. The program of entertainment continued for sixteen days, and for this festival Servandoni contributed sixteen decorations.

Back in Paris during his later years, Servandoni saw his successful career diminish when his king, Louis XV, appointed Gabriel and Moreau his successors. But his name is still remembered today. On the Left Bank, a sign "rue Servandoni" indicates the name of a small street; the theatrical façade of Saint Sulpice records his architectural taste; and his painting of a ruin hangs in the Ecole des Beaux Arts. A few of his drawings survive in private collections, but little more remains of this artist whom Diderot referred to as *"grande machiniste, grand architecte, bon peintre et sublime decorateur."*

Servandoni's drawings are scattered among many private collections and museums, notably at Drottningholm. Some thirty colored models and sketches attributed to Servandoni and supposedly from the château at Versailles were acquired by the French government in 1939 and are preserved at the Château de Champs, Seine-et-Marne. This drawing is similar in style to another drawing attributed to Servandoni in my collection, of steps leading to a terrace before a circular temple all enclosed in clouds.

### Charles Michel-Ange Challe

Charles Michel-Ange Challe was a twenty-four-year-old student in the atelier of François Boucher in Paris when he received the Prix de Rome. For the next four years he lived in the Villa Medici set among its ilex-bordered gardens high up on the Pincio Hill, which was the traditional residence of the French Academy in Rome. Those four years (1742–1746) were significant in Challe's development. Like Fragonard and Hubert Robert, he was exhilarated by the classical monuments and shadowed ruins of Rome, and they became the stimulus of the new aesthetics of his art. His French classical style embodied a free adaptation of the Doric and Ionic orders embroidered within Roman urns, obelisks, and sundry ornaments. Of all the artists he came to know in Rome, he most admired Giovanni Battista Piranesi, only two years older than Challe, who had but recently deserted the lagoons of Venice for the hills of Rome. Piranesi's sense of heroic scale, his feeling for the grandeur of Roman monuments, and his free-wheeling *rovinistica* style were to exert a lasting influence on Challe's later career in France.

Back in Paris, Challe's drawing and painting reflected his predilection for the antiquarian and mannerist traditions of classicism he had assimilated in Rome, and his work was prophetic of nineteenth-century neoclassicism and romanticism. His reputation as an accomplished artist brought him increasing recognition, though the mediocrity of his painting technique was harshly criticized by the Parisian intellectuals, especially by Diderot. His talent in architecture, and in devising and arranging fêtes, found favor with the court, however. In 1765, Louis XV appointed Challe *Dessinateur du Cabinet du Roi*, and, as with Berain before him, his responsibilities included designing for the theatre and opera as well as supervising illuminations, royal fêtes, and *pompes funèbres*. Challe excelled in his funeral arrangements for royalty throughout Europe—for Don Filippo, Infante of Spain, for Elizabetta Farnese, the Queen of Spain, for the Dauphine of Saxony, for Queen Maria Leszczinska, and, in 1774, for his royal master, Louis XV.

*Illustration 65.* Challe's designs for the royal theatre and *fêtes publiques* were never conceived on a small scale, and many of his scenes were architectural fantasies inspired by Piranesi, whose drawings were never intended to be confined by a proscenium arch. Challe possessed the discipline to accommodate his lofty designs to the scale of the theatre in which he worked. This drawing of Challe is

(65) Challe, Charles Michel-Ange, 1718–1778
France, Paris
Classical Hall with Stairs, c. 1765–1775
Pencil, pen, and bister with gray wash, 208 x 282 mm.
Collections: Malaussena, Alliance des Arts (Paris), Scholz

(66) Unknown artist, eighteenth century
France
Ballet for a Court Fête, 1730–1740
Pen and black ink with gray wash, 213 x 194 mm.

derived from Piranesi's print of a classical hall. There is no record of Piranesi ever working in the theatre, though he designed one print of a scene for a great classical hall and called it *Un Disegno per il Teatro*. In scale it surpasses all eighteenth-century-Italian scenographers. Challe freely recomposed and adapted this Roman design of Piranesi to his own French purposes.

*Illustration 66.* This drawing represents an open-air performance of a ballet in a temporary theatre erected in a courtyard of a maison royale or a château de plaisance in the environs of Paris. The artist has presented this lively scene as though viewed through a proscenium arch. The setting consists of a series of formal exterior palace wings which terminate in a perspective backdrop. Above the wings appear the actual rooftops of the enclosing courtyard, providing a harmonious background for the stage scene. The means of illuminating this open-air production

are not indicated, but light or no light, the artist has animated the scene with fifty members of the corps de ballet wearing costumes in the impeccable style of Louis-René Boquet, who was Louis XV's *Dessinateur des Habits*. Shepherds and shepherdesses appear together with dancers dressed *à la chinois*. The latter reflect the taste and curiosity of the French court for the tantalizing world of the Orient—as remote to Paris then as the lunar landscape is to our world today. Yet all over Europe, oriental motifs were borrowed without hesitation and applied to chinaware, lacquer, fabrics, costumes, furniture, and tapestries. Pavilions and pleasure houses in the Chinese taste, like those at Brighton, Drottningholm, and Czarskoe Selo, became the fashion.

In theatre as well, the West has often been receptive to the stimulation of Eastern sources of pictorial influence. Costumes for masquerades, carousels, and processions were fashioned by Burnacini, Vigarani, Berain, and Boquet in Turkish, Persian, Indian, and Chinese styles. Rameau composed the spectacular oriental ballet *Les Indes Galantes*; and Noverre created ballets in various oriental styles. Fokine and Bakst contrived for Diaghilev the ballet *Scheherezade* with shocking oriental splendor, and more recently, Peter Brook presented *Orghast*, his

(67) Unknown artist, eighteenth century
France
Costume Design, c. 1730
Pencil, 472 x 319 mm.

version of Aeschylus' *Prometheus Bound*, with an international group of actors speaking a new language on a stage on a mountaintop above the ruins of Persepolis, the ancient capital of Persia. This was about as strange a theatrical occasion as the eighteenth-century shepherds and shepherdesses indulging in a minuet with those French courtiers *à la chinois* in a classical stage scene.

*Illustration 67.* In the archives of the Opéra in Paris are three large volumes from the collection of the *Menus-Plaisirs du Roi*. They contain original costume designs and copies or counterproofs by Jean I Berain for l'Académie Royale de Musique. For twenty years after his death in 1711, no records were kept of the costume drawings for dancers and singers. During this period, costumes were designed in the style of Berain by Boucher, Gillot, Watteau, J. B. Martin, and by anonymous artists. This costume design for the character of Hercules is in every detail a French traditional theatre costume.

### Jacques de Lajoue

Jacques de Lajoue derived his interest in drawing and painting architecture, landscapes, and ornament from his father, who was a working architect. He early allied himself with the *Indépendants*, a group of artists oppressed by the conventional austerity and weight of the arts of the latter years of the eighteenth century. Gillot, Lancret, and Meissonier were among his friends, and he was actively engaged in collaboration with Watteau and Boucher.

He was accepted by the French Academy when he was twenty-four and exhibited his work for over thirty years. He became closely associated with the court as a protégé of Madame de Pompadour and received many important commissions to decorate palaces and other royal buildings. He depicted promenades and assemblies in gardens, courtly recreations, and characters of the Commedia dell'Arte.

The architect Jean François Blondel called Lajoue, Pineau, and Meissonier the three original inventors of the *genre pittoresque*, the most extreme expression of French rococo decoration to assert itself during the decades of 1730 to 1750. Their art was the ultimate extension of Berain's grotesque *capricci*, the free inventions of Callot and della Bella, and the ideal *perspettive* of Juvara and Piranesi.

Jacques de Lajoue's creations were singular and very elegant flights of fantasy. Favorite motifs in his decorative, ornamental compositions were fountains, consoles, curving stairways, treillages, canopies, and grottoes. His rococo drawings, which are unfortunately rare, are charged with verve, and his designs are infused with a singular intensity of expression. They exemplify the brilliant tradition of French eighteenth-century art.

*Illustration 68*. Jacques de Lajoue may have designed this illusionistic setting for a revival of Monteverdi's *Orfeo* in the court theatre of Louis XV. How theatrical and sophisticated Hell has become in the hands of Lajoue! Pluto is enthroned in an eighteenth-century royal *caldarium*, surrounded by spirited minions. Fire and smoke issue from vents in rococo clouds that partially obscure the throne hall.

During the 1730s, Jacques de Lajoue made a number of stylish suites of *rocaille* drawings for the *ornamentistes* of Paris, particularly for the engraver Cochin. His designs represented a variety of fanciful subjects—a theatrical scene, a buffet, a Bacchic fountain, a shipwreck. One print of 1736 represents the throne hall of Pluto, who brandishes aloft his two-pronged pitchfork above demons and damned in a contemporary setting ablaze with brimfire. The striking similarity of that engraving with this scene design supports the attribution of this drawing to Lajoue. Very likely the engraving was a souvenir of Lajoue's setting for *Orfeo*.

### Giuseppe Valeriani

The Empress Elizabeth, who ruled Russia from 1741 to 1762, had a passion for life and a passion for the arts. While the court in Saint Petersburg rocked with intrigue and her scandalous love affairs, she opened wide her palace windows on the cultural vistas of Western Europe. Diderot and Voltaire, those protagonists of the Enlightenment, were her advisers in acquiring fabulous collections of books and art to adorn her Winter Palace. They persuaded her to invite the sculptor Falconet and the painters Lorrain and Moreau le Jeune to work in her court. Her

(68) Lajoue, Jacques de, 1687–1761 (attributed)
France, Paris
Throne Hall of Pluto, 1730–1735
Black pen with gray and rose watercolors, 280 x 410 mm.

primary obsession was to build new and more stately palaces, theatres, and public works. Under the direction of Rastrelli, her architect-in-chief, Peter the Great's master plan for the new capital on the banks of the Neva was expanded. The fourth and final reconstruction of the sumptuous Winter Palace, as it stands today, was to become an enduring monument to Elizabeth's taste and vanity, though, ironically, she never occupied it since it was not completed until the year after her death.

Those imperial pleasure houses required an army of interior designers and painters capable of converting triumphal scenes of gods and goddesses into flattering expressions of homage to the empress. Rastrelli attracted many Italian artists to adorn the interiors of these palaces, and in 1745 Giuseppe Valeriani arrived in Saint Petersburg in the vanguard of this company. In Russia he was given opportunities to display his talents that he had only dreamed of while working on the frescoes of Juvara's Stupenigi Palace in Turin. The empress was pleased with Valeriani's gifts and showered him with her favor. He was among the foremost of her court painters and decorators, providing a procession of designs for his collaborators and assistants Perecinatti and Angelo Car-

(70) Valeriani, Giuseppe
Palace Hall with the Crest of Empress Elizabeth I Amidst Clouds (Left Half), 1745–1761
Pen and black ink with brown ink wash, 241 x 235 mm.
Collections: Member of the Russian imperial family; Max Eugène Joseph Napoleon de Beauharnais, Duc de Leuchtenberg; Edmund Fatio
Five drawings by Giuseppe Valeriani in the Oenslager Collection come from an album of 143 drawings which was purchased from the Fatio sale by Colnaghi of London and subsequently broken up.

(69) Valeriani, Giuseppe, c. 1690–1761
Italy, Northern (active in Russia)
Half of a Palace, 1745–1761
Pencil, pen, and brown ink with ink wash; pricked for transfer; 335 x 437 mm.
Collections: The Russian imperial family; Max Eugène Joseph Napoleon de Beauharnais, Duc de Leuchtenberg; Edmund Fatio

boni to execute. Soon he found himself arranging banquets, devising fireworks, planning festivals, and designing scenes for opera.

*Illustration 69.* J. Byam Shaw in a letter to the author noted: "This drawing, which is exactly the same style as S-1 [another drawing of Valeriani], evidently had the same inscription, although only the tops of the letters appear on the lower margin on the back [of S-1]. If you overlap the back of this drawing with the back of S-1, you will see that the remaining parts are clearly the G and the top of the V of the artist's name."

This sketch by Valeriani is the working drawing for the palace setting of the opera *Il Generoso di Tito.* An engraving of the design is reproduced in M. Konopleva's monograph, *Giuseppe Valeriani* (1948).

Valeriani made this working drawing to explain clearly to the Russian scenic artists how he wanted his scene to be executed in their studio. The drawing is perforated by hundreds of pin pricks for "pouncing" (transferring for reproduction) all parts of the design to another sheet. By this procedure, which is sometimes employed by designers today, identical scale sections of this master drawing could be used in blowing up or enlarging the original design to the full scale of the stage scene. All the elements of the total scene are included in Valeriani's drawing: the front grand drapery, the number one cutout for the two side balconies, the number two cutout drop of the ceiling and the arch enclosing the central stairs, and finally, the perspective backdrop itself.

*Illustration 70.* J. Byam Shaw, in a letter, writes: "This drawing [with the arms of the Empress Elizabeth I, which was one of the finest in the book] has only the inscription 'R.10' [for roubles 10?] in an early hand on the back. I notice a certain difference in style between this and drawing numbers S-1 and S-2 [in the Oenslager Collection], but on the whole I am inclined to think that by comparison with other inscribed sheets in the book, this is by the same hand, that is to say by Giuseppe Valeriani again."

Valeriani made this sure and sensitive drawing for a palace scene for the court theatre in Saint Petersburg. If the empress did not herself participate in the production, her double-eagle crest, engulfed in glamorous cloud machines, symbolized on the stage her glorious presence in the imperial box.

### Bernardo Belotto

Bernardo Michiel Antonio Eugenio Belotto, called Il Canaletto, worked in the studio of his distinguished Venetian uncle, the painter Giovanni Antonio Canale (known as Canaletto), whose father, Bernardo Canale, had been a scene painter in the public theatres of Venice. Bernardo Belotto was trained as a *vedutista*, which literally means "view painter" or "view renderer." The *vedutisti* captured the declining Venetian scene in their nostalgic glorification of the past of Venice.

Belotto traveled over much of the continent, serving as court painter successively to the Emperor of Austria-Hungary, the Elector of Saxony, and the King of Poland. His canvases, executed with virtuosity and style, constitute a remarkable pictorial record of the architectural delights and pleasures of their capitals. Today, most of these collected *vedute* of Belotto are in the national galleries of Vienna, Dresden, and Warsaw. After the destruction of Warsaw by the order of Hitler during World War II, Belotto's accurate views of eighteenth-century Warsaw served as invaluable historical documents for the restoration of that ancient city.

Theatre never played a major role in Belotto's painting career, even though his Venetian training in handling space and perspective surely equipped him to design for the theatre. As court painter, he was probably inveigled by his sovereigns into designing scenes for opera and other entertainment. The scene designs in the sketchbooks in my collection might very well have served for such occasions. The only proof of Belotto's connection with the theatre is a single engraving of a performance of the ballet-pantomime *Le Turc Genereux*, choreographed by Noverre in the Hofburg Theatre in Vienna in 1758. At that time, Belotto was resident painter in the Hapsburg court, and the engraving states that it was he who designed the very un-Turkish garden scene.

H. A. Fritsche, in his monogram on Belotto (1936), has identified a small group of drawings or *ideal-veduten* as scenic inventions intended for the theatre. Among the drawings in the Mayr Collection, János Scholz notes that he "found a small group of stage sets with Italian inscriptions and measurements, some of which have been marked by an eighteenth century hand in black chalk: *Canaletti*. After further study I was able to construct quite an *oeuvre*, of which the Courtyard of a Palace [now in the Oenslager Collection], drawing number 80 in *Baroque and Romantic Stage Design*, is the most important item having on the verso the fine Roman set similar to the one reproduced by Fritsche on plate 30, and with all the inscriptions in Belotto's own hand."

Stefan Kozakiewicz, in Volume I of his *Bernardo Belotto*, 1972, hazards the opinion "that both the attribution of the drawings [in the Oenslager Collection] to Belotto and the assumption that he did any work for the theatre, require a more positive foundation than has been offered to the present time. . . . In the absence of concrete evidence either way, however, the hypothesis cannot be altogether rejected."

Hopefully, the theatre designs in these sketchbooks will help to establish Belotto's active association with the course of the theatre of Central Europe. This group of *vedute* for the theatre offer interesting possibilities for further theatre research.

*Illustrations 71–73.* These drawings come from three loose-leaf sketchbooks which contain stage designs of all kinds—prisons, fortresses, palaces, landscapes, city squares, and architectural fantasies. Janos Scholz believes the Belotto drawings must have passed from Belotto to his younger friend and fellow Venetian scene designer, Lorenzo Sacchetti, who thriftily used many of the notebook's empty pages for his own designs. Later, anonymous collector-designers added their rough sketches to the notebooks. These additions are very apparent, for they lack both the style and grace of Belotto's drawings and the virtuosity of Sacchetti.

### The Quaglio Family

The Quaglio family, after the Bibienas, was the second celebrated family of Italian scenographers. This dynasty carried on in an unbroken line from Giulio Quaglio I, who practiced in the mid-seventeenth century, to Eugen Quaglio, who died in Berlin in 1942. For seven generations, some fifteen Quaglios were engaged in the family's traditional occupation with the theatre. Sons and grandsons, like heirs apparent of a royal line, bore numbered given names like Angelo III and Giulio IV. The Quaglios came from the town of Laino, set in the scenic region between the lakes of Como and Lugano. They worked mostly in the theatres of northern Italy, southern Germany, and Austria. Munich became the Quaglios' home base, as Bologna had been the Bibienas'. Quaglio sons learned their craft from fathers, and fathers and sons and brothers labored together in their scenic studios inventing and handing on the changing scenic patterns from the baroque era down to the twentieth century.

Giovanni Maria Quaglio I was the first member of the Quaglio family whose achievements are recorded in any detail. He spent his productive later years in Vienna working in the imperial theatres and arranging entertainments and garden fêtes for the imperial court. His most important work was done during the last decade of his life, following the appointment in 1754 of Christoph Willibald Gluck as Hofkapellmeister and of Count Durazzo as Oberdirektor of the Hofoper. During the regime of this theatrical trinity, Giovanni Maria was the principal designer of most of the operas and ballet pantomimes that Gluck composed. *Le Cinesi* was presented by Prince Friedrich at his summer retreat, Schlosshof, during a visit of Emperor Franz I, Maria Theresa, and the children of the court. The transparent scenes, prismatic lights, and mechanical effects so pleased the emperor that at the conclusion of the performance he asked that the curtain be raised so that he might further inspect with his opera glasses Quaglio's eye-filling decor. Quaglio made a "command" drawing of the scene, and, in return, the emperor rewarded the designer with a snuff box containing a hundred ducats.

In 1762, Gluck's new opera *Orfeo ed Euridice* opened the new Burgtheater. With this opera, Gluck launched his program for the drastic reform of music and drama. The music underscored the human qualities of the opera's characters with unadorned simplicity. Quaglio presented his innovative interpretation of the scene for the Elysian

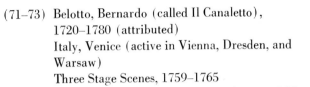

(71–73) Belotto, Bernardo (called Il Canaletto),
1720–1780 (attributed)
Italy, Venice (active in Vienna, Dresden, and
Warsaw)
Three Stage Scenes, 1759–1765
(71) Classical Atrium, pen and ink, 197 x 245 mm.
(72) Palace Stair Hall, pen and ink, 197 x 245 mm.
(73) View of a Walled City, pen and ink, 245 x
394 mm.
Collections: Sacchetti, Mayr, Fajt, Scholz

Fields with "a brilliance which dazzles the eyes." The trees and flowering plants were not represented as fresh and living; they were the autumnal colors of fading leaves! As an artist, Giovanni Maria Quaglio brought éclat to his family name, and as a collaborator with Gluck, prestige to the Austrian theatre.

Lorenzo Quaglio I was trained by his father, Giovanni Maria, as an architect and scene designer. At twenty-three he departed from Laino to take up residence in the enlightened court of Carl Theodore at Mannheim. In five years, Lorenzo became court architect in this active center of opera and ballet. He was involved in the construction of the National Komödienhaus and enlarged and renovated Alessandro Bibiena's Schlosstheater, which had opened only twelve years before. As court architect he was borrowed for various theatre projects in neighboring towns. In 1776 he decorated the new ducal theatre at Zweibrücken; in 1780, the Theater im Junghof at Frankfort on the Main, and also the new theatre at Lowingen on the Danube.

In 1778, Carl Theodore became Elector of Bavaria, and Lorenzo was transferred to the elector's more impressive court in Munich and given greater opportunities. Lorenzo

(74) Quaglio, Giovanni Maria I (Sometimes referred to as Giulio III), 1700–1765 (attributed)
Italy (active in Vienna)
Courtyard of a Fortress, c. 1750
Pencil, pen, and black ink with gray washes, 395 x 520 mm.
On the verso are both a pencil sketch and a pen sketch of a royal corridor, probably by Josef Platzer, who might have obtained this drawing from one of Quaglio's sons for his own collection.
Collections: Mayr, Fajt, Scholz
This drawing is one of a group of ten drawings in the Oenslager Collection which are obviously all by the same hand. Most of them are prisons or fortresses. One of these drawings, a prison with a palace courtyard, carries the signature "Julio Quaglio Inv."

(75) Quaglio, Lorenzo I, 1730–1804
Italy, Northern (active in Mannheim, Dresden, and Munich)
Forum, 1760–1770
Pencil, pen, and bister ink, 240 x 335 mm.
Collection: Scholz

Quaglio became one of the noted masters of scenography of his day and enjoyed the same recognition as the librettists and composers who were in attendance in the elector's court. Among Lorenzo's many distinguished productions in Munich were his settings for Mozart's *Idomeneo*, commissioned by the elector and opened during the Carnival of 1871. This "new and strange" first *opera seria* of Mozart was splendidly received at its premiere. In 1931, *Idomeneo* was rewritten by Wolf-Ferrari and presented in the Munich State Theatre to celebrate the music of Mozart. The ephemeral scenes of Lorenzo Quaglio could never celebrate their sesquicentennial.

The scenic work of seven generations of the Quaglio family, extending over a period of two hundred years, exerted a long and powerful influence on the course of the visual theatre of Italy, Germany, and Austria.

*Illustration 74.* Janos Scholz has made a reasonable attribution of this drawing to the first recognized designer of the Quaglio family. Among a recently discovered group of theatre drawings listed in the catalogue titled *XVIII and XIX Century Stage Designs from the Mayr-Fajt Collection* (New York, Seiferheld Gallery, 1962), are two drawings inscribed "J.M. invenit" (both are now in the Oenslager Collection). Mr. Scholz writes, ". . . there is a similar example by this very able Bibiena follower (also in the Oenslager Collection). The Catalogue of the Thea-

tre Collection of the National Library in Vienna describes a sheet of almost identical dimensions as 'School of Galli-Bibiena,' signed Joa. . . Mich. . ." Scholz calls the artist simply "J.M." and notes a certain affinity to the etchings of Vincenzo Mazzi. Another drawing of a prison scene attributed to Giovanni Maria Quaglio was formerly in the Kaufman Collection (#52) and is now in the Metropolitan Museum. The Kaufman catalogue, *Fantastic and Ornamental Drawings* (Portsmouth College of Art and Drawings, 1969), states, "It appears to be a fair assumption that the initials J.M. of the Mayr-Fajt drawings refer to the same artist—J.M. (Johann Marie) representing a German equivalent of the Italian G.M. (Giovanni Maria); he was known popularly in his lifetime as *Bibiena redivivo*." Most of the work of the Quaglio family is preserved in the Theatre Museum in Munich. Signed examples of Giovanni Maria I are in the Landesmuseum at Darmstadt.

*Illustration 75.* For many years, this drawing was attributed to Filippo Juvara. The correct attribution has recently been established through its association with Quaglio's finished drawing, in pen and gray and pink watercolor, in the Uffizi collection (reproduced in Ricci, fig. 122). The scene may have been intended for the 1769 Dresden production of Naumann's *La Clemenza di Tito*.

This lively pen drawing, the *primo pensiere* of Lorenzo Quaglio for the scene of a Roman Forum, is of consider-

able interest. It reveals the speed and completeness with which an eighteenth-century master envisioned a full-scale, two-point perspective scene. Every line is set down with clarity of thought. The designer knew exactly what he was up to. The proscenium opening is represented by a working hatched line, and the scale is indicated along the lower margin of the drawing. The artist reworked minor details of this preliminary drawing for his more organized and finished drawing in the Uffizi. Two sculptured groups on the left became one, and the slender obelisk in the foreground was eliminated. The questionable dome of the building in the central distance was changed by the artist, who substituted the penciled detail in the sky above. Several steps add dimension to the right entrance. This drawing provides an insight into Lorenzo Quaglio's way of thinking. As court architect, he became a master scene designer—the first of the third generation of the Quaglio dynasty.

The principal collection of the work of all the members of the Quaglio family is preserved chronologically in the Theatre Museum in Munich.

### The Galliari Family

The Galliari dynasty was the last notable Italian family of scenographers to appear on the European scene. For two generations they were referred to as the Galliaris, *"Inventori e Pittori dello scenario,"* or as the Signori Fratelli Galliari because they almost always collaborated with one another, sometimes to the point of working on the same sketch together. Thus they might have established the impression among their contemporaries that the collective style of several Galliaris must be better than that of a single Galliari. This accepted Galliari style makes the attribution of drawings to individual members of the family sometimes difficult to establish. Mercedes Viale-Ferrero, in her definitive work *Scenografia del '700 e i Fratelli Galliari*, admirably analyzes the characteristics of the more prominent members of the family, and with her authoritative scholarship reconstructs the oeuvre of this influential family of talented designers.

The initial appearance of the first generation of three designing brothers was unheralded. Bernardino (1707–1794), Fabrizio (1709–1790), and Giovanni Antonio (1714–1783) were destined to become a remarkable designing team, executing a prodigious number of scenes for opera and ballet. After Filippo Juvara died in 1736, their design style dominated the Piedmont and Lombardy and Germany.

The Galliaris were Piemontesi from Andorno, but their training in the arts was in Milan. When their father, Giovanni Galliari, a provincial painter-decorator, died in 1722, the elder brothers settled in Milan, followed a few years later by young Giovanni Antonio. All became apprentices in the scenic studio of the Teatro Regio Ducale, Bernardino learning painting from Medici and Crosato, Fabrizio absorbing architecture and perspective from Barbieri, who with Pietro Righini was the established scene designer of the ducal theatre. After their apprenticeship, the brothers Galliari were soon designing scenes in collaboration with their masters.

In 1738 the Galliari trio had their big chance. They were summoned to Innsbruck to design the elaborate wedding festivities of Charles III of Bourbon and Maria Amalia of Poland. Happily, the decorations were a great success and established the reputation of this burgeoning triple entente. Several years later, Barbieri died and Fabrizio succeeded him at the Teatro Regio Ducale, and in turn Bernardino succeeded Medici. Giovanni Antonio, in his early twenties, became scenic coordinator. The Fratelli Galliari "combine" was launched in Milan. Among them existed a felicity of taste and unity of intention. Bernardino, trained as a *figurista*, seems to have had the painter's and designer's eye and to have been the guiding spirit among his brothers. Fabrizio was a master of perspective and architecture, and Giovanni Antonio possessed the technical knowledge required in coordinating the execution of their settings.

In 1748, Bernardino and Fabrizio returned to the Piedmont and were appointed court designers of the Teatro Regio in Turin. They were also active in other theatres, including the Teatro Carignano, and Turin became the center of their activity for the remainder of their lives. They were assiduous designers, providing settings in some seasons for five or more productions between 1748 and 1792.

Giovanni Antonio remained in Milan in charge of settings for the Teatro Regio. This venerable house was destroyed by fire in 1776 and was replaced within a year by Piermarini's more commodious and splendid La Scala, built on the site of the collegiate church of Santa Maria della Scala. The Fratelli Galliari designed the inaugural opera, Salieri's *L'Europa Riconosciuta*. La Scala became the recognized "pilot theatre" of Italy.

Giovanni Antonio was all of forty-seven when his son, Gaspare Galliari, was born in 1761 to become his designing heir apparent at La Scala. His father was the recognized scenographer of the establishment in Milan. Gaspare, early endowed with the grace of filial piety, could not have avoided following in his distinguished father's footsteps. Brought up in the hectic milieu of designing uncles and cousins, he soon became indoctrinated in the studio traditions of the confraternity. When he was twenty-five, a share of the family enterprise was allotted to him. He first designed for the theatres of neighboring towns. Then he supervised the festivities for the wedding of the Duke d'Aosta. Commissions for settings followed in rapid succession in Vienna, Venice, Genoa, and finally back again in Milan, where he would preside at La Scala for the remainder of his life as a master designer fired with his own challenging ideas and his vision for a new Italian theatre in the vanguard of the nineteenth century.

For a hundred years, the Galliaris dominated the theatre of their day, and the theatre in turn dominated their lives. Their work reflected the era of the great social and political transformation that occurred during the French Revolution and its aftermath in Italy and Europe. As a family of artists they were unique, working almost exclusively behind the theatre's proscenium arch. Perhaps that is why their sketches were often enclosed, almost like a trademark, within a linear indication of a proscenium

(76) Galliari, Bernardino, 1707–1794
    Italy, Northern (active in Milan, Turin, and Berlin)
    Marriage of Bacchus and Ariadne, 1756
    Crayon, pen, and bister wash, 290 x 420 mm.
    Inscribed along lower margin on contemporary paper:
    "École Italienne, Galliari (Bernardino)"
    The drawing has a pencil overlay of ruled squares.

drapery. They clung proudly to their family scenic traditions even as they sought to give neoclassic rationale and romantic direction to the art of the theatre.

*Illustration 76.* This drawing is Bernardino Galliari's preliminary cartoon of Bacchus and Ariadne which he made in 1756 for the theatre curtain of the new Teatro Regio of Turin. The more finished oil sketch for the curtain is preserved in the Galleria Sabaudo in Turin. This curtain was acknowledged to be one of Bernardino's finest works.

Bernardino considered himself as much a painter as a scenographer. He painted at least six important theatre curtains; one he executed for the Hoftheater of Frederick the Great in Berlin. His style of painting was clearly influenced by the Venetian Giovan Battista Crosato, who worked in Milan as a scenographer and painted several splendid theatre curtains. Crosato's admiration for Tiepolo's brilliant compositions and color shines through Bernadino's cartoon. But his conception of the subject lacks sophistication and is rather self-conscious in its symbolic and mythological rhetoric. The year Bernardino painted this curtain, Giuseppe Bartoli felt impelled to publish a four-page leaflet for the enlightenment of the citizens of Turin, describing the curtain and explaining the actions of the bride and groom's attendants. Early theatre curtains were invariably adorned with spectacular scenes, swarming with a dedicated population of divine, mythical, and historical personages.

All subsequent painters of theatre curtains after Bernardino Galliari worked in the great tradition of Italian decorative painting, which reached a glorious finish with Tiepolo. Through the nineteenth century, their curtains continued to sport nymphs and warriors and the pompous ladies and gentlemen from Parnassus and the world of ancient history. In every opera house of Italy, a populous curtain, like a visual prelude, rose to reveal practically the same cast of characters suddenly come to life on the stage.

*Illustration 77.* Among collections of Galliari drawings, two or more design solutions for the same scene are sometimes found. Possibly these variations on a scenic theme were the result of composite thinking after brief conferences by those particular Galliaris involved on a given production, though it is likely that many of the duplicate designs were made in the Galliari studio and dispatched to other opera houses for productions of the same opera under the supervision of a member of the Galliari family.

Several preliminary studies exist for this bold scenic design of Bernardino Galliari. The Friend Collection at Princeton has one study of a straight colonnade *al angolo*, meeting a more open temple on the left, and in my collection there is a second exploratory study in pen and gray wash with a pale blue sky. That study is more formal and confined than this enclosing circular colonnade enhanced by dramatic light and shade.

*Illustration 78.* This fragile pencil drawing with a ruled ink overlay explains Fabrizio Galliari's coherent method of achieving a balance of architectural and pictorial forms which his brother Bernardino might thereafter enliven with figures and embroider with decorations. Subsequently, the design would be turned over to Giovanni Antonio for supervision of the scenic execution.

This working drawing affirms Fabrizio's preference for the *scena quadro*—a scene consisting chiefly of painted flat scenery within a square picture frame. Beyond the frame he continues the wing and border masking. In the upper right corner of this sketch is the plan of the scene in ink; related explanatory numbers and letters are disposed over the drawing. On the left of the center-line is drawn the large-scale central arch with an open space between columns, forming the foreground of the scene. Right of the center-line is the smaller-scale central arch with terrace and trees forming the middle distance. Beyond is the backdrop of the continuing terrace with stairs and central fountain.

The composition of the design is based on a linear perspective construction. This scheme of spatial composition was still unusual at this time, but it was put to increased use by the Galliaris. In the Oenslager Collection, a design by Fabrizio for an arched hall for "*Tamerlane,* Turino, 1757," is developed on the same *scena-quadro* system which he employed the previous year in designing a walled city for the opera *Emira* (Viale-Ferrero plate #49). The artist embellished these precise constructions with his own style of drawing. Within his square frame he was free to display his eclectic taste in scenes derived from the baroque, or from neoclassicism or naturalism—or, if he chose, all three together!

*Illustration 79.* This pen-and-wash drawing of a setting for the Elysian Fields has not been identified with any of the Galliaris' later designs for the opera in Turin. Possibly it was intended for a production of *Orfeo* in Innsbruck or Vienna. This naturalistic grove of trees, freely arranged in orderly perspective, is for a square frame, a device often employed by Fabrizio, with the tree wings indicated in the foreground right and left.

The composition is constructed on the Galliaris' favored device of interlocking lines of perspective to achieve both a spacious and theatrical design.

A spattering of scene paint along the lower margin of the sketch is positive proof that this design was put to practical use in the scenic studio. It also corroborates the suspicion that scene painters have traditionally displayed little regard for the designer's sketch as a work of art. For them it is a practical working sketch. A notable exception to this traditional attitude was the case of Chagall's scenes for the Metropolitan Opera's 1970 production of *The Magic Flute.* While the scenes were being painted in the opera's scenic studio, his sketches were not only protected by cellophane when they were used on the paint bridge, but for good reasons they were returned to the Metropolitan's safe when not in use!

*Illustrations 80–82.* This design for Roccaforte's popular opera libretto *Caius Marius,* with music by Scolari, was presented at the Teatro Regio Ducale in Milan during the Carnival of 1765. The settings were credited to those omnipresent Fratelli Galliari. Bernardino's and Fabrizio's base of operations at that time was the Teatro Regio in Turin. Which brother made this sketch? Both Bernardino and Fabrizio were treating architectural interiors with a new severity. Wynne Jeudwine notes that their "arches become flatter, straight lines take over from curves, ornament is suppressed. An austere angularity begins to take the place of the former luxuriance, and there is less concern with producing a stunning piece of illusionism."

This design is confusing because three separate versions of a prison background are superimposed through the central arch of the scene. One is drawn in black ink and a second in sanguine. By tracing these two versions, the former (82) presents a flight of stairs leading to balconies below a beamed ceiling; the latter (81) presents an arched hall receding in perspective. A third, hatched version indicates an arch framing stairs leading upstage. Were these three versions separate prison scenes? Or does this drawing possibly indicate where Giovanni Antonio, the resident designer-technician of the Teatro Ducale, might have assisted his brothers from Turin in determining the appropriate technical solution of this single scene? The question opens up interesting possibilities in understanding the working relationships of the Galliari brothers.

*Illustration 83.* When Giovanni Galliari was twenty-six, his uncle Bernardino took him to Berlin where Bernardino was briefly resident designer in the court of Frederick the Great. There Giovanni must have assisted his uncle in painting the new curtain for the Hoftheater and working on the scenes for Graun's *Demofoonte* and Hasse's *Arminio.* Returning to Turin, Giovanni fell into his family

(77) Galliari, Bernardino
　　　Circular Colonnade with Temple, c. 1745
　　　Pen, sepia, and gray wash, 220 x 322 mm.
　　　Collections: Mayr, Fajt, Scholz

(78) Galliari, Fabrizio, 1709–1790
　　　Italy, Northern (active in Milan, Turin, Innsbruck,
　　　Paris, and Vienna)
　　　Garden Terrace, 1750–1760
　　　Pencil and pen, 263 x 395 mm.
　　　Collections: Mayr, Fajt, Scholz

(79) Galliari, Fabrizio
Elysian Fields, 1760–1770
Pencil and bister pen with gray wash, 375 x 455 mm.
Collections: Mayr, Fajt, Scholz

slot in the Teatro Regio, working for many years as a team with his brother Giuseppino, his father, and his uncle Bernardino.

This drawing by Giovanni for a vestibule with far-reaching double stairways has both scale and authority. The design is constructed on a Bibienesque composition and overlaid with neoclassical detail typical of the Galliaris. Two contemporary critics, Algarotti and his disciple Milizia, were not opposed to the basic principles of the older rococo Bibienesque style which this drawing exemplifies, but they wanted noble forms repeating those of antiquity, strong color with contrasting light and shade, and naturalistic scale appropriate to contemporary aes-

thetic standards. The scenic style of the Fratelli Galliari conformed with their ideals.

*Illustration 84.* Gaspare Galliari inherited his uncle Fabrizio's concern for ingeniously constructed compositions and engineered architecture. Gaspare eliminated all unessential details of architectural decoration. He envisioned this scene for an *aula sepolcrale* as a highly theatrical place.

Gaspare's deft use of chiaroscuro, like that of Pietro Gonzaga, helped to make this scene a place of pure artifice. While the structural vaults of his design are neoclassical, he lighted these vaults so arbitrarily and

(80–82) Galliari, I Fratelli
Italy, Northern (active in Milan, Turin, and Berlin)
Prison, 1765
Pencil, pen, and black and red inks, 284 x 415 mm.
Inscribed in ink along bottom margin:
"*Jugurta usurpator del regno della Numidia e
tiranno, Mario lo conduce il trionfo e poi lo fece
morir di fame in prigione con due suoi figli*"
Collections: Mayr, Fajt, Scholz
(81, tracing of red ink version of prison;
82, tracing of black ink version of prison.)

OVERLEAF

(83) Galliari, Giovanni Antonio, 1746–1818
Italy, Northern (active in Berlin and Turin)
Vestibule with Double Staircase, c. 1775
Pen and brown ink with gray wash, 205 x 280 mm.
Inscribed in ink at lower left: "Galliari"
Collections: A. Perrera, Rome; E. Fatio, Geneva

dramatically that the scene succeeds in establishing a romantic impression of the nobility of happenings long past. It is this nostalgic mood that addresses itself directly to the future and to romanticism. This was Gaspare Galliari's great step forward into the nineteenth century.

*Illustration 85.* This is Galliari's drawing for the engraving number XVIII, Logge Terrene, in *XXIV Invenzioni Teatrali di Gaspare Galliari*, Milan, 1814. Four oversize drawings in the Oenslager Collection (Mayr-Scholz, *Baroque and Romantic Stage Design*, plates #61, #62, #63, and #64) have a monumental scale similar to this drawing. Probably these were not intended for the theatre. They may have belonged to a projected second series of *invenzioni teatrali* to follow his first series published in 1814. The frontispiece of the 1814 *invenzioni* ironically portrays the title of the volume carved on a classical mortuary monument nine years before Gaspare died!

The late eighteenth and early nineteenth centuries witnessed the emergence of genuine dramatic talent among opera librettists and composers. In place of the outmoded heroic characters and plots derived from antiquity, librettists Goldoni and Metastasio, and composers Paisiello and Cimarosa, introduced into their operas characters and plots from contemporary life. This breakthrough provided the designer with a new opportunity for collaboration with librettist and composer, and Gaspare Galliari accepted this challenge with alacrity. Gaspare was able to indulge his taste for the picturesque and the fictitious, and his artist's concern for the background of a changing contemporary society.

(84) Galliari, Gaspare, 1761–1823
Italy (active in Vienna, Venice, Genoa, and Milan)
*Aula Sepolcrale*, 1800
Pen and gray wash, 463 x 645 mm.
Collections: Collector's mark on verso not in Lugt;
R. Gunter

(85) Galliari, Gaspare
Magnificent Roman Hall, 1814
Pen and gray wash, 203 x 273 mm.
This is Galliari's drawing for engraving number
XVIII, Logge Terrene, in *XXIV Invenzioni Teatrali di Gaspare Galliari*, Milan, 1814.
Collection: Mayr-Scholz

104

Gaspare Galliari could devise the smallest or the largest scene on a super scale. He delighted in achieving a massive, picturesque effect whether the scene be heroic or minuscule, unreal or natural. The very subjects of his scenes forecast the new taste in scenic design. Out of respect for the past there were palaces and forums, prisons and subterranean locales. The neoclassic design for a magnificent Roman hall illustrated here has the scale and the ambience of Caracalla's baths and Diocletian's basilica. But far more avant-garde were his scenes of contemporary villages, courtyards and barns, inns and kitchens, villas and gardens under the hot sun, waterfalls, mills, and bridges by moonlight. These dictated the new order of design.

As an intuitive artist working on the stage with the limitation of oil and candle, Gaspare Galliari was actually the forerunner of the modern designer's use of arbitrary light in scene design. He substituted dramatic light and shade for architectural detail, which gave sweep and power to his designs.

*Illustrations 86 & 87.* These drawings are two studies for the same scene. The picturesque villa with its forecourt is typical of all of those *barochetto* villas that dotted the countryside of northern Italy in 1817.

Gaspare filled his sketchbook with all kinds of informal scenes. They reveal how disciplined and coordinated were the trained eye and the flexible mind of the designer. From his travels through the rural countryside, Gaspare recalled and set down these two quite different design solutions for the same scene, using in each the essential elements of kiosk and villa entrances required by the libretto for the dramatic action of the scene. How informal and sunny and natural they appear, seeming like free architectural sketches of an actual villa, actually lived in, and accurately recorded. In these informal studies, Gaspare has gone a long distance from the geometric artifice and the fantastic perspective *scena al angolo* of the Bibiena dynasty. These scenes appear to be viewed through the peephole of Gaspare's camera obscura.

### Francesco Orlandi

Francesco Orlandi, a successful architectural and decorative painter in Bologna, inherited his talent for the theatre from his father, Stefano Orlandi, a prominent Bolognese scenographer who designed settings for many major theatres in Italy. Francesco may have undertaken his apprenticeship in the art of the theatre with Antonio Bibiena, whom he very much admired when Bibiena was working in the theatre of Bologna. He became professor

*giardino*

of architecture in the Clementina Academy, the chair once held by Ferdinando Bibiena. Many churches of Bologna contain monuments and *trompe-l'oeil* decorations by his hand, though, according to the accepted eighteenth-century practice of many architectural designers, Francesco's figures were filled in by the hand of another artist.

*Illustration 88.* Francesco Orlandi designed settings for many theatres of towns surrounding Bologna as well as in Livorno and Trieste, but few examples of his theatrical work have survived. Unfortunately, this design for the pompous entrance hall of a palace lacks personal flair, and, even though precisely balanced and carefully organized, it is static and its decoration seems derived from an accepted formula. The drawing is nevertheless expert in its professional execution.

*Illustration 89.* It is difficult to attribute this drawing to a single designer-architect. Richard Wunder has ascribed it on stylistic grounds to Lorenzo Quaglio the Elder (1730–1804), who was active in the theatre of Mannheim and Munich. It is probably best to assign it to an Austrian or German follower of Giuseppe Bibiena.

The drawing confirms the belief that the sumptuous eighteenth-century proscenium frame did not really detract from the stage scene or overpower the performers on the stage. Most of the European theatres were small intimate court theatres accommodating several hundred

(86 & 87)  Galliari, Gaspare
Before a Villa (Two Studies), 1817
Sepia pen and gray wash, 155 x 215 mm.
Collection: Charles Loeser
These two drawings, and several other sheets in the Oenslager Collection, are from a sketchbook of scene designs inscribed by Gaspare Galliari and dated 1817. The title page and ten sheets are in the Victoria and Albert Museum. Unfortunately, the remaining sheets have been dispersed among private and public collections.

spectators with a proscenium opening that averaged twenty-five to thirty feet wide. Exceptions to their charming small-scale intimacy were a few large and famous theatres such as the San Carlo in Naples, the Argentina in Rome, the Teatro Communale in Bologna, and La Fenice in Venice.

In every opera house, small or large, the proscenium was the pride and joy of the house. The proscenium and the auditorium candelabra and chandeliers flickered and glowed throughout the evening and gave the occasion a festive air. The scenes on the stage were illuminated with a greater concentration of oil and candle power. Stage lighting was controlled with reasonable though, to our electronic eyes, rather primitive methods. This eighteenth-century theatre drawing suggests the constant glow that flattered both spectators and performers and also enhanced the solid theatre architecture and the painted scenery. The proscenium frame was common to both areas of the theatre. Its massive mission was to serve as the visual link, the ideal junction between fact and fantasy, uniting the reality of the world of the spectators in the auditorium with the unreality of the world of the performers on the stage.

To the purists, this exuberant display of theatre architecture comes dangerously close to that tasteless extravagance of the late rococo style of Central Europe. Nevertheless, here is the source of the tried and true traditional theatre architecture whose flamboyant style persisted in our theatre and opera-house interiors until the turn of the twentieth century.

### Carl Schutz

The drawing on page 109 is probably the original design by Carl Schutz for *The Persian Fair*, a ballet devised and choreographed by Jean George Noverre in the Hofburg Theatre of Vienna, April 15, 1796. Maria Theresa, two years before, had diplomatically arranged for Noverre's transfer to Vienna, and for seven years, as *maître de ballet*, he was one of the theatrical luminaries of the queen's court; he was able to create more than fifty ballets

there. He also served as *maître de ballet* for Frederick the Great and Marie Antoinette.

As reformer of the French balletic tradition, Noverre elevated dance to new heights of achievement and perfection. He discarded outworn routine in favor of style, created the *ballet d'action*, amplified the corps de ballet with pantomime, and introduced reforms in the costume of the dancers. In many of his ballets he exploited the eighteenth-century taste for the customs and color of the Near and Far East.

Carl Schutz was already an active young designer in the Viennese theatre when Noverre arrived in 1794. He no doubt had read Lessing's newly published translation of Noverre's *Lettres* in preparation for his scenic collaboration with the great Noverre himself on *The Persian Fair*.

*Illustration 90.* The drawing is strikingly similar in style to a signed drawing in the Oenslager Collection which Carl Schutz made for an artificial grotto with fountains for the garden of Baron de Vries at Voeslau in 1777. An engraving of this drawing is listed in the Berlin Catalogue, as are two theatre drawings made by Schutz in 1774.

Schutz's descriptive notations in German for the execution of his Persian setting and all the properties suggest a brief dialogue with Noverre. Notes inscribed at

bottom: "The landscape with steep mountains, the city very mild and bright. The middle tent white and light orange-red with gold, and the white worked with silver. The feathers on same white and black. The steps practical with iron grill. The second tent green with gold. The 3rd white and lilac. The 4th lacquered red the lining white and gold. The 5th tent white and gold and inside red lacquer with porcelain decoration. The sixth yellow and silver. . . ." Note inscribed at upper right: "Sedan chair warm lacquered red and gold bordered, the festoons silver, [indecipherable], white and black feathers." Notes lower down: "The chariot blue with silver, the festoons gold, the wheels of the chariot red lacquer." (The chaise) "green and gold." (The fan) "silver with peacock feathers."

These notations are illuminating, for they provide an invaluable clue to the all-important role that color later played in the eighteenth-century stage scene. Color could never be indicated in the traditional pen-and-ink sketch of the scene designer. Here it is—a verbal sketch. All the colors are specifically noted down in detail by the quill of the designer himself.

(88) Orlandi, Francesco, 1725–1769
Italy, Bologna
Royal Entrance Hall, c. 1750
Pen and bister ink with bister and gray washes, 382 x 464 mm.
Inscribed in ink at lower left corner: "Orlandi"
On additional sheet pasted along lower margin: *"Atrio Magnifico che introduce Alli Appartamenti Reali/Disegno di Francesco Orlandi di Bologna A[ccademia] C[lementina]."* This inscription suggests that this design was intended to be an engraved illustration for an unpublished volume of scenic designs.
Collection: Alexandre Benois

(89) Unknown artist, eighteenth century
Austria or Germany
Proscenium Framing a Garden Scene, c. 1750
Pen and black ink with gray wash, 455 x 582 mm.

(90) Schutz, Carl, 1745–1800 (attributed)
Austria, Vienna
The Persian Fair, 1796
Pen and black ink, 207 x 318 mm.

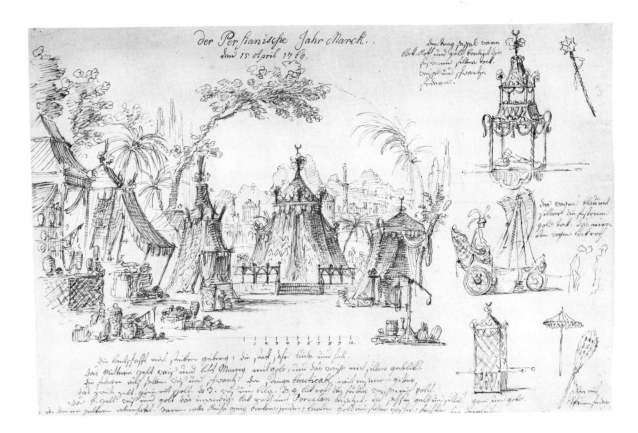

### Jean George Köpp

A theatrical drawing frequently turns up with no clue to establish its identity. The drawing for the *Ballet de l'Astrologue* (Illus. 91) is a companion piece to the bucolic landscape for the *Ballet du Philosophe* by the same artist in the Oenslager Collection. The drawings do carry the artist's name, but he remains for the present just this side of anonymity. Thieme-Becker briefly mentions a Swiss painter named J. G. Kopp (without the umlaut) active in the second half of the eighteenth century. Köpp's rather original Alpine talent was not influenced by the distinctive airs of the contemporary Italian, French, or German schools of theatrical design.

His work has a *gemütlich* Austrian air, but Marian Eames, dedicated balletomane and scholar of the dance, finds no record of these two ballets or reference to these sketches in the Vienna Jahrbuch. She has found, in Mooser's records of eighteenth-century theatrical performances in Russia, an intriguing entry: *"Gli Astrologi immaginari"*—see *"Gli Filosofi immaginari."* The latter was a *dramma giocoso* with book by G. Bertati and music by Paisiello, performed in Moscow and Saint Petersburg in 1779, 1782, and 1796. These are intriguing scraps of reference—Italian librettist, Italian composer, Swiss de-signer, and Russian performances. Hopefully, the mystery of the astrologers and the philosophers of these two ballets may some day be solved. Jean George Köpp might then be rescued from anonymity and regain his proper place as a designer.

*Illustration 91.* The perspective scene for the *Ballet de l'Astrologue* is an ornamental terrace set amidst greenery and trees. Downstage are two sets of wings representing splashing fountains supported by *putti*. Left is a garden laboratory equipped with telescopes and globes. On the roof, four youthful astrologers scan the skies and observe fifteen large stars shining in a sunny sky! Center stage, the master astrologer has obviously just cracked open a large globe with his dividers. From this globe has burst forth a beautiful maiden who dances toward a young lover, much to the astonishment of several groups of male and female eighteenth-century amateur astrologists.

In this drawing, Köpp has not only indicated the setting in all its enchanting detail, but he has also incorporated in the design a climactic moment in the choreography of the ballet. This dramatic introduction of choreographic action into the scene is unusual in eighteenth-century ballet designs.

BALLET DE L'ASTROLOGUE

(91) Köpp, Jean George, c. 1740–1800
    Switzerland
    The Astrologer's Garden, c. 1780
    (See also color plate 5)

Pen and watercolor, 305 x 470 mm.
Title in script above: *Ballet de l'Astrologue*
Inscribed lower right margin: "de signer Jean George Köpp"

# Neoclassicism to Realism

In Europe, the nineteenth century marked a hundred years of protest and revolt in social systems, politics, industry, science, and the arts. Four generations of writers and artists, each with progressive insight and an analytical eye, left their impact on the century's aesthetic theme of truth to nature. Stage design reflected the onrushing course of the arts during that century.

The baroque and rococo traditions of scene design persisted beneath the formal polished veneer of neoclassical decoration. The romantics, indulging in the freedom of nostalgic expression, picturesque contrast, and local color, assaulted the rigid formulas of the neoclassicists. The romantics believed in neither rules nor models; or rather, as Victor Hugo proclaimed, "There are no other rules than the general laws of Nature."

The victory of the romantic movement was no sooner a *fait accompli* than a rebel group of younger adherents, under the guise of thinly veiled naturalism, felt impelled to examine and analyze in greater depth the social and personal problems of their generation. They tagged naturalism to their "slice of life" interpretation of truth to nature.

The naturalists, with their increasing interest in imitating nature, ultimately established a school of realism which dominated Europe during the last quarter of the century. Their theatre stressed ensemble playing and the pictorial significance of scene and costume to achieve total illusion behind the proscenium. After a hundred embattled years, an authentic theatre "of the people, by the people, for the people" finally arrived. Ibsen, Strindberg, Shaw, Hauptmann, Tolstoi, and Chekhov found understanding audiences in those free and assertive art theatres that sprang up unannounced in Paris, Berlin, London, Dublin, Stockholm, and Moscow during the closing years of the nineteenth century.

(92) Panfili, Pio, 1723–1812 (attributed)
Italy (active in Bologna)
Monumental Vestibule with Staircase, c. 1757
Pen and blue-gray wash, 193 x 288 mm.
Collection: Alexandre Benois

(93) De Gaspari, Pietro, 1718/20–1785
Italy, Venice (active in Munich)
Roman Public Square, 1750–1775
Pen and black and bister ink with ink washes, 292 x 458 mm.
Collection: L.B. (not in Lugt)

### Pio Panfili

During the eighteenth century, Bologna claimed an impressive number of well-trained easel painters with a propensity for powerful design and endowed with uncommon technical facility. Vittorio Bigari, Mauro Bracciola, Vincenzo Mazzi, Stefano Orlandi, Pio Panfili, and Mauro Tesi all had theatrical flair. None was inspired and not one was famous, but their combined healthy proliferation in all areas of art made this Bolognese school one of the most influential schools of Italian eighteenth-century art.

Pio Panfili was a primary exponent of this school. Born in the coastal town of Fermo, he made his own self-trained way and by 1767 he had succeeded in establishing himself in Bologna, where he became the head of both the Accademia Clementina and the Accademia di Belle Arti. Little is known of his actual work, except that he decorated the great hall in the Palazzo Pubblico in his native town of Fermo and undertook numerous commissions for religious orders, such as the decoration of the refectory of the Capuchins in Rimini. Panfili was a skillful engraver, and in 1783 he executed two series of prints illustrating elements of architecture and ornament. The only record of Panfili's indulgence in the visual theatre is a small group of his scenic designs.

*Illustration 92.* Corrado Ricci reproduced two of Pio Panfili's drawings for scenes of royal stairhalls in *La Scenografia Italiana*, one of which is now in the Oenslager Collection and is signed and dated [17]57. This drawing is certainly by the same facile hand.

This design reveals the high quality of draftsmanship and technical capability that Panfili shared with all his contemporary Bolognese artists. He well understood the dramatic contribution of painted light and shade on the stage. He was influenced directly by the Bibiena family and by their theatrical activities that surrounded him in Bologna. The spaciousness and handling of chiaroscuro so apparent in Ferdinando Bibiena's royal stairhalls (see Illus. 30, 31) must surely have inspired Panfili in this drawing, which is a splendid example of his generation's feeling for the traditional royal stairhall.

### Pietro de Gaspari

Pietro de Gaspari and his older brother, Giovanni Paolo, were architects, painters, and scenographers. They were trained by their father in his architectural atelier in Venice—excellent preparation for their careers in the theatre. In 1753, Pietro and his brother were invited as a team to design the settings for the new opera house in Munich. Giovanni Paolo, probably the more skillful and practical of the two brothers, was appointed Hoftheater-maler and Hoftheaterarchitekt. Some years before, he had gained experience working in Giuseppe Bibiena's theatre in Bayreuth. Later, both brothers were also associated together designing for the Bavarian court in Munich. There they worked in the enchanting Residenz Theatre which Cuvilliés had designed. A number of settings by the de Gaspari brothers are included in Cuvilliés' oeuvre, *Ecole de l'Architecture Bavaroise* (Munich, after 1777).

The proscenium of the Residenz was probably too small to contain the scale of Pietro de Gaspari's theatrical vision; in any case, he decided to return to Venice and there established himself as a painter and engraver. A number of his perspective paintings are in the collection of the Accademia where he taught architectural and perspective painting.

As a stage designer, Pietro de Gaspari must be included among a large group of *bibieneschi*. He followed the traditional baroque formula of the *scena al angola* and the diagonal line. However, he was more sympathetic to the mannered architectural *capricci* of the Bolognese perspective painters Bigari, Mazzi, Panfili, and Stefano Orlandi, whose work supported his own goals and the spatial complexity of the neoclassicists.

*Illustration 93.* This uninspired drawing for a Roman public place is highly theatrical though it was not made for actual use in the theatre. Even the figures reduced to the scale of midgets do not resemble actors. A similar drawing of a classical court attributed to Pietro de Gaspari in my collection is also an eighteenth-century Roman wonderland. Originally, the finished perspective drawing contained no figures, and subsequently, underscale figures were pasted onto the drawing to boost and enhance its scale.

The enormity of these eighteenth-century scenic *capricci* of Pietro de Gaspari impressed the following generation of Italian scenographers which included Antonio Basoli, Giorgio Fuentes, Lorenzo Sacchetti, and Alessandro Sanquirico. These men were full-fledged stage designers working on a large scale within the limitations of the proscenium frame. They knew what they wanted from Pietro de Gaspari; he gave them theatrical grandeur.

### Pietro Gonzaga

Pietro Gonzaga was one of those rare designers who was successful from the beginning of his long theatrical career. He designed the scenes for three hundred and twenty productions of opera and ballet. His versatility as

a painter and decorator, and also as a theatre architect and scenographer was praised by knowing critics and applauded by an avid public. Highest honors were bestowed upon him as an artist.

As a youth of sixteen, Pietro was captivated with the personality and the work of Carlo Bibiena, who at that time was renovating a theatre in nearby Treviso, though his early hopes for working with Bibiena were never fulfilled. Gonzaga continued drawing and painting and soon moved on to Venice, where he studied perspective painting with the accomplished *quadraturisti* Visentini and Moretti at the Accademia.

After three years, and armed with ambition, he invaded the theatrical citadel of Milan and was admitted to the scenic workshop of the famous Galliari brothers. In six years, he advanced from apprentice to collaborator with the Galliaris in their work at the Scala. In 1779 he joined the Scala organization as inventor and painter of stage scenes, and for thirteen years he was *scenografo principale*. During these years, his services were in great demand. He took temporary leaves of absence from the Scala to design productions for the Teatro San Agostino in Genoa, the Teatro Alibert in Rome, the Teatro Pubblico in Crema, and the Teatri Ducali of Parma, Monza, and Mantua. In 1792, he received an official invitation to return to Venice to design the theatre curtain and also the

(94) Gonzaga, Pietro, 1751–1831
Italy, Milan (active in Saint Petersburg)
Necropolis, 1775–1790
Pen and bister with gray wash, 403 x 520 mm.

scenes for the ballet *Amore e Psiché* along with *Il Giardino d'Agrigento*, which his friend Francesco Fontanesi was designing. This double bill inaugurated the beautiful new Teatro La Fenice, which remains today one of the glorious opera houses of Europe.

Prince Yousupoff, Russian ambassador to the court of Turino and an aficionado of the performing arts, had persuaded Gonzaga in 1789 to journey to Moscow and design a theatre on his estate at Archangelskoe. When Catherine II appointed Prince Yousupoff director of all the imperial theatres in 1792, he arranged for Gonzaga's permanent transfer to Saint Petersburg, where the empress appointed him *Peintre en Chef avec autorité sur les autres peintres*. Pietro Gonzaga thus assumed the august role of court designer, traditionally held by an Italian, and decorated palaces, laid out parks, designed theatres and entertainments complete with mise-en-scènes for the imperial family. For three decades, he arranged the pomp and designed the circumstances for the coronation festivities of three czars: Paul I (1797), Alexander I (1801), and Nicholas I (1826). Czar Nicholas bestowed on Gonzaga the elevating title, "Architect of the Highest Order." At length he received a pension and died in Saint Petersburg, the city whose public buildings, theatres and scenery, churches and palaces, and even shops are a monument both to Russian imperialism and to Italianate taste.

Pietro Gonzaga overlaid his Venetian *vedutista* style with the grand manner he so admired in the work of the Galliaris and in the theatrical designs of his baroque predecessors, though his taste was generally eclectic. In his designs for tragedy, comedy, melodrama, and *opera seria* he assimilated the classic, the Gothic, the Renaissance, and the baroque. So many of his designs reveal hints of his admiration for a variety of favorite monuments, among them the mausoleum of Halicarnassus; in Rome the Pantheon, the baths of Caracalla, Vignola's Villa Farnese at Caprarola; Palladio's project for the

Rialto bridge in Venice; and the Lombard Certosa of Pavia. He liked to design big scenes—the entrance to an acropolis, a triumphal square, a monumental forum, a garden of vaulted foliage, or an *aula sepolcrale*. But he could also concoct, with equal felicity, a modest interior of a rustic inn or a barn. The specific locales of many such scenes are realistic in detail, allowing no room for grandiose austerity.

*Illustration 94.* This necropolis is a veritable city of the dead—chock full of tombstones and sepulchres set amidst mournful cypresses. Overhead, an arched bridge leads to a domed pantheon. This design of gloomy disarray is skillfully bound together by Gonzaga's strong chords of perspective.

*Illustration 95.* This drawing is a scene for an *aula sepolcrale* designed in a pseudo-Lombard grand manner— spacious and theatrical in its studied composition. The

(95) Gonzaga, Pietro
   *Aula Sepolcrale,* c. 1800
   Sepia pen and bister wash, 208 x 348 mm.
   Collections: Oreste Allegri, Alexandre Popoff,
   Alexandre Benois
   In 1937, Alexandre Popoff acquired the entire
   Allegri collection of Gonzaga's sketches and presented
   this and another Gonzaga working sketch to the
   Russian designer Alexandre Benois.

scene is a triumph of dramatic light over the shades of death. Possibly Gonzaga conceived it as the finale for a *Romeo and Juliet* opera. Or perhaps he conceived it as a place for his own fancy to rest. Pietro Gonzaga possessed the inquiring eye of an explorer. His neoclassic vocabulary equipped him to pursue the picturesque and indulge in a semiarchaeological restoration of both the ancient world and the world of the Middle Ages. His nostalgic concern for recreating these worlds of a dead past presaged the advent of romanticism and a new epoch in stage design.

Every country of Europe boasts of a shrine where rest the nation's famous dead—Westminster Abbey, the Pantheons of Paris and of Rome. Vast crypts or gloomy *aula sepolcrale* contain the mortal remains of generations of royal lines neatly laid away in rows of sarcophagi. The crypt of the Escorial, the Hapsburgs' Capuchin crypt in Vienna, the House of Savoy's Superga in Turin, and the crypt of the Popes beneath Saint Peter's are melancholy abodes of the dead biding their time, waiting upon eternity. Small wonder that opera librettists could seldom resist introducing in their plots such a traditional emotion-packed scene of life and death as the *aula sepolcrale* provided. In the eighteenth and nineteenth centuries, this scene was often an essential ingredient of grand opera, and so the setting was a favorite one in the scenic repertory of every opera house.

### Francesco Chiaruttini

Francesco Chiaruttini did not contribute new directions to the development of scenography. He did, however, effectively embrace the scenic tastes of his generation.

Brought up in Venice, he frequented the halls of the Accademia di Belle Arti. He learned his craft in the workshops of many Venetian painters and scene designers —Marieschi, Fontebasso, Colonna, and Fossati. He composed architectural scenes in the manner of his contemporary Pietro Gonzaga and also looked to the artists of the past for help and inspiration. The Cooper Union Collection contains several of his drawings for settings of ancient ruins after the fashion of Giovanni Paolo Pannini.

Chiaruttini worked as scene designer in the Teatro Argentina in Rome between 1786 and 1788. In Rome he developed an admiration for Canova, and he also succumbed to the potent spell of Piranesi's masterly *Carceri* prints.

*Illustration 96.* This drawing of a prison scene could have been made during Francesco Chiaruttini's sojourn in Rome. The spare grandiose design reveals only one segment of the total structure. The setting moves off in all directions. An air of nostalgic reverie haunts the scene, as though Chiaruttini recalled once in Venice passing from the Doge's Palace over the Bridge of Sighs and descending to the subterranean dungeons, where he found basic elements of prison settings by every designer whose work he had ever admired.

### Domenico Fossati

Domenico Fossati di Morcate belonged to an old Venetian family of architects and artists, a few of whom had worked occasionally as scenographers. Domenico would surpass them all, because literally all of Venice became his stage. He was a fresco painter and a *vedutista*, consequently very knowledgeable in the ways of perspective. In company with Domenico Tiepolo, Canaletto, and Longhi, he moved in the sunset orbit of the great Venetian painters of the eighteenth century, adorning the walls and ceilings of palaces and churches with his spacious decorations.

Save for brief excursions to Germany and Russia, he spent his brief career working in the Veneto, Friuli, and Carnia. His heartbeat was attuned to the rhythm of the Venetian scene of Gozzi and Goldoni, to the bright spectrum of the Venetian spectacle along canals and lagoons, and to the Commedia dell'Arte animating the timeless setting of the Piazza San Marco.

Fossati helped to create this wealth of scenic wonderment that graced the City of the Doges, for essentially he was a man of the theatre. He designed a triumphal arch and a scenic palace for the Piazza San Marco, machines for outdoor shows and spectacles at carnival time, a loggia in the Campo of SS. Giovanni e Paolo for the state visit of Pope Pius VI. He devised golden gondolas for sumptuous regattas staged on the Grand Canal.

Every parish of Venice boasted its church and its theatre, and Fossati knew them intimately. He designed and painted scenes for the Teatro San Moisé, the Teatro San Benedetto, and the revered Teatro San Cassiano, Venice's first public opera house, built more than a hundred years before Fossati was born. His scenic talents were, however, employed principally in the Teatro San Samuele. He was only eighteen when he painted the scenes for Gozzi's *The Love of the Three Oranges*—an allegorical fairy tale adapted for the stage. Carlo Gozzi had made a present of this work to Sacchi's company of comic players, and it was produced with huge success in the Teatro San Samuele during the Carnival of 1761. Subsequently, during the latter twenty years of his young life, Fossati designed the scenes for more than sixty operas and other dramatic works for the theatres of Venice.

*Illustrations 97 & 98.* A theatre artist is often known by the apprentices he attracts to his studio. Domenico Fossati had many assistants working with him in the theatres of Venice, among them Francesco Chiaruttini and Lorenzo Sacchetti. His albums of drawings preserved in Australia, England, and the United States, and his drawings in public and private collections, reveal his magnetic authority and explain his infectious influence on the imagination of younger designers.

Fossati's drawings are sensitive, fresh, sparse in line, and spontaneous, enhanced with revealing luminous washes. His drawings have the aerial enchantment one associates with Venetian eighteenth-century draftsmanship.

His subjects were frequently fantastic evocations of palaces and piazze, triumphal arches and ruins. He delighted in combining picturesque motifs with exotic

(96) Chiaruttini, Francesco, 1748–1796 (attributed)
Italy, Venice (active in Rome)
Prison Complex, c. 1786–1788
Sepia pen with gray washes, 235 x 334 mm.
Collection: Bittner

evocations derived from the East, just as this eighteenth-century caprice of rocks and bridges (Illus. 98) recalls, or suggests, the conventions of Chinese landscape painting.

*Illustration 99.* In designing this operatic scene of a picturesque, many-towered town, Domenico Fossati was the experienced *vedutista* working with concentrated planes of foreground and distance. The result is highly pictorial and dramatic for what is essentially a representational setting.

### Bartolomeo da Verona

Bartolomeo da Verona's mother, Elizabetta, was a sister of the first three illustrious Galliari brothers. Under these auspicious circumstances, Bartolomeo's career in the theatre was assured. In 1773, his uncle Bernardino was appointed court scene designer to Frederick the Great, and Bartolomeo accompanied him to Berlin as his chief assistant.

Bernardino's first production was Hasse's opera *Armenius*. He had early discovered that the royal budget for court entertainment in Berlin was excessively frugal, and thus mindful of economy, Bernardino proceeded to costume the opera's Royal Army in armor of papier-mâché. His "paper" soldiers seemed a ridiculous spectacle to Frederick the Great, who was not pleased, and Bernardino was quick to disengage himself from Berlin and to return happily to Turin. His nephew Bartolomeo remained behind as court designer for forty years during the reigns of three successive Prussian kings.

(97 & 98) Fossati, Domenico, 1743–1784
Italy, Venice (active in Germany and Russia)
Sketchbook of Stage Designs, c. 1775
Triumphal Arch
Rustic House with Cliffs and Bridges
Red chalk, pencil, pen, and bister ink with gray
washes, 241 x 295 mm; 23 leaves, some drawn
on both sides (modern binding)
Collections: Sacchetti, Mayr, Fajt, Scholz
A number of Fossati's drawings, and this
sketchbook, passed into the hands of his pupil,
Lorenzo Sacchetti, who took them with him to
Vienna. Before coming into Michael Mayr's
possession, this sketchbook evidently belonged to
a Viennese stage designer named Janitz, who
"improved" many of the drawings with a
generous use of black ink, even adding his
signature to pass them off as his own work.

(99) Fossati, Domenico
Approach to a Fortified Town, c. 1775
Pen and bister ink with gray washes, 245 x 390 mm.
Collections: Sacchetti, Mayr, Fajt, Scholz

If Frederick the Great exerted economy in his production budget for the performing arts, he was liberal with his artists' salaries. Bartolomeo received a thousand thalers a year and was housed in style at 17–18 Unter den Linden. He worked hard for his salary, however. He provided Italianate designs for all the king's German theatres: the Court Opera House, the French Theatre of Berlin, as well as the royal theatres in Charlottenburg and Potsdam. He also became the fashionable interior decorator of the royal establishment and for the Prussian aristocrats in Berlin. His Italian influence on the arts of Germany was impressive even though the king, an ardent francophile, made his court an ostentatious corner of France. Frederick the Great was an ardent amateur in literature and the performing arts, applauding both French plays and Italian operas. At the opera house he was wont to stand directly behind the *maestro di capella*, following the score and playing the role of director-general of the opera house as he played the role of generalissimo on the battlefield.

For want of appropriate funds, Bartolomeo must often have been obliged to settle for the commonplace; indeed, reference was frequently made to his productions being part new, part stock, and part renovation. In spite of this handicap, he enjoyed great success in Berlin and his work received the plaudits of the Prussian court.

Fortunately for Bartolomeo, Friedrich Wilhelm III, his third royal patron, on his accession to the throne, appointed August Wilhelm Iffland director of the National Theatre. Iffland, who brought about a resurgence of German theatrical activity, commissioned Bartolomeo da Verona to design the new National Theatre of Berlin. Heretofore, the plays of Schiller and Goethe had not been sponsored by the Prussian kings. With Iffland, Verona created successful romantic designs for Schiller's *Piccolomini* and the *Jungfrau von Orleans*.

The two compelling drawings illustrated show that Bartolomeo da Verona was a most facile and highly original scene designer. He was an eminent emissary who, in his Berlin outpost, spread the scenic gospel of the Galliari family throughout the Prussian theatre.

*Illustrations 100 & 101.* Unfortunately, few drawings remain of Bartolomeo da Verona's forty years of labor in the Prussian theatre. An album and a group of drawings are in Berlin collections. A second album is in Princeton. The Oenslager sketchbook contains many vigorous drawings of gardens and parks, villas and architectural fantasies.

### *Paolo Landriani*

In 1805, Paolo Landriani, a designer interested in all theatrical events, might have witnessed Napoleon dramatically crown himself in the Duomo of Milan with the iron crown of the old Lombard kings, saying "God gave it to me. Let him beware who touches it." Thanks to Napoleon, Milan became the neo-aristocratic capital of the Kingdom of Italy. The "new" Milanese society readily accepted Paolo Landriani as a distinguished neoclassical *architetto pittore scenico* and considered him an adornment to their new cultural establishment.

As a youth in Venice, Landriani had affected the *vedutista* style of Canaletto, but as an incipient theatre artist, he soon rallied to the side of Pietro Gonzaga, his elder by six years. At length, however, the Galliari "method" became the springboard for his own style of scenography.

With his talents tested and sharpened, Landriani introduced the North Italian neoclassic tradition into Rome at the Teatro Argentina during brief sojourns between 1790 and 1796. In 1792, he established himself in Milan, and for twenty-five years he worked consistently and congenially at La Scala with other designers, among them Giovanni Pedroni and Giorgio Fuentes. During his long residence at La Scala he trained and influenced a whole generation of younger scene designers, among them Giovanni Perego, Alessandro Sanquirico, and Pasquale Canna.

After years of designing scenes for the stage of La Scala, Landriani grew discontented with the opera house's deficiencies in production, the faulty construction and equipment of the stage, and the ineffectual practice of scene painting. So he finally severed his relations with

(100 & 101)  Da Verona, Bartolomeo, d. 1813
                Italy, Northern (active in Milan and Berlin)
                Sketchbook (Two Sheets), 1775–1780
                Bridges and Fountains
                Royal Pavilion (Two Schemes)

Pencil, pen, and brown ink with brown and gray washes, 315 x 316 mm. and 255 x 360 mm. These drawings are from a sketchbook of stage designs consisting of ninety-three leaves, some drawn on both sides (contemporary binding).

(102) Landriani, Paolo, 1757–1839
      Italy, Venice (active in Milan, Rome, and Vienna)
      Roman Temple, 1814
      Pen and ink with gray wash, 403 x 550 mm.
      Inscribed in lower right corner: "Pa. Landriani"

La Scala in 1817. He then devoted his time to writing, teaching perspective at the Accademia di Brera, and advising on the activities of the Accademia delle Belle Arti of Milan.

His magnum opus, *Osservazioni sui Difetti Prodotti nei Teatri*, was written in four parts between 1815 and 1824 and includes numerous copper-plate engravings to illustrate his arguments. *Osservazioni* is fundamental to understanding Landriani's ideas since it contains the thoughtful and scholarly observations of the architect and scene designer on the theatre of his day. It begins with a critique of late-baroque stage design and its extravagances, and proceeds through an exposition of practical rules to the affirmation of neoclassic theory.

Landriani became increasingly interested in theatre architecture. He used his knowledge of architecture and perspective in his analysis of the relationship of the stage and the auditorium and their ideal proportions.

Landriani's career in the theatre was divided in two parts. In his earlier years at La Scala he became one of the foremost neoclassic exponents of scenographic art in Italy. His later years were recalcitrant years—years consumed with his desire as an artist and architect to free the "official" Italian theatre from its outworn traditional mold. Landriani's significant contribution to the Italian theatre was his own scenic art, and his training of a younger generation of designers. Ironically, they attained their success in the traditional Scala whose mold their master could not break.

*Illustration 102.* The classical opera for which Landriani summoned this meticulously drawn neoclassical vision could have been Rossini's *Aureliano in Palmira*, which Landriani designed when the opera was performed at La Scala in 1814. The engravings of the ruins of the temples of Baalbeck may have impressed Landriani more than those of nearby Palmyra. Certainly Landriani derived this scenic composition from the Temple of Bacchus

(103 & 104)  Landriani, Paolo
        Sketchbook of 211 Stage Designs, c. 1817
        Ships in Harbor, for *Le Danaidi*, La Scala, 1795
        Great Square, for *La Crudeltà di Pisaro*,

La Scala, c. 1800
Pencil, pen, and brown ink with gray washes,
270 x 175 mm. (225 leaves; in contemporary
binding)

at Baalbeck. He adorned his stately scene with columns, statues, and a wealth of architectural detail. On the tympanum at the back, Minerva stands among wounded warriors and trophies of war.

*Illustrations 103 & 104.* This collection includes several early designs of Landriani for the opera *Il Trionfo di Aviace*, probably executed for the Teatro Argentina. Other drawings are for the Scala during the Carnival in Milan of 1794 and 1795 and for the Carnival in Rome of 1795 and 1796. Miscellaneous designs are dated as late as 1800. Some others, undated, were probably executed before 1817 when Landirani left the Scala.

The drawings in this sketchbook of stage designs vary in technique from swift linear impressions of sets to sketches executed in great detail. Many of the sheets carry informational notations of technical interest.

### Lorenzo Sacchetti

When Lorenzo Sacchetti abandoned Padua for Venice, the ardent young artist in no time lost his heart to the Queen of the Adriatic. He became a loyal Venetian, dedicated to the high traditions of its artists. He admired the visionary vistas of Piranesi and was enchanted with Canaletto and his magic circle of *vedutisti.* He accumulated drawings of Belotto and Fossati; in fact, Janos Scholz discovered that the cover of Sacchetti's treasured sketchbook of Fossati drawings (now in the Princeton Theatre Collection) carries the inscription "Domenico Fossati; maestro del Lorenzo Sacchetti." Sacchetti worked with Fossati as an apprentice in the Teatro S. Giovanni Crisostomo. Out of season, when the theatre was closed, Sacchetti nourished his art with various commissions for frescoes and interior decorations in Padua and Venice and was elected a member of the Accademia. But the theatre, like the tireless tides of Venice, flowed in his blood stream, and for ten years he refurbished and designed changing scenes for the repertoire of the theatres of San Samuele and San Moisè.

When the alluring theatre world of Vienna beckoned to him, he prayed to San Samuele and San Moisè that he would someday follow in the footsteps of all the notable Italian scenographers who had found success in Vienna. Sacchetti was all of thirty-five in 1794 when the choreographer Salvatore Vigano arranged for his transfer to Austria. He became an assistant in the Hoftheater to Josef Platzer, considered the most talented Austrian-born stage designer in the second half of the eighteenth century.

In 1818, Emperor Francis I appointed Sacchetti court painter and designer of the Hoftheater, and as *Architetto di Corte* Sacchetti decorated the Redoutensaal and other buildings in Brno. He must have enjoyed Bohemia, for from 1817 to 1830 he resided chiefly in Prague and was appointed the designer of the National Theatre. During his residence in Prague, Sacchetti wrote a practical handbook on matters scenographic, *Quanto Sia Facile l'Inventore Decorazioni Teatrali,* which was published in Prague in Italian (1830) and in Vienna in German (1834), based on his years of theatre experience.

The existing collections of Lorenzo Sacchetti's drawings and sketchbooks are proof that he was a remarkably productive artist in the theatre of his time. Over two hundred drawings in my own collection (mostly of his Austrian period) make it clear that he never entirely lost his Venetian training and style. However, having once crossed the Italian frontier, his designs began to reflect the more onerous responsibilities of his varied Hapsburg theatrical commitments. His focus changed, and soon he overlaid his Venetian heritage with the stencil of eclecticism. He became a master of many styles, which ranged over several centuries of theatrical inspiration from baroque to rococo, from neoclassic to romantic to realistic. Sacchetti's reliance on selective eclecticism has become common procedure among many designers working in today's theatre.

*Illustration 105.* The explicit and powerful pen drawing displays Lorenzo Sacchetti's frequent reliance on diagonal perspective to achieve a highly theatrical design. On the verso is a searching pen study for this smashing composition.

*Illustrations 106 & 107.* This group of drawings contains seventy-seven sheets of uniform size with drawings on one side. Binding thread perforations are identical and indicate that the drawings, still very Canalettian in spirit and free in execution, are from several dismembered early sketchbooks. On the first drawing, "L. Sacchetti," written by Michael Mayr, is an authentic attribution.

The Oenslager Collection contains 218 drawings by Lorenzo Sacchetti. The National Bibliothek in Vienna and The Gallery of Fine Arts of Budapest contain large collections of his work.

*Illustrations 108 & 109.* These two late, rather florid operatic designs carry Sacchetti's signature. Possibly he made them for an elaborate stage project when he was the designer for the National Theater in Prague. They suggest a scenic bridge connecting the baroque productions of Ferdinando and Giuseppe Bibiena with the later romantic extravaganzas and pantomimes of the nineteenth century. See the "Court of Venus" (Illus. 152 and color plate 13) for a later extravaganza in America.

*Illustration 110.* No Roman architect would have had the courage or displayed the theatrical flair which Sacchetti exhibited in this high-vaulted, triple-templed model of neoclassic art. It is pure theatre. As a scene for grand opera, it is an assertive tour-de-force of monumentality, and as a study in theatrical scale, the scene anticipates the later scenic vision of Gordon Craig.

*Illustrations 111 & 112.* This drawing illustrates a scenic "break-away." Sacchetti's painter's elevation of the Gothic tower (*111*) contains two pasted flaps which, when folded back on themselves, reveal the tower after destruction (*112*). This old trick was executed exactly like the sketch and is just as startling on our stage today as when Sacchetti used it.

(105)  Sacchetti, Lorenzo, 1759–1834
       Italy, Padua (active in Venice, Vienna, and Prague)
       Vaulted *Aula Sepolcrale*, c. 1810
       Pencil and bister pen, 370 x 485 mm.
       Collections: Mayr, Fajt, Scholz

(106 & 107)
Sacchetti, Lorenzo
Drawings from Several
Sketchbooks, c. 1785–1790
Palace Courtyard
Garden
Pen and bister wash, 187 x
225 mm.
Collections: Mayr, Fajt, Scholz

(108 & 109)
Sacchetti, Lorenzo
Recto: Temple in a Park with
Fountains, 1817–1830
Verso: Pleasure Hall Framed
within Clouds
Pencil on green paper, 201 x
260 mm.
Collections: Mayr, Fajt, Scholz

(110) Sacchetti, Lorenzo
Vaulted Temple Hall, 1815
Pen and sepia wash, 300 x 397 mm.
Collections: Mayr, Fajt, Scholz

(111 & 112)  Sacchetti, Lorenzo
Gothic Tower, 1815
Pen and sepia wash, 264 x 173 mm.
Collections: Mayr, Fajt, Scholz

## Josef Platzer and the Austrian School

Josef Platzer was the most talented Austrian-born stage designer of the second half of the eighteenth century. His father was a noted architect of Prague who worked on the design of Schönbrunn, and Josef was brought up in the cultivated tradition of the Austrian baroque and rococo styles, though he also inherited the Italian theatrical traditions of the Bibienas and Juvara. However, Austrian taste and vision enabled him to found an independent school of theatrical design which would dominate the theatre of Vienna throughout the nineteenth century. Along with Prud'hon, Fueger, and lesser Austrian artists of pre-Napoleonic Vienna, Platzer heralded the close of the resplendent Austrian baroque and rococo era, and opened wide the windows of Vienna to the fresh breezes of neoclassicism from Italy and France.

Platzer's first important scenic commission was for G. E. Lessing's *Emilia Galotti* for the inauguration of the new Nostitzsches Divadlo in Prague in 1783. Henceforth, this national theatre, the gift of a Bohemian aristocrat, would remain the center of theatrical life in Prague. Joseph II admired Platzer's work and appointed him *Theatraldekorateur* of the imperial court theatres of Vienna: the Hoftheater, the Burgtheater, and a few years later, the new Kärntnertortheater. Platzer continued to rise in imperial esteem. In 1793 he became *Direktor der Theatermalerei*, and in 1795 *Kaiserlichen Kammermalers*. At this time Lorenzo Sacchetti arrived from Venice, and for a dozen years collaborated with Platzer on the scenic investiture of the court theatres. For a brief time, Gaspare Galliari from La Scala worked as guest designer in the Hoftheater. Plays of Iffland, Goethe, and Kotzebue were in the drama repertory, and the opera repertory included works of Salieri, Cherubini, and Mozart. Platzer, a close friend of Mozart, designed the first production of *The Marriage of Figaro* in 1786 for the Nostitzsche Divadlo in Prague, and shortly before Platzer died, he designed the scenes for *Idomeneo* for the Kärntnertortheater.

In addition to his scenic responsibilities for the three imperial theatres, Platzer also worked for other Viennese theatres, and he designed settings for the private theatres of Count Fries, Count Kinsky, and Prince Liechtenstein. In Bohemia, he devised many productions for the minuscule court theatre in the Castle of Litomysl as well as for the commodious National Theatre of Prague, where he had designed his first major work.

Platzer had a vast knowledge of the traditions of his predecessors in scene design. When he decided to eschew his baroque background, he was equipped aesthetically to clothe all styles from Greece to romanticism with his balanced robes of neoclassicism, and romantic neoclassicism became his adopted and self-proclaimed style, a style of elegance and proportion. He insisted that theatrical lighting was essential to the establishment of pictorial atmosphere, which led him to expand the function of the painted backdrop in order to achieve broader vistas with greater depth. This new direction led to far greater representationalism in the stage scene.

Certain drawings of Platzer clearly indicate that he experimented in the development of effective use of the "simultaneous scene." This was a genuine novelty which more than a century later would become common practice in the modern theatre. In a single stage setting, he sometimes incorporated three individual scenes—a cave, a forest, and an inner room—or a front door and balcony with two separate interiors. The planning of these simultaneous scenes required close collaboration between designer and director in both the lyric and dramatic theatre. As an Austrian innovator, Platzer exerted advanced, even radical, changes in the evolution of stage design.

During the time of Platzer's activity in the theatre of Vienna, a group of fledgling Austrian designers were growing up, fired with enthusiasm for his advanced ideas. With the liberation of Austria that followed the Congress of Vienna in 1814, these young designers became dedicated to Platzer's espousal of a true Austrian tradition of scene design.

By great fortune, one designer among this Austrian group of more than a dozen artists was Michael Mayr, who collected drawings by practically all of his contemporary designers, including a large group of unidentified drawings by lesser artists. The bold theatrical drawings of Johann Biederman and Matthais Gail indicate that they were true practitioners of the Austrian scenic tradition. Their contemporaries Beringer and Poetzl and Johann Scharhan were also first-rate draftsmen with a theatrical lien on romantic realism. Herman Neefe was a Bonn painter who succumbed to the theatrical flair of Viennese stage design. Antonio Arrigoni, a Viennese by birth and an easel painter, frequently exercised his talent in the theatre. Little is known about the gifted Hungarian N. Institoris who was very active in the theatres of Vienna and West Hungary, but technical and theatrical expertise are everywhere evident in his explicit notes and colorful sketchbooks.

The Austrian portion of Mayr's collection of drawings constitutes a unique record of the Viennese school of scene design of the first half of the nineteenth century.

*Illustration 113.* The Oenslager Collection contains over two hundred drawings of Josef Platzer which probably came right from his atelier, no doubt acquired by Michael Mayr through Norbert Bittner, who had engraved and published Platzer's designs in ten portfolios in 1816, ten years after Platzer's death. These drawings, many with marginal notations, include preliminary pencil studies for scenes, working drawings, cut-out scenes, and finished drawings. He was a first-rate easel painter and a first-rate scene technician. Both sides of some sheets have three or four first-idea sketches overlapping one another. These hasty drawings are the work of an artist bursting with ideas who conversed freely with his pencil and pen.

This drawing by Platzer shows him working as an easel painter on a stage picture. His scenic composition of ancient tombs amidst a shadowy moonlit glade boldly obliterates the stage floor and retreats without benefit of perspective into atmospheric distance of eerie reverie.

(113)  Platzer, Josef, 1751–1806
         Bohemia, Prague (active also in Vienna)
         Monuments in Forest by Moonlight, 1775–1800
         Pen and bister ink with ink washes and watercolors,
         390 x 480 mm.
         Signature lower right corner: "Platzer"
         Collections: Mayr, Fajt, Scholz

(114) Platzer, Josef
Atrium of a Temple, 1775–1800
Pen and sepia wash, 225 x 283 mm.
Collections: Mayr, Fajt, Scholz

(115) Platzer, Josef
Proscenium Curtain for Theatre in
Castle of Litomysl, 1797
Pen and watercolors, 191 x 227 mm.
Collections: Mayr, Fajt, Scholz

(116) Arrigoni, Antonio, 1788–1851
    Italy (active in Vienna)
    Shipyard, 1830–1850
    Pen and black ink on gray-green paper, 275 x 402 mm.
    Signature lower right corner: "Arrigoni f."
    Collections: Mayr, Fajt, Scholz

*Illustration 114.* This drawing of a neoclassic scene is a typical example of Josef Platzer's swift, spontaneous sketching technique. Janos Scholz, a distinguished connoisseur of drawings, writes with pleasure of Platzer's draftsmanship: "He respects the past while inventing one set after another, allowing his pencil to roam over the surface of the paper, driven by an over-charged temperament, while his mind subconsciously checks his hand, commanding it to follow ruthlessly the supreme law of perspective. His lines may sometimes be considered superfluous, but they are never faulty. After studying literally hundreds of Platzer drawings, I cannot find a major slip in construction or perspective, a feat rarely observed in XVIIIth century architectural drawing, save in the work of a genius like Piranesi, or perhaps Juvara."

*Illustration 115.* Platzer made this design for the proscenium curtain of the small court theatre in the Castle of Litomysl in Bohemia. The theatre holding 150 spectators was designed with classical decor by Dominik Dvorak when the Renaissance castle was renovated in 1796–1797. A photograph of Platzer's curtain, hanging in the theatre today, and an engraving of this design by Bittner are reproduced with a study on the Litomysl Castle theatre by Jiri Hilmera, Curator of the National Museum in Prague, in the magazine *Zpravy Pamatkove Pecé* (numbers 3 and 4, 1957). Platzer's scene for a Gothic hall, six wings deep, still occupies the stage. Other Platzer settings, including a prison, a palace, a peasant kitchen, a town square, and a country road, are preserved in the theatre's scene dock. His drawings with Bittner's engravings hang in the theatre foyer. Platzer's pencil and pen study for this design is also in the Oenslager Collection.

*Illustration 116.* Antonio Arrigoni was much admired as an easel painter in Vienna before he was appointed court painter in 1826 to the court of Saxony at Dresden. Working in the theatre, he sketched with a clean realistic line and established a feeling of actual locale in his scenes. In this design he achieved a three-dimensional effect by cutting out the first of two sheets with the foreground elements of the scene and placing it before the second sheet representing the backdrop.

*Illustration 117.* Antonio de Pian, after leaving Venice, settled in Austria as a very able landscape painter. Attracted to the theatre, he assumed the characteristics of the younger Viennese group of theatre artists. This remarkable neoclassic interpretation of a votive shrine in a precinct sacred to a Greek deity has a spacious air and theatrical bravura. Janos Scholz contributes interesting comments on de Pian's occupation with the theatre: "Adapting a good measure of Platzer's style, he success-

fully combines Italian heritage and Austrian impressions. This artist was also quite well known as a theatre architect and, judging from the series of engravings in the Oenslager Collection (de Pian-Bittner), he completed many sets for Mozart operas during the two decades immediately following the composer's death."

*Illustration 118.* Little is known of the Hungarian artist Institoris. He worked for numerous theatres in Vienna including the Kärtnertor, the Leopoldstadter, and the Theater an der Wien. His many drawings and fabulous notes in the Oenslager Collection, and his sketchbooks in the theatre collection of the New York Public Library, indicate he played a very active part in the theatre of his day. Michael Mayr eagerly collected his work.

(117)  De Pian, Antonio, 1784–1851
      Italy, Venice (active in Vienna)
      Greek Shrine with Celebrants, c. 1840

(See color plate 7)
Pen and black ink with watercolors on gray paper, 378 x 488 mm.

(118) Institoris, N., d. 1845
   Hungary (active in Vienna)
   Roman Garden with Fountains, c. 1830
   (See also color plate 6)
   Pen and black ink with watercolors, 242 x 402 mm.
   Collections: Mayr, Fajt, Scholz

Institoris' precise sketch technique resembles that of colored engravings. His interest in design seems that of a scene painter and craftsman. He could have been the steward of Vienna's principal scenic studio. His style was strongly influenced by the work of Antonio de Pian. Indeed, this garden setting is derived from a design of de Pian. On the verso of the drawing is a detailed description (in German) of the scene and how it should be painted. Inscribed over the design are many numbers in black ink. These numbers refer to the numbered colors used by the scene painter. This precise procedure, still used today to expedite work in the studio, seems to have been formulated by Institoris.

*Illustration 119.* This vaulted ice cavern of frozen stalactites and stalagmites was a scenic tour de force devised by the magic brush of Institoris. The stage designers of the early nineteenth century restored the tradition of the lavish scenic wonderland so popular on the stages of the High Renaissance in Italy—a realm of strange places, extravagant novelty, and never-never fantasy.

*Illustration 120.* Institoris had a custom of making elaborate notes for the scene painter. He filled eleven leaves on both sides with detailed instructions and sketches for his production of *The Magic Flute*. Often, designers themselves painted scenes for Viennese theatres—providing paints, glue, whiting, the paint-spreader, and even the canvas—the theatre providing the place to paint. Institoris set down the following instructions for the scene painter to follow in executing this red and gold house curtain for the Kärntnertortheater in Vienna.
   1) The drawing is cartooned with "Bolus."
   2) The folds are laid in with burnt sienna and umber.
   3) Then, after it is laid in with "Bolus" and painted with burnt sienna and umber, it is painted with a dark

135

(119)  Institoris, N.
Neo-Gothic Ice Grotto, c. 1830
Pen and ink with watercolor heightened with white,
292 x 451 mm.
On the verso is a fragment (in ink) of a score of an
opera overture.
Collections: Mayr, Fajt, Scholz

varnish which has been mixed with potash.

4) This drawing of the grand-drape, covered with dark varnish, is now laid in with varnish and vermillion, and finally it is highlighted carefully with pure vermillion. Finally it is deepened with "Cologne earth." The golden ornaments are painted in a yellow-green color.

*Illustration 121.* Norbert Bittner was an expert Viennese engraver and an accomplished scenic designer. He emulated and probably studied with Josef Platzer and possibly Antonio de Pian. In 1810, he published ten portfolios with 160 plates of the former's scenic designs, and in 1818 ten portfolios of de Pian's designs.

Most of Bittner's drawings have the precise linear style associated with an engraver. During his career his scenic style varied greatly. This drawing follows the prototype for illusionistic landscape established by Platzer. The drawing has a charming, picturesque, colorful style bordering on naturalism. It reveals a mastery of scenic technique acquired from his years of association with Platzer.

*Illustration 122.* Michael Mayr was a popular and successful, though routine, stage designer in Vienna and a landscape painter of some consequence. The main interest in his theatre drawings derives from his knowledge of and reliance on those theatre artists whose work he avidly collected and admired, rather than from his own originality and imagination. Consequently, his designs seem uninspired and lacking in theatrical excitement.

This drawing is probably for the final scene of Gluck's *Orpheus and Euridice*. The central opening in the clouds would reveal the *deus ex machina*, a Vistavision of Love appearing before Orpheus and Euridice amidst the flower bank in the foreground of this classical landscape—"classical" only because of the two flaming urns right and left.

(120)  Institoris, N.
       Red and Gold Curtain for the Kärtnertortheater,
       c. 1830
       Pen and ink with watercolors, 263 x 360 mm.
       Collections: Mayr, Fajt, Scholz

(121) Bittner, Norbert, 1786–1851
Austria, Vienna
Temple in Forest with Four Nymphs, 1820–1840
Pen and ink with watercolors, 267 x 342 mm.
Signature lower right corner: "Bittner Inv."
Collections: Mayr, Fajt, Scholz

(122)  Mayr, Michael, 1796–1870
       Austria, Vienna (active also in Eisenstadt)
       Tropical Landscape with Clouds, c. 1820–1825
       Pencil, pen, and brown and blue ink, 269 x 455 mm.
       On the verso is a fragment (in ink) of a musical score.
       Collections: Mayr, Fajt

### Antonio Basoli

Small wonder that Antonio Basoli practiced his art with confidence and security. He was the son of a talented Bolognese painter and was trained by four master specialists: scenographer Mazza in architecture and perspective, Martinelli in landscape and painting, Fancelli in color and chiaroscuro, and Bracciola in scenography at La Scala. Together with scenographer Pelagio Pelagi, he conducted theatrical research in the library of Count Aldrovandini, which was rich in theatrical holdings. His two brothers, Luigi and Francesco, worked at his side as collaborators on a varied number of projects. As a decorator and designer, Basoli would exceed even his own ambitions.

By 1800 Basoli had decorated palaces at Cento, Trieste, and Saint Petersburg. When he canceled his Russian contract and returned to the sheltering arcades of Bologna, he received many commissions for decorating and theatrical jobs in Rome and Naples, among them a number of theatre interiors.

Basoli's original scenic style made him the logical leader of the post-Bibiena school of Bologna. Later, he succeeded the illustrious Alessandro Sanquirico as principal designer at La Scala. Two handsome collections of Basoli's engraved designs, many of them for La Scala, were published in Bologna. *Raccolta di 50 Scene Teatrali*, with Francesco Cocchi's engravings of Basoli's decorations, appeared in 1810. *Collezione di Varie Scene Teatrali*, containing 102 stunning aquatints, was published in 1821 for the edification of "patrons, professors, amateurs in the arts, and friends." His mature designs reflect the changing aesthetics of neoclassicism and romanticism. He nurtured a taste for archaeological verisimilitude combined with a cultivated indulgence in the exotic. His was a two-way highway. He applied his experience as a painter and decorator to scenography, and as a scenic designer he applied his experience to decoration. His personal performance proved rewarding to him and significant in both the visual and the performing arts.

*Illustration 123.* Antonio Basoli's theatre curtain depicting a small classical amphitheatre, like that at Tusculum above Frascati, is framed within a draped proscenium and two sculptured figures of Pegasus. Minerva appears on her cloud machine above two Roman figures.

*Illustration 124.* This album is a unified collection of eighteen classical theatre designs probably made by Basoli when he was residing in Rome. While they are cold as Thorvaldsen's marbles, they depict, with considerable spirit and charm, grandiose exterior and interior scenes

(123) Basoli, Antonio, 1774–1848
Italy, Bologna (active in Milan, Rome, and Naples)
Curtain for a Theatre, c. 1820–1840
Pen and bister ink with watercolors, 338 x 433 mm.
Inscribed lower right corner: "A.B."
Collection: Ercole Casanova

(124) Basoli, Antonio
Album of Eighteen Classical Theatre Designs
City Scene, c. 1830
Pen and sepia wash, 120 x 174 mm.
Collection: E. Fatio

of squares, peristyles, and atriums of temples and palaces. It may have been Basoli's intention that this integrated group of carefully executed perspective drawings be published in a single portfolio of engravings.

*Illustrations 125 & 126.* It is difficult to believe that Antonio Basoli never traveled beyond the borders of his own country. Many of the drawings in this album are steeped in nostalgia for times past, and colored with a romantic fascination for remote and picturesque places— Egypt, the Levant, Turkey, India, and China. He had a traveler's curiosity, but recorded his journeys only from hearsay. Most of the designs in this album are derived from impressions and descriptions recorded by others' eyes, and they have an unspoiled charm of their own, not overburdened with archaeological accuracy.

Some of these drawings were for opera and ballet, some for plays; others seem to be source or research material preserved for future use in designing scenes and fantasies.

*Illustration 127.* Antonio Basoli, after completing numerous studies, made a sequence of splendid finished drawings of religious ceremonials. This drawing depicts a mammoth Hindustani temple festival. In my collection is another drawing, dated 1840, of an Egyptian temple festival, *Il Gran Memnonia di Egitta*. Other collections have drawings of a fire ritual of Zoroaster in Persia, or of a sacrificial ritual in Mexico. These colossal, eye-filling religious spectaculars with thousands of participants were obviously not conceived by Basoli for any imaginable theatre. They were marvelous fantasies beyond the dreams of Barnum.

Basoli put his imaginative best into these drawings, and he inscribed them with full titles, his signature, and date. Probably he invented them between 1830 and 1840 as a series of splendid religious occasions with the expectation of their being published as a set of engravings. It would have been a noteworthy monument to his notable theatrical talent.

142

(125 & 126) Basoli, Antonio
Album of Fifty-two Stage Designs,
1830–1840
Before a Turkish Palace
Before an Egyptian Palace
Pen and ink with gray washes,
148 x 193 mm.

(127) Basoli, Antonio
Hindustan Temple Fantasy, 1837
Pen and bister ink with gray washes on cream paper,
366 x 462 mm.
Inscribed bottom margin: "1837 *Basoli fecit.*
*Invenzione delle Pagode dell'Indostan*"
Collection: A. Benois

### Unknown English Artist, Eighteenth Century

A handful of minor Italian decorators and painters were practicing their craft in the theatres of London during the second half of the eighteenth century. Nevertheless, the London stage of this period remained, on the whole, isolated and untouched by the neoclassical examples of scenic art that nightly graced the stages of Naples and Milan, Berlin and Munich, Paris and Vienna. The provincial London theatre remained aloof to such continental avant-garde artists as the Galliaris and Landriani, Percier, Sacchetti, and Platzer. These high-ranking designers were never summoned to the Court of Saint James's to display their talent in the Haymarket, Drury Lane, or Covent Garden.

David Garrick did, however, import Philip de Loutherbourg, an Alsatian pioneer of romantic scene design who had worked in Paris and Italy, and engaged him as scene designer of Drury Lane. After ten years (1771–1781) of treating London to miraculous "set scenes," lighting effects, technical tricks, and transformations achieved with gauze, de Loutherbourg deserted the stage of Drury Lane for the galleries of the Royal Academy, where he found easel painting more rewarding than scene making. London relapsed into the old scenic doldrums of stock wings in groves as shown in Illustration 128. Not until after the turn of the century would scenes and machines begin to assume any importance in the English theatre, thanks to the combined efforts and influence of the Grieve family—father and two sons—who were pioneering and versatile scene painters.

*Illustration 128.* The handwriting has not been identified with a known English scenic artist.

This drawing for a presence chamber is a designer's sketch of about 1790. It is not a good drawing: the scene's perspective has not progressed much beyond Moxon's *Practical Perspective; or Perspective Made Easier*, the first original work in English on perspective, published in 1670. Nor was its design affected by the aesthetics of Hogarth's *The Analysis of Beauty* written in 1753 "with a view of fixing the fluctuating Ideas of Taste." The artist's marginal note indicates that "The order is Corinthian according to Palladio," but the design

146

suffers by comparison with the modish neoclassic creations of the continental designers seen elsewhere in this book.

The drawing's primary interest lies in the copious marginal notations from which one learns exactly how the English studio executed this scene. "It consists of three pairs of wings, a flat and three [pieces?] in the roof as I have marked." There are also detailed directions for painting the scenery. Sybil Rosenfeld, knowledgeable authority of the English playhouse and its designers, has studied the measurements of this scene and judges the opening to be 32 feet wide and 22 feet high. The proscenium of the later Drury Lane of 1794 and that of Covent Garden were much too large for the scene, though the Haymarket could have accommodated it. Perhaps this presence chamber of a royal palace was intended for a provincial theatre, but it would seem rather elaborate for the provinces unless it were for Dublin or Edinburgh!

English designers' drawings of the eighteenth century are hard to find, since most scenes were improvised from stock, and relatively few sketches were made. Most of these have been gathered together in the Victoria and Albert Museum and in the University of London library.

### *Giuseppe Borsato*

Giuseppe Borsato, after studying stage design with the Venetian Francesco Bagnara, went on to pursue his classical studies in Rome. His Venetian background in painting, architecture, and theatre faded under the magic spell of ancient Rome and her classical monuments, and when the time came to return to work in Venice, he was thoroughly prepared to perform in the classical style. In Venice, Borsato found challenging decorative and theatrical projects to test his newly acquired resources. He was sought out to provide scenic investiture for many theatres of Venice.

When Napoleon planned his state visit to Venice for the autumn of 1807, Giuseppe Borsato was honored with the commission to redecorate the Palazzo Napoleonica in the Empire style. The city's artists and craftsmen were called upon to invent and design all the elaborate decorations for the festivities. This republican gesture on the part of Venice was in the true baroque tradition of European royal occasions. Processions, regattas, theatrical entertainments, and banquets and balls were planned. A sumptuous illustrated festival book, *Descrizione delle*

(129) Borsato, Giuseppe, 1771–1849
     Italy, Venice
     Mausoleum, 1799
     Pen and sepia wash with green watercolor, 298 x 409 mm.

Inscribed in ink along lower right margin:
"G. Borsato F. l'anno 1799"
Collection: A. Benois

*Feste Celebrate in Venezia per la Venuta di S.M.I.R. Napoleone il Massimo Imperatore*, records all the events of the ten days of celebration tendered Napoleon, King of Italy, by Venice, Queen of the Adriatic. The emperor's royal entry into Venice on November 7, 1807, was worthy of a doge's coronation. The stately aquatic procession of specially designed gondolas passed through a massive triumphal arch designed by the architect Antonio Selva. This monument in the neoclassical style served as the royal gateway to the splendors of the Grand Canal. Borsato, in the role of theatrical designer, supervised the execution of this spectacular triumphal entry—a dramatic triumph of neoclassicism for Borsato, for Venice, and for Napoleon.

*Illustration 129*. The design of a mausoleum with its stark classicism and supernatural dramatic mood shows how

(130)  Unknown artist, nineteenth century
Italy, Venice
Theatre Curtain—Glorification of Napoleon in Venice, 1807
Pen and brown ink with watercolors, 357 x 417 mm.
Inscribed at top in ink: "*Nee andairon disuit, sed vivej Cie*"; scale at bottom in "*Piedi Veneti*"
Official stamp of the Fine Arts Commission of the Venetian Republic, lower left.

completely Borsato's new style had taken over. This drawing, made after his return from Rome in 1799 when he was twenty-eight, was probably for one of his first productions for the new Teatro la Fenice. This ultramodern theatre designed by architect Antonio Selva had opened only seven years before. Between 1810 and 1823, Borsato was the official scenographer of this most beautiful neoclassical theatre of Venice.

*Illustration 130*. It is reasonably certain that this drawing was made for the theatre curtain of Teatro la Fenice when it was redecorated for the performance of a cantata, *The Judgment of Jupiter*, by Lauro Algarotti, on November 30, 1807. The cantata was presented as a feature of the ten-day program of festivities given by the city of Venice in honor of Napoleon's state visit. The emperor is here portrayed approaching the city on a shell drawn by seahorses, as was Neptune. On an island in the foreground are the allegorical figures of the Four Arts: Music, Sculpture, Architecture, and Painting. In the upper left, accompanying the figure holding Napoleon's shield, are Victory and Minerva, Goddess of War. Napoleon must have been pleased with this allegorical scenic tribute from an unknown scenic artist.

### Giovanni Perego

Giovanni Perego, like almost all Italian scenographers, was trained as a painter and architect. He pursued his

studies in the Accademia Brera of Milan and was a promising pupil in scene design of Paolo Landriani.

His brief life granted him only a few active years of splendid accomplishment in the opera house of Milan. In 1807, he was in Venice working with Bassi and Pellandi on opera designs for La Fenice at the time when Borsato was one of La Fenice's designers. The same year, he was back again in Milan collaborating with Canna, Monticelli, and Vacconi on their neoclassical decorations for La Scala. The last ten years of his life, he was most active designing his own specialized style of productions for the stage of La Scala. In the eyes of his admiring fellow designers, he was a dedicated advocate of neoclassicism. A memorial monument to Giovanni Perego was placed in the atrium of the Accademia Brera after his death.

Perego was a sensitive artist. His neoclassical drawings have a purity of line and form, yet his scenes lose their sharp definition beneath a muted diffusion of light. They have a breadth and dignity that evoke a poetic atmosphere reminiscent of William Blake. Perego was blessed with an intuitive sense of theatre that made him one with the inner mood contained in the newer drama and opera. His ability to capture and envision this inner mood placed him as a designer ahead of his time and set his work apart from the accepted style of his contemporaries.

*Illustration 131.* A number of Perego's designs, including this one, were engraved by Stucchi and Angeli and published in a collection of contemporary settings for La Scala (see Stanislao Stucchi, *Raccolta de Scene Teatrali,*

(131)   Perego, Giovanni, 1776–1817
        Italy, Milan (active also in Brescia and Venice)
        Entrance to a Castle, 1810–1815
        Pencil, brush, and bister ink wash, 280 x 380 mm.
        Signed in black ink at lower right:
        "Giovanni Perego"

c. 1822–1830, Vol. I, plate #72 entitled *Professo*, probably a forgotten music drama). The drawings of Perego's designs for La Scala are in the Museo Teatrale alla Scala, the Museo Caccia in Lugano, and a few private collections.

### Alessandro Sanquirico

Alessandro Sanquirico was a born Milanese. He never left Milan for a foreign assignment in the theatre (as did his friend Fuentes) to enjoy the pleasure of returning home. La Scala was Sanquirico's first and only home, and in this noble lyric theatre he spent most of his life designing scenery.

Alessandro was a pupil of Paolo Landriani. He learned perspective, architecture, and painting from Giovanni Pedroni, whom he assisted in La Scala and from whom he inherited the august traditions of the Galliari family. Sanquirico designed a prodigious number of settings for opera and ballet for La Scala from 1806 until 1832. Landriani, Canna, Perego, and Fuentes were fellow designers with whom he frequently collaborated. For the

(132) Sanquirico, Alessandro, 1780–1849 (attributed)
Italy, Milan
Royal Square in Alexandria, 1829
Pen and brown ink with opaque watercolors, 374 x
532 mm.

last fifteen years of his affiliation with the opera house he was given the title of "Chief Resident Scala Designer." In 1829, he redecorated the auditorium of the opera house (formerly decorated by Perego in 1807) in the stylish new Pompeiian vogue.

While the celebrated stage designer consistently served his muse at La Scala, outside of the opera house he could divert his theatrical talents to designing courtyards and gardens and stylish interiors for the new aristocracy of Milan. Even more important, he was occasionally called upon to serve the royal family of Lombardy-Venice. In 1835, he devised the *pompe funèbre* of Francesco I in the Duomo. Three years later, he provided the luxurious decorations for the coronation of the Emperor Ferdinand I as king of Lombardy-Venice. The brilliant decorations for the festivities which Sanquirico designed included the tough assignment of decorating the neo-Gothic Duomo, which for many resembles a gigantic wedding cake. He provided the decor for the royal palace and the reception pavilion; he even designed the coronation carriage, the costumes, and all the insignia of state, a few of which are preserved today in the Imperial Treasury in Vienna. A commemorative festival book was issued, and the spec-

tacular engravings illustrate that the royal occasion was pure theatre and might well have been framed within the proscenium of La Scala.

In the first half of the nineteenth century, during forty years of uninterrupted activity at La Scala, Sanquirico observed the gradual decline of the Bolognese and Venetian schools of scene design in favor of the ascendant Milanese school. During this era at La Scala, singing, acting, direction, and design reached a high level of perfection. The ballet found new expression in the heroic pantomimes and choreodrama with Vigano and Taglioni. The spectacular productions of La Scala became renowned throughout the lyric theatres of Europe.

As a designer, Sanquirico was trained to embrace the academic limitations of neoclassicism. Inevitably his youthful work adhered to this strict formula. However, he did succeed, with considerable brio, in reconciling the more rigid academic manner with the fresher pictorial solutions of the new romantic trends which were considered so out of humor and harmony with the spirit of classicism. Sanquirico learned how to combine the solemn grandeur of Graeco-Roman art with the nostalgic, picturesque taste for the art of the Middle Ages. He also

150

understood the pathos and mood that pervaded the new operatic creations of the contemporary lyric repertory of Bellini and Rossini, Donizetti and Pacini. He sought to achieve a closer relationship between the character of the opera and that of his decor. In designing for choral masses in war and peace, or devising scenic effects for fire and storm, he planned his scenes so that the dramatic action should occur downstage.

The composite harmony of his classical and romantic styles established a new trend in theatrical design. Whether his vast scenes were set in ancient Rome or in modern Milan, whether they reproduced the fiery spectacle of Pacini's *Last Days of Pompeii*, or the sombre atmosphere of a sepulchral Gothic hall, they were all designed with skillful articulation of architectural masses, with perspective to achieve spacial depth, and with chiaroscuro to dramatize light. Always a glorious, if theatrical, authenticity haunted his designs. His insistence on pictorial verisimilitude heralded the advent of naturalism.

*Illustration 132.* The *Nuova Raccolta di Scene Teatrali (Fascicolo 26)* contains six engravings of scenes for the ballet *Ottaviano in Egitta* presented at La Scala in 1829. This design is very similar in style and character to those six scenes, and may well be a drawing for an additional scene for that same ballet.

*Illustration 133.* An aquatint of this drawing was made by Biasioli and published by Antonio Bassi in Milan. Much of Alessandro Sanquirico's mature work has survived in collections of color plates. Two handsome collections of designs for La Scala were edited and published by Stanislao Stucchi. *Raccolta di Scene Teatrali* contains a large number of settings designed by the most celebrated scenic artists of Milan between 1819 and 1824. Many of Sanquirico's designs are included in this publication. Another work, *Raccolta di Varie Decorazioni Sceniche*, was published in 1827 and contains a selection of settings designed only by Sanquirico for La Scala. This publication was one of the most splendid illustrated books to appear in Italy during the nineteenth century. The plates constitute a record of the monumental achievement of Sanquirico at La Scala. A group of Sanquirico's hundreds of drawings which he made for La Scala are in Giuseppe

(133) Sanquirico, Alessandro
Roman Hall: Setting for the Ballet *Numa Pompilio*, 1815
Pen and black ink with opaque watercolors on blue paper, 280 x 382 mm.

Inscribed in ink on mount below drawing:
*"Appartamenti d'Ersilia. Questa scene fu eseguita per Ballo eroico-favoloso, Numa Pompilio inventato e posto sulle scene dell' I. R. Teatro alla Scala dal Sig. Salvatore Vigano"*

Fiocco's collection in Padua, another is in the Fondazione Cini, and a third group is in the Museo Teatrale alla Scala.

### Giorgio Fuentes

Goethe, in letters to Schiller and to Duke Karl August in Weimar, was enthusiastic about the work of Giorgio Fuentes. As manager of the Duke's court theatre, Goethe stopped off in Frankfurt en route to Switzerland in 1797, visited Fuentes in his studio, and saw his new production of Salieri's *Palmira, Queen of Persians.* Goethe admired his settings because "embedded within them is solid architecture and because they are opulent without being overladen." He attempted, with no success, to attract Fuentes to the court theatre in Weimar, and later had to be content with Fuentes' gifted pupil Friedrich Beuther.

Fuentes had been a pupil of Pietro Gonzaga in Milan's Accademia di Belle Arti and later was apprenticed to the celebrated Alessandro Sanquirico and worked in La Scala.

In 1797, with the best of credentials from La Scala, he was appointed designer in the National Theatre of Frankfurt. All critics agreed that his designs for *Palmira* (1797) and Mozart's *La Clemenza di Tito* (1799) were landmarks in the progress of German eighteenth-century scenic design. His six scenes for *Palmira* were aided and abetted, or more likely overrun, by crowds of extras, horses, two camels, and one elephant. In 1805, he packed up his paints and brushes, bid farewell to the National Theatre of Frankfurt, and departed for Paris. But designing in Napoleon's imperial capital offered no great attraction to Fuentes, and within the year he was happily home again in Milan, permanently ensconced in the scenic studio of La Scala, designing operas and ballets, sometimes alone, other times collaborating with his fellow designers, Canna or Pedroni.

Because of Fuentes' knowledge and experience, his designs have resounding authority. He was a neoclassicist devoted to historicity. His designs, while frequently aus-

(134) Fuentes, Giorgio, 1756–1821
Italy, Milan (active also in Frankfurt and Paris)
Before a Palace, c. 1799 (See also color plate 8)
Pen and black ink with watercolors, 300 x 393 mm.

(135)  Beuther, Friedrich, 1777–1856
       Germany, Frankfurt (also active in Weimar,
       Braunschweig, and Kassel)

Hall in Old German Style, c. 1825
Pen and gray wash with watercolors, 224 x 370 mm.
Collections: Mayr, Fajt, Scholz

tere, suggest thoughtful restorations of large-scale Roman monuments. Yet, by not adhering to the strict formulas of geometric proportion, a cool romantic air pervades his scenic compositions. His carefully contrived color-value contrasts of light and dark made his architectural perspectives more grandiose and his flat spatial areas more dramatic.

*Illustration 134.* This design may have been for the production of Mozart's *La Clemenza di Tito* in Frankfurt in 1799. The drawing has the same character and style of a Fuentes design (plate #8) in Franz Rapp's *Süddeutsche Theaterdekorationen aus drei Jahrhunderten.*

### Friedrich Beuther

Friedrich Beuther's talent and his significance in the German theatre have not been sufficiently recognized. As a designer, he played a dynamic and forceful role in the German theatre of the first half of the nineteenth century. A youthful actor greatly interested in scene design, he became in Frankfurt a pupil of Giorgio Fuentes and inevitably fell under the influence of his master's strong neoclassical style. Thereafter, for a number of years he and his young actress wife were members of itinerant

theatrical companies that barnstormed over Germany. In 1812, he gained practical experience designing scenes for the theatre in Bamburg, and the following two years he worked in Würzburg. It became clear that designing scenery, not acting, would be Beuther's way of life, yet his designs would always reflect his concern and experience with acting.

Goethe as manager of the Hoftheater in Weimar thought well of Fuentes' pupil and invited Beuther and his wife to join his Hoftheater company in Duke Karl August's classical citadel of culture. His distinguished court theatre catered to a well-balanced fusion of aristocrats and middle class. In assuming his new scenic responsibilities, Beuther enthusiastically adopted Goethe's principles of excellence in artistic presentation and homogeneity of style in production. With the support of Schiller, Goethe had long campaigned against realism, and Beuther formulated proposals for reform in scenery and its role in the Ducal Theatre that Goethe welcomed and endorsed. Beuther believed in the integrated totality of stage art, including also music and poetry. He anticipated many of the ideas later developed fully by Wagner in his doctrine of *Gesamtkunstwerk.*

Goethe recorded in his *Annals* for 1817 his impressions

153

(136)
Schinkel, Karl Friedrich,
1781–1841
Germany, Berlin (active also
in Hamburg and Weimar)
Palace Hall: Setting for
*König Yngurd*, Act I, 1817
(See also color plate 9)
Pen and black ink with
watercolors, 475 x 521 mm.
Collection: R. Gunter

of Beuther's scenic contributions during the last years of his regime in the Hoftheater: "Exactly at the right time we gained an excellent artist in the designer Beuther, who was trained in the school of Fuentes, and who, by means of perspective, was able to enlarge our small spaces endlessly; by characteristic architecture, to multiply them; and, by taste and ornament, to render them highly agreeable. Every kind of style he subjected to his perspective skill. In the Weimar library he studied the Egyptian as well as the old German architecture, and thereby gave to the pieces requiring such illustration new attraction and peculiar splendor."

Beuther designed impressive productions of Mozart's *Titus* (1815) and *The Magic Flute* (1817) for Goethe at Weimar. Every designer derives an idea from another artist and adopts and translates it into his own visual language. Beuther's Kapitol for *Titus* surely sprang from his master Fuentes' 1799 Frankfurt design for the same scene (see Illustration 134). And if Beuther was influenced by the very original, style-setting production that Schinkel devised for *The Magic Flute* in Berlin the previous year, he did nonetheless design his Weimar *Magic Flute* according to the dictates of his own studies—antique yet modern, archaeological yet imaginary, and particularly appropriate to the small scale of the Hoftheater proscenium.

After twenty-six years of dedicated service, Goethe relinquished the direction of the Weimar theatre in 1817. The following year, Beuther, with his wife, also left Weimar and accepted a new contract with Klingemann, the talented impresario of the theatre in Braunschweig, where he worked for six years, taking time out occasionally to work as a guest designer in other cities of Germany.

For the last thirty years of his full career, Beuther served as *Hoftheatermalerei* in Kassel, a position which carried with it the privilege of designing for other theatres of Germany, notably Leipzig and Hamburg. Beuther was the first of a long line of peripatetic German designers some of whom today continue to overload the capacity of their time and talent by accepting too many commissions for too many lyric theatres.

Always, Beuther was acclaimed a modernist. He fought for integrated totality in the art of the theatre. He converted the neoclassic and the neo-Gothic modes to his own contemporary style. His free adaptation of linear perspective, his theatrical penchant for a warm neutral palette, his experimentation in the use of color and light scales, marked him as an influential innovator and a superior master in scene design.

*Illustration 135.* In his *Conversations with Eckermann*, Goethe described his ideas on the use of color in theatrical costumes and stage settings: "Generally the scenes should have a tone favorable to every color of the dresses, like Beuther's scenery, which has more or less of a brownish tinge, and brings out the color of the dresses with perfect freshness." Beuther's sketch for this theatrical setting of an unrealistic Gothic hall is rendered in tones of gray with the exception of pale rose and yellow in the rear translucent window. From examining similar scenes of Beuther one can see that he probably used several vaulted wings in front of this design to achieve an even greater effect of depth.

In Braunschweig, a Beuther portfolio of only four

colored engravings, *Dekorationen für die Schaubühne*, was published as a theatrical gesture in 1824 to encourage the practice of German scenography.

Otto Jung's excellent study, *Der Theatermaler Friedrich Christian Beuther*, contains Dr. Rudolph Beuther's working catalogue of Beuther's designs and notes the many private and public collections in Europe which contain his work.

### Karl Friedrich Schinkel

Winckelmann's seminal treatise, *Reflections on the Imitation of Greek Art*, appeared in 1755. He urged artists to forsake the colorful, painterly traditions of the rococo style and "through careful analysis and self-conscious imitation of ancient Greek works to develop a painting style that stressed the supremacy of line and the importance of design." Winckelmann's treatise became the cornerstone of the neoclassic movement. A generation later his ideas found their perfect expression in the architecture and painting, decorations and scene designs of Karl Friedrich Schinkel.

Schinkel the neoclassicist was truly a Renaissance man. Everything from classical antiquity aroused his curiosity. Of Greek civilization he wrote, "Among the uncountable mistakes of our days, it is a relief to recall that beautiful and enlightened time, and an irrepressible tendency grows among the better of us to pick up the old threads again and to create according to the old methods and style so far as we may." Schinkel could devote his talent with equal enthusiasm to reforming the stage or designing a salt cellar.

After two years of travel among the cultural centers of Europe, he returned to Berlin and studied with the arch-classicist Friedrich Gilly at the Academy of Architecture. There he learned to worship the Doric and Ionic orders and discovered a new world through the polished glasses of neoclassicism.

Schinkel's career was primarily as an architect. King Friedrich Wilhelm appointed him state architect of Prussia at the age of thirty-four. What Inigo Jones had achieved in creating an urban façade for London, Schinkel aspired to achieve for Berlin. Schinkel contributed a new look to German architecture, basing his innovations

(137) Percier, Charles, 1764–1838 (attributed)
France, Paris
Napoleonic Fête, c. 1802
Pen and black ink with gray and blue washes on tan paper, 326 x 474 mm.
Collection: R. Gunter

and reforms on the strict doctrines of classical rhetoric, pompously austere and uninspired. He gave Unter den Linden, the heart of the Prussian capital, an urban Teutonic style of architecture. He designed the royal Schloss and the palaces of Prince Albrecht and Prince Karl Wilhelm complete with interior decor, furniture, and glassware. He also designed, in accordance with the cold precision of his neoclassical style, several churches, a royal library and a royal museum, bridges, and monuments. He was immensely interested in the theatre and sought to reform the architecture of concert halls and theatres with maximum optical and acoustical efficiency. In his theatres for Hamburg and Berlin he incorporated his own ideas of audience-actor relationship based on previous experiments by architects Dumont, Cochin, Morelli, Roubo, and Quarenghi. In the Royal Theatre of Berlin he introduced a generous forestage which, with orchestra pit rising to stage level, transformed his proscenium theatre into a classical amphitheatre.

An unmistakable sense of theatre pervaded much of Schinkel's architecture, painting, and decoration. During his youth, he must have witnessed many productions of the foremost neoclassic designers of Europe and carried back to Berlin vivid memories of rewarding evenings spent in the Hofburg, La Scala, La Fenice, the Argentina, and the Comédie Française.

After returning to Berlin, his career in the theatre rose to meteoric heights. He first painted dioramas for Wilhelm Gropius. These immense scenic inventions depended upon skillful perspective and optical illusion for their success with the viewing audience, and the great popularity of the diorama as a form of theatrical entertainment in Europe and America was phenomenal. Schinkel's cycloramas (the curved walls enclosing the dioramas) were painted in semitransparent watercolor and opaque tempera, and were animated with mobile theatrical lighting from in front and from behind. For the audience, the total effect was awesome.

So appealing were his dioramas as theatre that in 1815 he was entrusted by the Royal Theatre in Berlin to design a new production of Mozart's *Magic Flute*. This was one of the most original and brilliant theatrical productions of the nineteenth century in Germany, and it exerted unmistakable influence on contemporary continental scene design. It also established Schinkel as a major theatrical designer in the German theatre. The next year he designed *Undine*, followed by Schiller's *Maid of Orleans* and *Don Carlos*. Later he designed Goethe's *Iphegenia*, Shakespeare's *Macbeth*, and Gluck's *Armide*. His final and crowning work for the theatre was his marvelous scenic investiture for Goethe's *Faust*. Between 1815 and 1832 he designed over thirty productions of plays and operas.

As a scenographer, Schinkel excelled in landscape and architecture. At times he arbitrarily melded both into a single composition to achieve an esoteric scenic effect of romantic mysticism. As a neoclassicist, Schinkel was cold, precise, and formal in his drawing technique, and he affected the detailed style of an architect's rendering. Whether his setting was Greek or Egyptian, Roman or Romanesque, Gothic or Oriental, Schinkel always aspired

to simplicity, the straight line, gravity, and virility. His concern for bare, sometimes stark, but meaningful classical forms, and his use of geometric shapes, were revolutionary and modern. In the bourgeois German theatre, his virtuous nobility, his scale and grandeur, were nourished on the sunny philosophy of enlightenment but also required the protective shade of his romantic umbrella. Neoclassicism in the German theatre achieved its triumphant fulfillment thanks to Schinkel's empathy for the romantic.

*Illustration 136.* Müller's tragedy *König Yngurd* was first performed on January 16, 1816, in the Burgtheater in Vienna, and the following year it was presented, with Schinkel's designs, by Intendant Graf Brühl in the Royal Theatre in Berlin. The colored aquatint of this setting, entitled *Saal in dem Trauerspiel König Yngurd, Act I,* varies in several details from this sketch, notably in the perspective view through the right arch. The engraving was one of a group of Schinkel's designs first published in five portfolios by L. W. Wittich between 1819 and 1824. It was republished in *Sammlung von Theater-Dekoration Erfunden von Carl Friedrich Schinkel* (plate #26), which appeared in three editions after Schinkel's death: 1847–1849, Potsdam; 1861, Berlin; and 1874, also Berlin. This is fitting recognition throughout Germany and the continent of the prestigious talent of Karl Friedrich Schinkel and of his lasting contribution to the German stage. Many of Fuentes', Beuther's, and Schinkel's more popular designs were preserved in miniature settings. To the delight of German children, these engraved scenes, along with their casts of characters, could be cut out and assembled complete behind the proscenium of their toy theatres.

### Percier and Fontaine

Charles Percier and Pierre François Léonard Fontaine formed a lifelong partnership when they were Prix-de-Rome students in architecture (1785–1794) at the French Academy in Rome. With the success of their first collaborative publication, *Palais, Maisons et d'Autres Edifices Modernes, Dessinés à Rome,* "Percier-Fontaine" soon became synonymous with the empire style. Their elegant taste and superior skill in creating a repertory of neoclassic ornament and decoration made them the most sought-after Parisian designers of public buildings, dwellings, and furnishings for the newly prosperous society of the Directoire and Consulate.

As official architects and personal favorites of Napoleon, they were awarded the most important design commissions of the day, and consequently dominated the French taste in the visual arts. With the emperor's sanction came the restoration of golden splendor and luxury, symmetry and order. The published engravings of the interior decor of the remodeled residences of their imperial patron—the Louvre and the Tuileries, Malmaison, Compiègne, and Fontainebleau—brought Percier and Fontaine international recognition. Their empire style was adopted by rulers of dependent states from Stockholm to Naples.

(138) Lequeu, Jean-Jacques, 1757–1849 (?)
France, Rouen (active in Paris)
Happening in a Village Square, c. 1795
Pencil and black ink with gray washes, 367 x 550 mm.
Inscribed on lower left margin: *"Dessiné par Jn. Jqu. Le Queu"*

Below border in large script: *"Décoration du théâtre, projetté par Jn. Jques. Le Queu, Architecte"*
On verso the artist's monogram stamp: "JLQ"

Their predecessors, the Vigaranis, Berain, and Servandoni, had surrounded their royal masters with a regal display of elegant opulence. Similar responsibilities fell on Percier and Fontaine, who supervised the emperor's splendid occasions and the celebrations honoring his military victories. For political anniversaries they provided symbolic decor—statues of Liberty, altars of Nature, and fountains of Regeneration. In 1804, they sheathed the Gothic Notre Dame with sumptuous neoclassical decor for Napoleon's marriage to Marie Louise and their coronation ceremonies.

Napoleon considered theatricals essential to his program for the propagation of Republican ideals. The traditional art of the theatre, however, he considered essential to the well-being of the state. Playwrights and actors, architects and artists, should serve the state on the highest level. David designed *The Triumph of the French People* for the theatre curtain of the Théâtre de l'Opéra. The Comédie Française frequently performed in the court theatres of his majesty's imperial residences. Napoleon also saw to it that the members of the Comédie traveled abroad as honored ambassadors of French culture. On October 15, 1812, from the Kremlin in distant Moscow, Napoleon forwarded to Paris his extraordinary "Décret Imperial sur la Surveillance, l'Organization, l'Administration, la Comptabilité, la Police et la Discipline du Théâtre Française." Today this document continues to serve as the organizational instrument for the affairs of France's National Theatre.

Napoleon never lost his enthusiasm for the theatre—whether it was the special brand that Percier and Fontaine provided or the classical drama of Voltaire, leavened with *William Tell* or *Gaius Gracchus* at the Comédie Française.

*Illustration 137.* This design, attributed to Charles Percier, was probably for a theatrical extravaganza honoring the First Consul on the occasion of his return to Paris from a victorious campaign. All the trappings of a Roman Triumph are present. Massive Corinthian columns dwarf two phalanxes of Roman soldiers massed between choruses of ladies of the French Republic. Center stage, drummers and cymbalists precede the entrance of Mars, born aloft on a triumphal car with his emblems of war and flags flying. Nothing of pomp and circumstance was omitted—Percier and Fontaine, as the all-seeing eyes of Napoleon, saw to that. Edmond de Goncourt noted that "the Revolution made fêtes the complement of education. It was no longer a matter of only amusing the people. It was necessary to instruct while amusing." Napoleon understood the potential of lavish parades and state spectacles. The citizens of the young Republic were soon to learn where their authority rested.

### Jean-Jacques Lequeu

Jean-Jacques Lequeu first studied architecture in his native Rouen; in Paris he became a pupil of Soufflot and later continued his studies in Rome. On his return to Paris, the Revolution left him without direction or resources except for his wealth of talent, which he found difficult to convert to the needs of official architecture. Along with Etienne Louis Boulée and Claude-Nicolas Ledoux, Lequeu was one of the three remarkable visionary architects who lived through the reign of Louis XVI and survived the vicissitudes of the French Revolution, as prophetic designers of fantastic and surrealist architecture. Boulée and Ledoux achieved fame and success, however, while Lequeu found only poverty and solitude. As a frontispiece to the collection of his drawings in the Bibliothèque Nationale, Lequeu painted a brooding portrait of himself as a spectator, alone with his portfolios and drawings, gazing out of a darkened theatre box upon a world which failed to applaud his genius and passed him by.

Lequeu exemplified the new style of romantic classicism, and his architectural drawings display a grandiose feeling for the theatrical. There is no evidence that Lequeu ever designed settings for the theatre, but he did participate in the preparations for the gigantic Fête de la Federation, staged in Paris on the Fourteenth of July, 1790, which was the first of many subsequent large-scale political celebrations of the French Revolution.

*Illustration 138.* Lequeu probably considered this unique *décoration du théâtre* an excursion into a scenic world of political propaganda. Lequeu himself had narrowly escaped the guillotine. The setting is for no identifiable play. It represents a medieval village square set among Roman ruins and antique towers. In the background, behind a pair of obelisks, a pristine neoclassical villa with a Renaissance dormer appears to rise from ruins. An ancient villa and fortress dominate a surrounding hill. The scene symbolizes the new order rising from the old. Here is surreal scenery of life and death, of the sinister and symbolic into which Lequeu has carefully introduced specific characters in a dramatic situation. A husband and wife of the *ancien régime* with their attendants are served with a warrant of arrest by three guards romantically attired. The parents' four children, looking like winged *putti*, are frightened. One appears to be picking up the shattered fragments of the past. Life in this village has come to a poignant end. In the dawn, it awaits the new order of the Revolution—the future of a new society.

### Pierre-Luc-Charles Cicéri

Alexandre Dumas saluted Cicéri as "father of modern decoration," and Cicéri was indeed an innovator who fixed the characteristics of theatrical decor in France for almost a century.

In 1793, at the tender age of eleven, Pierre-Luc-Charles Cicéri arrived in New York from France, driven from his homeland by the Reign of Terror. He began painting scenery for New York's first and only theatre of the time, the John Street Theatre located near Wall Street. William Dunlap, contemporary art historian and theatre manager, observed that in the post-Revolutionary days, "the scenic decorations of the American Theatre had been lamentably poor," but when in 1794 Cicéri painted the scenes for an operatic spectacle called *Tammany*, the scenes took on a different look. "They were gaudy and unnatural, but had a brilliancy of colouring, reds and yellows being abundant. Cicéri afterwards made himself a better painter and proved himself an excellent machinist."

Four years later in 1798, New York's second playhouse, the splendid Park Theatre, opened. Cicéri was that theatre's scene painter, assisted by a Mr. Audin. New York's two newspapers gave the theatre and the inaugural production glowing notices. "The scenery was executed in a most masterly style," said one of them. "The extensiveness of the scale upon which the scenes are executed, the correctness of the designs, and the elegance of the painting presented the most beautiful views which the imagination can conceive. The scenery was of itself worth a visit to the theatre." The budget for Mr. Cicéri and his department was sixty dollars!

Having given a lift to the New York scene, Cicéri returned to Paris. He studied landscape painting with Bellangé, and entered the Opéra's Academy of Music and Dance as a scenic artist. In 1810, he succeeded Isabey as head of the studio, and within a few years he became uncontested scenic master of this great stage.

In 1821, the new Paris Opéra opened with the extravagant *Alladin or the Wonderful Lamp*. The "wonderful lamp" was the introduction of gas light in the French theatre. In its early use, Cicéri was greatly aided by Daguerre, who, by dimming the auditorium and using new sources of theatrical light, revolutionized the traditional conception of scenery and stage lighting.

Cicéri experimented also with scenic innovations such as cycloramas on the stage of the Paris Opéra during an era of great historical operas—*Alfred the Great, Robert le Diable*, and *Gustave III*. In *La Belle au Bois Dormant* (1825), Prince Charming appeared to float on a boat down a river before a moving panorama. Cicéri's eruption of Vesuvius for *La Muette de Portici* (1828) was the celebrated *coup de théâtre* of the time; the previous year, he had journeyed to La Scala to observe Sanquirico's miraculous effects for *The Last Days of Pompeii*.

In 1825, Baron Taylor, the playwright, was appointed Commissaire Royal at the Comédie Française, and Cicéri was appointed *Peintre de l'Empereur*. *Leonidas* with Talma was a smashing success. Cicéri based the scene of Xerxes' Tent on David's classical painting, but romanticism won its first scenic victory with his expansive design for the Pass of Thermopylae. The production of Victor Hugo's *Hernani* with Cicéri's settings marked the climactic victory of the forces of romanticism over those of classicism. Victor Hugo, as a man of letters and an artist, was a powerful influence in the theatre, and the manuscripts of his plays are filled with sketches and notes to serve as guidelines for the designer. In *Hernani*, the epic scale of the battlefield and the Romanesque great hall with its central flight of steps descending to Charle-magne's crypt indicated the changing directions of the "new movement." A century later, in the theatre of the Russian Revolution, Vakhtangov would use a similar flight of steps for *Hamlet* with comparable dramatic effect.

In order to execute his scenic commissions for all these theatres, Cicéri opened a scenic studio and called it *"Menus Plaisirs."* In this atelier he trained a corps of talented designer/scenic artists. Lavastre and Desplé-chin, Carpezat, Séchan, Philastre, and Cambon collaborated with Cicéri on his major productions. For the spectacular settings of *Gustave III*, Cicéri required the assistance of no less than six designers. In time, his collaborators established rival ateliers and became aggressive competitors; their studios produced relatively sterile historical and naturalistic decors. During the latter half

(139) Cicéri, Pierre-Luc-Charles, 1782–1868
France, Paris (active in New York, Paris, and London)
Hall of an Oriental Palace, c. 1818
Pen and watercolor, 247 x 350 mm.
Inscribed along lower margin: "Ciceri—Etude"

of the nineteenth century in Europe and America, scenic studios provided proficient, packaged scenic productions for opera, ballet, and theatre. In that routine world, Adolphe Appia and Gordon Craig were rocking in their cradles, biding their time to assault the theatre's lethargic, lackluster formula for art.

*Illustration 139.* Cicéri designed the scenes for the production of Cherubini's *Ali Baba* at the Paris Opéra in 1818, and with Philastre and Cambon for the revival in 1833. This drawing might be a study for a scene in one of those productions.

### William Clarkson Stanfield

William Clarkson Stanfield spent his youth along the northeast coast of England, enamoured with ships and tales of foreign ports. At twelve, he learned to draw and paint as an apprentice to a heraldic painter in Edinburgh. Later, he joined the Royal Navy and occasionally painted scenes for his ship's entertainments. He sailed in the East India trade but after fifteen years retired from the sea, and his captain recommended him as a scene painter at the Royalty Theatre, which was a "sailor's theatre" in Wellclose Square in East London. After three years, he moved to Edinburgh and painted scenery in the Pantheon Theatre, where he met another artist, David Roberts, who also was painting scenery at the Theatre Royal. Both were young scene painters who aspired to easel painting, and as artists they were congenial and were to become lifelong friends. Together they decided to assault the London art world, but to make ends meet, they painted scenery for the Coburg Theatre.

Stanfield's fresh canvases began to attract attention at exhibitions of the Royal Academy. He became a charter member of the Society of British Artists. Ensconced in the paint room of Drury Lane, Stanfield continued to develop his scenic work. In 1829, at thirty-six, Stanfield decided to give up scene painting for picture painting and a more lucrative income, but his canvases never lacked that romantic feeling for "painted illusion" which he had discovered as a scene painter in the theatre. His new paintings were soon honored at the Royal Academy, and before long, Stanfield was one of England's leading marine and landscape painters.

Stanfield never really gave up his scenic practice in the London theatre. In 1833, at Charles Kean's funeral, he met the great William Charles Macready, actor-manager of Covent Garden and later Drury Lane. They became close friends, and during the next eighteen years they made a dozen productions together. In 1836, in order to expand the capability of Covent Garden's stage, Stanfield installed a diorama for their production of *Ion.* This made possible a "moving picture" of the "progress of a ship from the building yards to its wreck"! For Macready's Christmas Pantomime, *Harlequin and the Peeping Tom,* the diorama displayed an eye-filling selection of Stanfield paintings—"Scenes at Home and Abroad." To show off this scenic masterwork more effectively, Macready installed gaslight in Covent Garden. Macready was well aware of the value of Stanfield's audience attraction. The

name "Clarkson Stanfield," with lyric descriptions of his scenery, would appear in the program above the names of leading actors. On occasion, Macready publicly expressed his gratitude and indebtedness to his friend Stanfield.

Stanfield became a close friend of Charles Dickens and the members of his admiring circle, all of whom shared an affection for the theatre. During twelve years, Dickens found time to indulge in amateur dramatics both in London playhouses and at home in Tavistock House. For these occasional amateur theatricals, Stanfield would desert his studio to fill Dickens' "office of scene painter" with exemplary professionalism. In the tradition of the artist of the Renaissance, this nineteenth-century English artist enjoyed escaping from his studio's easel to fashion scenes for the theatre. For him, the proscenium frame and the picture frame served one and the same purpose: Both framed and enhanced his popular and romantic view of nature.

A few years after Stanfield died, *Lloyd's Guide to Scene Painting* happily noted that "Stanfield experienced as much pleasure in listening to the public applause bestowed upon a scene of his in the theatre as in hearing the most lavish praises awarded him for any of his grandest academical pictures." Stanfield, in his dual role, never lost his sense of theatre.

*Illustration 140.* This drawing is a design for a London pantomime. After Stanfield retired from the sea in 1818, his travels were confined to Europe. Therefore, he must have concocted this romantic oriental scene from other travelers' engraved views of the East.

Most of Stanfield's drawings for the theatre are in the Victoria and Albert Museum.

### Simon Quaglio

Simon Quaglio was surrounded by family throughout his life. He was ten when his great-uncle, Lorenzo I, died. He trained for the theatre with his father, Giuseppe, and his older brother, Angelo I. When Simon was nineteen, he succeeded his brother Domenico II in supervising the restoration of the romantic Schloss Hohenschwangau for the King of Bavaria. Returning to Munich, he worked with his father, whom he soon succeeded as chief designer of the Hoftheater. For thirty-two years he held this position while his son Angelo II acquired from him the family's designing know-how. At sixty-five, Simon arranged for the transfer of his authority as *Hoftheatermaler* to his son, beside whom he continued to work until he died in 1878 at eighty-three.

Simon Quaglio's technical knowledge and theatrical experience in the Bavarian court theatre commended him as adviser and theatrical consultant to many opera and theatre centers of Germany. At twenty-three, he designed a highly original production of *The Magic Flute* for the Munich Hoftheater. With these designs he came of age. His earlier neoclassic persuasions became suffused with romantic overtones. Twenty years later, he devised the scenes for a new *Magic Flute* steeped in the mood of fantasy. Still later, with his son, he led the German avant-garde scenic movement with explorations in the use of

(140) Stanfield, William Clarkson, 1793–1867
England (active in Edinburgh and London)
Oriental Landscape for a Pantomime, c. 1825
(See also color plate 10)
Watercolor, 187 x 253 mm.
Inscribed on verso: "C. Stanfield—given to A. Betz
by Alfred Crowquil"
Collections: Crowquil, Betz

color and in projecting naturalism. Simon Quaglio had vision. He never stood still.

*Illustrations 141 and 142.* In the design by Simon Quaglio, a windswept robe of stars and a crescent moon shelter the Queen of the Night from a ghostly assemblage in a shroud of encircling clouds. Compare this design, made for the Munich Opera when he was twenty-three, with the design that Karl Friedrich Schinkel invented for the same scene only two years before in Berlin (Illus. 141). Schinkel's Queen of the Night stands on her immaculate crescent moon, serene amidst silver clouds beneath a classical dome of ordered stars. Mozart's rococo opera offered to

each of these two court-theatre painters an opportunity to display their opposing principles of theatrical style— romanticism vs. neoclassicism.

The Theatre Museum in Munich possesses eleven drawings by Simon Quaglio for scenes of the 1818 Munich production of *The Magic Flute*, including Quaglio's drawing for "The Queen of the Night." This design is identical with the Munich drawing except for a freer distribution of clouds and background figures. He might have made this slight variant of his original design for another production of the opera. Possibly he made it for Saint Petersburg, since Andreas Roller, designer for the imperial court theatres in Saint Petersburg, once owned the drawing. A

(141) Schinkel, Karl Friedrich
       "Queen of the Night" for *The Magic Flute*, 1816
       Aquatint by Jugel and Thiele (1819)

model of the scene is in the Mozart Museum in Salzburg.

*Illustration 143*. This imposing setting was executed in the new style of "built" scenery that Simon Quaglio introduced and developed in the Munich Hoftheater. However, lighting equipment and its control had not advanced to the stage where moonlight could be achieved by directional light. Therefore, accepting the conventional illumination provided by borderlights and footlights, Quaglio painted the shadows cast by the visible full moon on his three-dimensional scenery, and thus achieved the atmosphere of a realistic castle bathed in moonlight.

### Angelo Quaglio II

Angelo Quaglio II was trained in his father Simon's Munich studio. He also studied with Franz Adams, and in Berlin with Gropius. To complete his preparation for designing scenery, he was sent from Germany to the famous scenic atelier of Cambon in Paris. At twenty, Angelo returned to Munich to assist his father in the Hoftheater. While working on *Tannhäuser* (1855) and *Lohengrin* (1858), he came in contact with Richard Wagner. Informal discussions with Wagner laid the groundwork for his later close collaboration with the Meister who was deeply concerned with every detail of

(142) Quaglio, Simon, 1795–1878
Germany (active in Munich)
"Queen of the Night" for *The Magic Flute*, 1818
Pen and watercolor, 196 x 288 mm.
On verso: a rough outline of the sky drapery in
pencil; also several Russian collectors' notes in
Cyrillic.
Collections: A. Roller, S. Ernst, A. Benois

the visual aspects of the presentations of his operas.

Angelo II succeeded his father in 1860 as chief designer in the Bavarian Hoftheater. In 1867 he designed
scenes for new productions of *Tannhäuser* and *Lohengrin*,
followed four years later by a second revival of the latter
opera. So picturesque, in the eyes of Ludwig II, was his
Act II setting for *Lohengrin* that the Dream King wanted
the courtyard of his grandiose Schloss Neuschwanstein
(the model for the Disney castles) to be constructed to
resemble Angelo's romantic design for the Burghof.

A quixotic mutual admiration developed between King
Ludwig II and Richard Wagner on the first occasion they

met in the spring of 1864. At once, the royal patron paid
off all of the composer's debts, settled a residence and income on him, and proceeded to finance the productions of
his new operas. Between 1865 and 1870, the Bavarian
Hoftheater presented the world premieres of *Tristan und
Isolde*, *Die Meistersinger*, *Das Rheingold*, and *Die
Walküre*. Angelo II enthusiastically assisted Wagner on
the settings of these productions and complied with all of
his difficult scenic demands. Heinrich Döll and Christian
Jank also participated with Quaglio in the design and
preparation of these first performances. All were dedicated to realizing on the stage Wagner's doctrine of
*Gesamtkunstwerk* and his views on realistic, scenic illusion for music-drama constructed on romantic themes.
Quaglio's pictorial style of *inscenierung* particularly
pleased King Ludwig. By royal command, he designed
many private performances for the king. He also decorated many of the interiors of the fabulous Schloss Her-
renchiemsee which the king built in emulation of the Sun
King's palace at Versailles. Ironically, Ludwig II occupied this unfinished dream house for only twenty-three
days before his tragic death.

(143) Quaglio, Simon
   Ramparts before a Castle, c. 1850
   Pen and watercolor, 195 x 285 mm.
   Collections: A. Roller, A. Benois

(145) Materelli, Niccolo, nineteenth century
   Italy, Florence
   Two Costume Designs, 1873
   Pencil and watercolor, 243 x 167 mm.

Angelo II was not only the scenic attaché of Wagner; as *Hoftheatermaler* he collaborated on designing the full repertory of Mozart, Weber, Meyerbeer, Rossini, and Gounod. He devoted himself mainly to designing architectural settings. He had a staff of specialists who worked with him on landscape, decoration, and costume. In

(144) Quaglio, Angelo II, 1829–1890
   Germany, Munich (also active in other German cities
   and Belgium, Bohemia, and Russia)
   Interior of a Bavarian House, 1860–1875
   Pen and black ink with watercolors, 162 x 189 mm.
   On the white mount is the stamp: "Angelo Quaglio
   Hof Theatermaler Kol. Bayr"
   On the verso is a pencil drawing of a town which
   suggests the exterior backing for the window.

technical matters, he relied on the able assistance of the Hoftheater's *machiniste*, Karl Lautenschlager.

Angelo II was one of the most resouceful and successful members of the Quaglio clan. Commissions for new projects came from Dresden, Hanover, Berlin, Brussels, Prague, and St. Petersburg. He was cosmopolitan. His style in design was broad and comprehensive—romantic, mythical, historical and lyrical, of epic scale, with naturalistic atmosphere.

*Illustration 144.* The mount of this design for a Bavarian interior carries Angelo Quaglio's official stamp as court theatre painter, and the drawing itself bears the stamp of his craftsmanship and his skill as an artist.

*Illustration 145.* This dancer's costume for the *corpo di ballo* in the scene of the Piazza del Duomo in Florence, and Averardo in armor for Act I, Scene 2, were designed

(146) Zarra and Laloue, mid-nineteenth century
France, Paris
Rustic Interior, 1854 (See also color plate 11)
Watercolor and gouache, 408 x 593 mm.
Inscribed center left margin: "Zarra et Laloue";
inscribed lower right corner: "Zarra et Laloue—
1854"
Collection: A. Benois

(147) Cicéri, Pierre-Luc-Charles
Rustic Interior, 1836
Watercolors, 186 x 234 mm.
Inscribed lower right margin: "Ciceri 1836"

(148) Hobin, Franz, mid-nineteenth century
Austria, probably Vienna
Rustic Interior, 1832
Watercolors, 310 x 399 mm.
Inscribed lower right corner: "Franz Hobin 1832"
Collection: R. Gunter

for the opera-ballet *Niccolo dei Lapi* with music by Giovanni Pacini. The work was presented in the Teatro Pagliano, Florence, in 1873. A collection of thirty-eight costume drawings by Niccolo Materelli, seven designs and plans by C. S. Lessi, choreographic direction and musical documents for this opera are in the Oenslager Collection.

### Zarra and Laloue

In the eighteenth century, the scenic dock of every theatre and opera house in Europe housed a repertory of stock scenes that usually included a military encampment, a street, a forest, a garden, a prison, a palace, and a humble rustic interior. Additions were made to these basic scenes to suit the play's or the opera's varying requirements.

The eighteenth-century theatre in Drottningholm preserves a number of these stock scenes, including the rustic interior. They were composed of wings, borders, and a backdrop. Practical properties were used when required. The audience was never disturbed by the painted reality of a chair beside a real chair on which the performer sat. Such a compromise in illusion was an accepted convention in the theatre of that day, just as today on our space stage we accept a block with a cushion as a period chair.

The theatrical tradition of painted reality persisted through the nineteenth century in the provincial theatres of Europe and America. Zarra was an almost unknown French scenic artist who, like so many scenic artists before him, was trained in the craft of painting "painted" scenery. Zarra is not recorded in Bapst's listing of French nineteenth-century scenic artists in his *Essai sur l'Histoire du Théâtre*, but it is known that he and Cheret designed and painted the decor for *Joseph Balsamo* at the Odéon in 1878. Also, he certainly worked with Ferdinand Laloue, *l'ordonnateur des spectacles* of the Cirque Olympique where he was responsible for all sorts of scenic inventions.

In Illustration 146, Zarra, possibly at the instigation of Laloue, employed the new style of *le décor fermé*, first introduced on the stage of the Comédie Française in 1827 for Picard's comedy *Les Trois Quartiers*. The open Italian-style setting of wings and borders became a box set—closed on all sides. Even before the box set with painted detail became a formula, it established the theory of "the fourth wall" and became de rigueur for the presentation of the popular comedies and bourgeois dramas of Augier and Hervieu.

*Illustrations 146–148.* Each of these three drawings of rustic interiors carries the date and the signature of the artist. Each attests to the pride of the scenic artist in the execution of his craft. All employ a common scenic approach—the rude walls, the beamed ceiling, the fireplace with the painted fire and the window with the painted light, storage alcoves and shelves filled with "still-life" studies of bottles and crockery and domestic utensils. The details of the rustic interior varied little in Europe, England, and America. It served equally well for Ulrica's hut in *The Masked Ball*, the inn for *The Merry Wives of Windsor*, Rip Van Winkle's kitchen, or Uncle Tom's cabin.

With the twentieth century, painted scenery was thrown out of the theatre because it was believed to be too artificial by those who cared more for expensive solidity than painted fragility. Yet surely it has a real place in the theatre today, if only because it is theatrical and artificial. The technique of the old-style scene painter can open up a new world of invention for today's designer if he will put its ancient traditions to new use.

### H. Willbrandt

Little is known about Willbrandt and his work in the theatre. His style resembles some of those very modish German interiors that the painter and engraver Karl Blechan, who was scenic artist of the Königstadt Theater for three years, designed and published in Berlin in 1824.

By the middle of the nineteenth century, the sophisticated box set, with its enclosing walls and ceiling, had superseded the traditional open system of wings and borders. J. R. Planché is credited with having used the first box set for *London Assurance*, which the forward-looking actress-manager Mme. Vestris successfully introduced in her Olympic Theatre in London in 1841. She had an interest in offering the public realistic plays with "improved" scenery, appropriate furnishings, and correct costumes. Planché was more than a discerning artist; he was also an authority on English costume and heraldry, a musician, and a playwright. He believed that the box set, properly executed, should be "the product of a harmonious picture." It also proved to be a first-class accommodation for naturalism.

Before the development of photography, French graphic artists often did newspaper illustrations of actors animating the boxed interiors that the leading scenic ateliers of Paris provided for the naturalistic plays of Dumas, Balzac, or Scribe. For the growing audience of wealthy bourgeoisie, the old proscenium became the new frame in which the new society of London, Paris, Berlin, or Vienna was pleased to see itself mirrored in stage drawing rooms.

For Willbrandt, the box set belonged to the new establishment. Going further, this "slice of life" scene required a flat stage because "in real life we do not live our lives on ramped floors." That was yesterday's forecast for today's flat stages.

*Illustration 149.* This realistic setting for a drawing room could not have been executed in the time-honored method of painted wings and a backdrop. The enclosing walls of this new type of setting, called a box set, indicate precisely the ground plan on the flat stage which the cornice repeats on the ceiling. Willbrandt has not made the downstage walls, right and left, a part of the box set. They are two-fold wings that rise higher than the set itself and serve to mask the downstage front edge of the actual box set. The box set becomes the real thing—an actual room with the fourth wall removed.

The doors open and close with real handles. Real draperies hang at practical windows which admit actual light on actors using real furniture. The three-dimensional mantel is painted to imitate real marble and is adorned

(149) Willbrandt, H., mid-nineteenth century
Germany
Drawing Room, 1853
Watercolors, 209 x 327 mm.
Inscribed in ink at lower right corner:
"H. Willbrandt 1853"
Collection: R. Gunter

with a ticking clock and candelabra purchased in a fashionable shop, as were the ornaments on the consoles. The family portraits are antiques, actually framed and hung on green walls painted to look like flocked paper.

In executing this new-style setting, the scenic artist's responsibilities were forced to change with the changing styles of the times. He became a craftsman transforming built wood and canvas scenery into admitted imitations of every material and texture known to man since the ice age. The dubious art of faking every aspect of the real world became the new realism in the visual theatre of 1853.

### Andreas Leonhard Roller

Andreas Leonhard Roller was a German artist who studied with the stage designers de Pian and Neefe in Vienna. He then designed scenes for theatres in Munich, Vienna, Kassel, and Berlin. At twenty-eight, he left Berlin for Saint Petersburg. There he became resident designer in the Imperial Theatre for the remainder of his life and was known as Andrei Ivanovitch.

Eight of his drawings for scenes and costumes are in the Oenslager Collection. These were formerly in the collection of Alexandre Benois, who may have inherited them from his family, who had long been associated with the Russian theatre.

*Illustration 150. Sic transit gloria mundi* is obviously the theme of this sweeping design of Roller. It consists of four cut-out paper legdrops, two cutrows, and a backdrop, which, when arranged behind one another, make an accurate model of the stage setting.

The dramatic convolutions of this cavernous composition embrace a romantic assemblage of crumbling tombs and monuments memorializing heroes of the ancient world. The swirling clutter of rocks and tombs in the foreground, and the backdrop of a circular mausoleum and mortuary bridges, recall that fantastic necropolis which Pietro Gonzaga had also once designed for the imperial opera of Saint Petersburg (Illus. 94).

*Illustration 151.* Gounod's *Faust* was first performed in Saint Petersburg in 1864. It appears logical to assume from the sentiment of Roller's design that this drawing was used for the Apotheosis in the first Russian presentation of the opera. The scene is fraught with saccharine sentimentality. Marguerite, in prison, awaits death on her rude pallet, then miraculously she is redeemed by her appeal to Heaven. The prison walls fall away, and in purity of spirit she ascends on the wings of Gounod's music to the skies above. For this transcendent episode, Roller resorted to the traditional airways of the cloud machines. Arms raised high, Marguerite is wafted up among mauve clouds by a chorus of heavenly aides, some with harps, to a golden, garlanded *tempietto* encircled by

an aerial colonnade bathed in radiance. Many artists such as Murillo had used this device before Roller in depicting the Assumption of the Virgin; Bernini performed a similar elevating feat with the Ecstasy of Saint Theresa. The Bibienas frequently took Venus and her retinue on a theatrical tour of cloudland for a change of scene, and Torelli transported a wedding party to a pleasure dome amidst the clouds. Roller, like those unabashed showmen before him, played shamelessly on every heartstring with every known theatrical device to achieve a smashing Apotheosis for Marguerite.

### Unknown American Artist, Nineteenth Century

A few theatre drawings by journeyman scenic artists reveal, under the guise of fantasy, the presence of American primitive art in the musical theatre. Their drawings are naïve and crude, but they do succeed in conveying the

(150) Roller, Andreas Leonhard (Andrei Ivanovitch),
1805–c. 1880
Germany (active in Saint Petersburg)
*Aula Sepolcrale*, c. 1850
449 x 634 mm.
Collection: A. Benois

(151)  Roller, Andreas Leonhard
       Apotheosis of Marguerite for Gounod's *Faust*, Act IV,
       1864 (See also color plate 12)
       Pencil and watercolors, 258 x 349 mm.
       Inscribed on verso: "*Apothéose de Marguerite dont
       l'être pure est portée aux cieux*"
       Collection: A. Benois

scenic style of the American musical extravaganza, just as the spare and brilliant drawings of Inigo Jones define the scenic style of a Stuart court masque. The success of the American extravaganza, like the masque before it, relied on the combined skills of composer, librettist, choreographer, costume designer, and scenic artist.

Ironically, the emergence of the American musical theatre occurred during the tragic era of the Civil War. At "444 Broadway," Tony Pastor, known as the father of vaudeville, was developing the popular formula of the variety show. A series of musical melodramas, recalling Planché's London pantomimes, attracted enthusiastic houses in New York. In 1860, in the renovated Old Bowery Theatre, Laura Keene hit the jackpot with her enticing *Seven Sisters*. The show was labeled "an operatic, spectacular, diabolical, musical terpsichorean burletta." Clearly, the New York extravaganza was in the midst of growing pains. A few years later, that trail-blazing epic, *The Black Crook*, opened at Niblo's Garden laden with so much lavish trick scenery that it required the installation of a new mechanical stage. *The New York Times* recorded that "such a stage was never seen in this country before. Every board slides on grooves and can be taken up, pushed down or slid out at will. The entire stage may be taken away; traps can be introduced at any part at any time, and the great depth of the cellar below renders the sinking of entire scenes a matter of simple machinery." More than disappearing scenery dazzled the eye of theatre-goers. The corps de ballet of a hundred pretty girls parading in tights and daring costumes freely displayed "the theatrical potential of the female form," which in nineteenth-century American art was considered acceptable only when clothed in virtue.

The format of the musical melodrama of the extravaganza was the source of inspiration from which evolved the future musical theatre of burlesque, minstrel shows, operettas, reviews, and musical comedies. Notable significant descendants of those earlier musical prototypes record the changing scenic styles: Charles Dillingham's land, sea, and air spectaculars at the Hippodrome, the glorious Ziegfeld Follies at the New Amsterdam through whose dingy stage door passed "the most beautiful girls in the world," *The New Moon, Oklahoma, Porgy and Bess*, and *Hair*. The American musical theatre of the twentieth century, supported by fresh scenic stimulus, became an original and unique contribution to the world theatre.

*Illustration 152.* This aqueous delight is a scenic example of Americana—a never-never land belonging to no time or place. It recalls the Venus Grotto, that habitation of nymphs and water sprites which Ludwig II created for himself at his villa of Linderhof, with swans, shell boats, water lilies, garlands, and giant flowers.

This early setting already suggests the American theatre's traditional delight in opulence. It could have been painted in a scenic studio, or it could have been concocted by an ambitious itinerant scenic artist attached to a theatre in New Orleans, Cincinnati, or Philadelphia. The stages of these theatres were equipped with sufficient machinery to handle the "transformation" which the scenic artist quaintly describes on the verso of this drawing: "The water lilies to open and girls to come up through them bearing horns (fountains) and strings of spangles to represent water. Large swan at bottom of wing with girl sitting on back, daisy chains hanging from mouth of swan —the end in the hands of girls. The center piece, the upper half (the fountain), to descend from the flies bearing four girls. Dangling muslin strips, white and blue, hang all around the back edge, strung spangles represent water hung from the front side. The lower part with the shell to come from the cellar—with six girls on two fountains to ascend from the cellar fastened on backing. Backing represents flowers and water fading away into mist."

### Joseph Clare

Joseph Clare began his career at fourteen painting scenery. He was apprenticed to William Bronson and worked in the paint room of the Theatre Royal in Liverpool. At twenty-five, he moved to New York and was engaged to direct the preparation of scenery for the plays produced by Lester Wallack. Wallack's theatre, with its excellent company of actors, was considered the most elegant in New York. Besides being chief scenic artist for Wallack's theatre, Clare also provided scenes for many other New York theatre managers.

(152)  Unknown artist, nineteenth century
       United States, probably New York
       Court of Venus, c. 1870
       (See also color plate 13)
       Pencil and watercolor, 187 x 237 mm.

The American scenic artists of the second half of the nineteenth century were proudly eclectic in their tastes. Charles Witham served the New York theatre well with his realistic productions for the Shakespearean revivals of Edwin Booth and Augustin Daly. He often derived his scenic arrangements from "location" photographs, or gave his scenes an added pictorial lift by basing them on famous paintings, using Veronese's *The Marriage at Cana* for *The Taming of the Shrew*, or Gérôme's *The Death of Caesar* for *Julius Caesar*.

Other scenic artists, in devising settings for Boucicault's or Daly's many-scened dramas, effected the popular, panoramic style of painting in which Frederick Catherwood, John Banvard, and their followers excelled. The panoramists, in depicting their unfolding narratives, employed the telling brushwork of the scenic artist. Their views of rivers and mountains, highways and rural scenes, often relied on naïve and popular stage effects. Other times they suggested homely scenic wall decorations or a medley of Currier and Ives color prints.

Sometimes, scenic artists working on operas or scenes for Rip Van Winkle, Davy Crockett, or Johnny Appleseed evoked the style of America's romantic landscape artists such as Asher Durand and John Cole, who, inspired by the unspoiled world of the Hudson River, possessed "a passionate faith in Nature as a key to Art." Albert Bier-

(153)  Clare, Joseph, 1846–1917
      United States, New York
      Hindu Pavilion, 1887
      Pen and watercolors, 329 x 437 mm.
      Inscribed in ink at lower right: "J. Clare, 1887"
      Collection: Studio Alliance, New York

(154)  Unknown artist, nineteenth century
      United States, probably New York
      Rocky Gorge with Bridge over Waterfall, c. 1875
      Watercolors, 155 x 244 mm.

stadt, too, was inspired by the luminous grandeur of the Rocky Mountains and Yosemite. Frederick Church believed art's truest and noblest function was "not to imitate Nature but to rival it." His canvases of Niagara rivaled the falls themselves. However, most scenic artists, restricted to the paint frames of their studios, only found time to imitate, not to rival, Nature. As a result, they rarely rose above scenic "grandomania" on the stages of their theatres.

Joseph Clare's work is reminiscent of the picturesque postcard scenes turned out by the successful continental studios of Europe in the last quarter of the nineteenth century. His detailed settings and theatrical effects were much admired by public and press. The critic of the *Herald* wrote that his settings "are all such masterpieces of the stage carpenter's and scene painter's art that whenever they claim the attention of the audience they do so thoroughly and completely." Joseph Clare was a theatre craftsman in search of theatre art.

*Illustration 153.* Joseph Clare made this drawing for Reginald De Koven's Hindu comic opera *The Begum*, presented by John McCaull at the Fifth Avenue Theatre in 1887.

Clare filled the stage with a golden glow of orientalia. His exotic decor, like an old picture postcard from India, was enriched by the painted grand drapery, which also conformed with the ornate decoration of the theatre's proscenium arch.

*Illustration 154.* This sylvan example of scenic art survives the forgotten melodrama it once served. In this design, an unknown scenic artist has sought to capture the grand style of America's romantic landscape school and reproduce it on the stage of the theatre of his day.

### Carlo Ferrario

Carlo Ferrario rose from a humble Milanese family to become the leading designer at La Scala for forty years during the second half of the nineteenth century, just as Sanquirico, Gonzaga, and Landriani had been the leading designers during the first half of the century.

At the Accademia di Belle Arti he studied painting and decoration, and perspective with the designer Vimarcati. But *scenografia* was what he wanted, and the Accademia had no stage, which was essential for learning the craft. At nineteen, he presented himself at La Scala's scenic studio, where he became apprenticed to Vimarcati and Peroni. He helped them to execute their scenes and even made many sketches for his master Peroni. In 1859, he succeeded Vimarcati at the Accademia di Belle Arti. He also took over some of Peroni's work, and when Peroni retired in 1867, Ferrario's career at La Scala was well under way.

In 1878, he deserted La Scala to design settings for the Teatro Argentina in Rome and the Teatro San Carlo in Naples. After nine years, the prodigal son returned to Milan. He was appointed director of La Scala's scenic studio. His initial assignment was to design the first production of Verdi's *Otello*.

Carlo Ferrario was the acknowledged designer of the operas of Verdi. He found a new scenic expression for contemporary opera. His solutions for the scenic problems of Verdi's operas remain valid today. While he was the major "Verdian designer," he also worked with Boito (*Mefistofele*) and Ponchielli (*La Gioconda*) and designed new settings for the revivals of opera and ballet in the Scala's changing repertory.

Ferrario's designs are captivating. They combine the technician's skill with the artist's appealing imagination and popular idealism. Designs as diverse as an ice grotto, a desert in Arabia, a natural arch by the sea, or a terrace above the Bay of Naples reflect his deep respect for nature. He possessed an exceptional knowledge of period style. He had a brilliant sense of color coupled with a capacity for achieving dramatic light in designs as varied as the interior of the Palermo Cathedral or the Circus in Corinth.

Twelve years after Ferrario's death, Vespasiano Bignami assembled five hundred of his sketches, and they were published in five monumental portfolios, *Cinquecento Bozzetti Scenografici di Carlo Ferrario*, by Ulrico Hoepli in Milan in 1919. This commemorative work is a splendid memorial to the "*glorificazione del suo nome*."

*Illustration 155*. Verdi's opera *Un Ballo in Maschera* was first presented in Rome in 1859. This design was for the first production of the opera at La Scala in 1861. A draw-

(155) Ferrario, Carlo, 1833–1907
Italy, Milan (active in Rome and Naples)
Ulrica's Hut for *Un Ballo in Maschera*, Act I,
Scene 2, 1861
Pen and watercolors, 214 x 298 mm.
Collection: R. Gunter

(156) Ferrario, Carlo
Festa di Campagna for Cagnoni's *Il Vecchio della
Montagna*, Act III, Scene 5, 1863 (See also color
plate 14)
Pen and watercolors, 206 x 270 mm.
Inscribed lower left corner: "Carlo Ferrario"

ing for an alternate scheme by Carlo Ferrario is included
by Bignami in *Cinquecento Bozzetti Scenografici di Carlo
Ferrario*, Vol. I, pl. #5 (Milan, 1919).

Ferrario devised this interior-exterior lair for the
sorceress Ulrica who practices the black art and foresees
events in the future. Fetishes and symbols of her magic
guard the runic entrance to her hut. Totems lend an
eerie air to the open place beyond.

A large collection of Ferrario's drawings is in La
Scala's Museo del Teatro and the Brera. Others are in
the Donghi Collection in Padua, and twenty-eight are in
the Oenslager Collection.

*Illustration 156.* This drawing is included by Bignami in
*Cinquecento Bozzetti. . .* (Vol. I, pl. #73). The opera
was first presented at La Scala in 1863. The setting is a
pleasant retreat in a forest glade with cushions, plumed

canopies, and an airy net supporting an oriental lamp held
up by a cupid. Ferrario has imbued his design with romantic idealism to create a scene of lyrical and picturesque realism.

*Illustration 157.* Giuseppe Ronchi was the machinist in
charge of La Scala's stage equipment. This drawing is a
sectional view of the interior construction of La Scala's
stage house in the 1850s. That stage was one of the most
advanced in Europe. This graphic drawing illustrates the
complex technical equipment required to handle the extravagant scenic inventions of Alessandro Sanquirico,
Filippo Peroni, and Carlo Ferrario. The method of lowering their finished scenery from the paint loft to the stage
is explained. Shown in detail are the gallery and the grid
with large headblocks and loftblocks for raising and
lowering scenery, as well as a system for transverse move-

(157) Ronchi, Giuseppe, mid-nineteenth century
Italy, Milan
Sectional View of the Stage of La Scala, c. 1850
Pen and ink and watercolor, 1090 x 875 mm.
Inscribed in upper left corner are nineteen descriptive
notes with the signature "Giuseppe Ronchi"

(158 & 159)  Lavastre, Jean-Baptiste, 1839–1891
France, Paris
Letter with Six Sketches for *Hamlet*, 1870
Pen and ink, 267 x 410 mm.
Recto of letter has one sketch; verso has five
sketches.

ment. The mechanism for raising and lowering platforms above and below the stage anticipates the modern elevator stage.

### Jean-Baptiste Lavastre

Jean-Baptiste Lavastre was an apprentice in the atelier of Despléchin, and, after learning his craft, he collaborated with his master on many notable productions for the Paris Opéra, the Opéra Comique, and the Comédie Française, as well as numerous theatres of the boulevards. In 1870, during his association with Despléchan, he designed *Hamlet* for the Comédie Française.

In 1873, the scenery for the operas which they had designed together was destroyed by fire. Shortly afterward, Lavastre joined forces with the atelier of his brother Antoine and the scenic artist Carpezat (see page 179). Lavastre had become an expert *machiniste*—a master at devising fires and tempests, transformations and trick effects. He designed, with Carpezat, *L'Ode Triumphale* for the plush *grande salle* of the Palace of Industry of the Exposition Universale in 1889. This pretentious "spec-

tacular" showed off every facet of Lavastre's inventive skill. Two years later, the ballet *La Rêve* became a famous novelty at the Opéra, not because of the Japanese ballet, but because of Lavastre's invention of a forty-five-foot Japanese fan that magically opened and closed on changing scenes. Except for his mechanical forays into the realm of *féerie*, Lavastre belonged to the traditional, naturalistic school of scenic decor. His designs were coated with historical overtones. They were grandiose and theatrical and always elicited applause.

Germain Bapst recounts Lavastre's story of how he added his touch to the backdrop for *Hamlet*, Act I, Scene 2—Elsinore in the distance by night. He was unhappy with the finished effect of the scenic artists' carefully rendered drop. It did not light up; it lacked life. After reflection, Lavastre dipped a brush into a pot of white paint and boldly attacked the castle with his powerful line. Suddenly the scene grew in depth, and the castle seemed to detach itself under the moonlight. With those few brush strokes, Lavastre had created the emotional note essential, he believed, to capturing the imagination of the spectator.

*Illustrations 158 & 159.* This letter with thumbnail sketches was written by the designer Lavastre to the director Duflocq in Paris outlining his first ideas for their forthcoming production of *Hamlet* at the Comédie Française in 1870.

Their *Hamlet* was played in six full-stage sets with no mention of time out for change of scenes. The ground plans indicate how the scenery was arranged, the designer's concern for the director's problems, and his feeling for the mood and atmosphere of each scene. This document provides an insight into the designer's methods of working in the Parisian theatre under the vicissitudes of the Franco-Prussian War.

Lavastre's stenographic notes supplement his sketches.

Act I, Scene 1—Scene where the ghost appears—
The Terrace of a Castle—small scene—moonlight—snow—door black.

Act II, Scene 1—Courtyard of a Castle—
Effect of evening—sunset—houses colored—autumn trees.

Act II, Scene 2—Scene of the Comedians—
Great Hall of a Castle—architecture Romanesque, Rhenish in character—warm-polychrome—huge chandelier above—long hall beyond—practical wooden platform covered with painting for comedians—garden—curtain.

Act III—The Queen's Chamber—
Muted and sombre—tapestried walls—moonlight out-

side the window—interior effect of hushed lamplight—
the ghost appears near the door.

Act IV—Scene of Ophelia's Death—
Springtime landscape of a tender fresh green—effect of
mist—in the distance one sees the Castle of Elsinore—
Ophelia's body passes by on the stream—the water is
contrived with metallic cloth—her body passes above.

Act V—Burial of Ophelia—
The Graveyard—the sky is red on the horizon, broken
with black ominous clouds and black cyprus trees—the
grave is practical.

### Auguste-Alfred Rubé

Auguste-Alfred Rubé studied with Pierre-Luc-Charles
Cicéri, and later, working together in Cicéri's atelier, they
devised elaborate, naturalistic scenes for opera and ballet.
Rubé eventually combined with Chaperon and as associates they formed their own atelier. The accuracy of
Rubé's period scenic reconstructions could be com-
pared with the painstaking architectural restorations that
Viollet-le-Duc was carrying out on many of France's his-
toric monuments. Fortunately for the theatre, however,
Rubé never lost his romantic taste for the picturesque
which he had inherited from Cicéri. Thinly veiled romanticism always charged his *tableaux véritables* with atmospheric mood.

Chaperon's and Rubé's successful atelier provided the
scenes for the premières of Meyerbeer, Gounod, Massenet,
and Saint-Saëns. Those grandiose scenic conceptions, provided by the top Parisian scenic studios such as Chaperon
and Rubé, were instrumental in putting the "grand" in
grand opera during the second half of the nineteenth century in France, and France set the style of grand opera for
Europe.

It was apparent that French decor for the theatre had
come of age. In 1878, scene designers' original drawings
were considered worthy of hanging not just in the flies of
a Parisian theatre, but also on the walls of the Paris
Exposition Internationale in harmonious company with
the finest arts. Theatrical decor in "the grand manner"
had arrived and come into its own with both the blessing
of art critics and the acclaim of a new-found audience.

(160) Rubé, Auguste-Alfred, 1815–1899
France, Paris
East Indian Hippodrome, 1870–1880
Pencil, gray washes, and Chinese white on gray-green
paper, 418 x 582 mm.

(161) Rubé, Auguste-Alfred
Tudor Stairhall, 1883 (?)
Pencil and Chinese white on sepia paper, 310 x
443 mm.

*Illustration 160*. Rubé's design for this Indian arena was in all likelihood made for an equestrian act at the Cirque Olympique. This popular theatre of the Parisian bourgeoisie was the one truly national theatre of France. Under the canny direction of the great Adolphe Franconi, it was famous for the quality of its scenic spectacles. Ferdinand Laloue was *l'ordonnateur des spectacles*, the Hazard Short, the general factotum, who managed all the scenic marvels: *tableaux vivants*, stately parades, *spectacles féeriques*, and *gloires militaires*. The auditorium was circular and surrounded the arena. On one side, the proscenium and an adjustable forestage connected the great stage (ten wings deep) with the ring. Almost all of the notable scenic ateliers, such as Philastre and Cambon (1850–1880), Séchan and Despléchin (during the Second Empire), and Chaperon and Rubé (the end of the nineteenth century), provided the scenery for the extravaganzas of the Cirque Olympique.

This topical, good-natured design could only be found at the Cirque Olympique. The scene consisted of two leg-drops and a backdrop. Arthur Saxon, authority on the circus, observes that "the archway formed by those leg drops would make a splendid entrance for a hippodromatic procession" from the stage into the arena. Look-ing closely, one discovers that all the spectators' boxes in Rubé's hippodrome are occupied by horses joyfully applauding with their proud hoofs the equestrian act taking place before them, sharing with the Parisian audience in their boxes the marvels of the equine world.

*Illustration 161*. The opera *Henry VIII*, with music by Saint-Saëns, was presented in the Paris Opéra during the season of 1883. Rubé designed some of the scenes for this production, and this drawing may be one of his designs for that opera.

### Carpezat

Carpezat was first a pupil of the scenic artist Cambon, and later his collaborator in designing many productions for the Paris Opéra; in 1876, he succeeded Cambon as designer at the Opéra. During the next thirty years he was closely affiliated with the activities of Lavastre's huge scenic atelier. Lavastre insisted that "we must know everything. One day we are asked for a Gothic Cathedral, the next the baths of the sultans of the Alhambra, and the next day a sunset in the pampas of America." Carpezat shared in his associate's enthusiasm for historicity in theatrical design. Carpezat was recognized as a master of

(162) Carpezat, c. 1836–1912 (attributed)
France, Paris
Egyptian Throne Hall for *La Mort de Cléopâtre*,
c. 1880 (See also color plate 15)
Pencil, watercolor, and Chinese white, 317 x 415 mm.

architectural reconstruction and complete illusion. Lessing once wrote, "all that does not favor illusion destroys it." This might have been Carpezat's credo. His opinion also was shared by Moynet, the recognized authority on scenes and effects for the theatre. He contended that the achievement of illusion on the stage was the primary purpose of theatrical art.

Stage decoration in France during the latter half of the nineteenth century had come under the domination of a number of influential scenic artists who became either collaborators, associates, or successors. In practicing their craft, they carried on the established formulas and procedures of the earlier ateliers. But they became powerful leaders who, perhaps without realizing it, initiated the industrialization of the scenic artists' profession. The traditional old-time atelier became a business house. New theatres were appearing. Production activity was spreading all over Paris with new scenic studios and construction shops, costume houses and huge warehouses for the storage of properties and mechanical effects. With the growing pressures of expansion, something had gone out of the individual scenic artist such as Carpezat. He had lost himself in imitating former innovations, and in his expanding workshop, while satisfying the demand for popular illusionist techniques, he fell into the trap of scenic cliché and pictorial pastiche.

*Illustration 162.* Carpezat must have become quite an authority on Egyptian architecture, for he worked on four productions that required Egyptian locales.

Ifan Kyrle Fletcher believed this drawing was made by Carpezat for a scene in Isabey's opera *La Mort de Cléopâtre* presented in Paris about 1880. In this drawing, Carpezat renders the colors and details of the scene with care. The characters, however, he briefly indicates in gouache. This drawing shows Carpezat organizing the stage picture at the moment when the queen, seated on her throne, receives officials advancing toward her.

The Bibliothèque et Musée de l'Opéra in Paris possesses a drawing very similar to this design but without the characters. That drawing is known to be for *La Mort de Cléopâtre*.

### Max Brückner

Max Brückner and his brother Gotthold were trained in Coburg by their father, who was scene painter and theatre master of the Hoftheater of Coburg-Gotha. The busy Brückners worked together as a team of designer-technicians in Coburg. They also exercised their skills in Berlin and Dresden, and in Weimar were entrusted with the supervision of those demanding naturalistic ensemble productions planned and directed by George II, Duke of Meiningen.

Max was in his early twenties when the Brückners were summoned to Bayreuth to work on the settings for the first performance of Wagner's tetralogy, *Der Ring des Nibelungen*. This stupendous work inaugurated the Festspielhaus in 1876. Ludwig II's generosity and admiration for Wagner had finally made possible the dream theatre of Der Meister. In dedicating the Festspielhaus, Wagner said, "The ideal relation, dreamed by me, of theatre and public, I found in the theatre of ancient Athens, the gates of which were thrown open on none but special sacred occasions. . . . In the arrangement of the seats, you will find expressed a new relationship between you and the play you are about to witness, the music coming from a mysterious source will prepare you further for the unveiling of visions seeming to rise from an ideal world of dreams, having the reality of a noble art's most skillful illusion." Wagner's innovations in the design of his stage and auditorium provided a fresh concept for new theatre architecture in Europe.

Unfortunately, Wagner's scenic ideas were bounded by the naturalism of his time, while his music was far in advance of it. For the settings of the *Ring* he turned to Joseph Hoffmann, a Viennese painter—not a man of the theatre. It seems illogical that Wagner should have searched outside the theatre for an "historical painter" to inspire the scenic artists accustomed to working within the theatre. His reasons were set forth in a letter to Hoffmann in 1872: "It was most important that we should be able to lay before the cleverest or most experienced scenic painters, sketches by genuine artists, in order that the former may be inspired to an idealization of their work." In spite of Hoffmann's sincere cooperation and willingness to alter his sketches to conform with Wagner's requirements, dissension was inevitable between Hoffmann and his theatrical co-workers. Much against Wagner's wishes, Hoffmann decided to withdraw from participation in the *Ring* in order to maintain harmony. His task was transferred to Max Brückner. Brandt, the technician of the theatre at Darmstadt, was engaged to execute Brückner's designs.

The scenic traditions of the *Ring*, established in that first Bayreuth production, would persist on opera stages for several generations. Wagner's poetic scenes, from the depths of the Rhine, by way of forest, hut, and great hall, to the mountaintop overlooking Valhalla, were overburdened with a false realism totally unsuited to the supernatural beings who inhabited them. All was flapping solidarity and papier-mâché. Those settings, startling as they may have been in 1876, bore little relation to the inner content of the text or to the musical motifs of the *Ring*.

One day after World War II, Wagner's grandson Wieland, confronted with the bare facts of economy in pre-

serving Bayreuth, would of necessity turn the tables on the traditional Bayreuth scenic establishment. He evolved his spare neo-Bayreuth style of staging Wagnerian opera. With head spots he lighted static singers often lost amidst impressive environmental symbols or camouflaged beneath light patterns projected onto the darkened stage of the Festpielhaus. Wieland Wagner's revolutionary productions received enthusiastic acceptance. In the hands of lesser directors who freely borrowed or adapted the neo-Bayreuth method, the results were less successful.

Most of us are in accord that Brückner's traditional designs displayed little imagination. However, as a designer, he was consciously concerned with projecting the Wagnerian actor-singers on their stage and maintaining a harmony between performer and setting. He felt that the neutral tonality of contemporary scene design absorbed the actor. For his settings he adopted a fresh color palette. His scenes glowed with reds and browns and blues, because he believed that settings contrived with a rich

palette would contrast with the performers and give them added emphasis. And so, in his own fashion, Brückner aided and projected the performers.

*Illustration 163.* Wagner believed he was an innovator in the scenic art of his day. When *Tannhäuser* was produced in Dresden in 1852, he wrote, "Only through an accurate knowledge of the whole poetic subject, and after careful agreement as to the scheme of its portrayal with both *régisseur* and *kapelmeister*, can the scene painter and the machinist succeed in giving the stage its needful aspect. The scene painter will then see how infinitely important—indeed how completely indispensible—is his intelligent collaboration, and also that I assign to him a certainly not indecisive share in the success of the whole; a success which can be won only through a clear and immediate understanding of the most unusual situations."

Brückner's design follows the sketch and plan of Wagner's original *Tannhäuser* Szenarium of 1853. A great grotto of stalactites, adorned with surrealistic flowers, crystal, and coral, affords a fantastic meeting place for Venus and Tannhäuser. The scene, enlivened by a waterfall, leads into a cavern with a lake, blue as Capri's romantic grotto, in which the Naiads bathe.

Max Brückner made this design for the 1891 revival of *Tannhäuser* in Bayreuth.

(163) Brückner, Max, 1855–1912
Germany, Coburg (active in Berlin, Dresden, Weimar, and Bayreuth)
Venusberg Scene for Wagner's *Tannhäuser*, Act I, 1891
Oil on canvas, 404 x 455 mm.
Inscribed lower right corner: "Max Brückner"
Collection: Sakellaropoulos, Cantalis, Athens

# Modern

The first decade of the twentieth century was a shattering period of creative tension for the world of all the arts. Escape from the prisons of naturalism and realism occurred in all directions. Imitationalism and literalism succumbed to opposing, negative forces—nonrepresentational and nonobjective art. Paris was stirring with yeasty ferment, attracting young artists and writers, architects and musicians, from all over Europe and America.

*Les Fauves*, led by Matisse, declared their independence of nature and the traditional Western ways of representation. Only a year before, Picasso and Braque had arrived in Paris, and within three years Cubism was created. In dismissing nature they rearranged her shapes and colors in more revealing order. The German expressionists chose to distort nature as an expression of the artist's innermost self, "the Art of Inwardness." Léger, the high priest of the machine, subjected the orderly world of nature to the orderly abstractions of his new-found mechanistic world. In these same years Frank Lloyd Wright and Le Corbusier tore down the staid façades of Beaux-Arts eclecticism. Richard Strauss shocked the civilized ears of Western society with the turbulent abstractions of his monumental score for *Elektra*.

New cults of the dance appeared. Loïe Fuller was worshipped by the symbolists; Isadora Duncan charged the ancient classical dance forms with the electricity of her vibrant personality; and in 1908 Diaghilev brought his Ballets Russes from St. Petersburg to Paris. The company was a dazzling, disciplined group of young choreographers and dancers, musicians and artists.

And what of new movements in theatre? Two young visionaries, unknown to one another, appeared on the scene —Gordon Craig, the zealous reformer in London, and Adolphe Appia, the shy prophet in Geneva. Both were disenchanted with the theatre they grew up in, and set out to release the theatre from the tyrannous hold of tradition and realism. Both believed the theatre must be retooled, renovated, recharged. Each in his own fashion invented simplified, sculptural stages with abstract scenic forms, designed for the movement of performers and fluid light, which would become the modern theatre's fourth dimension. The ideals and vision of Appia and Craig influenced three generations of European and American directors and designers, actors and dancers who would formulate the changing directions of the modern stage—symbolism and impressionism, expressionism and constructivism, and the avant-garde groups of today who seek a form of theatre appropriate to the pattern of our changing society.

(164) Appia, Adolphe, 1862–1928
   Switzerland, Geneva (active in Paris, Hellerau, Milan,
   and Basel)
   Rock of the Valkyries (at the rise of the curtain) for
   Wagner's *Die Walküre*, Act II, 1892

Black crayon with gray and white chalk on bluish
paper, 314 x 481 mm.
Inscribed in crayon at lower right: "Appia—1892"
Collection: Fondation Edmond Appia

### Adolphe Appia

Adolphe Appia as a youth was absorbed in the theatre, yet he never actually attended the theatre until he was nineteen. His father was a puritanical doctor in Geneva and a founding father of the Red Cross, and he saw no place in the theatre for his frustrated son. When it was agreed that young Appia might embark on a musical career, Adolphe was relieved, for he knew instinctively that opera could become an entree to a theatrical career.

In 1881, with music in his heart, Appia left Geneva. He studied with Liszt in Weimar and continued his studies in Leipzig and Dresden, Paris and Vienna. He was always on the move attending concerts and operas. In Bayreuth, Appia was initiated into the Wagnerian "mysteries" with *Parsifal*, and overnight he became an ardent disciple of the master. He steeped himself in the music of Wagner's word-tone dramas and assimilated Wagner's theories of the relation of music, drama, and poetry in *Opera and Drama* and also of *Gesamtkunstwerk* in *The Art Work of the Future*. Appia was not, however, impressed with Wagner's romantic, realistic scenery that cluttered the stage of the Festspielhaus; indeed, he detested it and felt he must do something about it.

He returned to Switzerland in 1890 and established his studio in a secluded town overlooking Lake Geneva and the Alps. Henceforth, studying and creating would go hand in hand. He set himself the "imperative task" of preparing detailed scenarios for the staging of the *Ring* and *Parsifal* and composed a series of revolutionary designs for these operas. In 1895 he completed a booklet, *La Mise en Scène du Drame Wagnerien*, which he published in Paris with the hope that it would call attention to the searching questions raised by his investigations. Full of hope, Appia returned to Bayreuth. The composer's widow, Cosima, received Appia at Villa Wahnfried, but she firmly rejected his highly original ideas and designs, comparing the latter to empty polar ice fields. Four years later, in 1899, his manifesto of the modern movement, *Die Musik und die Inscenierung*, was published in Munich.

When in 1906 he met Émile Jaques-Dalcroze in Geneva, Appia was eager to experiment in the theatre with Dalcroze's "rhythmic gymnastics." He designed a series of liberating *espaces rythmiques* for Dalcroze to use with his pupils, and in 1913 designed the unique theatre for Dalcroze's new school at Hellerau near Dresden. With this intimate rectangular hall of luminous muslin walls and ceiling, he sought to release the theatre from the stranglehold of the proscenium arch, behind which he believed everything was fictitious and tentative. The freedoms of the three-dimensional space stage would restore the classical balance between spectators and performers.

Claudel's *Tidings Brought to Mary* and Gluck's *Orpheus and Eurydice* were experiments which attracted an international audience to Hellerau, including the designers Alfred Roller, Robert Edmond Jones and Gordon Craig, Copeau and Rouché from Paris, Granville Barker, Max Reinhardt, and Diaghilev. Exciting plans for the future were projected with Dalcroze and Appia, but the year was 1913 and World War I shattered all hopes for their realization.

In 1923, Arturo Toscanini and Appia collaborated on a notable production of *Tristan und Isolde* at La Scala. The simplistic approach of Appia in modernizing Wagnerian staging received scant applause from the traditional Milanesi; nevertheless, Toscanini insisted on keeping their production in the repertoire.

The next year, the Stadttheater of Basel summoned Appia to create a new production of the *Ring*. He was assured of far greater rapport than he had received at La Scala. *Das Rheingold* and *Die Walküre* opened with a storm of opposition to Appia's stylized scenic reforms from the city's die-hard Wagner Verein, and production plans for *Siegfried* and *Die Götterdämmerung* were canceled. Appia's *Ring* became a *cause célèbre* in Basel's cultural establishment.

Appia was absorbed with the spatial possibilities of the stage. He once admonished a student to "design with your legs, not with your eyes." By doing so, the designer becomes the performer's alter ego and harmoniously constructs out of steps, ramps, and levels, the sculptured formation of the performer's rhythmic stage. "Stairs," wrote Appia, "by their straight lines and breaks maintain the necessary contrast between the curves of the body and the sinuous lines of its evolution. Their practical use offering at the same time distinct facilities of expression."

(165) Appia, Adolphe
Rock of the Valkyries (engulfed in clouds after Wotan's arrival) for Wagner's *Die Walküre*, Act III, 1896

Black crayon with gray and white chalk on bluish paper, 406 x 500 mm.
Inscribed in crayon at lower right: "Appia—1896"
Collection: Fondation Edmond Appia

Appia sought to establish a fusion of the actor and the setting, with the actor a part of the scene but prominent. "In *Siegfried* not a forest is wanted but the feeling of a man walking through a forest." With this statement, Appia introduced psychology into the designer's world. Appia would have the audience see the forest not through the eyes of Wagner, but through the eyes of the young hero Siegfried. This point of view was a totally new concept and a revolutionary contribution to modern stage design.

Appia's contemporaries employed light in the theatre to make their scenes as real as nature, but Appia thought of light as a fifth sense in the theatre. His sketches are suffused with a luminous energy which gas and Edison's new incandescent lamp could only approximate on the stage. He anticipated the imaginative projection of light in space, knowing that mobile light and a plastic stage are essential to display fully the character and movements of the actor.

Appia was ever at heart a classicist, with the humanistic point of view that man on his stage is the measure of all things. His theories have logic and his designs have inner organization. Like Prometheus, he "taught us how to know the waking vision from the idle dream." His writ-

ings regenerate themselves for each generation, and his prophetic designs will ever remain a point of departure for changing directions in the theatre of tomorrow.

*Illustrations 164 and 165.* These are two of seven studies which Adolphe Appia made for the Rock of the Valkyries and included in *Die Musik und die Inscenierung* (1899) to illustrate his solution for the design of this difficult setting. The 1896 drawing is also reproduced in *L'Oeuvre d'art Vivant* (1921). This complex setting is used four times in the Ring—*Die Walküre, Siegfried,* and twice in *Die Götterdämmerung.* Appia organized all of Wagner's demanding requirements into this dynamic composition: a stormy mountaintop to be encircled with fire, a great pine, and a grotto.

Appia's design solution for this complicated setting remained the prototype accepted by designers for two generations.

*Illustration 166.* Appia describes the mountain in the foreground as a sculptured construction with two ominous entrances—the one on the right leading down to the dark depths of Alberich's realm; the other leading down to Erda's grotto. Beyond, ominously looms Valhalla, built

Mountain Overlooking Valhalla for Wagner's
*Das Rheingold*, 1892
Black crayon with black and white chalk on buff
paper, 393 x 531 mm.
Inscribed in crayon at lower right: "Appia—1892"
Collection: Fondation Edmond Appia

by the Giants overnight on Wotan's order as the mighty fortress of the gods. At the left, Froh is indicated. On the rocky platform to the right, Donner disperses his storm clouds and reveals Froh's rainbow bridge, briefly outlined, over which the gods will ascend to Valhalla.

On the paper of this drawing, Appia pricked the mass of Valhalla with a needle so that he could redraw variations of the foreground in subsequent studies and retain the form of Valhalla, which presumably satisfied him. Appia first drew his sketches in pencil. They were "spontaneous to begin with," he stated, "and directly and somehow chronologically derived from the score, my vision accidentally implied the theories which I discovered only later on." He worked on his sketches as a craftsman, changing and altering as he progressed. The luminosity and the repose of his drawings he achieved by smudging, rubbing, and erasing until very little of the original drawing remained. "I design with my eraser," he explained. Appia thought in terms of neutrality, never color.

The major collection of Appia's drawings is in the Schweizerische Landesbibliothek in Bern. A few drawings are found in the Victoria and Albert Museum. The Beineke Library at Yale University has an important collection of Appia material. A portfolio of fifty-six splendid reproductions of Appia's drawings was issued as a memorial to Adolphe Appia in 1929.

### Edward Gordon Craig

Edward Gordon Craig grew up in Henry Irving's Lyceum Theatre in London. He had little schooling and no training and always claimed that "my real school and my real master" was Irving. For eight years he acted in the Lyceum company, but in 1897 Craig became disenchanted with the star system, the authority of the actor-manager, the photographic look for the productions, and the commercialism of the London theatre, so he struck off on his own. He began to draw and sketch for the theatre, though he never forgot that "acting is the essence of the whole business of Theatre." He discovered that to draw and to act were to see a piece in the theatre as a whole. All his life, Craig identified himself with Hamlet. He designed projects for *Hamlet* with a new poetic style and played Hamlet in several productions. His production of *Hamlet* with Stanislavski's Moscow Art Theatre was a landmark in the theatre. He cut the woodblocks and designed an edition of *Hamlet* for Count Kessler which is one of the most beautiful illustrated books of the twentieth century.

In three years (1900–1903) Craig produced and designed six productions in London, which together with the four more he designed later in his career represent the sum total of his experience in the theatre. The early productions bore the mark of Craig's unique talent. His innovations in the use of suggestive scenery replaced the current theatrical "realism," and his scenic effects were both imaginative and practical. There was stylization in his symbolic use of light, and beauty in his unification of sound, movement, light, and color. Here was the revelation of a new and distinct art in which everything was larger than life.

Craig's instinct told him that in England he had reached a dead end. The operas and plays he had designed were artistic successes and commercial failures. There was little understanding of Craig's ideas on the part of the English managers.

Count Harry Kessler, a cultivated German amateur in the arts, was enthusiastic about Craig's designs and invited him to Weimar to produce a play at the Hoftheater. The project never came off, but Kessler opened many doors for Craig in Berlin. He met poets and musicians and the avant-garde artists of the *Jugend Stil*. He designed the ill-fated *Venice Preserved* for Otto Brahm, and Max Reinhardt was eager to have Craig work with him in his Deutsches Theater.

Craig found intimate and understanding friendship with Isadora Duncan, who was then living in Berlin at the height of her success. In 1905, she recorded in her notes: "I have just finished reading a book even now published entitled *The Art of the Theatre* by Ed. G. Craig. This book seems to me to contain the bomb for an immense explosion of all things which exist as we know them in the theatre. An upheaval so general and deadly at first it represents to our mind's eyes the entire theatres of the world suddenly heaved sky high into the air in one wild chaotic bang. . . . Step up Mr. Edward Gordon Craig. Step up now and show us—What's To Happen Next. What has the theatre become."

With this small bible written in a few weeks, Craig, the Reformer, set out to free the theatre from the tyrannous hold of literature. The theatre must be retooled, renovated, recharged. Only then would the true theatre be restored. The unifying spirit of the theatre must be the artist, the director, who should be capable of working in all areas of the theatre. Thus the true theatre would be restored and "stand self-reliant as a creative art, and no longer as an interpretive craft."

Craig awoke overnight to find himself the spokesman of a new movement in the theatre. Craig's activities during 1905–1910 revealed what was to happen next—where the theatre was going. These five years were probably the most fertile of Craig's career.

Gordon Craig had succeeded in breaking through the

(167)  Craig, Edward Gordon, 1872–1966
England, London (active in Berlin, Florence, Moscow,
and Copenhagen)
Throne Hall for Shaw's *Caesar and Cleopatra*, Act I,
Scene 3, 1906 (See also color plate 16)
Colored chalks on tan board, 684 x 494 mm.

old barriers of naturalism. He had introduced a new vision of theatre to the continent. In his writings, through his magazine *The Mask*, with his drawings and prints, with his screens for Yeats at the Abbey Theatre, and with his work for Stanislavski in the Moscow Art Theatre, Craig had become the bright hope of the century's new generation in the theatre.

As Craig was dreaming of the ideal actor and the *Uber-Marionette*, he was also exploring the possibilities of the ideal place where theatre could happen. For several of his London productions, he had remodeled halls to enhance the immediacy of stage and auditorium. In Florence, he introduced an intimate open-air theatre in his Arena Goldoni. In Paris, he was briefly involved in a new theatre for music and dance for Isadora Duncan. For Bach's *Saint Matthew Passion* he envisioned a theatre structure with nave, crypt, and chancel united by flowing steps. He invented a Shakespearean stage with a variable proscenium and movable portals.

He became more concerned with a theatre in which abstract movement of scene could harmonize with the controlled movement of the actor or dancer. His experiments resulted in his treatise *Motion* and two portfolios of etchings which he published in Florence in 1908. The etchings were studies for moods of movement. He envisioned a "Space Stage" equipped with elevators, steps, and platforms rising and falling, and utilizing flexible screens to create perpendicular abstract forms—mobile and capable of infinite variety—"A Thousand Scenes in One" requiring the coordination of actor, scene, light, color, and movement. He called these scenes "architectonic" as opposed to "pictorial." Craig delighted in the scenery of hillsides of vineyards and olive groves, in cloud shadows moving over mountains. But on his stage there was no room for the scenery of Nature, only the ideas of Nature.

Craig had an artist's and scholar's enthusiasm for architecture. The books of Serlio, especially his treatise on theatre perspective, were the key volumes in his library, as were the works of Palladio, Vignola, and Pozzo. But his own designs were not shaped by these canons of architecture. They were free of cornice, finial, and period detail. They recall the blank, textured walls and abstract shapes of Indian pueblos, pierced with openings for doors and windows. Walking along the parapets or through the narrow stepped streets of medieval *Tourettes-sur-Loup* in southern France, Craig, carrying Irving's cane, would point enthusiastically to the plain, up-rearing walls of sun-washed buildings, unadorned like his mobile screens in changing light. "*That* is real scenic architecture," he would explain. "There is *Julius Caesar* and over there is an idea for *Macbeth*."

Through his long and active life, Craig could never conform. He endured loneliness and frustration. He thrived on it. While he was thwarted at every turn, his humor never failed him—he was witty, sly, and sardonic. He knew everyone in the theatre of his time, but he had few close friends. He feared that other designers would convert his ideas into their own successes, as indeed they often did. Yet these men were his ardent admirers and disciples—there are now three generations of them and still multiplying.

Craig was an inveterate letter writer, and with his inimitable hand he seemed to sketch as he wrote. It was with his hands that he fulfilled himself in so many ways—not so much through his ten ephemeral productions but through his prodigious work on paper which he dispatched from his embattled tower—his sketches, his hundreds of wood engravings and etchings, his letters and essays, *The Mask*, and his books on the theatre, whose ideals and vision brought about the evolution of theatrical art in the twentieth century.

There are large collections of Craig's drawings in the Victoria and Albert Museum, the Biblioteque Nationale, and the Austrian National Library.

The Oenslager Collection contains twenty-two drawings of Gordon Craig for settings and costumes.

*Illustration 167.* The year after Craig came to Berlin, Max Reinhardt inaugurated his repertory season in the Deutsches Theater. Always on the lookout for new talent, he approached Craig to design *The Tempest*, *Macbeth*, and Shaw's *Caesar and Cleopatra*. Craig was put off by the thought of Reinhardt borrowing his schemes, taking over his ideas, and changing his plans.

Craig included this drawing and two others for *Caesar and Cleopatra* as illustrations in *Towards a New Theatre* (1913). These indulgent notes about his drawings are typically Craig:

Although I really designed this and the following two scenes for myself, it may be more exactly said that I designed them for Professor Reinhardt. How many scenes I have not designed both for myself and Professor Reinhardt it would be difficult to say, but in 1905, he asked me for the fifth or sixth time to produce him a play, and of course, the moment anybody asks one to produce a play one gets excited. . . . I set to work, and in a couple of days had put down in colour eight or ten projects for the production.

If you have read the play, you will know that this is the scene which culminates in Caesar and Cleopatra being seated side by side on the throne, and she turns to him and asks him to point out to her where is Caesar. I put the bars all round to keep out the mob and the soldiers, so that we have Caesar and Cleopatra quite alone in the scene. And yet the

actors say I never think of the leading actor and actress. They would be more exact to say that I sometimes let my eyes wander from the center of the stage. . . .

I am very sorry I have not talked about this design, but you see the moment I think of the scene it makes me think of the actor.

*Illustration 168.* Craig made this drawing in 1904 and included it in his major work, *On the Art of the Theatre* (1911). Craig describes his feeling for the mood of the scene: "This design depends much on its color to enforce the exact feeling I wish to convey. So think of it as bathed in a warm yellow light—the only other color being the touches of green in the dresses of the Italian gentlemen who are awaiting the arrival of their guests. The large seat is silver white—upon this the two lovers are soon to find themselves seated side by side."

*Illustration 169.* Sir Herbert Beerbohm Tree had great admiration for Craig's mother, Ellen Terry, and for his father, Edward William Godwin, who had designed a number of productions for him. In 1908, Beerbohm Tree considerately sought out Craig to design *Macbeth*, and Craig proceeded to make sketches and models for his production. Craig was thirty-six and Tree was fifty-five. Edward Craig, in his book on his father, *Gordon Craig*, described the denouement of this project: "The scene painter Joseph Harker was called in, and he, seeing a threat to the future of scene painting in Craig's three-dimensional scenes 'painted with light,' vigorously attacked them as being unpractical in every way. The models were eventually confined to his care and some of them got smashed. This later led to a tragic misunderstanding between Craig and Tree."

The contract was torn up but not Craig's sketches. They

(168) Craig, Edward Gordon
Hall in Capulet's House for Shakespeare's *Romeo and Juliet*, Act I, Scene 5, 1904
Pen and gray wash on sepia ground, 203 x 228 mm.
Inscribed lower left corner: "EGC—1904"
On verso: An unfinished sketch by Craig.

(169) Craig, Edward Gordon
Castle Hall for Shakespeare's *Macbeth*, Act II, 1908
Black crayon, white and brown chalk on gray paper,
238 x 312 mm.

Inscribed lower left corner: "EGC—1908"
Inscribed in pencil along lower margin: "Macbeth's
Castle"
Collection: Gordon Craig

would become the rallying point for the battle between the old guard and the avant-garde of the English theatre. This drawing is one of Craig's designs intended for that production of *Macbeth*.

### M. A. Schiskov

For centuries, Russian theatre and music were retarded by czarist absolutism and the hostility of the church. Until the nineteenth century, Russian culture was traditionally derived from the cultivated taste of foreign countries to the west, but the defeat of Napoleon created a new climate. Russian theatre asserted itself with the genius of Pushkin, Tolstoi, Gogol, and Ostrovski, and opera and ballet with Tchaikovsky, Musorgski, and Borodin. Even though they worked under imperial surveillance, they succeeded magnificently in incorporating into theatre, opera, and ballet the historical, political, and social themes close to the heart of Russia and her storehouse of legends and folklore. With this change of heart, the stages of Saint Petersburg and Moscow no longer needed to house the customary sophisticated foreign scenes. Those traditional architectural settings which Giuseppe Valeriani and Pietro Gonzaga had introduced into the Russian court theatres became a lost art in the nineteenth century. In their place were substituted realistic, documentary Russian scenes of the czarist court, or, as in Schiskov's scene, the square of a provincial town. This in its visual way was aggressive nationalism, and in its blind way was revolutionary.

*Illustration 170.* This design was probably made for the première of Tchaikovsky's *Oprichnik* in Saint Petersburg in 1874. Perspective lines in pencil, probably by M. A. Schiskov himself, were drawn over his complicated ink drawing as simple guide lines for the scene painters. All of the unorganized details of this realistic Russian town add up to a distracting background with which the cast had to compete for the attention of the audience.

### Konstantin Korovine

Konstantin Korovine became a painter in the Moscow School of Painting, Sculpture, and Architecture in 1882. He was a brilliant colorist, and his landscapes reflect the strong influence of the French impressionists. Korovine's work also indicated a flair for the theatrical. At twenty-three he became exposed to Savva Mamontov's new ideas for the theatre and discovered his own special aptitude and talent for designing settings and costumes. Mamontov was a Muscovite Mycaenas, a nationalist and social idealist, who had made his fortune in railroads. He was an enthusiastic patron of the theatre arts, and one of his dreams, which only a generous tycoon could realize, was to regenerate Russian opera. He believed that the realistic, outworn scenic conventions of the Bolshoi Opera needed to be changed, and the production of opera should become an integrated artistic enterprise in which director and designer could establish with performers (such as Chaliapin, whom Mamontov had discovered) a unified style and atmosphere for each opera. In 1885, Mamontov built his private opera house in Moscow and launched his opera program. He turned his stage over to the younger directors and the recognized easel painters of the day. Among the artists were Vasnetzov, painter of Russian history; Vroubel, a leading modernist; Golovine; and Korovine the impressionist. Within a few years, Mamontov had brought about the renaissance of Russian opera through the combined talents of the *régisseur* and painter.

Korovine went on to become artistic director of both the Bolshoi and the Maryinski theatres, and naturally designed many productions of opera and ballet in both. Later, he also designed many plays for Moscow's progressive Mali Theatre. Diaghilev admired Korovine's impressionistic brushwork and commissioned him to design decor and costumes for his first sensational season in

(170)  Schiskov, M. A., 1831–1897
Russia, Saint Petersburg
Village Square for Tchaikovsky's *Oprichnik* (The Guardsman), 1874
Pencil and pen on tan paper, 220 x 380 mm.
Inscribed lower left corner: "Schiskov"; title cut from upper left corner and pasted on verso.

Страница Красавицы "Панорама"

Konstantin Korovine 1915.

(171) Korovine, Konstantin, 1861–1939
Russia, Moscow (active also in Saint Petersburg and Paris)
"Panorama" for Tchaikovsky's *La Belle au Bois Dormant*, 1915 (See also color plate 17)

Gouache, watercolor, and crayon on heavy cardboard, 362 x 440 mm.
Inscribed (in Cyrillic) upper right corner: "Sleeping Princess 'Panorama' "; lower left corner: "Konstantin Korovine—1915."

Paris. At the height of his career, in Paris in 1909, little did Korovine dream that in fourteen years, with the Communists established in power, he should emigrate forever from Russia and find a new life as a painter in the French capital. Save for half a dozen design commissions for several expatriate Russian ballet groups, the great days of Korovine's impressionist triumphs in the Russian theatre had passed. The memories of seventeen plays, thirty-seven ballets, and eighty operas are nevertheless impressive reminders of a distinguished career.

*Illustration 171.* Konstantin Korovine was a master designer of scenes requiring atmospheric stage effects and uncluttered suggestion like this misty, unfolding *"panorama du Bois Dormant"* before which the prince embarks on his journey to the enchanted castle. Korovine's swift and deft brush strokes wove his impressionist observations into tapestried scenes of charming refinement and subtle imagination.

### Alexandre Benois

The Benois family was for many years associated with the theatre. Alexandre Benois's great-grandfather had been the director of La Fenice in Venice, and his grandfather had been the architect of Moscow's beautiful Bolshoi theatre. His family was entrenched in the intellectual circle of Saint Petersburg society, and Alexandre himself was interested in all spheres of knowledge and art. He was a connoisseur of Russian culture from Scythian gold to the explosion of modern art in the twentieth century. He was also an art historian and later became the Director of the Hermitage museum. During the Revolution, he helped safeguard the priceless treasures of Russian art. First and foremost, however, was Benois the artist, who devoted his imagination and talent to book illustration, the decorative arts, and design in the theatre.

Benois was a leading spirit in a group of gifted young artists who attended the same private school, Mai's Academy in Saint Petersburg. Among them were Bakst, Bilibine, Filosofov, Roerich, Somov, Golovine, and Korovine. Serge Diaghilev was not one of these artists, but he was a born impresario, a critic, and an aesthete, and he was enthusiastic about projecting their art. In 1898, in collaboration with Benois, he founded and edited an art review, *Mir Isskustva* (The World of Art). Their magazine would restore the neglected arts of Russia's cultural heritage and at the same time encourage the contemporary arts. Benois thought that "The whole art of our time lacks direction—it is uncoordinated, broken up into separate personalities." Benois and his circle of artists were contributors to the magazine and formed the World of Art group. *Mir Isskustva* served as a catalyst in coordinating this group and gave it a sense of purpose. While they were an avant-garde group of artists, they had no sympathy with the rising revolutionary currents that would sweep

away their world in 1917. "None of us was in the least democratic," Benois remembered. "We all felt, quite consciously, an absolute indifference to politics and every shade of it." Between 1897 and 1906, Diaghilev, with his canny perception of the art world, organized a series of exhibitions of these Russian artists together with Western European artists. In Paris, he advanced his front with several seasons of carefully coordinated Russian concerts and operas. *Boris Godunov* with Chaliapin and Golivine's decor had an overwhelming reception at the Paris Opéra in 1908.

For several years, Diaghilev as impresario and Benois as art director formulated their innovative plans for a cohesive ballet company with private financial guarantees and independent of the czarist theatre. They would restore the eighteenth-century tradition of putting the

(172) Benois, Alexandre, 1870–1960
Russia, Saint Petersburg (active also in Moscow, Paris, London, Milan, Vienna, Copenhagen, New York, and Buenos Aires)
Argan's House for Molière's *Le Malade Imaginaire*, Act I, 1911

Pencil, watercolor, and gouache on cardboard, 424 x 664 mm.
Inscribed (in Cyrillic) lower right corner: "A. Benois—1911"

(173) Benois, Alexandre
"The Apparition of the Grail" for S. Miguel's *Fée de Sagesse*, 1949 (See also color plate 18)
Pencil, pen, watercolor, and gouache on cardboard, 494 x 647 mm.

Inscribed lower margin: "Alexandre Benois" with the dedication in Cyrillic: "In memory of good friendship from Benois to Mr. Boris Romanoff"
Collection: Romanoff

painter to work in the theatre. Russian painters of the World of Art group found release in adapting their own ideas and painterly style to the design of scenery and costumes for opera and ballet. Diaghilev, "the man with an eye," would himself designate the artist, composer, and choreographer to work as a collaborative team for the creation of each new ballet.

In 1909, Diaghilev brought his Ballets Russes from Saint Petersburg to Paris on its initial tour. The company was a dazzling, disciplined group of young choreographers, artists, and dancers—Pavlova, Karsavina, Nijinski, Bolm, and Fokine—in works of Rimsky-Korsakov, Musorgski, and Borodin, with breathtaking productions designed by Bakst, Benois, Golovine, and Roerich. Diaghilev and Benois had set out to do something in the theatre that had not been done before, and they succeeded brilliantly. Every evening their Russian miracle astounded the cultivated eyes of Western Europe. The Diaghilev Ballet was the first "synthetic" movement in the realm of modern European art. This concept in which all of the arts played a part became the fashion in the years before

World War I. Sharing in this common impulse were Stanislavski, Reinhardt, Appia, and Craig. Many of the theatrical designs of Appia and Craig were conceived for dance and movement, and they should have appealed to Diaghilev's eye, but apparently the vision of these artists extended beyond the spectrum of the Russian's temperament, for he never used their work.

From 1917 onwards, Diaghilev forsook most of the Russians of the World of Art group and commissioned modern French, Spanish, and Italian artists to design his ballets. Only a few of the early Russian stage designers remained in Russia. Most found careers in various capitals of the continent and in America, where unfortunately they were persuaded to repeat frequently their original Russian successes.

After 1927, Benois's position in the Hermitage was abrogated. He emigrated to Paris, never to return to Russia, and thereafter devoted himself principally to the theatre. He designed many ballets for Ida Rubinstein at the Paris Opéra and for the Ballets Russes de Monte Carlo. During his later years, Benois became a peripatetic international designer, highly honored and much sought after for opera and ballet. Through his eighties he migrated from Paris to La Scala, the Vienna Opera, the Royal Copenhagen Opera, and Covent Garden. Wherever he went, Benois the designer always left in his wake a legacy—processions of beautiful costumes and stages full of his scenic wonderment.

*Illustration 172.* Benois made this carefully prepared drawing for Stanislavski's production of *Le Malade Imaginaire* in the Moscow Art Theatre. He based the character sketch of Argan at the table on Molière's own description of his costume. Another smaller design for this same scene (which was the scene actually used) is in the Museum of the Moscow Art Theatre.

*Illustration 173.* Benois often made several drawings for the same design. A preliminary drawing (identical size) was illustrated in Sotheby's Catalogue (#70), *Diaghilev's Ballet Material*, July 18, 1968. Benois completed this finished drawing when he was nearly seventy-nine, adding the throne and side entrances, vaults, and draperies which result in a more cohesive design.

### *Léon Bakst*

Who has not been enchanted by the work of Léon Bakst? One of Russia's most celebrated artists, he was a meticulous draftsman and painter who could define with clarity the imaginative realm of his unique art.

After graduating from the Academy of Arts in Saint Petersburg, Bakst went to Paris to study but returned in

(174) Bakst, Léon, 1866–1924
Russia, Saint Petersburg (active also in Paris and London)
Prologue for *Les Orientales*, 1910 (See also color plate 22)
Watercolor, 330 x 440 mm.
Inscribed lower left corner: "Bakst"

1900 to devote himself to portraiture, book illustration, and especially to designing decor and costumes. He worked first for Prince Wolkonsky in the Hermitage theatre (the imperial family's private theatre) and later for the great imperial theatres of which the prince was director.

Bakst had always adored the theatre. He became a prominent member of the World of Art group that met around the samovar in Diaghilev's elegant apartment, and he found great stimulation as well as headaches in collaborating with Diaghilev on many schemes. 1909 was a fateful year for both Diaghilev and Bakst. Diaghilev declared his independence from the czarist theatre and had his first smashing success with his Ballets Russes in Paris. Bakst, in spite of all of his influence at court, was exiled from Saint Petersburg as a Jew without a resident permit. He re-established himself in an old studio at 110 Boulevard Malesherbes in Paris, where he continued his career in the theatre designing for Diaghilev and Ida Rubinstein. Overnight, Bakst became the fashion in Paris. His exotic oriental color and opulent imagery exerted great influence on interior decoration, illustration, and fashion for a generation.

Because Bakst was trained as a painter, he thought of his stage scenes as paintings in which he had not yet painted in the performers. As a painter, Bakst knew how to release color in a stage scene to visualize the sound of music and also how to employ color symbolically in order to convey to the audience specific impressions and emotions. He explained, "I have often noticed that in each color of the prism there exists a gradation which sometimes expresses frankness and chastity, sometimes sensuality and even bestiality, sometimes pride, sometimes despair. This can be felt and given over to the public by the effect one makes of the various shadings. This is what I tried to do in *Scheherazade*. Against a lugubrious green, I put a blue full of despair, paradoxical as it may seem."

Bakst's impeccable draftsmanship is ever apparent, whether in a brief sketch of Delphi or in his nude studies and line portraits of poets, artists, and dancers. The exquisite line and the voluptuous curvilinear forms of his finest costume designs assuredly admit him to membership in that exclusive master company of great draftsmen. With his facility for drawing, Bakst understood the peculiar problems created by moving figures on the stage. The dancers were never dwarfed by his settings. In costume and scene he combined his dramatic sense of line and mass with his flexible color palette to establish an optical unity of production, regardless of the period and subject of his decor.

André Levinson, critic and friend of Bakst, believed that Bakst inhabited four worlds or spheres of influence: archaic tragic Greece and the bucolic Greece of Pan; the mysterious East where Russia, Persia, and Arabia meet; and the Vienna of Biedermeier, and Balzac's Paris; included also might be the rococo court of Saint Petersburg. Like visual motifs, these sources of inspiration, of emotion and erudition, recur to form his sophisticated world of artistic expression.

The ephemeral sketches of Bakst alone survive to recall the excitement of evenings long vanished in the theatre. Collections of his drawings have been dispersed; and they are avidly sought by balletomanes in Russia, France, England, and America. And well they might be, for his stage designs represent the glorious sunset of the ancient tradition of scene painting. Bakst had an innate sense and love of theatre. He, probably more than any of his Russian fellow artists who found release in the theatre, was the scene painter's painter. His scenes magically lifted ballet design from the groundswell of diverting entertainment to a stylish theatrical art.

*Illustration 174.* This drawing by Bakst for the Prologue of *Les Orientales* was unrealized, probably because its style did not harmonize with Korovine's decor for this dance suite which Diaghilev presented during his 1910 season at the Paris Opéra. The bold colors show Bakst's predilection for exotic painted fabrics and extravagant curtains arranged in impossible folds. In dramatic contrast these overscale curtains frame an architectural court reduced in scale and keyed in neutral tones. Bakst may have intended these curtains to frame an inner drop; or the complete design could serve as a show curtain, a pictorial device used by Diaghilev's designers to establish the mood of the ballet and also to serve as a unifying visual transition between the ballet's changing scenes.

This design is reproduced in André Levinson's *Bakst* (1924) and in Camilla Gray's *The Russian Experiment in Art* (1970).

*Illustration 175.* This spontaneous drawing in grisaille is Bakst's preparatory study for a color sketch and appears as plate 36 in a sumptuous fête book, *La Belle au Bois Dormant,* with a preface by André Levinson and fifty-four color plates, published in 1922. The ballet was presented by Diaghilev in 1921 at the Alhambra Theatre in London. Bakst had performed the herculean task of designing and supervising the execution of six scenes and three hundred costumes in six weeks. The production was a rapturous success and a financial catastrophe. Diaghilev lost his shirt, and Oswald Stoll, the London manager, took over Bakst's scenery and costumes, which severed the old friendship between Bakst and Diaghilev. Never again would they collaborate. This open palatial hall of lofty arches borne on twisted columns has the soaring lines, upward thrust, and aerial enchantment that had made the

later Bibienas supreme in theatrical decor. The entire scene was a light golden monochrome beneath a cerulean sky with cumulus clouds. Levinson called this design "one of Bakst's most notable successes as theatrical architecture."

In 1968, Sotheby & Co. of London sold at auction the original backdrop, legs, and borders of this regal setting. The scenery was tarnished and tired, but it revealed all the old scenic craftsmanship which O. Allegri, Bakst's favorite scene painter, had once lavished on it.

### Mstislav Doboujinsky

Mstislav Doboujinsky grew up in the small town of Nizhny Novgorod, and memories of this town with its wealth of Russian folk art and architecture would recur frequently in his theatre designs. He studied in Munich and later in Saint Petersburg where he allied himself with Benois's World of Art group. Stanislavski felt that the artists of the World of Art group best suited the special needs of his theatre, which accounts in part for his admiration of Doboujinsky as a genuine artist of the theatre.

In Saint Petersburg, Doboujinsky found many assignments in the theatre. In 1911, Diaghilev commissioned him to design decor and costumes for his ballets. He participated in early experimental productions with Meierhold, Komisarjevski, and Granovsky, and their avant-garde dramatic groups. During those pre-revolutionary years, Doboujinsky was an active co-worker with these young directors who, without realizing it, were already at work forging their formulas for what would be the theatre of the new proletariat. In Moscow, those men later became powerful leaders of the theatre of the Bolshevik Revolution, and for a time Doboujinsky worked closely with them.

After the Revolution of 1917, the visual and performing arts became essential instruments of the propaganda campaign, for Lenin had proclaimed that "Art must belong to the people." Overnight, alert artists and bourgeois intellectuals shifted to the left and became adherents of the Bolshevik regime. Meierhold, the former progressive stage director of the Imperial Theatre in Saint Petersburg, became the director of theatre under the experienced leadership of Lunacharsky, First Commissar of Education. Meierhold charted the complex organization of the proletariat theatre of the Revolution. Overnight, "Playwrights, designers, directors and actors found their profession reoriented," observed John Mason Brown. "Everything they had remembered in the practice of their own art they were asked to forget. They were speaking to a new audience in a world where everyone was of one class." Men and women with a talent for the theatre, discovered in factories and collectives from the Ukraine to the steppes of Asia, were selected for training in Theatre Tecnicums of the Central Theatre Combinate.

Many theatres were stripped of their decoration. Auditorium and stage became a single theatrical structure to accommodate peasants and workers. Never having been in a theatre before, they sat spellbound before the actors in productions that also incorporated radio and cinema. The brick walls of the stage served as proud backgrounds

(176) Doboujinsky, Mstislav, 1875–1957
       Russia, Saint Petersburg (active also in Moscow,
       Europe, and America)
       Blue Sitting Room for Turgenev's *A Month in the
       Country*, Act I, 1919 (See also color plate 19)
       Watercolor and gouache, 355 x 444 mm.
       Inscribed lower right corner: "D. 1909, 1919"
       On verso: The artist mounted his sketch on a sheet
       of a contemporary Russian newspaper. In red ink:
       "E.O.D. 22–1919" and in black ink: "(*Une Mois à
       la Campagne*) *app. à Acte I*"
       Collection: Artist's widow

for exciting constructions and platforms of functionalism, with intrusions of machine and industrial technology.

Meierhold introduced his system of bio-mechanics into the Russian theatre schools as a universal method of training actors. "The trained body, the well-functioning nervous system, correct reflexes, vivacity and exactness of reaction, the control of one's body—in other words," explained Korenyev, "the general feeling for space and time, and coordination of movements with each other—such are the results of the application of bio-mechanics." Meierhold's results with actors suited the avant-garde scenic experiments which the Russian artists of the constructivist and cubo-futurist groups carried out on their stages during the years just prior to 1917. Among those

distinguished artists were Exter, Larionov, Gontcharova, Vesnin, Annenkov, and Tatlin. It was a tragic moment for Russia's culture when their efforts in behalf of Russian modern art fell victim to Stalin's decree inaugurating the doctrine of socialist realism. It could have been a unique moment in time when a liberal, revolutionary movement in the arts marched hand in hand with a great social and political revolution.

In 1921, Doboujinsky, plotting his own career, decided to emigrate to Europe, where he continued to design settings and costumes for plays, ballets, and operas, and Balieff's *Chauve Souris*. He worked with gusto in the theatres of such diverse cities as Dresden, Dusseldorf, Riga, Kaunas, Amsterdam, Brussels, Paris, and London.

During his long career as a scene designer, Doboujinsky had wandered far with his wide knowledge of the arts and the theatre. Everywhere he roamed, he eagerly took on new commissions. On a foreign stage, the complication of executing the designs for *Eugene Onegin* or the technical problems of *Pique Dame* never disturbed him—they stimulated him. At sixty-four, he finally "retired" to New York but only, as he soon discovered, to labor with his overflowing talent in the vineyards of the American theatre until he was eighty-two. The American theatre was the richer for his labors and his talents.

*Illustration 176. A Month in the Country* was the first of many plays that Doboujinsky designed between 1909 and

1919 for Stanislavski and Nemirovich-Dantchenko in the Moscow Art Theatre. Stanislavski's *My Life in Art* contains a chapter (62) in which he discusses the scenic and directorial problems he encountered with this production of *A Month in the Country*.

### Serge Soudeikine

Serge Soudeikine "fell into" stage design while working part-time under Serov and Korovine in the Moscow School of Painting, Sculpture, and Architecture. In 1910 he was in the Academy of Arts in Saint Petersburg, and with his exposure to the World of Art group, the theatre soon beckoned to him. He assisted Meierhold on Maeterlinck's *Sister Beatrice* and Komisarjevski on Shaw's *Caesar and Cleopatra*. He then went to Paris and, in connection with Diaghilev's exhibition of Russian painters, was asked to work on the scenes for three new ballets which Bakst had designed. Diaghilev then com-

missioned Soudeikine to design two new ballets for him, but with the outbreak of war in 1914, only *The Tragedy of Salome* was produced.

Soudeikine then returned to Russia, and in Moscow Tairov gave him the chance to design Beaumarchais's *The Marriage of Figaro* and Benavente's *Inside of Life* in the Kamerny Theatre. For several years he served in the Russian army. During the revolution he did not participate in Russia's changing theatre, but retreated to the Crimea and Tiflis.

In 1919, Soudeikine emigrated to Paris in search of a new world and a new theatre. He was doubly fortunate in that he found an opportunity to work with Antoine and also with Jacques Copeau in his exciting new Théâtre du Vieux Colombier. As a Russian expatriate, he was commissioned to design scenes and costumes for Anna Pavlova's company. Nikita Balieff, having once used Soudeikine, knew how much his kaleidoscopic color and

(177) Soudeikine, Serge, 1882–1946
Russia, Moscow (active also in Saint Petersburg, Paris, and New York)
Traveling Show for *Chauve Souris*, c. 1922
Pencil and watercolor, 342 x 481 mm.
Inscribed lower right corner: "Soudeikine"

(178) Gontcharova, Natalia, 1882–1962
Russia, Moscow (active also in Paris, Berlin, London, and New York)
Battlements of a Castle for Balakirev's *Thamar*, c. 1925 (See also color plate 21)

Pencil and watercolor, 463 x 679 mm.
Inscribed lower right margin: "Gontcharova"
On verso: a variant for the same sketch in pencil.

his stylized design glamorized the "look" of his *Chauve Souris*. When Balieff took his troupe from Paris to New York in 1922, Soudeikine was included as staff designer.

Once he had landed in New York, Soudeikine eagerly cast his lot with America and became a member of the Designers' Union. He soon made a successful place for himself in the New York theatre. The Metropolitan Opera engaged him to design a number of Russian operas and ballets, and he was also associated with four ballet companies. For three years he devised spectacles for the Radio City Music Hall as well as colorful scenery for Broadway musicals and operettas.

In 1935, he designed for the Theatre Guild a genuine American background for George Gershwin's American opera *Porgy and Bess*. Soudeikine had been accustomed to play on the primitive color and decoration of Russian folk art. Living in a Hudson River town, Soudeikine succeeded in balancing the peasant art of his past with the folk art of his new world.

*Illustration 177.* Nikita Balieff's *Chauve Souris* was a popular vaudeville-type intimate review. The skits and dances had gaiety, sardonic humor, peasant ebullience, and romantic schmaltz. Soudeikine invented a unique scenic style for them.

This compact scene for the *Chauve Souris* springs right from the Commedia-dell'Arte stage. Soudeikine adorns familiar barrels and stage trappings with his own brand of decoration. The tattered backcloth, lantern, and poster are covered with comic graffiti. Set against an ultramarine sky, all is just as temporary as the brief sketch the platform stage was designed to support.

### Natalia Gontcharova

Natalia Gontcharova, daughter of an architect, was an important scenic designer as well as an easel painter. Her early pictures were inspired by the primitive vigor and bold color of Russian folk art and by the mystical austerity of Russian ikons. She also took up sculpture under

Prince Paul Trubetzkoy in Moscow's School of Painting, Sculpture, and Architecture, where she met a young artist named Mikhail Larionov. Henceforth, they would share in everything together. In 1906, both contributed paintings to Diaghilev's Russian Exhibition in the Salon d'Automne in Paris.

At that time, under the infectious influence of Diaghilev, Gontcharova became strongly attracted to the theatre. Her initiation to the theatre was her legendary production of Rimsky-Korsakov's opera *Le Coq d'Or* done by Diaghilev in 1913 as a pantomime. Her lavish settings (realized simply with legdrops and backdrop) were stylized houses and palaces of old Moscow, alive with fantastic floral designs in flaming reds, chrome yellows, and blue. Following Gontcharova's stunning success with this opera-ballet, Larionov too became one of Diaghilev's favored artists, and in the future would advise on many of Diaghilev's production plans.

In that epochal Salon of 1906, cubism and futurism revealed a new reality to the young artists of Western Europe, and to Gontcharova and Larionov as well. Out of their impetuous experiments in geometrical forms and abstractions, they evolved the Rayonnist style of painting. In 1913, Gontcharova, with Larionov and nine other young Russian artists, signed their *Rayonnist Manifesto*. "We consider ourselves the creators of Modern Art. The future is with us . . . we do not need popularization—our art will take its place in life fully." In their revolutionary art they sought to express new concepts of time and space —to produce "a sensation of the fourth dimension."

Gontcharova's early involvement with the theatre provided an important extension and application of the conclusions she reached in her search to achieve a new dimension with Rayonnism. In 1915 she experimented with Tairov in his Kamerny Theatre in Moscow. Her abstract decor for Goldoni's *The Fan* ignored all precedent by disregarding the time and place of this eighteenth-century Venetian comedy.

That same year, with the Germans occupying much of France, Gontcharova and Larionov courageously decided to sever their artistic ties with Russia and settle permanently in Paris. Shortly after her arrival, she set to work on Stravinsky's *Liturgie* in Lausanne for Diaghilev. She designed hieratic Byzantine costumes moving before a stylized iconostasis, fragmented with religious figures and ikons of the Orthodox church.

Gontcharova was a dynamic artist of great creative energy. She divided her time in such a way that there should be enough for painting and enough for the theatre. "These are of course inseparable," she believed, "but painting is an inner necessity for theatrical work, and not vice versa." Her scenic resolution for *Les Noces* was sculptured austerity. Between two pairs of grand pianos were a backdrop, framed in black, and several wooden platforms, unadorned to emphasize the dancers wearing work clothes—skirts, tunics, and pants of a coarse brownblack linen. After Diaghilev's death, Gontcharova continued to design decor for various international dance companies, but she always alternated her work in the theatre with her easel painting. One fed the other, just as

she and Larionov had always shared a world of stimulating associations. Finally, at seventy, they decided to celebrate their lifetime of mutual successes and were married. Gontcharova's achievements in the theatre were progressive markers leading to those peaks of theatrical art which she discovered.

*Illustration 178.* This design by Gontcharova for *Thamar* is much simpler than the elaborate decor that Bakst invented for the 1912 Diaghilev production. For this later revival, probably by Serge Lifar, she changed the setting from the interior of the castle's tower to its battlements. Ignoring the use of perspective, she invented a cubistic design based on the rigid, angular forms of the Caucasus Mountains. Her novel treatment enhances the Russian folk elements of the ballet's theme.

### Aleksandra Exter

Aleksandra Exter was twenty-six when she journeyed from Moscow to Paris to continue her art studies at the Académie de la Grande Chaumière in 1908. She remained in Paris through six formative years, and with her friends Picasso and Braque, Marinetti and Pappini, she became absorbed in investigating new dimensions in cubism. Her destiny, however, was the theatre, which became a laboratory in which she explored the possibilities of converting tenets of cubism to the theatrical idiom. In working with a basic three-dimensional or "constructed" stage scene, she discovered a new harmonious relationship between actors in abstract costumes and the abstract shapes and forms of the scene in which they moved. Little did Exter realize how close in principle she came to Adolphe Appia's contemporary experiments in his new theatre at Hellerau, nor how far beyond Appia her own experiments would lead her!

In Moscow in 1914, Alexandre Tairov founded the Kamerny Theatre with his wife, Moscow's favorite actress Alice Koonen. In this intimate playhouse, he hoped to revive the great theatre of the past for an audience of students and intellectuals. With his theory of formalism he sought to restore the stature of the hero in heroic plays; also to establish pictorial and internal harmony on his stage with the actors masked and moving in prescribed rhythms after the fashion of Craig's *Über-Marionette*. "Remember you are on the stage," he always admonished his actors.

In 1914, Exter returned to Moscow, where she met Tairov a year later. They discovered that each had independently arrived at very similar aesthetic conclusions. During those few years preceding the Russian Revolution, constructivism became a modernist movement of artistic consequences. Exter's spatial abstractions were stage architecture based on form, not function; her constructivism complimented Tairov's formalism.

Their first collaborative effort in the Kamerny Theatre was a poetic play, *Thamira Cytharide* by Annensky, presented in 1916. Exter hoped to destroy the old realistic scenic formula and replace it with her "decor of atmosphere." Tairov sought to adopt her painter's vision by blending "emotions, words, gestures, music, dance, light

(179) Exter, Aleksandra, 1884–1949
    Russia, Kiev (active also in Moscow, Leningrad,
    and Paris)
    Construction for a Tragedy, c. 1925
    (See also color plate 23)

Pencil and gouache, 510 x 530 mm.
Inscribed lower right corner: "A. Exter"
On verso: "A. Exter, 152 Rue Broca; *Construction Théâtrale pour une Tragedie*—N. 1080"
Collection: Evreinov

and color" on her scenic forms. The nude bodies of the actors playing bacchantes and satyrs were painted in multicolored designs. Exter's and Tairov's first flight must have been a wild evening for the students and intellectuals of Moscow!

That experiment was followed the next year by Oscar Wilde's *Salome*, which further explored the capabilities of constructivism and the movement of actors. Constructivism, as Hilton Kramer has observed, constituted in some degree the aesthetic counterpart to the Russian Revolution itself. But the alliance of avant-garde art and revolutionary politics proved to be short-lived.

In 1920, amidst Moscow's crises of revolution, ap-

peared the Exter-Tairov revolutionary production of *Romeo and Juliet*. For the first time in any theatre, the stage's total cubic volume was divided vertically into a series of abstract playing areas that did not mean to create any lifelike illusion of the Capulets' great hall or Juliet's tomb. A stunning solution to the stage's spatial problems was achieved with Tairov's taut direction. The Exter-Tairov drama of ill-fated lovers was applauded by Moscow's modern reactionaries, but not by those who viewed it from the Kremlin.

Exter resolutely persevered with her theatrical activities. In 1924, she introduced with Mikhail Chekhov her bold techniques to the Second Studio of the Moscow Art

Theatre with her costumes and scenery for Calderon's *La Dama Duende*. That production celebrated a decade of Exter's intensive participation in the advancement of the Russian theatre. It was also her farewell production, for soon after, she emigrated from the Soviet Union and returned to Paris. There she could teach theatrical design in Léger's Académie d'Art Moderne and in her own atelier. With her customary drive, she continued to carry on her experiments in the French theatre, in the cinema, and also with marionettes.

Aleksandra Exter was one of the dominant artists and innovators of the modern stage for having pioneered and helped to introduce constructivism to the art of scenic design.

*Illustration 179*. This abstract constructivist setting by Aleksandra Exter logically extends the stage's plastic values beyond any association with the world outside the theatre. Within the theatre, this permanent construction could serve equally well for *Electra*, *Macbeth*, or *Phèdre*. The structure of soaring black vertical members and ascending diagonal orange-red ramps creates independent, yet interconnected, playing spaces on which tragedy could unfold.

A limited edition of a handsome portfolio of fifteen silk-screen prints of Aleksandra Exter's theatre sketches, with a preface by Alexandre Tairov, was published in Paris in 1930.

*Illustration 180*. Exter designed this costume for *La Dama Duende* which Mikhail Chekhov presented in the reconstituted Second Studio of the Moscow Art Theatre in 1924.

*Illustration 181*. In converting natural forms to their simplest geometric shapes, Aleksandra Exter employs steps, ramps, platforms, and poles in this constructivist design and limits them to white, gray, and black. In the rear, she contrasts a brilliant color projection on a white backdrop. This production was staged at the Teatro Tatiana Pavlowa, Rome.

### Mihail Fedorovitch Andreenko

Mihail Fedorovitch Andreenko was a lawyer and an artist who cast his lot with the cubo-futurist movement. As a painter, he was intrigued with the possibilities of the theatre. For five years he designed settings for theatres in Odessa, Bucharest, Prague, and Moscow. In 1924, like many other Russian artists of the theatre, he interpreted the warning of the dictator's writing on the wall and emigrated to Paris. Finding only scattered theatrical productions to design, the lawyer in him wisely advised giving up the theatre for painting.

For twenty years after the revolution, the greatest drama of the Russian theatre was the struggle to preserve the freedom of the theatre from state control. In 1937, *Pravda* attacked Meierhold, the former director of all Soviet theatres, as a deviationist who "cannot and apparently will not comprehend Soviet reality or depict the problems which concern every Soviet citizen." The next year, Meierhold's theatre, the most progressive, revolutionary theatre in all Russia, was closed. In June, 1939, the following year, the first all-Union Congress of Directors assembled in Moscow. Their official mission was to declare that the theatre must subordinate itself to the tasks advanced by the Party and the government. Meierhold, as an artist, valiantly spoke against Communist coercion in the theatre: "But the theatre is art! And without art, there is no theatre! Go visiting the theatres of Moscow. Look at their drab and boring presentations that resemble one another and are each worse than the others. It is now difficult to distinguish the creative style of the Maly Theatre from that of the Vakhtangov, the Kamerny, or the Moscow Art Theatre. Recently, creative ideas poured from them. Where once there were the best theatres of the world, now—by your leave—everything is gloomily well-regulated, averagely arithmetical, stupifying, and murderous in its lack of talent. Is that your aim? If it is—oh!—you have done something monstrous! . . . In hunting formalism, you have eliminated art!" This was Meierhold's farewell to the people of the Soviet theatre. The next day, he was arrested and disappeared behind the walls of the NKVD. Shortly after, his wife was found murdered under strange circumstances in their Moscow flat. Meierhold is believed to have been executed on February 2, 1940.

Organized fear, like a plague, spread throughout the corridors of the Soviet theatre. Dramatists and directors,

artists, actors, and critics were suddenly arrested and never heard from again. The lights of the theatre had gone out and a creative, subsidized theatre was reduced to the common denominator of state propaganda.

After their valiant defeat of the Germans in the Second World War, the Russians hoped and believed that with their heroic victory the visual and performing arts would be granted the freedom of expression that had been denied them for twenty years. They were sadly disillusioned. The dreary impact of totalitarian culture on the theatre remains as oppressive as ever. The Soviet theatre, with all its official vitality, suffers from malaise and is confined in its own isolation ward—out of contact with the advancing theatre of a free world.

*Illustration 182.* Andreenko designed this dance setting just ten years after the October Revolution. During this stormy decade, he had assimilated all the scenic vocabulary of the theatre of revolt: constructivist principles, Tairov's abstract formalism, and Meierhold's acrobatics for the actor.

### Nikolai Akimov

Nikolai Akimov was a leading Russian designer-director who found his early experience in the theatres of Leningrad and from 1927 in Moscow, where he enjoyed working in the atmosphere of the Vakhtangov Theatre group whose ideals were congenial to his own.

Like Gordon Craig, Akimov believed that one artist should be responsible for the synthesis of the visual and intellectual elements of a play. His love of artifice and dynamic deception enabled him to achieve startling and novel effects, often using unconventional techniques of the theatre and even the cinema.

One of his notable productions was Goethe's *Love and Intrigue*, which he dramatically staged on a huge silver disk steeply raked in blackness. Another was his adventurous *Hamlet* in 1936, which he directed as a grotesque, boisterous comedy. His "monstrous profanation" of Shakespeare's tragedy caused such controversy that it was "officially" withdrawn from the proletariat eye.

Akimov was one of the few prominent Russian designers and directors who remained active in the Soviet

(182)  Andreenko, Mihail Fedorovitch, 1894–
        Russia, Ukraine (active in Russia, Czechoslovakia, and Paris)
        Acrobats—Scene for a Ballet, 1927
        Pencil and gouache, 444 x 424 mm.
        Inscribed lower left corner: "Andreenko—'927"

(183)  Akimov, Nikolai Pavlovitch, 1901–1968
Russia, Karkov (active in Moscow and Leningrad)
Satirical Constructivist Setting for *Now for Hamlet,*
c. 1930
Pencil, black ink, and gold paper crown, 264 x
333 mm.
Collection: Evreinov

theatre after the thirties. He was honored as People's Artist of the USSR, and labored through the dreary decline of Russian theatre under the deadening domination of official ideology. The adventurous talent for design that marked his early aggressive productions was in his later years sadly leveled to picturesque, neo-decorative conformance.

*Illustration 183.* Akimov made this constructivist design for *Now for Hamlet* for Evreinov's Crooked Mirror Theatre in Leningrad. In his intimate cabaret theatre, Evreinov presented satirical parodies of important productions of dramatists, directors, and actors of the Russian theatre in the twenties. In 1965, Madame Evreinov wrote a letter with reference to this design: "As for Akimov's sketch, it is a satirical representation of *Hamlet* . . . The very 'avant-garde metteurs en scène' of that time, Eisenstein, Meierhold, etc., sometimes changed so much [of] the au-

thor that you could no more recognize the play. Ophelia is going up the ladder singing, 'It's a long way to Tipperary'; the King, each time asserting his kingship, runs under the crown, and so on. . . . Akimov was our dear friend." His presentation of *Now for Hamlet* may have influenced his own later, controversial *Hamlet* at the Vakhtangov Theatre in Moscow.

*Illustration 184.* Yozac Jankus' setting for *Porgy and Bess* is a medley of constructivism, expressionism, and abstract realism. This Russianized Catfish Row is rooted neither in the socialist realism of Charleston nor of Moscow. The locale is depersonalized; the design is standard abstraction in sombre violet-reds, yellows, and gray with flashes of metallic silver. Orange windows stare out from darkness, and black windows from lightness. If this setting was successful in 1967, it was because it reflected the lively experimentation of the golden period of the Soviet

(184) Jankus, Yozac, 1912–
Russia
Catfish Row for Gershwin's *Porgy and Bess*, 1967
(See also color plate 24)
Pencil, gouache, and metallic silver, 485 x 722 mm.
Inscribed lower left corner: "Jankus '67"

theatre of the twenties and early thirties.

One must not compare the socialist ways of Russian designers with the ways of designers of another country. However, one may question whether Jankus had the freedom of an artist to determine for himself whether his setting expresses the living essence of Porgy's marvelous world of black folk, pathos, song, and heart that permeates every corner of Catfish Row.

### N. N. Zolotaryov

N. N. Zolotaryov is one of the most active and gifted contemporary stage designers in the USSR. In a country that rejects rank, he has been called "one of the ablest of the Moscow artists." In recent years, he has been closely affiliated with the Moscow Art Theatre's Musical Theatre, working jointly with the director, L. Mikhailov, on new productions of Russian classical and modern Soviet works.

Several years ago in the Moscow Musical Theatre, Zolotaryov collaborated on *Carmen* with Walter Felsenstein, the meticulous stage director of the East Berlin Komische Oper. In praising this Soviet-Satellite collaboration, Sokolova writes with disarming satisfaction: "This friendship in creative work with the German Democratic Republic is another example of cultural relations between our people, it is again an example of mutual understanding in the struggle for peace, in which the artists of the socialist countries take part." But why stop at the Berlin Wall? Would that the artists of the Soviet theatre might be free to indulge in peaceful dialogue and harmonious collaboration with the artists of the theatre of the Western world.

*Illustration 185.* This production of *Boris Godunov* was presented in 1966 in the Paliashvili Georgian Opera House in Tiflis and also in the Ballet Theatre in Tbilisi. In designing this classic Russian opera, Zolotaryov managed to avoid the oppressive art of socialist realism. Here is an imaginative artist enhancing the meaning and the grandeur of *Boris* with his abstract manipulation of sultry blues on bold free forms, as a substitute for realistic architecture. By thus suggesting the immensity of Russia, Zolotaryov dramatizes the solitude of Pimen's cell with a solitary monk recording the revered chronicles of Holy Russia. This monastery is an impressive design, individual and free from the stamp of totalitarian art.

210

### Andrej Majewski

The Polish stage has attained a leading position in the international theatre. In spite of Poland's subjugation, her painful period of reconstruction (every playhouse in Warsaw was destroyed by the Nazis), and her distressing economy, the Polish theatre today is far from impoverished. The post-Marxist theatre is a healthy and vigorous institution—independent and original, exciting and bursting with vitality. The performing arts in Poland exert a strong cultural influence on the taste of the communities of both large cities and provincial towns.

Stanislaw Wyspianski (1869–1907) was the dramatist, director, and designer who first prepared the way for the modern Polish theatre. Like Gordon Craig, he was a true artist of the theatre. The ideas and principles he envisioned for the stage of the Cracow Theatre were mostly disregarded in Poland during his short lifetime. It remained for his ardent designer-successors, called the "Big Four"—Pronaszko, Fryz, Daszewski, and Drabik—to raise scene design in the first half of the twentieth century to the high artistic standards of all the contemporary arts of Poland.

A middle generation of "career" stage designers of Cracow and Warsaw stem from the "Big Four" and provide stimulating impetus to Poland's progressive theatre. There are the vivid stage designs of Roszkowska and Axer, the highly theatrical, neorealistic work of Kosinski, Stopka, Cybulski, and Zenobiusz Strzelecki. Strzelecki has written three enlightening volumes on the scenography of the modern Polish theatre and is himself one of Warsaw's most imaginative and original designers.

Many of the youngest group of stage designers appear to temper their abstractions by employing subtle yet realistic means to achieve suggestion and symbolism. Andrej Majewski is one of this group who has discovered unsuspected possibilities in the outer boundaries of surrealism. He finds that a detail of tree bark or a piece of worn carpet can be dramatized to provide new and significant

(185) Zolotaryov, N. N., 1915–
Russia, Moscow
Monastery of Tchudo, Pimen's Cell, for Musorgski's *Boris Godunov*, Act I, Scene 1, 1966 (See also color plate 25)
Gouache, 595 x 696 mm.

scenic meaning. The use of collage as a texture supports his mood. Strzelecki finds that Majewski "has a relish for violence, destruction and decay" which he injects into his settings for such unrelated plays as *Troilus and Cressida*, Ionesco's *Rhinoceros*, and *Hamlet*. In 1961, Majewski's highly charged designs for *Hamlet* were awarded the Prize of the Festival des Nations in Paris. In the Prague Quadrienale of 1968, his costume designs received the Gold Medal.

Majewski's eerie curtain for Stravinsky's *Firebird* and his "etched" costume drawings for Molière's *School for Wives* make it clear that as a designer he is not allied to any school of design. Majewski cultivates his own artistic concept of design in the theatre. So do all the other talented designers of Poland, who together constitute a dynamic nationalistic school of stage design.

*Illustration 186. Pulcinella* is a comic pantomime derived from an eighteenth-century scenario of the Neapolitan popular theatre, whose performers are the traditional characters of the Commedia dell'Arte. This *Pulcinella* was presented in the Wieller Theatre in Warsaw in 1966. Majewski, in his surrealist design, places center-stage a traveling show, like a two-story, windblown circus wagon with only one wheel! The surrounding square is a delicate and poetic collage of thin, cut-out paper details, playfully revealing glimpses of the construction of wings and borders meshed with houses and foliage. All is in moldy tones of rose, gray, and green. It is an original and engaging theatrical conceit, just right for the characters of *Pulcinella* and for Stravinsky's arrangement of Pergolesi.

### André Delfau

André Delfau, after completing his studies in the École des Beaux Arts, soon became an accomplished painter and a stylish Parisian illustrator. His theatrical style as an

(186)  Majewski, Andrej, 1941–
Poland, Warsaw (active also in Italy, Germany, and England)
Commedia-dell'Arte Stage for Pergolesi-Stravinsky's *Pulcinella*, 1966
Collage with watercolor, gold, and gouache, 475 x 369 mm.

(187) Delfau, André, 1914–
France, Paris (active also in Copenhagen and Chicago)
Abstraction for the ballet *Chantier*, 1961
(See also color plate 26)

Watercolor, 368 x 465 mm.
Inscribed lower right corner: "Delfau 61"
On verso: Preliminary sketch for a similar design.
Collection: The Artist

illustrator soon led to an important commission in 1947 to design the decor and costumes for *Sérénade* and *Apollon Musageté* with George Balanchine, who was embarking on his new commitment as choreographer of the Paris Opéra Ballet. Three years later, Delfau and Balanchine provided a picturesque, romantic ambience for their balletic version of Bellini's *La Sonnambula* for the Marquis de Cuevas' ballet company, the first of a number of ballets Delfau designed for the company. Outstanding were Tchaikovsky's *Tragédie à Vérone* and Schiffman's poetic *Annabel Lee* derived from Poe's poem. In 1955, Delfau was working again with Balanchine on *Night Shadow* for the Royal Opera Ballet of Denmark.

Decor for the ballet became Delfau's forte, and except for an occasional play such as Marivaux's *Les Serments Indiscrets* for the Comédie Française in 1956 and productions for the Opéra Comique, he has consistently maintained his allegiance to the dance. Since 1961, he has created many decors for Ruth Page's Chicago Opera Ballet. Ruth Page has been most successful making ballet out of operas. She explains, "I was dissatisfied with the way operas looked, yet loved the way they sounded." Delfau contributed to the "look" of her ballets with his decor and costumes for *Die Fledermaus*, *Pygmalion*, and *Romeo and Juliet*, among others.

André Delfau and many other leading contemporary French designers such as George Wakhevitch, Jean Denis Maclés, Cassandre, and before them, Christian Bérard and Jean Hugo, approach designing for the stage with the unfettered freedom of the painter. Diaghilev reestablished this tradition in Paris when he chose to exploit the talents of Picasso, Braque, Léger, Matisse, and Marie Laurencin by inviting them to collaborate as artist-designers in the creation of his ballets. Consequently, stage decoration in "the painter's style," sometimes for better and at times for worse, became traditional in the French theatre and today remains the hallmark of French theatrical decor.

Delfau as a practicing painter in the theatre insists that the designer create a pictorial climate and that he have the flexibility to adapt his personal style to the exacting requirements of the scenario. Sometimes his settings are abstract, sometimes they are neorealistic, but whatever their style, they always look like Delfau.

*Illustration 187.* This drawing is for *Chantier*, an unrealized ballet commissioned by the Marquis de Cuevas for his Ballet in 1961. Delfau's aerial design, typical of the painter's abstract approach to his canvas, consists of

213

(188) Walser, Karl, 1877–1943
Switzerland, Biel (active in Berlin, Munich, Vienna, and Bern)
Verona, a Public Place for Shakespeare's *Romeo and Juliet*, Act I, Scene 1, 1907 (See also color plate 20)
Crayon and gouache, 505 x 405 mm.
Inscribed lower margin: "Romeo u Julia—Karl Walser"

splintered constructions suspended in space above a bare stage within a cyclorama animated with changing light projections of violet, red, and orange.

### Karl Walser

Karl Walser was a Swiss artist who moved to Berlin shortly after the turn of the century and became a prominent member of the Berlin Sezessionist movement, a group of young avant-garde artists who broke with the tradition of realism. Walser was one of the first of this group to be enthusiastic about applying his painter's skill to designing settings for the theatre.

In the Berlin theatre, Max Reinhardt was making a place for himself as a producer-director. His interests carried him far beyond the naturalism of Otto Brahm with whom he had worked, and he sought out young artists of the Jugendstil, the Wiener Werkstätte, and the Sezessionist group to lend their fresh talents to his theatre. Munch, Nolde, Pechstein, Stern, Roller, Orlik, and Walser were among the distinguished artists whom he early introduced to the Berlin theatre.

In 1904, Reinhardt was impressed with Walser's initial scenic effort painted in fresh colors for a new play by Wedekind. The following season, Walser was designing fancy-free costumes for Reinhardt's first production of Shakespeare—an antinaturalistic, neoromantic production of *A Midsummer Night's Dream*. Following this great success, Reinhardt gave Walser free rein in designing decorative costumes and painted scenery for Kleist's *Käthchen von Heilbronn*. Another Reinhardt triumph was Wedekind's *Spring's Awakening* which he presented in his new Kammerspiel Theater. Walser's impressionist scenery, with psychological overtones, was a revelation to that generation. Curtains decorated with stylized flowers and leaves framed a draped gauze with appliqued flowers through which one glimpsed an impression of trees by a river bank. The whole conveyed a feeling of early spring and misty adolescence. Utterly different was Walser's literal production of *Romeo and Juliet* in 1907, which was freighted with detail far too rich for Shakespeare's poetic tragedy.

Walser remained one of Reinhardt's favored designers prior to World War I, but he also collaborated on many productions with other young German directors and for a number of seasons was Hans Gregor's resident designer of the Berlin Komische Oper.

After the war, in 1922, Walser returned to Berlin from Switzerland to design *Cyrano* for Eric Charell in the Deutsches Theater and *As You Like It* for Reinhardt. In Germany he found only confusion. The defeated German Empire had become an impoverished struggling democracy. The theatre was in revolt, too, and the old order was changing with a new breed of young expressionists. Reinhardt had built his Grosses Schauspielhaus, a theatre seating five thousand, and was experimenting with large-scale productions. With the changing economics of a new commercial theatre, Reinhardt was shifting his theatrical interests from Germany to Austria. Walser was no longer in the mainstream of the theatre and reluctantly returned to Switzerland to resume his career as an easel painter and graphic artist.

Unquestionably, Walser had been a major force in revitalizing the German theatre during the decade before World War I. He brought to that theatre a picturesque and refreshing painter's style, enhanced by his neoromantic vision of the theatre. It is noteworthy that Walser's countryman, Adolphe Appia, the great reformer of the modern movement, and Gordon Craig, its prophet, who was living in Berlin in 1905, exerted little influence on Walser's theatrical style. He was a Sezessionist painter, and in the theatre he designed as a painter.

*Illustration 188.* When Reinhardt took over the Deutsches Theater in 1905, he installed the first large-scale revolving stage in Berlin, which opened new avenues in design and technical efficiency. Entire scenes could be shifted within seconds.

214

Karl Walser designed the scenes and costumes for Max Reinhardt's production of *Romeo and Juliet* in his Deutsches Theater in 1907. Walser filled the revolving stage with two-storied realistic interiors and exteriors of Renaissance Verona. The scenes, executed in Walser's painted style, were picturesque and filled with colorful detail. This opening street scene with the encounter of the Capulets and Montagues served as an atmospheric prologue, quite as realistic as Serlio's Renaissance street scene of 1545 (Illus. 4).

### Emil Orlik

Emil Orlik, born in Prague, studied art in Munich and was strongly influenced by post-impressionist and symbolist movements. He displayed a particular talent for the graphic arts, especially woodcuts. In 1900, he journeyed to Japan and devoted a year to learning the techniques of the Japanese woodcut. In Japan he discovered the splendor of the Kabuki theatre and made many drawings of Kabuki actors. On his return, he settled in Vienna and fell in with a group of young actors from Berlin whose summer interest was putting on new plays to develop their talents. Orlik delighted in sketching their theatrical activities. One of those actors was Max Reinhardt.

In 1905, Orlik established his studio in Berlin, and like the Swiss painter Walser, he wanted to design settings for the theatre. Naturally, he approached Max Reinhardt, who commissioned him to design the scenes and costumes for seven plays between 1905 and 1911. Orlik's first project was *The Merchant of Venice*; the scenes were illusionistic and seemingly the work of a technician—buildings and bridges, canals with gondolas and high hedges. Having commissioned Orlik to design these realistic scenes, Reinhardt, the director, failed to utilize Orlik's recognized gifts as an artist.

That same year, Gordon Craig, the high priest of the New Movement, had deserted England and was living in Berlin. Craig was exhibiting his revolutionary designs in many German cities, and before long, his ideas would permeate a generation of rising European designers including Pirchan, Sievert, Stern, Linnabach, Roller, and Strnad, and in America, Jones, Geddes, and in spite of himself, Lee Simonson.

Max Reinhardt carried on a lengthy dialogue with

(189) Orlik, Emil, 1870–1932
  Czechoslovakia, Prague (active in Berlin)
  Forest in Bohemia for Schiller's *The Robbers*, Act
  II, Scene 3, 1908

Watercolor and india ink, 258 x 313 mm.
Inscribed lower right corner: "Orlik"
Below margin: *"Die Räuber: Böhmische Wälder"*
Collection: Max Reinhardt

Craig in his studio in the Tiergarten, but Craig was suspicious of Reinhardt's borrowing his schemes, taking over his ideas, and changing his plans. If Craig could not see his way to working with Reinhardt, Reinhardt and his designer Orlik could subject themselves to the influence of Craig! And they did. The following year, in their production of *A Winter's Tale* in the Deutsches Theater, they emphasized the theatrical simplicity of walls and draperies towering in perpendicular lines above the actors. Japanese influence was also evident in Orlik's studied placement of details in his scenic compositions. Unlike Craig, Reinhardt was not averse to introducing several scenic styles within a single production. Thus, for a sheep-shearing festival in Bohemia, Orlik, in striking contrast to his other scenes, designed a cartoonlike folk scene that might have illustrated a Czech fairy book, full of childlike gaiety, color, and sunshine.

*Illustration 189.* Emil Orlik designed the scenes and costumes for Max Reinhardt's production of Schiller's *The Robbers* in the Deutsches Theater in 1908. *The Robbers,*

Schiller's first play, was written in 1803, and in it the playwright challenged the social order of his own generation and rebelled against its regimentation and restraint. Count Dalberg accepted the play for production in his Mannheim Theater on condition that Schiller set the period of the play back three hundred years and tone down its more turbulent episodes.

For a Berlin audience a hundred years later, Schiller's romantic play of rebellion still had compelling political significance. Reinhardt and Orlik gave their production all the intensity and dramatic attack they could contrive. Orlik knew how to give meaning to a scene. He applied his rugged brush technique to a few massive tree forms and black silhouettes to suggest nature's last primeval stronghold against the encroachment of civilization.

### *Alfred Roller*
Alfred Roller and his circle of young artists in Vienna (which included Emil Orlik) formed an association in 1890, which seven years later became known as the Vienna Sezession, with the painter Gustav Klimt as its

(190)  Roller, Alfred, 1864–1935
      Austria, Brunn (active in Vienna, Salzburg, Munich, and Berlin)
      Before a Palace—Goethe's *Faust, Part II*, Act V, Scene 17, 1911

Pen and ink, watercolor, and gouache, 247 x 328 mm. Inscribed left and right portals: lower right corner "AR-II" and above: "see drawing B" (an alternate design).
Collection: Max Reinhardt

(191) Stern, Ernst, 1876–1954
Roumania, Bucharest (active in Vienna, Berlin, Munich, Paris, London, and New York)
Throne Hall for Schiller's *Don Carlos*, Act II, Scene 1, 1909

Pencil, watercolor, and gouache on tan paper, 350 x 470 mm.
On verso: "No. 43d. *Don Carlos* Stern"
Collection: Max Reinhardt

first president. Roller had studied architecture and painting in the Academy of Fine Arts but wanted most of all to design scenery for the theatre. His innovative ideas impressed Gustav Mahler, the director of the Vienna Hofoper, and in 1903 *Tristan und Isolde*, with Roller's settings of color and light, was their initial artistic collaboration. Roller then became the Hofoper's chief scenic artist during Mahler's regime and later also for the Burg Theater. No less important to Roller's career at that time was his meeting in 1906 with Max Reinhardt. That year he designed his production of von Hofmannsthal's *Oedipus and the Sphinx* in Berlin. Roller experimented with combining color and light to create pictorial, sensory impressions. This was the first of their many notable productions, and it launched Roller's career as a professional designer. The year 1911 was typical of the scope of his designing activities with Max Reinhardt. Five productions became landmarks in the theatre of the twentieth century: the première of Richard Strauss' *Der Rosenkavalier* in the Dresden Opera House; in Berlin, *Faust, Part II* in the Deutsches Theater and *Oedipus Rex* in the Cirkus Schu-

mann; and in two Munich festival halls, Aeschylus' *Oresteia* and von Hofmannsthal's *Jedermann*.

These exacting productions required a free and uncluttered scenic approach on the part of the designer. As a Sezessionist, Roller had turned his back on the naturalistic traditions of the previous generation, although he never entirely dismissed realism. Roller was perhaps the first artist to appreciate and put into practice the principles of Adolphe Appia and Gordon Craig. Their use of light, dynamic stage space and simplified forms are the basis of much of Roller's work in the theatre. He incorporated their aims in his "Roller Türme" for *Don Giovanni* in the Hofoper in 1906. These mobile scenic towers he frequently employed in flexible combinations for both artistic and technical purposes.

Roller achieved his scenic reforms because he was a sensitive, practical man of the theatre. For twenty-five years, he was the revered director of Vienna's excellent School of Arts and Crafts where he gave a course in stage design. The opera *régisseur* Herbert Graf took his course and recalled that "Roller was a precise, exacting teacher

217

and he never failed to explain the practical reasons that underlay his own designs. He insisted on his pupils' mastering the basics of their craft before setting out on wild flights of experimentation." Because Roller practiced what he taught, he could accompany Max Reinhardt to Stockholm and contrive a many-scened imaginative production for Strindberg's demanding expressionist *Dream Play*. Or, for the Vienna Staatsoper, he could invent astonishing transformations for the challenging first performance of Strauss' *Die Frau ohne Schatten*.

Outside of the theatre, Roller was respectful of nature. Inside the theatre, he freed the stage of illusionism and replaced it with simplified realism, *lebensraum* for the performers, a sense of poetry, suggestive color, and music —all integrated with his innate Viennese refinement and his modern expertise.

*Illustration 190*. Goethe's *Faust, Part II* is so vast in its philosophical conception that its symbolic panorama is almost impossible to encompass in the theatre.

In 1909, Max Reinhardt and Alfred Roller had done a successful realistic production of *Faust, Part I* with the help of the revolving stage of the Deutsches Theater. Two years later, they dedicated themselves to the challenging task of bringing Part II of this dramatic ritual to life on the same stage. To frame his drawings, Roller used a constant white portal to indicate the reduced proscenium opening which had to contain Goethe's continuous procession of fragmentary scenes. This design for a palace entrance is the seventeenth scene of the fifth act! For every scene, Roller used simplified forms, emphasizing only the reality of essential details and relying on dramatic lighting to swiftly establish the passing scene's brief mood.

### Ernst Stern

Ernst Stern, a member of both the Munich and Berlin Sezessionist groups, was an international stage designer, well-known in the theatre of Berlin, Vienna, London, Paris, and New York.

Stern wandered onto the theatrical scene of Europe as a young Roumanian from Bucharest who deserted commerce for the practice of art. The world of the theatre early intrigued him, and in 1905 in Munich he finally decided to cast his lot with the theatre and move to Berlin. There he supported himself by drawing theatre cartoons for the *Lüstiger Blätter*. After seeing Max Reinhardt's *Orpheus in the Underworld*, he ventured to write a critical appraisal. Reinhardt happened to read it and summoned young Stern to his office. Impressed with Stern's sense of theatre, Reinhardt concluded their discussion: "You've got a lot to criticize, Herr Stern. If you think you can do it any better, what about it?" Ernst Stern left that meeting as costume and scenery director of the Reinhardt theatres, and for sixteen years was the principal designer for Germany's major theatre reformer. Many other talented artists also worked with Reinhardt, and Stern always aided and abetted them. Reinhardt had a strict

(192) Stern, Ernst
Chinese Chamber for Gozzi-Vollmoeller's *Turandot*, 1911
Pencil and watercolor, 310 x 380 mm.
Inscribed lower left corner: "Stern"

method of working with designers. After making his own detailed prompt book, he discussed with the designer the play's requirements, its style and atmosphere, and his practical directorial problems, after which sketches were made. Reinhardt recognized Stern's talents, however, and often let him work things out for himself.

Stern was a prodigious scene and costume designer—organized and innovative. He could easily adapt himself to Reinhardt's mercurial changes in production style, whether working in the Kammerspiel Theater, the Deutsches Theater, a civic arena, or the Grosses Schauspielhaus which was designed by Hans Poelzig and opened in 1919. Within the immensity of this new thrust theatre, Reinhardt and Stern presented nine plays during the first season of six months, including *Oresteia, Lysistrata, Hamlet, Julius Caesar,* and *Danton.* These huge productions required experimenting in new lighting methods and scenic techniques. Some productions were not successful, many were criticized for their revolutionary innovations, but they were all courageous and adventurous and injected new life into the postwar theatre of Germany.

Stern's experience working with Reinhardt on more than one hundred and fifty productions of theatre, ballet, and opera was the foundation for his later activities and his international reputation. When Reinhardt decided to relinquish control of his Berlin theatres, Stern became the art director for Ernst Lubitsch's motion-picture studios outside of Berlin. After the burning of the Reichstag, Lubitsch transferred his activities to Hollywood. Stern became associated with the director-producer Eric Charell and designed spectacular musicals such as *The Whitehorse Inn* and *The Three Musketeers* in Berlin, London, Paris, and New York. In Berlin he worked with Bruno Walter on *Tannhäuser* in the Charlottenburg Opera.

With Hitler's rise to power, Stern and his wife commuted from London and New York to Hollywood to work with Lubitsch; then back again to work in London's West End with C. B. Cochran, Basil Dean, and Tyrone Guthrie. In 1936, he designed theatrical decor on a grand scale for the façade of Selfridge's for the coronation of Edward VIII, with only slight alterations for George VI. During World War II, he was confined in an English internees' camp and was later released, only to be bombed out of his London flat in 1944. After the war, Stern chose to reside in England.

In 1951, he wrote a wry, witty book, *My Life, My Stage,* enlivened with his inimitable drawings recounting the mercurial career of a famous designer whom His Majesty George VI honored with a Civil List pension for his distinguished contribution to the art of the theatre.

*Illustration 191.* In his drawings for Reinhardt's 1911 Deutsches Theater production of Schiller's *Don Carlos,* Ernst Stern captured the stark, sombre mood of Philip II's court in the Escorial, and the oppressive air of impending tragedy that hung over Spain in the sixteenth century.

In all of Stern's "sketch like" designs for *Don Carlos,* washed white walls, with architectural elements lined in black, serve as background for dark doors and minimal

properties such as the stark throne. A weakling and mentally ill, Philip II was torn during his whole life between religion and humanity. Stern's recurring scenic visual reminder is the cross or the crucifix.

*Illustration 192. Turandot* is the old Venetian comedy by Carlo Gozzi set to music by Karl Vollmoeller. The locale is the faraway court of the Emperor Altoun in Peking. The oriental costumes and decor of Ernst Stern were variously described as grotesque, splendid, sumptuous, monstrous, and marvelously beautiful—Chinese fantasy out of a German's dream world.

This is the imperial couch of the princess Turandot, almost lost beneath a glowing canopy of huge Chinese lanterns suspended before Craig-like screens.

"Herr Stern has certainly let himself go," wrote an English critic of the production when *Turandot* was transferred in 1911 from Berlin to the Saint James's Theatre in London. A designer can often be his own best critic, and Ernst Stern later agreed: "Both in decor and costumes I had 'let myself go.'"

### Ludwig Sievert

Ludwig Sievert belonged to a new generation of German designers who studied stage design preparatory to a professional career. In Coblenz, he pursued his formal training in the Kunstgewerbschule and simultaneously learned the craft of executing costumes and scenery in the studios of the Stadttheater. As a young artist, he was strongly influenced by the French impressionists; as an incipient designer, he fell under the spell of Adolphe Appia.

When Sievert was only twenty-five, he was appointed to the responsible position of artistic adviser for the Stadttheater of Freiburg. On Freiburg's stage he could experiment in all the new artistic trends of the day. His first season, he designed a simplified production of the *Ring* very much in the manner of Appia, his hero.

During World War I, Sievert was working in the Mannheim Theater with the aggressive director Richard Weichert. Impressionism could no longer contain Sievert's strong reactions to the civilization rapidly disintegrating around him, and he became an ardent member of the German expressionist movement. Expressionism was a phenomenon that came to Germany in that generation, with artists and writers revolting against the sorry social environment of the previous generation. They were passionate advocates of a new humanity and a better and more peaceful society opposed to war.

In 1919, Richard Weichert became Intendant of the prestigious Stadttheater in Frankfurt, and Sievert accompanied him from Mannheim as staff designer. For eighteen years, their theatre was one of the most influential, vital, and experimental postwar theatres of Germany. The repertory included expressionist plays by Hasenclever, Kaiser, and Von Unruh, audacious productions of Goethe, Schiller, and Shakespeare, and operas by Mozart, Wagner, Strauss, and Hindemith.

By the mid-twenties, expressionism had run its course. Sievert turned his expressionist eye to old matters and

LUDWIG
SIEVERT·
1913·

new directions. He explored the fresh fields of stylization. The neorealistic Sievert "look" had simplicity and refinement, and his drawing found the freedom of the baroque line. He confined himself almost exclusively to designing operas.

During the period of political and military pressures in Germany between 1937 and 1943, Sievert was on the design staff of the Staatsoper in Munich. There were political pressures within the opera house which caused grave unrest among all the artists behind the scenes. Sievert once again was faced with the same wartime economies which he had experienced in Mannheim during World War I. After his years in Munich, with his country spiritually and economically defeated, Sievert became relatively inactive and removed from the mainstream of the German theatre.

Ludwig Sievert made a significant contribution to the development of German scenography between the two world wars. The body of his work reflects all the changes in the visual theatre of that vital period—from impressionism to expressionism, from stylization to the new realism.

*Illustration 193.* Ludwig Sievert was twenty-six when he designed the production of *Parsifal* for the Freiburg opera house. He sought to dramatize in visual terms his responsive impressions of Wagner's transcendent music,

(193)  Sievert, Ludwig, 1887–1966
        Germany, Hannover (active in Freiburg, Mannheim, Frankfurt, and Munich)
        Holy Forest near Monsalvat for Wagner's *Parsifal*, Act I, Scene I, 1913
        Pastel, 310 x 359 mm.
        Inscribed lower left corner: "Ludwig Sievert 1913"
        Collection: The Artist

and also to capture the poetic mood of Adolphe Appia's *Parsifal* drawings which he deeply admired. Sievert's impressionist approach to this mystic legend of redemption imbued his scenes with a depth of religious mood akin to ecstasy.

In this opening scene of spring awakening amidst the holy forest, Gurnemanz and two esquires are engaged in their devotionals. A flowery sward with bowing tree forms leads down to the sacred lake encircled by the blue-green sheltering forest.

To accompany Gurnemanz' and Parsifal's ascent from this forest glade to the castle of Montsalvat and the hall of the grail, Sievert did not employ the traditional moving panorama. His towering tree-trunks, like columns, slowly pivoted in full view to become the Gothic shafts supporting the dome of the hall of the grail. Sievert combined scenic imagination with visual intelligence.

(194) Sievert, Ludwig
Besieged Fort for Kokoschka-Hindemith's *Murderer,
Hope of Women*, 1922

Watercolor and charcoal, 391 x 487 mm.
Inscribed lower right corner: "L. Sievert, 1922"
Collection: The Artist

*Illustration 194.* The German expressionists chose to distort nature as an expression of the artist's innermost self; "The Art of Inwardness," they called it. In his first expressionist play, *Murderer, Hope of Women*, written in 1908, Kokoschka fused dialogue, design, and movement into his own concept of total theatre. This timeless play of dark symbols, dealing with the eternal polarity of the sexes, was frequently revived in Germany before embattled audiences and demonstrations.

Hindemith made an opera of Kokoschka's play which was performed in the Staatsoper of Frankfurt in 1922 under the direction of Ernst Lert with the setting and costumes of Ludwig Sievert.

Kenneth Macgowan, in *Continental Stagecraft*, describes Sievert's expressionist design as "strong and arresting with dark surfaces massed in triangles symbolic of the feminine element dominant in the piece, and with a successful, if not very subtle, use of red and red-orange on the pylon surfaces guarding the prison door."

Sievert's sketch dramatizes the moment of confrontation between the armed warriors and the helpless women.

His dramatic solution of space for this opera was not only a high achievement for himself as a designer, but also for the German expressionist theatre of the twenties.

### Helmut Jürgens

During the early years of the German Republic, Helmut Jürgens, like most of the stage designers of his generation, learned to design scenery and costumes under the economic pressures that beset every government-subsidized theatre. While all the German state theatres were nightly crowded with hungry audiences, they operated on a shoestring. Old scenery from the storehouse was cut to a new style, black curtains or the stage's white cyclorama enclosed constructivist steps and platforms or expressionist scenic symbols. Yet startling advances in projected scenery and arbitrary stage lighting were made. German designers compensated for bareness by using theatrical invention and imagination. Thus they were released from the formulas of accepted scenic practice and free to exercise their individual talents.

Jürgens' knowledge of the new approach to scenic

design was acquired from years of experience in many of Germany's leading state theatres. In 1948, he finally settled in Munich and became a permanent designer on the staff of the redoubtable Staatsoper. For seventeen years, he found the freedom and opportunity to design many of the Staatsoper's notable modern productions in its restored neoclassical house.

Jürgens was one of Europe's significant designers, and his death in 1965 was a great loss to the German theatre. Jürgens never opted for constructivism, expressionism, or realism. For him, every play or opera was its own designer. His productions always bore the stamp of his elegant and graphic style. German artists from Dürer on have rarely handled color subtly. Like the color of Emil Nolde and other expressionists, Jürgens' color had to have reason and make a statement, even though sometimes it bordered on the obvious and self-conscious.

Jürgens had the curiosity of the artist-craftsman. In his search for new dimensions in theatre technology, he experimented with the theatrical capabilities of materials associated with other crafts and industries—metals, acrylics, fiber glass, fabrics, and meshes. This inquiring concern gave a contemporary, exciting look to his settings and contributed to the unmistakable character of his distinguished style.

*Illustration 195.* Helmut Jürgens fashioned this ominous setting for the 1963 revival of Strauss' *Elektra* at the Staatsoper in Munich. Jürgens' design is pure theatre with no intention of reconstructing the art of ancient Mycenae—only its tragic glory.

The main action of the opera is confined to a purpled-red ramp receding to a pair of towering, sculptured silver doors which solemnly admit to the palace. The back wall is a dark coarse gauze, striated with a plastic web which gives the transparent wall an etched texture. Only once were the interior terraces revealed, as shown in this sketch, with servants rushing frenetically through the palace by torchlight. Jürgens' coherent design heightened the emotional impact of the stark action of von Hofmannsthal's spare libretto and served as a brooding foil to Strauss' violent score.

(195) Jürgens, Helmut, 1902–1965
Germany, Westphalia (active in Munich, Coblenz, Dusseldorf, and Frankfurt)

Palace of Agamemnon at Mycenae for Richard Strauss' *Elektra*, 1963
Tempera, acrylic, and metallic paint, 435 x 590 mm.
Collection: Dr. Claire Jürgens

### Ansel Cook

Ansel Cook's name first appears in the program of the Castle Square Theatre in Boston in September 1898. The Boston City Directory listed him as "Scenic Artist" of the famous Castle Square Stock Company between 1897 and 1902. Afterwards, he moved to Chicago and was engaged in the Sosman & Landis Studio where he was recognized as "a fine drapery painter."

*Illustration 196.* This sketch for a palace, attributed to Ansel Cook, harks back to neoclassical European palace settings. Ansel Cook gave his "old-world" palace a turn-of-the-century American look with his pink "grand drapery" framing the beige and gold hall adorned with sculptures and yucca-filled urns. This palatial scenic style was the precursor of America's ornate movie palaces.

### Claude Bragdon

Claude Bragdon was an American architect, artist, author, and philosopher who endured the exquisite pleasure of subjecting his work to the controlling principles of dynamic symmetry. After studying architecture at Cornell and designing a number of important buildings in Rochester, Claude, the artist, decided to move to New York City and find a new world for himself.

The desultory theatre of Broadway did not excite him. Having absorbed Gordon Craig's ideas, he would champion the New Movement in the theatre with all its promise as a corrective for the wayward commercial theatre. He applauded Reinhardt's revolutionary productions and Diaghilev's sensational Russian Ballet. A few other isolated Americans, sharing Bragdon's vision, were also seeking to revolutionize American stagecraft. Sam Hume, who had studied with Craig in Florence, put on the first American exhibition of the new stagecraft in 1914 and later directed the Arts and Crafts Theatre in Detroit. In 1916, Sheldon Cheney launched *Theatre Arts Quarterly,* the mouthpiece of the new movement. Winthrop Ames, a proper Bostonian, was dreaming of plans for a National Theatre. A handful of young playwrights, including Eugene O'Neill, were putting on their plays in an impoverished theatre on a wharf in Provincetown on Cape Cod. At Harvard, Professor George Pierce Baker was offering a pioneering course to aspiring playwrights and also laying the foundations for the educational theatre in America.

Claude Bragdon set out to establish artistic coordination on the American stage. David Belasco's calculated realism left no room for freedom of imagination. Bragdon's stage settings would have the stylized simplicity of dynamic symmetry. When Thomas Edison invented his carbon filament lamp, he bequeathed to the theatre a fourth dimension. For three summers, because of his contribution to the Song and Light Festival in New York's

(196) Cook, Ansel, d. c. 1915 (attributed)
United States (active in Boston and Chicago)
Palace Drop, c. 1905

Pen and ink with watercolor, 305 x 458 mm.
Inscribed lower right with the studio's code number for the drop: "No. 656 DWP"

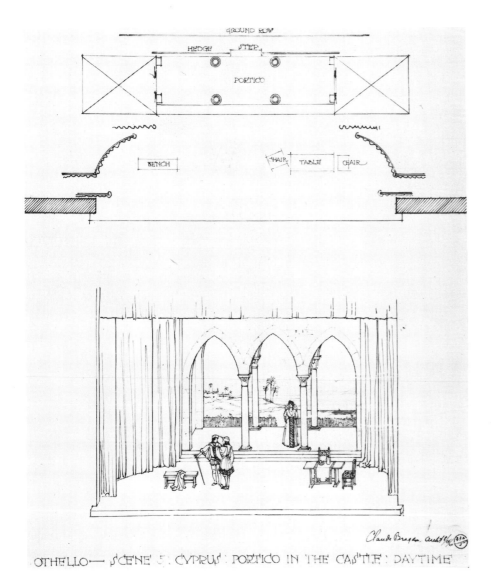

OTHELLO— SCENE 5 : CYPRUS : PORTICO IN THE CASTLE : DAYTIME

(197)
Bragdon, Claude, 1866–1946
United States (active mostly in New York)
Cyprus—Portico in the Castle for Shakespeare's *Othello*, 1924
Pen and ink on transparency, 477 x 377 mm.
Inscribed lower right corner: "Claude Bragdon, Arch 8/14/24"
Collection: Henry Bragdon

Central Park, Claude Bragdon was called the "Master of Light." He was among the first artists in America to convert this new force to aesthetic and imaginative use. In the theatre he promised a revolutionary use of mobile color and a dramatic role for stage lighting.

Bragdon's ideas greatly impressed the distinguished actor-manager Walter Hampden, who asked Bragdon in 1919 to collaborate with him on a production of *Hamlet*. Bragdon designed an elaborate but ingenious unit setting for *Hamlet* with neutral draperies, steps and levels, and movable units that could be rearranged swiftly yet maintain a unity of style in production. That simplified production of *Hamlet* was considered by most critics to be as fine as anything yet seen on the American stage. In the following years, Claude Bragdon campaigned for his scenic simplicities as design associate for many of Walter Hampden's revivals, including *Macbeth*, *Cyrano*, *Othello*, and *Caponsacchi*.

In retrospect, Claude Bragdon's productions may seem bland and static, formal and uninspired; but in their time, they swept the stage of realistic scenic conventions and emphasized simple pictorial values and arbitrary lighting, and thus provided the actor with a free, unobtrusive stage. Bragdon's contribution to the American scene has not yet been sufficiently recognized.

*Illustration 197.* Claude Bragdon made precise, mechanical drawings for his settings and accompanied them with informative ground plans. This insistent linear clarity was the result of his architectural training. His customary signature was "Claude Bragdon, Arch." For Walter Hampden's *Othello*, Bragdon framed stylized settings within simple masking curtains. He used a few architectural elements and only those properties essential to the dramatic action.

Compare this design made in 1924 for *Othello* with the accepted Palace Interior by Ansel Cook (Illus. 196), which Bragdon might have seen in his younger years of theatregoing. How revolutionary were the new directions that Bragdon helped to bring about in American stage design.

### Thomas G. Moses

Had Thomas G. Moses heeded his father, he would have been a tanner in England. But he was an aspiring artist, and as a lad he left Liverpool, sailed for America, and ended up as a scenic artist in Chicago after studying with various artists in Chicago, New York, and California.

In Chicago, Moses was hired to paint scenery in the Sosman & Landis Scenic Studio (1877–1929) which was one of the largest studios in the country. While he managed the studio for many years, and later became its vice-president, he never gave up scene painting. He designed and painted scenery for Buffalo Bill, Edwin Booth, Edward Barret, and Sarah Bernhardt. A model stage with more than a hundred wings and drops executed by Moses for Masonic initiation ceremonies is in the theatrical collection of the University of Texas.

Arthur Oberbeck, a respected elder scenic artist, continues to carry on the great tradition of scene painting in the Peter Wolf Studio in Dallas, Texas. In the nineties, he was hired by the Sosman & Landis Studio for six dollars a week as an apprentice, cleaning palettes and washing paint pots. Oberbeck recalls a number of well-known scenic artists working there at that time, each a specialist in his field: "There was Ansel Cook, who was a fine drapery painter; Mr. Hartson from New York, who was one of the best exterior painters I ever knew; Mr. Evans, who was a street painter; Mr. William Nutzhorn, who painted only interiors; Mr. Strong, who was the only man allowed to paint Masonic scenery at that time; and, of course, Mr. Moses, who also painted exclusively exteriors. I worked under Mr. Moses for eleven or twelve years. In my opinion, Mr. Moses was not nearly as versatile an exterior painter as Mr. Hartson. Mr. Moses had difficulty painting ornament. His style, while quite fine, was very stereotyped; distinctive, but repetitive and easily recognizable."

When the Sosman & Landis Scenic Studio changed hands and became the Chicago Studio, Moses took his leave and "went around the country touching up Masonic scenery." Moses' exit from the theatre symbolizes the end of the era of the scenic artist as a force in American scene design.

*Illustration 198.* This sketch for a vaudeville olio drop is a scenic artist's moonlit idyll—a world serene, without sorrow. A golden drapery frames the marble terrace and sculptured grand staircase bordering an Italian lake. Moses shared with the audience his belief that the romantic world of the theatre was created for the greater happiness of all. About the same year that Moses made this design, Ziegfeld, in New York, set out to achieve this same ideal with his more stylish and sophisticated *Follies.*

### Erté (Romain de Tirtoff)

Erté's stylish hand made everything that he touched fashionable. He was an artist in tune with the era which his art helped to create. He was a cosmopolitan illustrator and an acclaimed fashion designer; he even designed jewelry, shoes, and fabrics; and most important, he designed lavish costumes and scenery for a theatre of luxury.

Romain de Tirtoff studied with the Russian painter Repin in Saint Petersburg. His special tastes were only peripheral to the ideas of the World of Art group. In 1912, when only twenty, he left Russia and settled in Paris. Soon he found a place for himself in the fashionable atelier of Paul Poiret, where he gained experience

(198) Moses, Thomas G., 1856–1931
England, Liverpool (active in Chicago)
Terrace by Moonlit Lake—An Olio Drop, c. 1910
(See also color plate 27)
Watercolor and gouache, 450 x 594 mm.
Inscribed lower right corner: the studio's stock
number, "No. 554"
On verso: "Painted in the Chicago Studio of Sosman
& Landis Co."
Collection: New York Studio Alliance

(199) Erté (Romain de Tirtoff), 1892–
Russian-French, Saint Petersburg (active in Paris,
Monte Carlo, Naples, London, New York, and
Hollywood)
Gold Scene for *The Ziegfeld Follies of 1923*
Gouache and metallic paint, 140 x 215 mm.
Inscribed lower right margin: "Erté," and on verso:
"No. 664 Decor L'Or, 1923" with Erté's stamp.
Collection: The Artist

working with Poiret on costumes for the theatre. In 1916, Erté embarked on his own professional career as a costume and scene designer for spectacles in Parisian music halls and for reviews such as the Folies-Bergère.

For a generation, Erté enjoyed the prestige of a designer's royal progress. His spare yet sumptuous style brought him international recognition. During the twenties, George White engaged Erté to glamorize his editions of the *Scandals* for Broadway. For Ziegfeld he designed *tableaux* for the *Follies*. M.G.M. lured him to Hollywood. In London he designed spectacular shows for those Roman pleasure domes the Coliseum, Palladium, and Hippodrome. In Paris he designed many operas, among them Poulenc's *Les Mamelles de Tiresias* for the Opéra Comique, and also productions for Monte Carlo and the San Carlo in Naples.

Erté had panache. He could convert the arts of Greece or Rome, Persia or China to his individual style of art moderne—costumes with billowing lace and bows and trains, and costly curtains and draperies caught up by sumptuous tassels. On occasion, his decorative costumes could become scenery, and his scenery could become animated costumes. His scenes had the felicitous, flowing lines of the illustrator. He created many arresting covers for *L'Illustration*, *Harper's Bazaar*, and the *Illustrated*

*London News*. Unfortunately, his style was often debased in the hands of lesser artists, and his popular influence became responsible for the debauched and sterile style associated with "movie-palace" stage presentations of that epoch. However, in his own hands, Erté's style had unique originality, and it set the fashion for a generation in Europe and America.

*Illustration 199*. As the Great Glorifier, Ziegfeld understood "the promise of romance and excitement and all the things a man dreams about when he thinks of the word 'girl.'" In *The Playbill*, Eugene Boe described Ziegfeld's "finishing school" for his girls of the *Follies*: "He taught them the statuesque stance and the art of descending a staircase or crossing the stage with a certain elegant, aloof, gliding grace that became the distinguished mark of the Ziegfeld girl. He swathed their bodies in lavish gowns and jewelry and positioned them against luxurious backdrops."

Erté, in this be-tasselled production number in gold and black, contrived to regiment the ladies of the ensemble into a stunning climax of draped pulchritude that nightly evoked spontaneous cheers from the audience.

A collection of two hundred drawings of Erté was acquired by the Metropolitan Museum of Art in 1967.

### Joseph Urban

In sixty-one years, Joseph Urban managed to live two full lives in the theatre, first in Austria and then his "second coming" in America. Like Alfred Roller a brief generation before him, Urban studied in the Vienna Academy of Fine Arts and also attended the Polytechnical School. He, too, was an outstanding member of the Viennese Sezession movement. He always had a deep interest in the visual theatre, but he did not surface until 1905 with his first designs for a play of Schnitzler in the Hofburg Theater. His next challenge was designing Parts I and II of *Faust*. In 1908 he was designing for Gustav Mahler at the Hofoper along with Roller. He also found time to design the *Ring* in Budapest, and operas for many lyric theatres in Germany.

In 1911, Urban accepted the Boston Opera Company's invitation to become artistic director and design a half dozen operas for the following season. The originality and craftsmanship of his settings impressed the Bostonians, but after a second Boston season, Urban felt the lure of Broadway. He took a chance and opened his Urban Scenic Studio in New York. The American custom of painting scenery on huge frames that slid up and down did not appeal to Urban's feeling for the craft of scene painting, so he staffed his studio with a group of European scenic artists who introduced the continental traditions of their craft to America. With long-handled brushes they painted their scenes on the flat floor of his studio. They also used starch with tempera colors and analines to achieve atmospheric, translucent drops. Urban adapted the system of pointillism, perfected by Monet and Seurat, to scene painting. This method of painting with texture gave the surface of a drop or scene any desired color with proper handling of lighting. As a designer, Urban literally "painted" with light. Urban's method of scene painting was adopted by many New York scenic studios, notably the innovative studio of Robert W. Bergman, favored by the younger generation of American designers.

Within a few years, Joseph Urban had become the most active designer of plays and musicals on Broadway. Florenz Ziegfeld was the first producer to recognize his flair and taste, and he engaged him to design the *Follies* of 1915. For many years, Ziegfeld, the autocratic Mycaenus of Broadway, rarely embarked on a musical without Urban's guiding eye. During the twenties, "Settings by Joseph Urban" appeared on the houseboards of major producers of musicals by Jerome Kern, Sigmund Romberg, Vincent Youmans, George Gershwin, and Richard Rodgers. Urban brought many scenic innovations to the American musical theatre—plastic three-dimensional scenery, the show portal and permanent portals to frame the entire stage, revolving *periaktoi* to frame changing backdrops, and alternating swinging platform stages.

In 1917, Gatti-Casazza, general manager of the Metropolitan Opera, first commissioned Urban to design *Faust*. Previously, much of the Opera's scenery had been imported from the studio of La Scala in Milan. Thereafter, Urban settings in many styles added lustre to the Metropolitan's changing repertory. He moved from realism in *Norma*, to monumental simplicity in *Parsifal* and *Otello*, to pure decoration in *Don Giovanni*. In Liszt's *The Legend of Saint Elizabeth* he shifted stylistically from realism to abstraction and symbolism.

As an experienced stage designer, Joseph Urban was a knowledgeable theatre architect, and the drawings in his book *Theatres* (1929) reveal his versatility and skill in devising new theatre forms that brought stage and auditorium into closer relation. In the intimate theatre of the New School for Social Research, he eliminated the proscenium and favored side stages, while in the Ziegfeld Theatre in New York the audience sat beneath a richly frescoed egg-shaped dome, separated from the stage by a bold golden cyma molding. In 1927, with the encouragement of Otto Kahn, Urban designed a unified, total plan for a new Metropolitan Opera House some years before its move to Lincoln Center. This plan was never realized.

In 1920, Urban decided to undertake designing for motion pictures in Hollywood, and for ten years he applied his theatrical and architectural experience to designing some forty pictures, principally for Hearst's Cosmopolitan Studios and Fox Films.

Joseph Urban brought to America the traditions and advanced taste of continental stagecraft. He was not essentially an innovative designer, but the American theatre was ready for and receptive to his practical reforms. He brought to the theatre such versatility and energy that for every Broadway season, in addition to his work in architecture and motion pictures, he designed more than ten productions. For a score of years Jo Urban's name was legendary in the entertainment world of New York.

*Illustration 200*. Joseph Urban designed *Parsifal* for the Metropolitan Opera's season of 1919–1920. With occasional face-lifting, Urban's production of *Parsifal* re-

(200) Urban, Joseph, 1872–1933
    Austria, Vienna (active in Austria-Hungary,
    Germany, and the United States)
    Klingsor's Magic Garden for Wagner's *Parsifal*,
    Act II, Scene 2, 1919
    Gouache, 226 x 377 mm.
    Collection: Mrs. Joseph Urban

mained in the repertory for thirty-six years. This atmospheric sketch represents the final moments of Act II when Klingsor's magic castle crumbles into earth, and the sensuous tropical gardens wither into an arid desert. This is one of Wagner's demanding scenic transformations, and Urban made several studies for it. The drawing shown reveals the artist in his most imaginative and powerful style—freed of the decorative eclecticism of the Austrian *Wiener Werkstätte* which was identified with so much of his work.

The major collection of Urban's drawings is in the Columbia University Library in New York.

### Lee Simonson

Lee Simonson as a young man had two spiritual godfathers: Maxfield Parrish opened his eyes to the world of art, and George Bernard Shaw inducted him into the modern theatre. At Harvard, he majored in philosophy and sat at the feet of his god, Santayana. From the heretical George Pierce Baker he learned that the theatre mat-

tered. Intellectually fortified, he went to Paris for three years of artistic stimulation where, he wrote, "art was redefined and recreated once a year." Cézanne, Matisse, and Picasso sharpened his eye for modern art, and with his "passion for galaxies of brilliant color" he happily pursued his painting in a crowded studio of L'Académie Julien. In Europe he discovered what Reinhardt and Diaghilev could do with artists in revivifying the theatre.

Back in New York, after playing the forlorn role of a painter of still life for three years, Lee Simonson fell in with a group of crusading theatre friends who called themselves the Washington Square Players. In 1915, on the diminutive stage of their Bandbox Theatre, he began his theatrical career designing a mountain for Andreev's *Love of One's Neighbor* with two pieces of scenery. This was followed by a stylized colorful setting for the French medieval farce *Maître Pathelin*, and America's first curtained interior for Susan Glaspell's psychological play *Overtones*.

After serving in World War I, Simonson returned to

229

New York in 1919, and with Lawrence Langner and several of the old Washington Square group he became one of the six founding directors of the prestigious Theatre Guild. For twenty years he remained the Theatre Guild's art director and principal designer of settings, costumes, and lighting. Some of his notable designs were for such varied plays as *Liliom, The Adding Machine, Back to Methuselah, Roar China, Marco Millions*, and *Faust*. He also contributed his versatile talent to many Broadway productions, and in 1948 he was commissioned to design the settings and costumes for the Metropolitan Opera's *Ring* cycle.

Lee Simonson's interests spread beyond the theatre. In 1927, he designed the very modern installation of the first International Exhibition of Modern Crafts at Macy's store. He organized the eye-opening International Theatre

Exhibition in 1934 for the Museum of Modern Art. He was an art critic and a magazine editor; he wrote three important lasting works on the history and the art of the theatre, *The Stage Is Set* (1932), *Part of a Lifetime* (1943), and *The Art of Scenic Design* (1950). With his knowledge of theatre mechanics and lighting, he served as a frequent consultant for new theatres.

However, first and foremost, Lee Simonson was a vital stage designer. His drawings for the theatre had the strict but proud limitations of the draftsman. He designed his scene from inside the proscenium looking out. Every detail was clearly set forth in his scale plans, sections, and elevations. His final setting was the visual expression of what he called his preliminary "plan of action." This was a detailed analysis of the playing areas which accommodated the movement of the actors in sustaining the dra-

(201) Simonson, Lee, 1888–1967
United States, New York
Street Scene for Molière's *School for Husbands*, 1933
Pencil and watercolor, 406 x 547 mm.

Inscribed on four sides of sketch are notations for the scenic artist; "Lee Simonson" along lower margin.
Collections: UCLA, Larsen

(202)  Simonson, Lee
Costumes for Athene and Tircis for Molière's *School
for Husbands*, 1933
Pencil, watercolor, and metallic paint, 321 x 404 mm.
Collections: UCLA, Larsen

matic action of the play. He designed as a director. He
was sensitive to the stage's spatial relationships and how
these areas could be lighted. "Much of my designing was
conceived in technical terms of gauze, projections or
translucent sheets, permanent frames, interchangeable
units."

For all of his manifest talent, Lee Simonson was very
modest—and so was his work for the theatre. He believed
that a stage setting was only a background of selective
detail—a heightened abstraction from reality. His work
always displayed versatility, taste, and technical skill—
occasionally uneven in style and not always inspired. As
an artist, he raised the craft of stage design in America
to a high level of professionalism.

*Illustration 201.* Molière's *School for Husbands* was presented by the Theatre Guild in New York in 1933, directed by Lawrence Langner with choreography by Doris
Humphrey and Charles Weidman. This working sketch
was Simonson's decorative backdrop for a street scene.

Painted houses were set on either side of the stage and
framed the drop. Simonson rarely made finished drawings
for his settings. He made detailed elevations, sections,
and plans of his scenes, then scale painter's elevations for
the scenic artists.

*Illustration 202.* These costumes were for a ballet interlude in *School for Husbands*. Simonson based these stylish
designs on the authentic pattern of French seventeenth-
century theatre costumes. As a practical man of the theatre, Simonson believed that costumes for the theatre
should be constructed so they could be worn easily and
comfortably not only as costumes but as clothes on an
actor in action.

*Illustration 203.* This street scene was the anonymous
work of a scenic artist early in this century. Customarily,
a studio salesman would travel cross-country with his
stock books of numbered sketches from which the theatre
manager selected his scenery.

(203)  Unknown artist, twentieth century
United States, New York
Olio Street Drop for Vaudeville, c. 1908
Watercolor, 303 x 480 mm.
Collections: New York Studios, Studio Alliance

Every vaudeville house in the United States boasted an olio street drop. Most were inventions, but this one is identified. The central portion reproduces a contemporary photograph (preserved in the Library of Congress) of Courtland Street in Lower Manhattan. Lining the street in perspective are hotels, stores, and office buildings including the Singer Tower, at that time the highest building in the world. Trolley tracks recede toward an elevated railway station. Advertising display boards and foliage form a gateway to this silent city whose only traffic was provided by the noisy vaudeville song-and-dance teams that played back and forth across the street.

The theatre of every age since Plautus and Terence has had its "street scene." Only one generation separates this scenic artist's New York street from Lee Simonson's stylized street of Paris for Molière's *School for Husbands*. But stylistically how far apart they are!

### Norman Bel Geddes

Norman Bel Geddes' life is the drama of a rebellious young genius who, with a hunger for theatre and no formal schooling after sixteen, worked his way through art school in Cleveland and Detroit and became the foremost designer in the United States.

When Geddes was nineteen, he spent a summer among the Blackfeet Indians in Montana. He wrote an Indian drama and called it *Thunderbird*. He designed the scenes and costumes for it and persuaded Charles Cadman to compose the incidental music. Aline Barnsdall, a pioneer in the little-theatre movement in the United States with her theatre in Los Angeles, which boasted a good acting company, agreed to produce *Thunderbird*, and also engaged Geddes as her designer for a year. His play was not produced, but his settings for her 1916 season were an artistic and economic success.

One day found Geddes on a park bench in Los Angeles discouraged with the progress of his career. Another bench-sitter had left his copy of the *Literary Digest* with a page open whose headline proclaimed "Millionaires Should Help Artists" and an interview with Otto Kahn, New York banker and patron of the arts. Geddes wired Kahn asking for two hundred dollars to get his family

(204)  Geddes, Norman Bel, 1893–1958
  United States, Adrian, Michigan (active in Los
  Angeles, Chicago, and New York)
  Project for the Dance, c. 1917 (See also color plate 28)
  Watercolor and gouache, 152 x 254 mm.
  Collections: Powell, Richmond Museum

and himself to New York to find a job in the theatre. Two days later the money arrived, and thanks to Otto Kahn, Geddes was off to New York and a fabulous career. Before long, he was designing operas for the Metropolitan Opera, plays for William A. Brady and Winthrop Ames, and for the Century Roof Theatre for Morris Gest.

Geddes' first real success was in 1919 with the Chicago Opera when he designed the ballet *Boudour* and Montemezzi's opera *La Nave*: both works displayed his uncompromising craftsmanship and exuberant originality. In 1920, George Tyler asked Geddes to design his revival of the old musical *Erminie* starring the original veterans Francis Wilson and De Wolfe Hopper. For his scenes, properties, costumes, and even makeup for *Erminie*, Geddes adopted the sketch technique that Inigo Jones used for his court masques. "Norman Bel Geddes' designs are as fine as has ever been seen in the American Theatre," wrote Boston's critic H. T. Parker; "his was the outstanding glory of the evening."

With all this glory, Geddes feared being typecast as only a designer of musicals. He wanted to work on a new play that might regenerate the American theatre. Such plays rarely came along. His future role in the theatre was beginning to take form in his mind: he wanted to be that ideal of Gordon Craig's, an overall artist of the theatre. He would search for a work that would show the theatre what he had in mind.

In 1921, Geddes embarked on his scheme for a theatrical presentation of Dante's *Divine Comedy*. He planned a vast, gray stage that ascended in stepped formation on all sides from a central deepening well. He designed the costumes and masks for 523 actors. The production combined movement, voices, sound, and light. Geddes, with his students, lighted the scale model for every minute of the production. This glorious production of *The Divine Comedy* has been preserved in a book of masterly photographs by Francis Bruguiére published in 1924 through the interest and assistance of Edith J. R. Isaacs by Theatre Arts, Inc. This project remains one of the exciting landmarks of the American theatre of this century.

Henceforth, Geddes produced, directed, and designed most of his own productions—among them, *Hamlet*,

*Lysistrata*, and *Dead End*. Often he designed as a sculptor, changing his plastic forms with dramatic lighting. The execution of these simple productions was often costly—curves fashioned of straight lines, straight lines achieved with entasis, or angles indented, frequently steps and platforms spilling down into the orchestra pit. Geddes was always escaping from the proscenium arch. He designed many indoor and outdoor theatres that broke with all conventions of theatre architecture.

Geddes' scenic bravura appealed to Max Reinhardt. The impresario Morris Gest brought them together in 1924 with *The Miracle*. Geddes transformed the stage and auditorium of New York's huge Century Theatre into an incense-laden medieval cathedral which nightly provided the prelude of a Mass to a vast morality play enacted by a lavishly costumed cast of several hundred, and with à vista changes of scene.

In 1927, after eight energetic years of shaking up the New York theatre, Geddes set out to apply his magic theatre formula to realigning the world in which we live. He opened an office of specialists offering architectural and industrial services and established the profession of industrial design.

At once he was designing an extraordinary variety of commissions in the field of art and industry. He gave the Geddes "look" to product packaging, to the TV set and the refrigerator, to the layout and typography of many magazines. In *Magic Motor Ways* (1940) he set forth his bold concept for today's urban and transcontinental systems of highway communication. He designed films with D. W. Griffith and Cecil B. De Mille. He styled the Ringling Brothers and Barnum and Bailey Circus. During World War II, he invented for the government a system for identifying enemy aircraft and ships. He designed prefabricated houses, factories and hotels, cafés and restaurants.

The enterprise of Norman Bel Geddes was prodigious. His was the world of tomorrow. Thanks to his forward-looking eye, this generation's everyday life is the richer in efficiency and economy, comfort and pleasure—and beauty, too. He imparted his inexhaustible sense of drama to everything he touched. In the theatre and out of it, he was a true pioneer.

*Illustration 204*. This drawing and a companion drawing in my collection were probably designs for the Festival and Ballet Stage which Norman Bel Geddes designed in 1917 for Ruth St. Denis in Los Angeles and called the Denishawn Dance Theatre. The spacious freedom and high walls of this stage project, along with his unfettered projects for *King Lear* and *Pelléas and Mélisande*, recall the strong influence that Gordon Craig exerted on the receptive imagination of Geddes in his early twenties.

The complete collection of Norman Bel Geddes' drawings for theatre and industry is preserved in the Theatre Arts Library of the University of Texas in Austin.

### Robert Edmond Jones

Robert Edmond Jones, during his years at Harvard, had little interest in the theatre—unlike his contemporary Lee Simonson, he did not fall under the theatrical spell of George Pierce Baker. He was concerned with the fine arts and drawing and painting. On occasion, he did indulge his theatrical taste by escaping to Keith's Vaudeville in Boston, where he was enamored of the theatrical allure of the Gibson girl Valesca Suratt and Gertrude Hoffman in her dance of the seven veils.

After Harvard, however, with the support of several friends, he went to Europe in 1913, where he heard assertive voices in a changing theatre and allied himself with those young insurgents. He went to Italy hoping to study theatrical art in Gordon Craig's new school in Florence; he was not enrolled, possibly because Craig suspected young Jones's enthusiasm for his innovations! Jones discovered potent theatre in Claudel's *Tidings Brought to Mary* performed in the radical theatre of Appia and Dalcroze at Hellerau, also in Paris with Jacques Copeau and his adaptable stage at the Vieux Colombier. In Berlin he associated himself with Max Reinhardt and his two designers, Emil Orlik and Ernst Stern, in the Deutsches Theater. Jones was engaged on a Reinhardt production of *The Merchant of Venice* when World War I broke out.

Jones returned to New York from his *wanderjahr* to attack the American theatre's stronghold of outworn tradition. Early in 1915 on the stage of Wallack's Theatre, the name of Robert Edmond Jones burst into public consciousness with his modest setting and exaggerated costumes for Granville Barker's production of Anatole France's *The Man Who Married a Dumb Wife*. Jones's decorative silver-gray housefront was posterlike in its abstract simplicity, with no indication of medieval ornament or architecture. That production became the manifesto of the insurgent New Movement against the theatre's traditional realism, stereotyped acting, and conventional direction. Within a few years, the revolution in American stagecraft instigated by the rebellious triumvirate of Jones, Simonson, and Geddes was a fait accompli, and their efforts established the profession of the stage designer in America.

For Jones, the scene designer was a man of many minds. According to the dictates of the drama, he thought in terms of realism or surrealism, of impressionism, expressionism, or symbolism. Each of his productions bore the lustrous magic of his own special style. "A good scene is not a picture," he asserted. "It is something seen, but it is something conveyed as well; a feeling, an evocation. A setting is not just a collection of beautiful things. It is a presence, a mood, a symphonic accompaniment to the drama, a great warm wind fanning the drama to flame. It echoes, it enhances, it animates. It is an expectancy, a foreboding, a tension. It says nothing, but it gives everything."

Jones relied enormously on the power and the flexibility of light to animate his scene. The setting of the Jones-Hopkins-Barrymore production of *Richard III* in 1920 was a courtyard reminiscent of the Tower of London. Jones played light like a chiaroscuro wash over those confining walls; exploring spotlights revealed the intimate drama of individual scenes—an arras or a prison cage trundled onto the stage. For the same trio's production of

(205) Jones, Robert Edmond, 1887–1954
   United States, Milton, New Hampshire (active in
   New York, Central City, Colo., and Hollywood)
   An Abstraction for Arnold Schönberg's Opera-
   Pantomime *Die Glückliche Hand* (The Hand of
   Fate), 1930
   Pen and black ink with ink wash, 306 x 540 mm.
   Collection: Joseph Hindle

*Hamlet* two years later, Jones designed an immense hall enclosing a flight of stairs which ran the full width of the stage and led up to a dominant Romanesque arch. There were no scene changes, only atmospheric changes of light. Light with Jones was a marvelous, sensitive medium of expression, so sympathetic that "the livingness of light" for him was a sixth sense.

Jones was always exploring new directions for the theatre of today and tomorrow. As early as 1913 in Florence, he designed a project for Shelley's *The Cenci* to be performed on the central raised stage of a boxing arena—the stage harshly lighted with white light from below and overhead. Within the surrounding darkness of the auditorium, the characters appeared externalized, stark, and theatrical. For the American premiere of Stravinsky's *Oedipus Rex* in 1931, he placed the opera-oratorio's singers in the orchestra pit. In the immense darkness of the empty stage of the Metropolitan Opera House, floating high above the robed chorus in eerie light, archaic Greek supermarionettes pantomimed the slow movement of the ancient drama of Oedipus. In designing Marc Connelly's spiritual fable, *The Green Pastures*, Jones brought simple reverence and exaltation to the production—as though he himself were an eager member of a black community in the deep South charged with making up the scenes and improvising the costumes from whatever he could lay his hands on.

In 1934, Jones was invited to try his hand at Hollywood. He designed for Pioneer Pictures the first color motion picture, *La Cucaracha*, followed by *Becky Sharp* directed by Rouben Mamoulian. These films in Technicolor became milestones in the development of cinematic art. Ten years earlier, he had sought to establish a synthesis between theatre and motion pictures. He explored many avenues in his search for a new form of theatre art —"a presentation of light, color, moving form, and sound —an abstract evocation."

Robert Edmond Jones' dreams for an American theatre live on. His influence on the younger generation survives and will continue to survive through his evocative *Draw-*

*ings for the Theatre* (1925 and 1970) and his inspiring ideas in *The Dramatic Imagination* (1941). "His settings were not reproductions of reality," observed John Mason Brown. "They were extensions of it. They had exaltation in them, too. Although the mood and meaning of a play lived in them, they lived a life of their own. . . The dream that was his walks in them, as summoning as ever, and the more welcome and needed in today's almost dreamless theatre, as reminders of what the theatre can be."

*Illustration 205.* Robert Edmond Jones designed this assemblage of abstract screens animated with light for the League of Composers' American premiere of Schönberg's *Die Glückliche Hand* at the Metropolitan Opera House. It was conducted by Leopold Stokowski and directed by Rouben Mamoulian, with Doris Humphrey as the Woman and Charles Weidman as the Man.

*Illustration 206.* In 1938, the Players Club of New York planned for their annual revival a series of scenes from the repertoire of Edwin Booth, the founder of the club, with a cast of distinguished performers from Broadway and Hollywood. Robert Edmond Jones was enlisted as director-designer. Because of their stage and studio commitments, the "cast melted away" and the decision was made: "No revival this year."

Jones probably made this dramatic drawing as an in-

ducement to Jane Cowl to play Lady Macbeth in the sleep-walking scene for that proposed revival.

*Illustration 207.* No other *Macbeth* drawings are known to accompany this design. Apparently, Jones was fascinated with the solution of the visual dramatization of this scene. This design, with its complex of mirrored reflections, appears to be a more refined resolution of the scene that he devised in 1921 for the Jones-Hopkins expressionist production with Julia Arthur and Lionel Barrymore. For that production, Jones contrived a series of cut-out, jagged arches symbolizing in outer embodiment the inner thoughts of Lady Macbeth as she walked in her sleep through this maze of arches.

### Eugene Berman

Eugene Berman and his brother Leonide were sons of a cultivated family in Saint Petersburg. At nine, Eugene was sent abroad, and he studied in Germany, Switzerland, and France. With the outbreak of World War I, he returned to Saint Petersburg and pursued his studies in painting and architecture until 1917 when he and his brother settled in Paris. There, a congenial group of artists, including les frères Berman, Bérard, and Tchelitchew, revolted against the main current of modern abstract art. In 1924, they held their first exhibition at the Galerie Druot; soon they were recognized in the Salon as the neoromantic group. They were influenced by the blue

(206) Jones, Robert Edmond
Sleepwalking Scene for Shakespeare's *Macbeth*,
Act V, Scene I, 1938
Pen and ink and black watercolor, 216 x 260 mm.
Inscribed by the artist on back of frame: "To be
played by Jane Cowl"
Collection: Gift of the Artist

(207) Jones, Robert Edmond
Sleepwalking Scene for Shakespeare's *Macbeth*,
Act V, Scene I, 1946
Pen and ink, black wash, and Chinese white, 189 x
305 mm.
Collection: Jones Estate

and rose works of Picasso, and captivated with the surrealists, especially de Chirico.

All through the twenties, Berman made pilgrimages to Italy, sketching and painting from memory her ancient landscape and ruins, and her aging architecture. He paid homage to the Renaissance architects—Palladio, Scamozzi, Peruzzi, Serlio, and Vignola; to the painters Mantegna, Carpaccio, and Gentile Bellini; to the later artists Piranesi, Tiepolo, Pannini, and Canaletto.

In 1935, Berman arrived in New York and was persuaded to apply his talent to the theatre. A. Everett Austin, with his eye for new talent, invited Berman to design his first settings for a music festival at the Hartford Atheneum. Berman also designed dramatic murals for his new patron James Thrall Soby, and he soon was commissioned to design ballets in Paris and New York. He created decor for the Monte Carlo Ballet's *Icare* (1938), *Devil's Holiday* (1939), and *Concerto Barocco* (1941); the last with choreography by George Balanchine. In New York he designed *Romeo and Juliet* (1943) and *Giselle* (1946) for the Ballet Theatre.

Berman's neoromantic decor had invention and fantasy. His designs for palace or inn, desert or cave were treated to the same spatter-and-hole treatment. Julien Levy observed that Berman's "holes painted in the surface of the canvas not only simulate decay and destruction, but also act as a two-dimensional counterpoint to the third dimension of illusionist perspective." Variations on the Bermanesque theme composed these timeless perspectives—ropes and tattered draperies, pyramids and obelisks, antique columns and arches, or crumbling stairways and balconies. In the theatre, his art found full expression in the sensitive designs for *Amahl and the Night Visitors*, Gian-Carlo Menotti's first opera for television, produced by NBC in 1952.

His later decor for opera reveals the assertive influence of the neo-baroque on his style—the sweeping line of assimilated architecture, chiaroscuro, and illusionistic atmosphere. During the fifties, Berman designed the scenes and costumes for four operas for the Metropolitan Opera—*Rigoletto*, *La Forza del Destino*, *Il Barbiere di Seviglia*, and *Don Giovanni*—and for the Piccolo Scala in Milan, *Così fan tutte*.

In 1972, after a long period devoted to painting, he returned to the theatre to design a new staging for the New York City Ballet's Stravinsky Festival at the request of George Balanchine and in memory of his close friend, the composer. That was the finale to twenty-two years of scenic activity in the United States and Europe.

*Illustration 208.* Eugene Berman made this drawing for the ballet company of Colonel de Basil with David Lichine's choreography. World War II intervened, and the ballet was never done.

This evocative design, based on Mendelssohn's *Symphonie Italienne*, is a neoromantic fantasy which in 1939 reflected Berman's fascination with Italian ruins. A series of arches provide depth amidst an aging Italian landscape. Living statues, tufted vegetation, an arm with a lamp, and tattered draperies are typical Berman motifs adorning timeless architecture. All is pink and blue, tawny beige and black. Confided Berman, "To me theatre is in this direction—Magic, Illusion, Enchantment!"

### Pavel Tchelitchew

Pavel Tchelitchew was the scion of an aristocratic, wealthy Russian family. He learned to draw by himself, and his youthful drawings of stage designs, influenced by Bakst, indicate his early interest in the theatre. In 1917, he went to Kiev, where it was his good fortune to study with the stage designer Aleksandra Exter. In 1921, a French warship transported him to Constantinople, where he designed costumes for cabarets in the Pera section, and then he made his way across the Balkans to Berlin. His original settings and costumes for a Russian emigré opera company, and especially his decor for *Le Coq d'Or* for the Berlin Staatsoper, received enthusiastic notices, but it was not long before Diaghilev persuaded Tchelitchew to settle in Paris.

Tchelitchew, with Eugene Berman and Christian Bérard, became a leader of the neoromantic group, which was dedicated to painting in a lyric realm of romantic melancholia. Their first exhibition at the Galerie Druot brought them recognition among the haute monde of the

arts, including Gertrude Stein and, later, Dame Edith Sitwell, who became his British patroness and helped open his way to success in the literary and artistic world of London.

Tchelitchew's figures were becoming increasingly distorted—interlaced and interchangeable with his backgrounds. He began experimenting with perspective. He painted pictures with double and triple perspective. This startling new style was referred to as "multiple image metamorphosis." In 1928, when he designed Nabokov's cosmic dance-drama *Ode* for Diaghilev, he experimented with projected film and light as an integral part of that adventurous work which combined speech, melody, pantomime, and dance. Five years later, in 1933, a lifelong rapport was begun with his fellow countryman George Balanchine with their collaboration on *Errante*, a ballet in which he carried his audacious experiments further, with mobile light on white settings and costumes in primary colors.

The next year, this vanguard artist sailed for America to arrange an exhibition in New York at the Julien Levy Galleries, where the work of Berman, Dali, and Tanguy had already been shown. His paintings at once attracted attention and were much sought after. He designed the decor for two new works with Balanchine: *Magic*, with Mozart's music for A. Everett Austin's Wadsworth Atheneum in Hartford, and Gluck's *Orpheus and Eurydice* at the Metropolitan Opera.

Much of his time in America, Tchelitchew lived through the drama of the changing seasons in Connecticut and Vermont. His little house and studio in Vermont he sentimentally designated *La Maison de Giselle*. Working in seclusion on hundreds of drawings and major canvases, he found time to experiment with his palette and his changing style. However, "the illusion, caprice and fantasy of the theatre still amused him." In 1939, he took time off to return to Paris to collaborate with Louis Jouvet on their famous production of Giraudoux's *Ondine*.

Back in New England again, he designed the decor with Balanchine for Stravinsky's *Ballustrade* and Hindemith's *The Cave of Sleep*; also, in 1942, for Stravinsky's *Apollon Musagete* and *Concerto*, the latter for the Teatro Colon in Buenos Aires. *Concerto* was Tchelitchew's last work for the theatre. Memories of his association with the world of theatre, however, persisted in his remarkable interior or anatomical landscapes, in his flowers of sight which he created in the forties, and in his brilliant linear space compositions which he invented during his last six years in Grottaferrata near Rome.

Tchelitchew was a sensitive and orderly artist of many minds, and his exploratory inclinations carried him from Russia over an arc that spanned forty years of creativity in Europe and America. From the logical course of his changing career, a vast oeuvre of his art survives, and a small part of this oeuvre happily belongs to the theatre.

*Illustration 209.* Giraudoux's *Ondine* was presented in the Théâtre Atheneé in Paris in 1939. This imaginative collaboration of Louis Jouvet and Pavel Tchelitchew received wide acclaim in Paris and was Tchelitchew's greatest theatrical success. The stage and interior of the theatre were altered to accommodate the fantastic aqueous effects which Tchelitchew envisioned.

This sketch was for the backdrop of the trial of Ondine. Tchelitchew repeatedly injected into this scenic production symbols of the power, the flow, and the magic of water. The strange anthropomorphic landscape is an isometric view of water interlacing shadowless multiple images of human and animal skulls in yellow and pink.

This drawing is a prelude to Tchelitchew's greatest painting, *Hide and Seek*, which he began the following year and completed in 1941. The composition of water and skulls foreshadows the branches of his great skeletal tree peopled with heads and limbs of children playing.

*Illustration 210.* Balanchine and Tchelitchew collaborated on this production of *Concerto*, a ballet in three movements to music of Mozart, which was presented in the

(208) Berman, Eugene, 1899–1972
Russia, Saint Petersburg (active in Paris,
New York, and Rome)
An Italian Place for Mendelssohn's *Symphonie Italienne*, 1939
Pen and black ink with watercolor, 266 x 367 mm.
Collection: The Artist

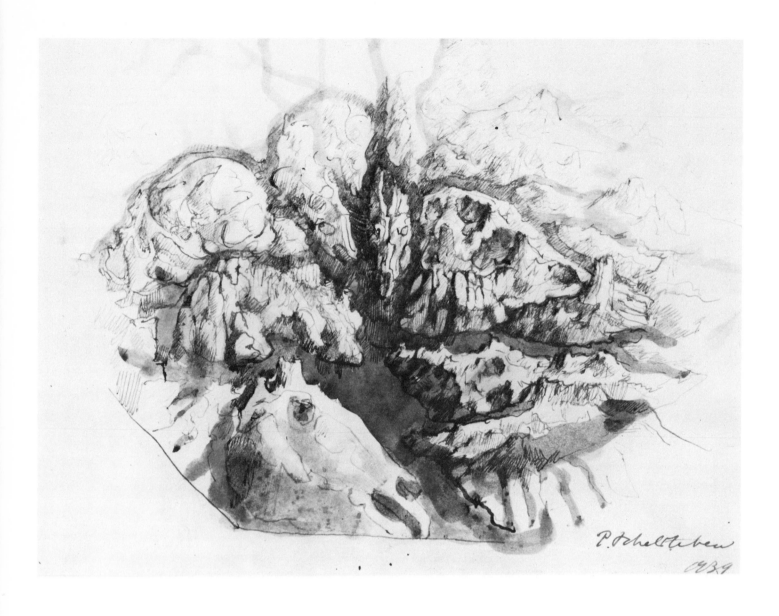

(209) Tchelitchew, Pavel, 1898–1957
      Russia (active in Kiev, Constantinople, Berlin, Paris,
      New York, London, and Buenos Aires)
      Backdrop for the Trial Scene in Jean Giraudoux's
      *Ondine*, 1939 (See also color plate 30)
      Pen and black ink with watercolor, 278 x 455 mm.
      Inscribed lower right corner: "P. Tchelitchew 1939"

Teatro Colon in Buenos Aires in 1942. This construction, departing from metamorphic abstraction to kinetic, linear space composition, represents a transitional phase in Tchelitchew's art. These spontaneous, wiry studies record the artist's experiment in devising a domed palace suspended in deep blue space, with translucent curtains and light to suggest changing locale and mood. Tchelitchew's harmony of interlacing lines achieves a spacious grandeur and simplicity.

### Rex Whistler

Rex Whistler was an English artist whose murals and conversation pieces, portraits, book illustrations, carpets and textiles, and settings and costumes for the theatre reflect not the slightest impact of abstract art. He had a positive preference for the eighteenth-century English scene, and his Fitzroy Street studio was a world of his own creation. "It was a world," wrote James Laver, "of tender fancy lightened and redeemed by wit. It could be gay or sombre, but never harsh or melodramatic. It was a world full of knick-knacks, and yet as fresh as a morning rose. There was no dust upon it—the phrase might almost be accepted as the criterion of a real personal style."

At the Slade School, he was drawn to the work of Inigo Jones and William Kent, and, like Jones before him, Whistler succumbed to the work of the great Italian Renaissance and baroque architects and painters, and to Cuvilliés' rococo Residenz Theater, which contributed to the flowering of Whistler's fluent style and decorative elegance.

From his growing interest in botany, he wove the vegetable world of trees, plants, and flowers into his poetic fantasies. After Milton, the English Romantic poets were his favorites. Poe and Walter de la Mare also held a special place in his hall of poets. He later confided to his brother Laurence that he would rather have been a great poet than anything else. His feeling for poetry pervaded all his work.

Whistler was inevitably drawn into the theatre as a stage designer. Sir Charles Cochran was attracted by Whistler's popular murals painted in the restaurant of the Tate Gallery under the sponsorship of Sir Joseph Duveen, and he commissioned Whistler to design his 1929 revue, *Wake Up and Dream*. Whistler designed three more Cochran revues before he ever designed a play, opera, or ballet, but he soon found himself deluged with theatrical commissions.

In his brief career, he designed the scenes and/or costumes for some twenty-seven productions, including twelve plays, seven ballets, and two operas—sometimes the program and poster as well.

Cecil Beaton, a close friend of Whistler's, pointed out that Whistler never thought of himself as a stage designer, though he designed for the theatre with great facility. He never indulged in theatrical dynamics nor in scenic experiments like his contemporary Tchelitchew. Beaton observed, "His stage rooms were of painted canvas but interpreted with more realism than reality." Whistler's realism was poetic—never spectacular. His notebooks for *Victoria Regina* reveal his painstaking care with every detail. His charming interiors were the result of arduous research in the social and artistic life of the Victorian era. They had atmosphere, taste, and great elegance. Settings and costumes reflected his love of craftsmanship and finish.

For two brief decades, he enlivened and elevated the visual and performing arts of England. His death in Normandy on his first summer morning in action with his

(210) Tchelitchew, Pavel
Studies for the Ballet *Concerto*, 1942
Pencil, pen, and black ink, 480 x 297 mm.

OVERLEAF
(211)
Whistler, Rex, 1905–1944
England, London
"Happy and Glorious, Buckingham Palace" for Laurence Housman's *Victoria Regina*, Act III, Scene 2, 1935
Pencil and watercolor, 209 x 349 mm.

tank division was a tragic loss not only for the theatre but for all the decorative arts of his time.

*Illustration 211. Victoria Regina* was presented by Gilbert Miller in the Broadhurst Theatre, New York, December 26, 1935. Helen Hayes and Vincent Price played Victoria and Albert.

The scene is the state reception hall of Buckingham Palace looking out on the Mall. The occasion is the celebration of Queen Victoria's Diamond Jubilee in 1897. The queen is being wheeled onto the balcony to receive the acclaim of her subjects.

In designing the scene, Rex Whistler must have had in mind the charm of the early Victorian toy theatre. His color, of course, is more subtle, and his sophisticated feeling for the reality of the scene avoids the naïveté of penny-plain twopence-colored scenery.

The largest group of Whistler's drawings for the theatre is in the collection of Laurence Whistler. Others are found in private collections in England and America. *The Work of Rex Whistler*, 1960, compiled by Laurence Whistler and Ronald Fuller, is a comprehensive illustrated catalogue raisonné of every branch of his work.

### John Piper

John Piper was twenty-five when he left his father's business and entered the Slade School to study painting. At home in rural Epsom, young John had developed a precocious taste for music and poetry, drawing and painting. He loved to explore the countryside sketching barns and churches and tracing stained-glass windows. He admired Frank Brangwyn and emulated the mannerisms of Lovat Fraser.

Piper realized it was not easy to rise from an amateur in the arts to a professional. After he left the Slade School, he labored day and night experimenting with textures and techniques in painting, entirely engrossed in developing his theatrical style of mottling and spattering his pictures to achieve an atmospheric effect.

In 1933, Piper went to Paris, not on a holiday but to discover and expose himself to the work of Segonzac, Braque, Picasso, and Brancusi. Back in England, he crashed into his abstract period with a series of inventive constructions followed by oil abstractions in blue, gray, and black. He learned to master the crafts of wood engraving, lithography, typography, etching, and aquatint, which he found congenial to his new style.

During World War II, Piper became a war artist, capturing brilliantly the haunting pathos of bombed-out desolation and charred, stark ruins. Ironically, during this cruel period, he found himself as an artist, and he also found recognition. In 1941 the Queen commissioned him to make a series of portrait sketches of Windsor Castle. King George VI, after examining these watercolors, observed, "I'm afraid you had very bad weather, Mr. Piper."

Piper was thirty-five before he was initiated into the theatre with settings for Stephen Spender's *The Trial of a Judge*. His mannerisms in drawing and painting proved singularly appropriate for ballet and opera. In 1946, he

began collaborating with Benjamin Britten on his opera *The Rape of Lucretia* at Glyndebourne, and since then he has designed most of the English productions of Britten's operas. Piper has worked jointly with many notable choreographers—Frederick Ashton, Ninette de Valois, and John Cranko—and with opera directors Carl Ebert and Basil Coleman. He believes that a living work of theatrical art can only be realized with the closest collaboration and visual unity of all parts.

Like the scene designs of Eugene Berman or Marc Chagall, Piper's designs cannot be divorced from his vigorous painter's style. Yet, for their full theatrical impact, they must be translated into scenic terms. Sometimes Piper's settings, with their color, luminous beneath charcoal skies, appear to be not scene designs but beautiful paintings, blown-up and animated by painted costumes.

*Illustration 212.* Benjamin Britten was commissioned to compose *Gloriana* in honor of the coronation of Elizabeth II. The presentation of the opera was a gala occasion in the Covent Garden Royal Opera House, June 8, 1953. The production was highly controversial. *Gloriana* was directed by Basil Coleman with choreography by John Cranko and settings and costumes designed by John Piper. The heightened theatricality of the design is suggested by the overscale, staccato brush work in this sketch. The scenes moved swiftly but failed to save the royal occasion.

### Jo Mielziner

Jo Mielziner started out to be an easel painter. His father, Leo Mielziner, was a gifted portrait painter in Paris, and Jo spent his youth drawing and painting in his father's cluttered atelier and absorbing his mother's dialogue on the arts. She wrote a monthly letter for *Vogue* on the state of the arts in Paris, and, born of a theatre family, was an enthusiastic theatre-goer, and often took her two boys along. When Jo was ten, the Mielziners moved to America, where he continued painting in his father's New York studio, at the Art Student's League, and later at the Pennsylvania Academy of Fine Arts in Philadelphia.

In 1921, Jo needed work and became an apprentice with the Bonstelle Stock Company in Detroit taking on every odd job—acting, scenery, and stage managing. He returned to New York in 1923 and got a job as an apprentice with the Theatre Guild. He was fortunate in working close to Lee Simonson, the Guild's art director, from whom he learned the significance of stage lighting. Later, while assisting Robert Edmond Jones on technical matters, he came to appreciate the meaning of theatrical style.

Mielziner was already twenty-two, and still in the back of his head was the idea that "Once I get a little money ahead, I'll give up the theatre and do nothing but paint." Fortunately for the theatre, he never got "a little money ahead." Somewhere along the way, Craig and Appia also intervened. In any case, the easel painter in Jo Mielziner died when he suddenly discovered that "the art of scenic design was a rich field in expression and emotionally satisfying. . . . Suddenly I no longer looked upon the

theatre as merely an economic expedient." Henceforth, the theatre was essential to his life and the focus of a notable career.

In 1924, the Theatre Guild commissioned Jo Mielziner to design his first Broadway production, Molnar's *The Guardsman*, which also launched Alfred Lunt and Lynn Fontanne on their felicitous career together. Since then, Jo Mielziner has designed well over 250 professional productions, including operas, ballets, plays, and musicals. He has designed productions ranging from *Romeo and Juliet* for Katharine Cornell, and *Hamlet* with John Gielgud for Guthrie McClintic, to the plays of major American playwrights of his generation including Eugene O'Neill's *Strange Interlude*, Sidney Howard's *Yellow Jack*, Maxwell Anderson's *Winterset*, Robert Sherwood's *Abe Lincoln in Illinois*, Tennessee Williams' *A Streetcar Named Desire*, and Arthur Miller's *Death of a Salesman*. His visual concepts for these plays attest to the versatility and imagination of his talent.

Through close collaboration with author, composer, director, and choreographer, he has contributed notably to the exciting evolution of the American musical theatre. Among the glamorous musical successes which he designed were the three *Little Shows, Of Thee I Sing, I Married an Angel, Carousel, South Pacific, Guys and Dolls, The King and I*, and *1776*. In all of his musicals, Mielziner, with his orderly organization, has always brought to the theatre a high standard of visual coordination of imaginative lighting, mechanical ease of movement, craftsmanship, and style.

With all this experience, Mielziner, like several other fellow designers who are weary of the cramped, antiquated theatres in which they have always labored, has devoted a great deal of research and time to working as a theatre consultant with architects to raise the standards of modern theatre planning with improved technical and lighting equipment for the professional, regional, and educational theatre. His book, *Shapes of Our Theatre* (1970), is an authoritative presentation of contemporary trends in theatre architecture.

245

(213)  Mielziner, Jo, 1901–
France, Paris (active in
New York)
Beneath the Brooklyn Bridge,
for Maxwell Anderson's *Winterset*,
1935
Pen and black ink with washes,
528 x 846 mm.
Inscribed lower right corner:
"JM"
Collection: Elizabeth Hudson

Jo Mielziner's greatest pleasure in designing scenery is the time he spends alone on his drawings. They contain the theatrical atmosphere of a dramatic artist, and always reflect the inner spirit and outer mood of his productions. His feeling for this "livingness" of a scene is embodied in the theatrical reality of *Street Scene*, the linear, aerial definition of *Summer and Smoke*, and the melding interior-exterior moods of *The Glass Menagerie*.

For nearly fifty years, Jo Mielziner has served the theatre as a dedicated theatre artist. Continually percolating in his subconscious is his insistence on simplification to imply the universal, his search for imaginative and suggestive scenic concepts, and his experimentation with new directions in lighting techniques for tomorrow's theatre.

His book *Designs for the Theatre* (1965) contains a portfolio of his designs.

*Illustration 213.* Maxwell Anderson's first script for *Winterset* placed the setting beneath the Brooklyn Bridge before a city backdrop. Jo Mielziner believed the play to be "a story of hope and faith and imagination," and he and the producer-director Guthrie McClintic finally persuaded the author that the cluttered backdrop of wharves and run-down buildings would confine the play and hold it earthbound. They felt that the massive bridgehead, with the span of the bridge high above thrusting into space across the East River toward Manhattan, was a more poetic setting for the play. Maxwell Anderson, still doubtful, resigned himself with "let's see what it looks like." In the published version of the play, the author's description of the scene follows the designer's sketch.

This drawing is one of Jo Mielziner's finest poetic settings and is a genuine contribution to the art of American stage design.

## Boris Aronson

Boris Aronson was born in Kiev of an old Ukrainian Jewish family. He liked to draw and paint, and his parents sent him to the State Art School, where he excelled in old-fashioned Russian realism. In the School of the Theatre in Kiev, Boris was exposed to Aleksandra Exter's theatrical stimulus and her principles of constructivism. Henceforth, stage design and painting would share equally in his creative work.

In 1921, he settled in Moscow and attended the School of Modern Art, where his theatrical style became an amalgam of burgeoning forces of change. The Jewish Theatre Academy and the Habima group stimulated him, and he thrilled to the productions of the new theatre of revolt, and to the paintings of Picasso, Matisse, and also Chagall, whose early cubist-fantastic style exerted a lasting influence both on Aronson's painting and on his sense of visual theatre.

In 1922, Aronson decided to leave Russia for Berlin, where he published a book on Chagall and another on modern Jewish graphic arts. In 1923, he arrived in New York as an immigrant, without a friend or a word of English, and settled in the Bronx, little dreaming of the opportunities that he as an artist would discover in America.

Aronson's beginnings were modest. When he was not painting, he was designing experimental scenery for plays by Pinski and Ansky for Yiddish theatre groups in the Bronx. His costumes and scenes were experimental—stylized, angular constructions far ahead of anything then being produced in America. Maurice Schwarz chose him to design *The Tenth Commandment* for his new Yiddish Art Theatre on Second Avenue. This was a musical play in fifteen scenes set between Paradise and Hell. Aronson set Paradise in tiers of white opera boxes; Hell, within the grim recesses of a man's head. This startling Off-Broadway production of the mid-twenties served to project Boris Aronson into the public eye, if not into Broadway's private ear. Further east on Fourteenth Street, he designed a rather naïve, simultaneous scene for Eva Le Gallienne's Civic Repertory Theatre's experimental production of *2 × 2 = 5*.

Five years later, Aronson was finally welcomed to Broadway with his scenes for S. J. Perelman's *Walk a Little Faster*. Before he knew it, he was riding high with George Abbott and *Three Men on a Horse*. During the thirties, he worked with the august Group Theatre on plays by Clifford Odets and Irwin Shaw. He was also designing for the vast stage of Radio City Music Hall as well as for Max Reinhardt's intimate production of Thornton Wilder's *Merchant of Yonkers*.

During the fifties and sixties came a procession of memorable plays and musicals with "settings designed by Boris Aronson"—*The Crucible*, *The Diary of Anne Frank*, *J.B.*, *Incident at Vichy*, *Fiddler on the Roof*, *Cabaret*, *Company*, and *Follies*; also, for the Metropolitan Opera, *Mourning Becomes Electra* and *Fidelio*. Each script he approaches quite individually. He must explore it, break it down, pull it apart in his effort to discover the hidden meaning, the insides. By extracting its essence, his imagination enables him to evoke on the stage his visual interpretation of the core of the playwright's script. Aronson constantly tries out new ideas. He rarely repeats himself even when he has succeeded with something. He finds change stimulating.

He approaches his assignments with great humility. His designs for scenes and costumes must be wedded to the mood and the meaning of the script. He works with painstaking care with the director and slowly evolves his plans, determining what mechanics best serve his purpose. Aronson designs as a painter in the theatre, and as a sensitive craftsman he is concerned with how the texture and the quality inherent in his painting can best be projected on the stage.

*Illustration 214.* Boris Aronson could not envision a universal music-drama of liberation in a Spanish prison. "The music sings of freedom, not of layers of granite." What kind of prison contains this music? In searching for ideas before beginning to design, Aronson urged the stage director, Otto Schenk, to meet him first in the Science Museum in Munich—in the collection of locks. He explained at length how he felt that keys and the mechanism of huge locks, and interlocks, and bolts of ancient types, and massive chains, linked ideas of imprisonment with modern sculpture and also could become the underlying, organic design element of his prison for *Fidelio*.

He planned his imaginative setting around a tilted central space to support changing prison elements and the opera's intimate action. The ever-present environmental prison is an ancient gray-green construction whose materials spring from folk art—wood, metal, and stone.

### Donald Oenslager

After Harvard and a year in Europe, exploring the Continental ways of stagecraft, I was given a job working with Robert Edmond Jones in the Provincetown-Greenwich Village Group under the direction of Jones, Kenneth Macgowan, and Eugene O'Neill. Imagination was the theatre's cornerstone—their manifesto, "The difficult is our special task, or we have no reason for existing." Here was the shrine of the New Movement. Together we shared an enthusiastic sense of discovery of new theatrical values.

One day I received a summons from Irene Lewisohn to the Neighborhood Playhouse on Grand Street, to design their next experimental production, *Sooner and Later*, a dance satire in three "states of existence." Creating the past, present, and future was a challenge that might never come my way again, and here it was my first production in New York. For the first time on the stage we introduced Thomas Wilfred's *Clavilux* to project the mobile rhythms of crystalline life, which even Havelock Ellis would never have recognized. Only the cognoscenti, the seers of the avant-garde, applauded those earnest overtones of 1925.

Since then, over 250 of my productions have come and

(214)  Aronson, Boris, 1899–
        Russia, Kiev (active in New York)
        Prison Courtyard for Beethoven's *Fidelio*, Act II,
        Scene 2, 1970
        Acrylic on black cardboard, 556 x 833 mm.
        Collection: Gift of the Artist

gone on Broadway. They have ranged from realism and expressionism to the minimalism of a bare stage with a lonely chair in a spotlight. I have designed settings and lighting for such musical successes as *Good News*, *Girl Crazy*, and *Anything Goes*, and such plays as *You Can't Take It With You*, *Born Yesterday*, *Of Mice and Men*, *Major Barbara*, *A Majority of One*, and *Coriolanus*. *Salomé*, *The Abduction from the Seraglio*, and *Otello* are among operas designed for the traditional Metropolitan; for the more adventurous New York City Opera, *Orfeo*, *Tosca*, and *Der Rosenkavalier*. I designed the first uncut staging in America of *Tristan und Isolde* by the Philadelphia Orchestra with Fritz Reiner and Herbert Graf, and *Orpheus and Eurydice* for the inauguration of Vancouver's Queen Elizabeth Opera House. I designed *Don Carlo* for the opening of the HemisFair in San Antonio,

and for the Central City Opera Festival in Colorado I have designed some twenty operas, ranging from Mozart, Verdi, and Beethoven to the premiere of Douglas Moore's *The Ballad of Baby Doe*. Central City provided an opportunity to experiment in new techniques of revitalizing the lyric theatre.

After World War II, New York theatres with their outmoded stages seemed more uncomfortable and antiquated than ever, and I became a theatre consultant associated with architects who were planning elaborate complexes for the performing arts—the Montreal Cultural Center, the New York State Theatre and Philharmonic Hall in New York's Lincoln Center, Washington's Kennedy Center, the Meeting Center of the Albany South Mall, and many educational and civic theatres mushrooming across the country.

(215) Oenslager, Donald, 1902–
United States, Harrisburg, Pennsylvania (active in New York)
The Harbor of Carthage for Purcell's *Dido and Aeneas*, 1953 (See also color plate 31)
Collage: photostat, marbleized paper, and gouache, 382 x 569 mm.

(216) Smith, Oliver, 1918–
United States, Wawpawn, Wisconsin (active in New
York and London)
Beneath the Brooklyn Bridge—Setting for *Kelly*,
1964
Pen and ink with watercolor, 330 x 525 mm.
Inscribed lower right corner: "Oliver Smith 64"
Collection: The Artist

Because the theatre is my life, I have participated in the changing directions of the performing arts in our changing society. I am confident that a virile theatre of new-found convictions will rise from today's ashen stage. During my forty-five years of teaching stage design in the Yale Drama School, I have always tried to set my course to conform with the changing directions of the theatre's compass. In this way, I discovered that teaching can be as exciting as designing. I have always thought that learning to design should be as exciting as teaching it. I have exhorted students to "give me ideas with resonance." I have always aligned myself with the dreams and beliefs of the NOW generation. Today, where might these dreams and beliefs be? Vanished? Be patient. Robert Frost wrote to an acquisitive, but insecure, young writer: "You can see the stars by day if you look down a well that's deep enough." I am confident that the rising generation will dig deep enough to see the stars and restore them to the theatre. These dreams and beliefs may communicate an idea to a director or designer, a young playwright or producer, for the newer ways of tomorrow's theatre. That is what the theatre should care about and search for, believing with Gordon Craig that "the Big Dream recurs again and again till it becomes in years the reality."

*Illustration 215. Dido and Aeneas* was a joint production of the Music School and the School of Drama of Yale University, presented in 1953.

Purcell's classic opera was given a contemporary production based on the scenographic methods of the baroque stage. A permanent portal of yellow, black, and white suggested a baroque proscenium arch framing a permanent

251

(217) Lee, Ming Cho, 1930–
China, Shanghai (active in New York)
Permanent Setting for Jakov Lind's *Ergo*, 1968
Collage: photostat, pen and black ink, and gouache,
340 x 270 mm.
Inscribed lower right corner: "M C Lee"
Collection: The Artist

ramped and stepped platform receding in perspective. Above hung alternating black and white swags which indicated positions for stylized inset wings and borders for forest or palace—in this instance, masts, with fluttering pennants against a projected seventeenth-century print of the harbor of Carthage. All changes of scene were *à vista*, accompanied by changing light and music.

### Oliver Smith

Oliver Smith left Wawpawn, Wisconsin, to study architecture at Pennsylvania State College. He meant to be an architect, but he was also stagestruck and ambitious, and Broadway became his goal. He was twenty-one when he settled in Brooklyn Heights. He painted, was an usher at Roxy's, and did odd jobs until he was admitted to the Scenic Artists' Union.

His first commission was designing *Saratoga* for the Ballet Russe de Monte Carlo at the Metropolitan in 1941. Agnes De Mille liked his settings and the next year asked him to design a corral among wide, rolling prairies for Aaron Copland's *Rodeo*. From the beginning, the problems of designing for ballet appealed to him. His free painter's style and color, his precise clarity of line, and his innate feeling for space have been particularly suited to the requirements of the musical theatre and the ballet.

In 1944, Oliver Smith and Jerome Robbins first collaborated on Leonard Bernstein's *Fancy Free* for the Ballet Theatre. He reduced his decor to a stunning minimum —a sailor's bar and the outline of a ship's prow against city lights. Out of *Fancy Free* came two significant developments for Oliver Smith. First, he turned *Fancy Free* into the successful musical *On the Town* with Paul Feigay, which launched the career of Oliver Smith, Producer. Second, he became associated with Lucia Chase as co-director of the Ballet Theatre. For both of them, the Ballet Theatre has always been a labor of love. With clarity of direction, they have maintained this brilliant company and planned its American seasons and European tours.

In rapid succession he designed very original decor for Jerome Robbins' ballets *Interplay*, *Facsimile*, and *Age of Anxiety*, and also for the Agnes De Mille-Morton Gould ballet-drama, *Fall River Legend*. During the forties, Oliver Smith worked closely with George Balanchine, David Lichine, and Michael Kidd for the New York City Ballet and the Ballet Theatre. Oliver Smith is a choreographer's designer. "In my work, I have tried to produce in ballet design an American style that is neither easel painting nor stage design in the architectural, dramatic sense. What I have tried to do is a combination of these two elements, not out of financial necessity, but out of a desire to create an air of elegance through the elimination of extraneous detail. I have tried to achieve a simplicity of design which allows the dancer to remain the most important object on the stage, which indeed he is."

Since the success of *On the Town* in 1945, Oliver Smith has co-produced many admirable musicals and plays on Broadway. While he concedes that the theatre is a business for egomaniacs, the playwright Jean Kerr notes that when working in the theatre "he is an island of calm in the sea of temperament." He is endowed with cool confidence and professional tact. Otherwise, he could never have handled the prodigious number of musicals he designed during the fifties and sixties, including *Brigadoon*, *Pal Joey*, *My Fair Lady*, *Auntie Mame*, *West Side Story*, *The Sound of Music*, *Camelot*, and *Hello, Dolly*, and the variety of plays, including *Five Finger Exercise*, *Becket*, *Luv*, *Cactus Flower*, and *Plaza Suite*. For diversion he also found time to design *Martha* and *La Traviata* for the Metropolitan Opera, and for Hollywood, the spectacular films *Band Wagon*, *Oklahoma*, and *Porgy and Bess*.

Along Broadway during those rich years, Oliver Smith seemed to be in everything and everywhere at the same time. From his workroom in Brooklyn Heights, he almost cornered the Broadway scenic market for several seasons. In 1965 *Time* magazine labeled him "a man for all scenes and the delight of all producers."

Oliver Smith has managed his talent and career with skill and artistic integrity. As a designer, he first thinks out his overall "scheme" for a production. His visual solution then emerges from his blueprints and appears in his precise, quarter-inch-scale color sketches and painter's elevations for the scenic studio. Thereafter, he allocates responsibility to the theatre craftsmen who build and paint his settings and light them.

Oliver Smith, like every designer, is not averse to financial reward in the theatre, but he is not interested in turning out polished design for pedestrian entertainment. Among all the plays he has worked on, he has probably received most satisfaction and inner reward from designing such challenging works as Sartre's *No Exit*, Michaels' *Dylan*, and Kopit's *Indians*—plays with which he felt as a theatre artist he could make a creative statement. The plays, the musicals, and the ballets which appeal most to his clear overall vision of the theatre are those that inspire his finest designs.

*Illustration 216. Kelly* was an opulent, panoramic musical which had the dual distinction of opening and closing on Broadway in one night, and also losing $650,000 for the producers.

This imaginative drawing of an urban fantasy beneath the Brooklyn Bridge is proof that eloquent scenery cannot turn a mediocre musical into a success. It is interesting to compare this drawing of Oliver Smith's with Jo Mielziner's design for *Winterset* (Illus. 213).

### Ming Cho Lee

Ming Cho Lee belongs to the younger group of American designers who have been working in the theatre for twelve or fifteen years. This generation of designers, playwrights, directors, and actors entered the theatre just as the high tide of the post–World War II theatre began to recede. They confronted the declining theatre on their own terms and clamored for recognition. They sought a theatre of greater scope and purpose to conform with the growing pains of a changing society.

Lee was born and brought up in Shanghai during the Japanese occupation, where he studied traditional Chinese landscape painting. Fortified with a student visa, he spent four years at UCLA in Los Angeles, where Edward Kook, who happened to be lecturing on stage lighting, generously said to those eager students, "If any of you ever come to New York, let me hear from you." Shortly thereafter, in 1955, Ming telephoned Kook from a pay station in New York, and soon miraculously found himself working in Jo Mielziner's studio, where he remained for five years, first as an apprentice and then as an assistant designer.

In 1958, he designed *The Infernal Machine* and *The Crucible* for the Phoenix Theatre and several backgrounds for José Limon. During the next few years, he was designing operas for the Peabody Arts Theatre in Baltimore, and *Peter Ibbetson* and the premiere of *Katya Kabanova* for the Empire State Music Festival. In 1961, he was appointed resident designer of the San Francisco Opera Company, and the following year he returned to New York and designed his first Broadway production, *The Moon Besieged*, which ran for one night.

Thereafter, his cluttered New York studio became the command center of all his varied theatrical activities. He had witnessed the emergence of many types of open stages across America—the result of economic pressures, new forms of plays, and young groups passionate about bringing audience and performers into a more vital relationship. This assertive theatre influenced Lee's stylistic attitude toward the design of opera, ballet, and theatre. He sought a new dimension in the theatre. Often he has invented a formal scenic skeleton—a multi-level setting that makes a single environmental statement, which he transforms with visual idioms and symbols into a flexible multiscene arrangement.

In 1962, Ming Cho Lee became Joseph Papp's principal designer for the New York Shakespeare Festival in Central Park, and for ten summers he mounted twenty-two plays of Shakespeare. For Papp's Public Theatre he devised exciting environmental productions for many plays, and also a mobile unit that has carried Shakespeare to the New York school system. As the principal designer for the Juilliard Opera Theatre, he has been able to carry out many experiments in opera production, and during six seasons at the New York City Opera, he has created arresting productions as diverse in style as *Julius Caesar* and *Bomarzo*.

Lee also enjoys the stimulation offered by theatres outside New York—Baltimore, Washington, and San Francisco. Abroad, he has been commissioned to design for the Hamburg Opera and for the Teatro Colon in Buenos Aires.

As an artist, Ming Cho Lee has become more sensitive to the bristling forces of social change which demand a higher volume of theatre resonance. Already, what he has achieved as a designer in twelve years, he feels, constitutes his early period. He is in the process of discovering what lies ahead, and how the naturalistic theatre might be the launching-pad for a fresh indigenous expression of the American theatre.

*Illustration 217. Ergo* was directed by Gerald Freedman and designed by Ming Cho Lee for the New York Shakespeare Festival Company at the Anspacher Public Theatre in 1968. The year before, the charming reading room of the old Astor Library of 1886 was converted into this modern space theatre with three hundred seats surrounding three sides of the acting area.

This stage challenges the imagination of the designer. *Ergo* was an expressionistic play dealing with the conflict between a disciplined, mechanized Prussian and a slovenly, romantic Austrian. The designer suspended a double eagle high overhead like a keystone. A skeletal arrangement of girders and poles provides three acting levels (connected with ladders and steps) and clearly divides the stage between the Prussian's stark white walls and the Austrian's area cluttered with junk and newspapers. This unobtrusive, yet highly theatrical framework is Lee's 1968 concept of scenic containment.

# Color Plates

**Errata**
The captions for Plates 3 and 4 are reversed, and the captions for Plates 6 and 7 are reversed.

(1) Sebastiano Serlio, The Comic Scene, c. 1550

(2) UNKNOWN ITALIAN ARTIST, Landscape with Volcano
in Eruption, c. 1620

(3) UNKNOWN ITALIAN ARTIST, Landscape with Rustic
Houses and Waterfall, c. 1620

(4) CHARLES ERRARD, A Deserted Landscape with Open Cave, 1647

(5)  JEAN GEORGE KÖPP, The Astrologer's Garden, c. 1780

(7) N. Institoris, Roman Garden with Fountains, c. 1830

(6) Antonio De Pian, Greek Shrine with Celebrants, c. 1840

(8) GIORGIO FUENTES, Before a Palace, c. 1799

(9) KARL FRIEDRICH SCHINKEL, Palace Hall: Setting for
*König Yngurd*, Act I, 1817

(10) WILLIAM CLARKSON STANFIELD, Oriental Landscape for a Pantomime, c. 1825

(11) ZARRA AND LALOUE, Rustic Interior, 1854

(12) ANDREAS LEONHARD ROLLER, Apotheosis of Marguerite
for Gounod's *Faust*, Act IV, 1864

(13) UNKNOWN AMERICAN ARTIST, Court of Venus for an
Extravaganza, c. 1870

(14) CARLO FERRARIO, Festa di Campagna for Cagnoni's
*Il Vecchio della Montagna*, Act III, Scene 5, 1863

(15) CARPEZAT,
Egyptian Throne Hall, c. 1880

(17)  KONSTANTIN  KOROVINE,  "Panorama"  for  Tchaikovsky's *La Belle au Bois Dormant*, 1915

(16)  EDWARD  GORDON  CRAIG, Throne Hall for Shaw's *Caesar
and Cleopatra*, Act I, Scene 3, 1906

(18) Alexandre Benois,
"The Apparition of the Grail" for
S. Miguel's *Fée de Sagesse*, 1949.

(19) MSTISLAV DOBOUJINSKY, Blue Sitting Room for Turgenev's *A Month in the Country*, Act I, 1919

(20) KARL WALSER, Verona, a Public Place for Shakespeare's *Romeo and Juliet*, Act I, Scene I, 1907

Karl Walser

(21) NATALIA GONTCHAROVA, Battlements of a Castle for Balakirev's *Thamar*, c. 1925

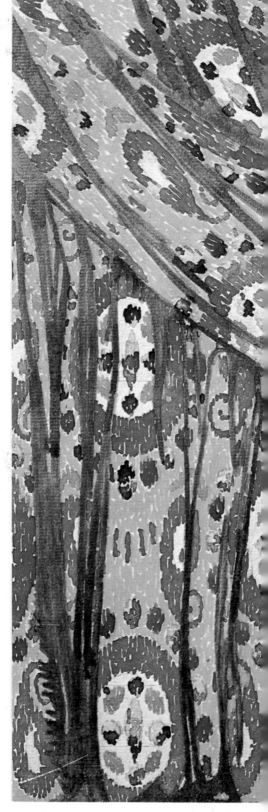

(22) LÉON BAKST, Prologue for *Les Orientales*, 1910

(23) ALEKSANDRA EXTER, Construction for a Tragedy, c. 1925

(24) YOZAC JANKUS, Catfish Row for Gershwin's *Porgy and Bess*, 1967

(25) N. N. ZOLOTARYOV, Monastery of Tchudo, Pimen's
Cell, for Musorgski's *Boris Godunov*, Act I, Scene I,
1966

(26) ANDRÉ DELFAU, Abstraction for the Ballet *Chantier*, 1961

(27)  THOMAS G. MOSES, Terrace by Moonlit Lake—An Olio
Drop, c. 1910

THE NEW YORK STUDIOS
1001 TIMES B'LD'G,  ·  NEW YORK

(28)  NORMAN BEL GEDDES, Project for the Dance, c. 1917

N°554

(29) JOHN PIPER, Street Scene for Benjamin Britten's
*Gloriana*, 1953

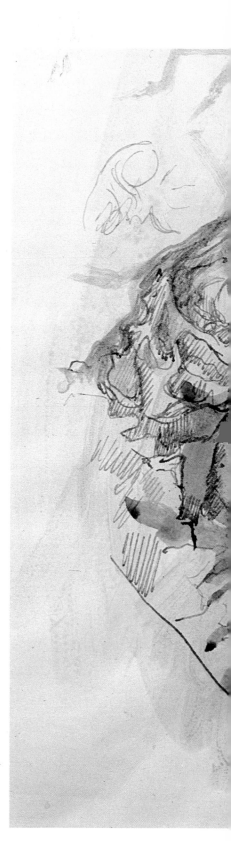

(30) PAVEL TCHELITCHEW, Backdrop for the Trial Scene in
Jean Giraudoux's *Ondine*, 1939

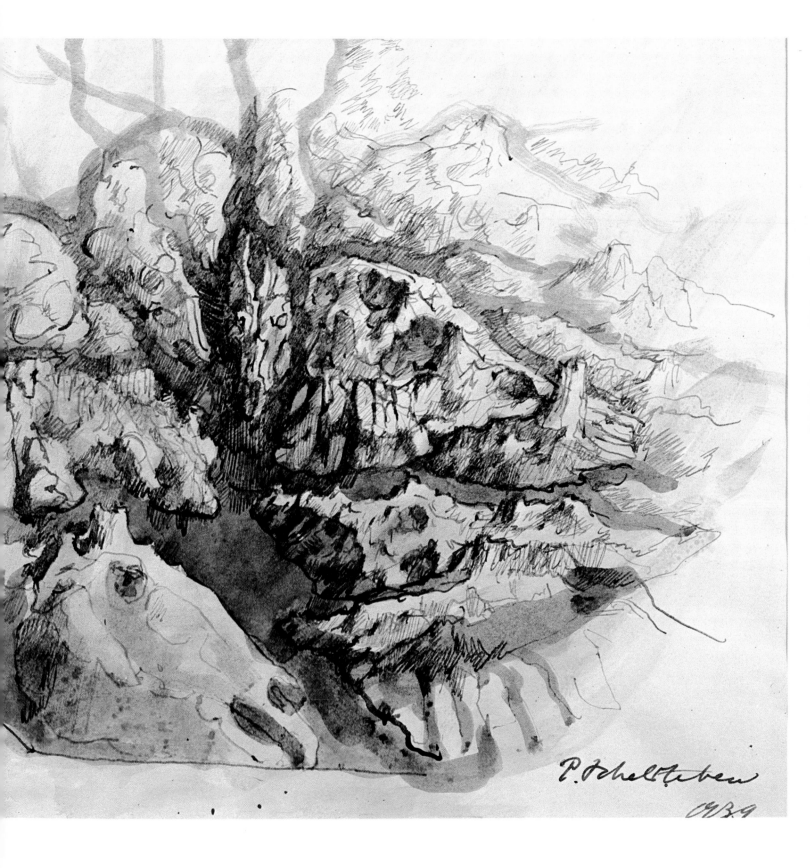

P. Schellenberg

1939

(31) DONALD OENSLAGER, The Harbor of Carthage for Purcell's *Dido and Aeneas*, 1953

# Bibliography

# Bibliography

## General

Altman, George, et al. *Theater Pictorial*. Los Angeles, 1953.

Amico, Silvio d', ed. *Storia del teatro italiano*. Milan, 1936, 1950.

Amorini, Antonio. *Vite dei pittori ed artefici bolognesi*. Bologna, 1843.

Ancona, Alessandro d'. *Origini del teatro in Italia*. Florence, 1877.

Bapst, Germain. *Essai sur l'histoire du théâtre*. Paris, 1893.

Beaumont, Cyril W. *Five Centuries of Ballet Design*. London and New York, 1939.

Berliner, Rudolf. *Stage Designs of the Cooper Union Museum*. New York, 1941.

Bieber, Margarete. *The History of the Greek and Roman Theater*. Princeton, 1939; Oxford, 1961.

Bischoff and Meyer. *Die Festdekoration*. Leipzig, 1897.

Brock, Allen. *A History of Fireworks*. London, 1949.

Brunelli, Bruno. *I teatri di Padova*. Padua, 1921.

———. *Scenografi italiani di ieri e di oggi*. Rome, 1938.

Buttafava-Garbagnati. *Architetture ne segno dei maestri*. Bergamo, 1962.

Chaloupka, Adolf. *Tschechische Bühnendekoration aus zwei Jahrhunderten*. Prague, 1940.

Chambers, E. K. *The Elizabethan Stage*. Oxford, 1923.

———. *The Mediaeval Stage*. London, 1903.

Cheney, Sheldon. *The Open-Air Theatre*. New York, 1918.

———. *Stage Decoration*. London and New York, 1928.

———. *The Theatre: Three Thousand Years of Drama, Acting and Stagecraft*. London and New York, 1959.

Cicognara, Conte. *Catalogo dei libri d'arte*. Leipzig, 1931.

Cohen, Gustave. *Histoire de la mise-en-scène dans le théâtre religieux français du moyen âge*. Paris, 1926.

———. *Le théâtre en France au moyen âge*. Paris, 1928.

Corsi, Mari. *Il teatro all'aperto in Italia*. Milan-Rome, 1939.

Croce, Benedetto. *I teatri di Napoli del Rinascimento alla fina del secolo decimottavo*. Bari, 1916.

Decugis, Nicole, and Reymond, Suzanne. *Le décor de théâtre en France*. Paris, 1953; London, 1954.

Diaz-Plaja, ed. *El teatro*. Barcelona, 1958.

Dubech, Lucien. *Histoire générale illustrée du théâtre*. Paris, 1931-1934.

Ducharte, Pierre L. *The Italian Comedy*. London and New York, 1929.

*Enciclopedia dello spettacolo*. Rome, 1954-1966.

Ferrari, Giulio. *La scenografia*. Milan, 1902.

Fisher, Carlos. *Les costumes de l'opéra*. Paris, 1931.

Flickinger, R. C. *The Greek Theater and Its Drama*. Chicago, 1936.

Freedley, George, and Reeves, John A. *A History of the Theatre*. New York, 1941, 1968.

Frette, Guido. *Stage Design, 1900-1954*. Milan, 1955.

Gascoigne, Bamber. *World Theatre*. London, 1968.

Gervais, A. C. *Propos sur la mise en scène*. Paris, 1943.

Gregor, Joseph. *Kulturgeschichte des Ballets*. Vienna, 1944.

———. *Monumenta scenica: Denkmäler des Theaters*. Vienna, 1924-1930.

———. *Wiener szenische Kunst: Die Theaterdekoration*. Vienna, 1924.

———. *Wiener szenische Kunst: Das Bühnenkostüm*. Vienna, 1925.

———. *Weltgeschichte des Theaters*. Zurich, 1933.

Hammitzsch, Martin. *Der moderne Theaterbau*. Berlin, 1907.

Hartnoll, Phyllis, ed. *The Oxford Companion to the Theatre*. London and New York, 1967.

Hewitt, Barnard. *Theatre U.S.A., 1668-1957*. New York, 1959.

Hilmera, Jiri. *Perspektivni scena 17 a 18 stoleti*. Prague, 1965.

Holsboer, S. Wilma. *L'histoire de la mise en scène dans le théâtre français*. Paris, 1933.

Hughes, Glenn. *A History of the American Theatre, 1700-1950*. New York, 1951.

Jullien, Adolphe. *Histoire du costume au théâtre*. Paris, 1880.

*Katalog der Ornamentstichsammlung der Staatlichen Kunstbibliothek Berlin*. Berlin, 1939.

Kennard, J. S. *The Italian Theatre*. New York, 1932.

Kernodle, George R. *From Art to Theatre*. Chicago, 1944.

Kindermann, Heinz. *Theatergeschichte Europas*. Salzburg, 1957-1965.

Kindermann-Dietrich. *Drei hundert Jahre österreichisches Bühnenbild*. Vienna, 1959.

Kochno, Boris. *Le ballet en France du quinzième siècle à nos jours*. Paris, 1954.

Komisarjevsky, Theodore. *The Costume of the Theatre*. London, 1931; New York, 1932.

Laver, James. *Drama, Its Costumes and Decor*. London, 1951.

Leclerc, Hélène. *Les origines italiennes de l'architecture théâtrale moderne.* Paris, 1946.

Loukomski, G. K. *Les théâtres anciens et modernes.* Paris, 1934.

Lugt, F. *Les marques de collections de dessins et d'estampes.* Amsterdam, 1921.

Mâle, Emile. *L'art religieux de la fin du moyen âge en France.* Paris, 1908.

Mancini, Franco. *Scenografia italiana.* Milan, 1966.

Mandler Raymond, and Mitchenson, Joe. *Hamlet through the Ages.* London, 1952.

Mariani, Valerio. *Storia della scenografia italiana.* Florence, 1930.

*The Mask.* Florence, 1908–1929.

Maurey, Gabriel. *Le livre des fêtes françaises.* Paris, 1930.

Mayor, A. Hyatt, et al. *Tempi e aspetti della scenografia.* Turin, 1954.

McKechnie, Samuel. *Popular Entertainments through the Ages.* London, 1931.

Monteverdi, Mario. *La Scala: Four Hundred Years of Stage Design.* Milan, 1971.

Moussinac, Léon. *Le théâtre des origines à nos jours.* Paris, 1957.

———. *Traité de la mise en scène.* Paris, 1948.

Nagler, A. M. *A Source Book in Theatrical History.* New York, 1959.

Nicoll, Allardyce. *The Development of the Theatre.* New York, 1927; 6th ed. London, 1966.

Niessen, Carl. *Das Bühnenbild: Ein Kulturgeschichte Atlas.* Bonn, 1924.

Odell, George. *Annals of the New York Stage.* New York, 1927–1949; Oxford, 1949.

Patte and Landriani. *Storia e descrizione dei principale teatri.* Milan, 1830.

Pirchan, Emil. *Bühnen Brevier.* Vienna, 1948.

Poudra, Noël Germinal. *Histoire de la perspective ancienne et moderne.* Paris, 1864.

Pougin, Arthur. *Dictionnaire historique et pittoresque du théâtre.* Paris, 1885.

Rapp, Franz. *Süddeutsche Dekorationen.* Munich, 1926.

Rava, Arnaldo. *I teatri di Roma.* Rome, 1953.

Reynaud, Charles. *Matériel de l'art théâtral.* Paris, 1900.

Ricci, Corrado. *La scenografia italiana.* Milan, 1930.

Ricci, Giuliana. *Teatri d'Italia.* Milan, 1971.

Rolland, Romain. *The People's Theater.* New York, 1918; London, 1919.

Rosenfeld, Sybil. *A Short History of Scene Design in Great Britain.* Oxford, 1973.

Scholz, Janos, and Mayor, A. Hyatt. *Baroque and Romantic Stage Design.* New York, 1950.

Schöne, Günter. *Tausend Jahre deutsches Theater, 914–1914.* Munich, 1962.

Sharp, Cecil J., and A. P. Oppé. *The Dance.* London, 1924.

Simoni, Renato. *Museo teatro alla Scala.* Milan, 1918.

Simonson, Lee. *The Stage Is Set.* New York, 1932, 1963.

———. ed. *Theatre Art.* New York, 1934.

Sonrel, Pierre. *Traité de scénographie.* Paris, 1956.

Southern, Richard. *Changeable Scenery.* London, 1952.

Stuart, Donald C. *Stage Decoration in France in the Middle Ages.* New York, 1910.

*Theatrical Designs from the Baroque through Neoclassicism.* 3 portfolios, intro. by George Freedley. New York, 1940.

Torelli, Luigi. *Il teatro italiano.* Milan, 1924.

Veinstein, André. *Bibliothèques et musées des arts du spectacle dans le monde.* Paris, 1960.

Vitruvius. *The Ten Books on Architecture.* Cambridge, Mass., 1914.

Vloberg, Maurice. *Les fêtes de France.* Grenoble, 1936.

Webster, T. B. L. *Greek Theatre Production.* London, 1956, 1970.

Wolff, Helmuth. *Musikgeschichte in Bildernoper.* Leipzig, n.d.

## Renaissance

Adams, John C. *The Globe Playhouse: Its Design and Equipment.* Cambridge, Mass., 1942; London, 1961.

Amorini, A. B. *Elogio di Sebastiano Serlio.* Bologna, 1823.

Baker, George Pierce. *The Development of Shakespeare as a Dramatist.* New York, 1907.

Barbaro, Daniele. *La pratica della perspettiva.* Venice, 1568.

Borcherdt, H. H. *Das europäische Theater im Mittelalter und in der Renaissance.* Leipzig, 1935.

———. *Der Renaissancestil des Theaters.* Halle, 1926.

Campbell, Lily B. *Scenes and Machines on the English Stage During the Renaissance.* New York and Cambridge, 1960.

Charvet, Leon. *Sebastiano Serlio.* Lyon, 1869.

Densmoor, William B. "The Literary Remains of Sebastiano Serlio," *The Art Bulletin.* 1942.

Doesschate, G. *Perspective.* Nieuwkoop, 1964.

Fasola, G. N., ed. *Piero della Francesca: De prospettiva pingendi.* Florence, n.d.

*Feste e apparati Mediceo da Cosimo I a Cosimo II* (catalogue). 1969.

Garrone, Virginia. *L'apparato scenico del dramma sacro in Italia.* Turin, 1935.

Gori, Pietro. *Le feste fiorentine.* Florence, 1926.

Harris, John, et al. *The King's Arcadia: Inigo Jones and the Stuart Masque* (catalogue). London, 1973.

Hewitt, Bernard, ed. *The Renaissance Stage.* Coral Gables, Fla., 1958.

Jacquot, Jean. *La vie théâtrale au temps de la Renaissance* (catalogue). Paris, 1963.

———. *Les fêtes de la Renaissance.* Paris, 1956–1960.

Jones, Inigo. *Festival Designs.* Washington, D.C., 1967.

Lawrence, W. J. *The Elizabethan Playhouse and Other Studies.* Philadelphia, 1913; Stratford, England, 1912–1913.

McGowan, Margaret. *L'art du ballet de cour en France, 1581–1643.* Paris, 1963.

Massar, Phyllis. *Presenting Stefano della Bella.* New York, 1971.

Molinari, Cesare. *Le nozze degli dei.* Rome, 1968.

———. *Spettacoli fiorentini del quatrocento.* Venice, 1961.

Montenari. *Del teatro olympico.* Padua, 1733.

Nagler, A. M. *Theatre Festivals of the Medici 1539–1637.* New Haven, 1964.

Nicoll, Allardyce. *Stuart Masques and the Renaissance Stage.* London, 1937; New York, 1938.

Orgel, Stephen, and Strong, Roy. *Inigo Jones: The Theatre of the Stuart Court.* Berkeley, 1973.

Pélerin, Jean (Viator). *De artificiali perspettiva.* Toul, 1505.

Pozzo, Neri, ed. *Il teatro olympico.* Vicenza, 1969.

Prunières, H. *Le ballet de cour en France avant Benserade et Lully.* Paris, 1914.

Sabbatini, Nicola. *Pratica di fabricar scene e machine*

*ne' teatri.* Ravenna, 1638; Rome, 1955.

Schöne, Gunter. *Die Entwicklung der Perspektivbühne.* Leipzig, 1933.

Schrade, Leo. *La rappresentazione d'Edipo tiranno au teatro olimpico.* Paris, 1960.

Serlio, Sebastiano. *Il primo (secondo) libro d'architettura.* Paris, 1545.

Sirigatti, Lorenzo. *La pratica di prospettiva.* Venice, 1596.

Strong, Roy. *Splendor at Court.* Boston, 1973.

Vasari, Giorgio. *Lives of the Painters, Sculptors and Architects.* London, 1912; New York, 1927.

Vignola, Giacomo Barozzi da. *Le due regole della prospettiva pratica.* Rome, 1583.

Walpole Society. *Designs by Inigo Jones for Masques and Plays at Court.* Oxford, 1924.

White, John. *The Birth and Rebirth of Pictorial Space.* London, 1957.

## Baroque and Rococo

Accolti, Pietro. *Lo inganno de gl'occhi: prospettiva pratica.* Florence, 1625.

Ademollo, Alessandro. *I teatri di Roma.* Rome, 1888.

Aghion, Max. *Le théâtre à Paris au XVIII^e siècle.* Paris, 1926.

Aguilonius, Franciscus. *Opticarum libri sex philosophis juxta ac mathematicis utiles.* Antwerp, 1613.

Angelis, Alberto de. *Il teatro Alibert o delle dame.* Tivoli, 1951.

Baur-Heinhold, Margarete. *Baroque Theatre.* London, 1967.

Beijer, Agne. *Bilder från Stottsteatern på Drottningholm.* Stockholm, 1950.

———. *Stottsteatarna på Drottningholm och Gripsholm.* Stockholm, 1937.

Biach-Schiffmann, Flora. *Giovanni und Ludovico Burnacini.* Vienna, 1931.

Bibiena, Fernando (Galli-Bibiena). *L'architettura civile.* Parma, 1711.

Bjurström, Per. *Feast and Theatre in Queen Christina's Rome.* Stockholm, 1966.

———. *Giacomo Torelli and Baroque Stage Design.* Stockholm, 1961.

Bouché, Jeanne. "Jean-Nicolas Servandoni," *Gazette des Beaux Arts,* vol. IV, no. 4.

Celler, Ludovic. *Les décors, les costumes et la mise-en-scène au XVII^e siècle.* Paris, 1869.

Chiaramonti, Scipione. *Delle scene e teatri.* Cesena, 1675.

Christout, Marie-Françoise. *Le Ballet de cour de Louis XIV.* Paris, 1967.

Croce, Benedetto. *I teatri di Napoli dal rinascimento alla fine del secolo decimottavo.* Bari, 1916.

Damerini, Gino. *Scenografi veneziani dell'ottocento* (catalogue). Venice, 1962.

*Disegni teatrali dei Bibiena* (catalogue). Venice, 1970.

Dubreuil, Jean. *La perspective practique.* Paris, 1642–1649.

Fabris, Jacopo. *Instruction in der teatralischen Architectur und Mechanique.* Copenhagen, 1930.

Ferrero, Mercedes Viale-. *Feste delle Madame Reali di Savoia.* Turin, 1965.

———. *Filippo Juvara.* New York, 1970.

———. *La scenografia del '700 e i Frattelli Galliari.* Turin, 1963.

———. *Scenografia-mostra del barocco piemontese.* Turin, 1963.

Fichera, Francesco. *Luigi Vanvitelli.* Rome, 1937.

Furttenbach, Joseph. *Architectura Civilis.* Ulm, 1628.

———. *Architectura Recreationis.* Augsburg, 1640.

———. *Mannhaffter Kunstspiegel.* Augsburg, 1663.

*Gonzaga, Pietro* (catalogue). Venice, 1967.

Gregor, Joseph. *Wiener Szenische Kunst: die Theater Dekoration.* Vienna, 1924.

Hadamowsky, Franz. *Die Familie Galli-Bibiena in Wien.* Vienna, 1962.

Hibbard, Howard. *Bernini.* Harmondsworth, England, 1965.

Holsboer, S. Wilma. *L'histoire de la mise en scène dans le théâtre Français de 1600 à 1657.* Paris, 1933.

Horányi, Mátyás. *Das Esterhazysche Feenreich.* Budapest, 1959.

Jeudwine, Wynne. *Stage Designs in Royal Institute of British Architects.* London, 1968.

Jullien, Adolphe. *La comédie à la cour.* Paris, 1888.

Kaufman Collection. *Fantastic and Ornamental Drawings* (catalogue). Portsmouth, 1969.

Kelder, Diane. *Drawings by the Bibiena Family* (catalogue). Philadelphia, 1968.

Konopleva, M. S. [*Stage Designs of Giuseppe Valeriani*]. Leningrad, 1948.

Lancaster, C. L. *Le mémoire de Mahelot, Laurent et autres décorateurs de l'hôtel de Bourgogne.* Paris, 1920.

Lawrenson, T. E. *The French Stage in the Seventeenth Century.* Manchester, 1957.

Magne, Emil. *Les fêtes en Europe au XVII^e siècle.* Paris, 1930.

Mancini, Franco. *Scenografia italiana.* Naples, 1966.

———. *Scenografia napoletana dell' età barocca.* Naples, 1964.

Marconi, Paolo. *Giuseppe Valadier.* Rome, 1964.

Mayor, A. Hyatt. *The Bibiena Family.* New York, 1945.

Meyer, Rudolf. *Hecken und Gartentheater in Deutschland im XVII und XVIII.* Emsdetten, 1934.

Muraro, Maria Teresa. *Scenografi di Pietro Gonzaga.* Venice, 1967.

Muraro-Povoledo. *Disegni teatrali dei Bibiena* (catalogue). Venice, 1970.

Palumbo-Fossati, Carlo. *I Fossati di Morcote.* Bellinzona, 1970.

Paradossi, Giulio Troili. *Paradossi per practicare la prospettiva senza saperla.* Bologna, 1683.

Pilon, E., and Saisset, F. *Les fêtes en Europe au XVIII^e siècle.* Sainte-Gratinée, n.d.

Pozzo, Andrea. *Perspettiva pictorium et architettorum . . . prospettiva de'pittori e architetti.* Rome, 1693–1700.

*Quarenghi, Giacomo* (catalogue). Venice, 1967.

Ricci, Corrado. *I teatri di Bologna.* Bologna, 1888.

Rouchés, Gabriel. *Vigarani.* Paris, 1913.

Rovere-Viale. *Filippo Juvara.* Milan, 1937.

Ruggière, Claude. *Les fêtes, les spectacles.* Paris, 1830.

Sabbatini, Nicolo. *Pratica di fabricar scene e machine ne'teatri.* Ravenna, 1638.

Schlumberger, Eveline. *Servandoni.* Paris, 1965.

Sirigatti, Lorenzo. *La pratica di prospettiva.* Venice, 1596.

Sofia-Moretti, Ugo. *Pietro Gonzaga.* Milan, 1960.

Sonneck, Oskar. *Catalogue of Opera Libretti before 1800.* Washington, D.C., 1914.

*Théâtre en France au XVII^e siècle.* Paris, 1957.

Tintelnot, Hans. *Barocktheater und Barocke Kunst.* Berlin, 1939.

Ubaldus, Guido. *Perspettivae libri sex*. Pesaro, 1600.

Vignola, Giacomo Barozzi da. *Le due regole della prospettiva pratica*. Rome, 1583.

Vsevolodsky-Gerngross. *Russky teatr vtoroi polovini XVIII*. Moscow, 1960.

Wollin, N. G. *Desprez en Suède*. Stockholm, 1939.

Worsthorne, S. T. *Venetian Opera in the Seventeenth Century*. Oxford, 1954.

Zucker. Paul. *Die Theaterdekoration des Barock*. Berlin, 1925.

## Neo-Classic and Romantic

Adami, Giuseppe. *Un secolo di scenografia alla Scala*. Milan, 1945.

Allévy, Marie-Antoinette. *La mise en scène en France dans le première moitié du XIX^e siècle*. Paris, 1938.

Bablet, Denis. *Le décor de théâtre de 1870 à 1914.* Paris, 1965.

Bapst, Germain. *L'histoire des panoramas et des dioramas*. Paris, 1891.

Castelucho, A. and C. *Escenografia, teatral-perspettiva*. Barcelona, 1896.

Celler, Ludovic. *Les décors, les costumes et la mise-en-scène*. Paris, 1869.

Chirodi, Luigi. *Disegni di Giacomo Quarenghi*. Venice, 1967.

Ferrario, Carlo. *Scenografia*. Milan, 1919.

Fouquières, Becq de. *L'art de la mise en scène*. Paris, 1884.

Gernsheim, H. and A. *Daguerre*. New York and London, 1956.

Ginisti, Paul. *Le théâtre romantique*. n.d.

Grisebach, August. *Carl Friedrich Schinkel*. Leipzig, 1924.

Grube, Max. *Geschichte der Meininger*. Stuttgart, 1926.

Hodge, Francis, ed. *Innovations in Stage and Theatre Design*. Austin, Texas, 1972.

International Federation for Theatre Research. *Anatomy of an Illusion*. 1969.

Jung, Otto. *Der Theatermaler Friedrich Christian Beuther und seine Welt*. Emsden, 1963.

Knudsen, Hans. *Goethes Welt des Theaters*. Berlin, 1949.

Landriani, Paolo. *Osservazioni*. Milan, 1815.

Leconte, L. H. *Napoléon et le monde dramatique*. Paris, 1888.

Moynet, Georges. *Trucs et décors*. Paris, n.d.

Moynet, M. J. *L'envers du théâtre*. Paris, 1888.

Nusser, Luitpold. *Schinkel und Brückner*. Würzburg, 1923.

Odell, George C. *Annals of the New York Stage*. New York, 1927–1949.

Petzet, D. and M. *Die Richard Wagner-Bühne Königs Ludwigs II*. 1970.

Phillips, I. Von Keith. *Clarkson Stanfield and Romantic Paintings in the English Theatre*. London, 1969.

Saxon, Arthur. *Enter Foot and Horse*. New Haven, 1968.

Schinkel, Karl Friedrich. *Dekoration auf den Königlichern Theatern in Berlin*. Berlin, 1819.

Scholz, Janos, ed. *Theatrical Designs from the Baroque through Neoclassicism*. New York, 1940.

Schank, Theodore J. "Shakespeare and Nineteenth Century Realism," *Theatre Survey*, vol. 4, (1963).

Stanislavski, Constantin. *My Life in Art*. Boston, 1924; London, 1962.

Trost, Brigitte. *Domenico Quaglio*. Munich, 1973.

Vaulabelle and Hemardinquer. *La science au théâtre*. Paris, 1908.

Waxman, S. M. *Antoine and the théâtre-libre*. Harvard, 1926.

Winter, Marian. *The Theatre of Marvels*. New York, 1964.

Zucker, Paul. *Die Theaterdekoration des Klassizismus*. Berlin, 1925.

## Twentieth Century

Adami, Giuseppe. *Un secolo di scenografia alla Scala*. Milan, 1945.

Alarma, S. *Escenografia*. Barcelona, 1919.

Aloi, Roberto. *Esempi architetture per lo spettacolo*. New York, 1959.

Amberg, George. *Art in Modern Ballet*. New York, 1946; London, 1947.

Appia, Adolphe. *Music and the Art of the Theatre*. Coral Gables, Florida, 1962.

———. *Portfolio of Drawings*. Geneva, 1929.

———. *L'œuvre d'art vivant*. Geneva, 1921.

Arent, Benno von. *Das Deutsche Bühnenbild 1933–1936*. Berlin, 1938.

Artaud, Antonin. *Theatre and Its Double*. Paris, 1938.

Bablet, Denis. *Edward Gordon Craig*. Paris, 1966.

———. *Le décor de théâtre de 1870 à 1914*. Paris, 1965.

Bakst, Léon. *La belle au bois dormant*. Paris, 1922.

Bayer, Herbert, et al., eds. *Bauhaus, 1919–1928*. Boston and London, 1952.

Beaton, Cecil. *Cecil Beaton's Scrapbook*. London, 1937.

Beaumont, Cyril W. *Design for the Ballet*. London, 1937.

Belasco, David. *The Theatre through Its Stage Door*. New York, 1919.

Bel Geddes, Norman. *Horizons*. Boston, 1932.

———. *Miracle in the Evening*. New York, 1960.

———. *The Divine Comedy*. New York, 1925.

Benois, Alexandre. *My Life*. London, 1960, 1964.

Bjurström, Per. *Theaterdekoration I Sverige*. Stockholm, 1964.

Boll, André. *Du décor de théâtre*. Paris, n.d.

———. *La mise en scène contemporaine*. Paris, 1944.

Bragaglia, A. G. *Del teatro teatrale*. Rome, 1929.

Bragdon, Claude. *Merely Players*. New York, 1929.

Brook, Peter. *The Empty Space*. London, 1968.

Brown, John Mason. *The Modern Theatre in Revolt*. New York, 1929.

Buckle, Richard. *Modern Ballet Design*. London, 1955.

Burian, Jarka. *The Scenography of Josef Svoboda*. Middletown, Conn., 1971.

Carter, Huntly. *The New Spirit in the Russian Theatre*. London and New York, 1929.

———. *The Theatre of Max Reinhardt*. London, 1914.

Cheney, Sheldon. *Stage Decoration*. New York and London, 1928.

———. *The Art Theatre*. New York, 1917; rev. ed. 1925.

———. *The New Movement in the Theatre*. New York, 1914.

Cogniat, Raymond. *Décors de théâtre*. Paris, 1930.

———. *Les décorateurs de théâtre*. Paris, 1959.

———. *Simon Lissim*. Paris, n.d.

Cooper, Douglas. *Picasso et le théâtre*. Paris, 1967.

Craig, Edward. *Gordon Craig: The Story of His Life*. London, 1968.

Craig, (Edward) Gordon. *On the Art of the Theatre*. London, 1911; reissued London and New York, 1968.

———. *Scene*. London and New York, 1923.

———. *The Theatre Advancing*. Boston, 1920; London, 1921.

———. *Towards a New Theatre*. London, 1913.

*Deutsches Theater—Ausstellung*. Magdeburg, 1927.

Dhomme, Sylvain. *La mise en scène contemporaine*. Paris, 1923.

*Les ballets russes de Serge Diaghilev* (catalogue). Strassbourg, 1969.

Drinkwater, John, and Rutherston, Albert. *Claud Lovat Fraser*. New York, 1923.

*Exposition internationale des arts* (catalogue). Paris, 1925.

Exter, Aleksandra. *Maquettes de théâtre* (portfolio). Paris, 1930.

Fischel, Oskar. *Das moderne Bühnenbild*. Berlin, 1923.

Fletcher, I. K., and Rood, Arnold. *Edward Gordon Craig: A Bibliography*. London, 1967.

Ford Foundation. *The Ideal Theater: Eight Concepts*. New York, 1962.

Fuerst, Walter R., and Hume, S. J. *Twentieth Century Stage Decoration*. London, 1928; New York, 1929.

George, Waldemar. *Boris Aronson et l'art du théâtre*. Paris, 1928.

*George W. Harris, 1878–1929*. London, 1930.

Goldschmidt, Alfons. *Das Moskauer Jüdische Akademische Theater*. Berlin, 1928.

Gontcharova-Larionov. *L'art décoratif théâtral moderne*. Paris, 1919.

Gorchakov, Nicolai. *The Theatre in Soviet Russia*. New York, 1957; London, 1958.

———. *Vakhtangov: School of Stage Art*. New York, n.d.

Gorelik, Mordecai. *New Theatres for Old*. New York, 1940; London, 1947.

Graf, Herbert. *The Opera and Its Future in America*. New York, 1941.

Gregor, Joseph. *Alfred Roller*. Vienna, 1940.

———. *Das Russische Theater*. Zurich, 1927.

———, and Fülop-Miller, René. *Das Amerikanische Theater*. Zurich, 1931.

Gröning, Karl. *Der Bühnenbildner*. Hamburg, 1962.

Grotowski, Jerzy. *Towards a Poor Theatre*. London, 1969.

Hainaux, Yves-Bonnat. *Le décor de théâtre*. Paris, 1935, 1950, 1963, 1973.

Haldane, Macfall. *The Book of Claud Lovat Fraser*. London, 1923.

Holme, Geoffrey, ed. *Design in the Theatre*. London, 1927.

Holzmeister, Clemens. *Werke für das Theater*. Vienna, 1953.

Houghton, Norris. *Moscow Rehearsals*. New York, 1936.

Houseman, John. *Run-Through*. New York, 1972.

Jones, Robert Edmond. *Drawings for the Theatre*. New York, 1925, 1969.

———. *The Dramatic Imagination*. New York, 1941.

Kirstein, Lincoln. *Pavel Tchelitchew* (catalogue). New York, 1964.

Kochno, Boris. *Diaghilev and the Ballets Russes*. New York, 1970; London, 1971.

Kodiček, Rutte, and Vydani. *Nové České Divadlo, 1918–1926*. Prague, 1927.

Komisarjevsky, Fedor, and Simonson, Lee. *Settings and Costumes of the Modern Stage*. London and New York, 1933.

Kostin, E. *V. F. Ruidin: Theatrical Work*. Moscow, 1955.

Kranich, Friedrich. *Bühnentechnik der Gegenwart*. Munich, 1933.

Larsen, Orville. *Designing for Stage and Screen*. East Lansing, Mich., 1961.

Laver, James. *Drama: Its Costumes and Decor*. London, 1951.

Levenson, André. *Bakst*. Paris, 1924.

Levy, Julien, ed. *Eugene Berman*. New York, 1946.

Ley, Maria. *The Piscator Experiment*. New York, 1967.

Lister, Raymond. *The Muscovite Peacock*. Cambridge, 1954.

Lobonov, Nikita. *Transactions of the Association of Russian-American Scholars*, vol. 2. New York, 1968.

Lobonov and Rostovsky. *Russian Painters and the Stage* (catalogue). New York, 1968.

Macgowan, Kenneth. *The Theatre of Tomorrow*. New York, 1921; London, 1923.

———, and Jones, Robert Edmond. *Continental Stagecraft*. New York and London, 1923.

Mello, Bruno. *Trattato di Scenotecnica*. Milan, 1962.

Messel, Oliver. *Stage Designs and Costumes*. London, 1933.

Mielziner, Jo. *Shapes of Our Theatres*. New York, 1970.

———. *Designing for the Theatre*. New York, 1965.

Motherwell, Hiram. *The Theatre of Today*. New York, 1925.

Moussinac, Léon. *La décoration théâtrale*. Paris, 1922.

———. *The New Movement in the Theatre*. London, 1931.

Nemirovitch-Dantchenko, Vladimir. *My Life in the Russian Theatre*. London and Boston, 1936.

Newmark, Maxim. *Otto Brahm*. New York, 1938.

Niedermoser, Otto. *Oskar Strnad 1879–1935*. Vienna, 1965.

Niessen, Carl. *Brecht auf der Bühne*. Cologne, 1959.

———. *Die Deutscher Oper du Gegenwart*. Regensburg, 1944.

———. *Max Reinhardt und seine Bühnenbildner*. Cologne, 1958.

Oenslager, Donald. *Scenery Then and Now*. New York, 1936.

———, and Rood, Arnold. *Edward Gordon Craig* (catalogue). New York, 1967.

*Orientamenti della scenografia*. Milan, 1959.

*Oskar Schlemmer und die abstrakte Bühne* (catalogue). Munich, 1961.

Otto, Teo. *Meine Scene*. Cologne, 1965.

———. *Skizzer eines Bühnenbildners*. Saint Gall, 1964.

Panofsky, Walter. *Wieland Wagner*. Bremen, 1964.

Parker, John. *Who's Who in the Theatre*. London, 1972.

Pendleton, Ralph, ed. *The Theatre of Robert Edmond Jones*. Middletown, Conn., 1958.

Pirchan, Emil. *Bühnenmalerei*. Ravensburg, 1950.

Piscator, Erwin. *Das politische Theater*. Berlin, 1929.

Rischbieter and Storch. *Art and the Stage in the Twentieth Century*. New York, 1969.

Rouché, Jacques. *L'art théâtral moderne*. Paris, 1910.

Rudiger, W. E. *Preetorius: Das scenische Werk*. Berlin, 1941.

*Russian Stage and Costume Design* (catalogue), intro. Georges Annenkov. Washington, D.C., 1967.

Rutherston, Albert. *Sixteen Designs for the Theatre*. London, 1928.

Sayler, Oliver. *Inside the Moscow Art Theatre*. New York, 1924.

———. *Max Reinhardt and His Theatre*. New York, 1924.

———. *The Russian Theatre*. New York, 1922.

*Scenografia italiana contemporanea* (catalogue). Naples, 1969.

Schilern, Eugen. *Scenografia romaneasca*. Bucharest, n.d.

Schlemmer, Oskar, et al. *Die Bühne im Bauhaus*. Mainz, 1965.

———. *Theatre of the Bauhaus*, ed. Walter Gropius. Middletown, Conn., 1961.

Schubarth, Ottman. *Das Bühnenbild*. Munich, 1955.

Sheringham, G., and Laver, J. *Design in the Theatre*. London, 1927.

Sievert, Ludwig. *Des lebendiges Theater*. Munich, 1944.

Silverman, Maxwell. *Contemporary Theatre Architecture*. New York, 1965.

Simonov, Ruben. *Eugene Vakhtangov*. New York, 1969.

Simonson, Lee. *Part of a Lifetime*. New York, 1943.

————. *The Art of Scenic Design*. New York and London, 1951.

Sokolova, N. *Design in Soviet Theatre*. Moscow, 1971.

————, ed. *Artists in the Theatre*. Moscow, 1968.

Stadler, Edmund. *Das schweizerische Bühnenbild von Appia bis Häute*. Zurich, 1954.

Stanislavski, Constantin. *My Life in Art*. Boston, 1924; London, 1962.

Stern, Ernst. *Bühnenbilder bei Max Reinhardt*. Berlin, 1955.

————. *My Life, My Stage*. London, 1951.

Stern and Herald. *Max Reinhardt und seine Bühne*. Berlin, 1920.

Strzelecki, Zenobiusz. *Polska Plastyka Teatralna*. Warsaw, 1963.

Symons, James. *Meyerhold's Theatre of the Grotesque*. Miami, Florida, 1971.

Tairov, Alexander. *Das entfesselte Theater*. Potsdam, 1923.

————. *Notes of a Director*. Coral Gables, Florida, 1969.

*Theatre Arts Monthly*. New York, 1916–1948.

Turgenhold, Jacques. *Aleksandra Exter*. Berlin, 1922.

Unruh, Walter. *A B C der Theatertechnik*. Halle, 1950.

Urban, Joseph. *Book of Theatres*. New York, 1930.

Veinstein, André. *La mise en scène théâtrale*. Paris, 1955.

Vohlbach, Walther. *Adolphe Appia*. Middletown, Conn., 1968.

Von Einam and Melchinger. *Caspar Neher*. Hannover, 1966.

Wagner, Ludwig. *Der Szeniker Ludwig Sievert*. Berlin, 1926.

Waxman, S. M. *Antoine and the Théâtre-Libre*. Cambridge, Mass., 1926.

Whistler, Laurence, and Fuller, Ronald. *The Work of Rex Whistler*. London, 1960.

Whistler, Rex. *Designs for the Theatre*. London, 1950.

Whitworth, Geoffrey. *Theatre in Action*. London and New York, 1938.

Zikes, Vladimir. *La Scena Moderna Ceco-Slovacca*. Prague, 1938.

Zinkeisen, Doris. *Designing for the Stage*. London, 1948.

# Index

Page numbers in italics refer to illustrations.

Abbott, George, 248
Adams, Franz, 162
Addison, Joseph, 14
Aeschylus, 13, 14, 15, 16, 88, 217
Agatharcus, 16
Akimov, Nikolai, 208–10, *209*
Albani, Francesco, 57
Alberti, Leon Battista, 23
Albrecht, Prince (Prussia), 156
Alcibiades, 16
Aldrovandini, Count, 140
Aleotti, Gianbattista, 43
Alexander I, Czar (Russia), 114
Algarotti, Francesco, 60, 61–64, 100
Algarotti, Lauro, 148
Alkamenes, 16
Allegri, O., 198
Ames, Winthrop, 224, 233
Amico, Silvio d', 9
Anaxagoras, 16
Anderson, Judith, 17
Anderson, Maxwell, 245, *247*, 248
Andreani, Andrea, 32
Andreenko, Mihail Fedorovitch, 202–208, *208*
Andreev, Leonid, 229
Angeli (engraver), 149
Anne, Queen (France), 44, 52
Annenkov (artist), 199
Annensky (playwright), 202
Ansky [Solomon Rappoport], 248
Antoine, André, 200
Appia, Adolphe, 160, 183, 184–87, *184*, *185*, *187*, 195, 202, 214, 217, 220, 221, 234, 244
Aretino. See Conti, Metrodoro (Aretino)
Ariosto, Lodovico, 23, 24–25, 61
Aristophanes, 16, 17

Aristotle, 15, 17, 23, 24
Aronson, Boris, 248–49, *249*
Arrigoni, Antonio, 130, 133–34, *133*
Arthur, Julia, 236
Ashton, Frederick, 244
Audin (scene painter), 158
Augier, Émile, 167
Augustus, Emperor, 16, 19
Augustus III, King, 84
Aureli, Mariano, 34
Austin, A. Everett, 237, 238
Axer, Erwin, 211

Bach, Johann Sebastian, 188
Bagnara, Francesco, 147
Baker, George Pierce, 9, 224, 229, 234
Bakst, Léon, 12, 87, 193, 195, 196–98, *196*, *197*, 200, 202, 238
Balakirev, Mili, *201*
Balanchine, George, 213, 237, 238, 239–40, 252
Balbus, Cornelius, 19
Balieff, Nikita, 199, 200–201
Balzac, Honoré de, 167, 198
Banvard, John, 172
Bapst, Germain, 167, 176
Barbaro, Daniele di, 29
Barbieri (architect), 96
Barnsdall, Aline, 232
Barnum, Phineas Taylor, 142, 234
Barret, Edward, 226
Barrymore, Lionel, 234, 236
Bartoli, Giuseppe, 97
Basil, Colonel W. de [Vassili Voskrensky], 238
Basoli, Antonio, 113, 140–42, *141*, *142*, *143*, *144*
Basoli, Francesco, 140

Basoli, Luigi, 140
Bassi, Antonio, 149, 151
Bean, Jacob, 9
Beaton, Cecil, 241
Beaumarchais, Caron de, 200
Beethoven, Ludwig van, *249*, 250
Begemann, E. Haverkamp, 9
Beijer, Agne, 9, 29
Belasco, David, 224
Bella, Stefano, della, 37, 89
Bellangé, Joseph Louis, 158
Bellini, Gentile, 237
Bellini, Giovanni, 27
Bellini, Jacopo, 23
Bellini, Vincenzo, 151, 213
Belotto, Bernardo (Il Canaletto), 68, 91–92, *93*, 124
Bembo, Pietro, 23
Benavente y Martinez, Jacinto, 200
Benois, Alexandr, 10, *115*, 168, 193–96, *194*, *195*, 198
Berain, Jean I, 11, 52–54, *54*, 58, 84, 86, 87, 88, 89, 157
Bérard, Christian, 213, 236, 238
Bergman, Robert W., 228
Beringer (artist), 130
Berliner, Rudolf, 9
Berman, Eugene, 236–38, *239*, 244
Berman, Leonide, 236
Bernhardt, Sarah, 226
Bernheimer, Richard, 9, 68
Bernini, Giovanni Lorenzo, 169
Bernstein, Leonard, 252
Bertati, G., 109
Betti, Ugo, *204*
Beuther, Friedrich, 152, 153–55, *153*, 156
Beuther, Dr. Rudolph, 155

Bevan, Frank, 251
Biach-Schiffmann, Flora, 51
Biasioli (artist), 151
Bibbiena, Cardinal Bernardo Dovizi da, 25, 57
Bibiena, Alessandro Galli, 57, 94
Bibiena, Antonio Galli, 12, 58, 60, 67–68, *68*, *69*, 84, 105–106
Bibiena, Carlo Galli, 58, 66, 70–72, *70*, *72*, 84, 114
Bibiena, Ferdinando Galli, 9, 35, 42, 57–58, *59*, 60, 61–64, *61*, 67, 72–73, 74, *75*, *75*, 84, 106, 112, 124
Bibiena, Francesco Galli, 57, 58, *61*, 64
Bibiena, Giovanni Maria Galli da, 57
Bibiena, Giovanni Maria Galli the Younger, 58
Bibiena, Giuseppe Galli, 57–58, 60, 64, *64*, *65*, 66–67, *66*, 70, 106, 113, 124
Bibiena family, 10, 11, 57–71, 92, 105, 112, 130, 140, 169, 198
Biederman, Johann, 130
Biedermeier, Joseph, 198
Bierstadt, Albert, 172–73
Bigari, Vittorio, 112, 113
Bignami, Vespasiano, 174, 175
Bilibine (artist), 193–94
Bisi, Luigi, *66*
Bittner, Herbert, 64
Bittner, Norbert, 130, 133, 134, 136, *138*
Bjurström, Per, 9, 44
Blake, William, 36, 149
Blechan, Karl, 167
Blondel, Jean François, 89
Boe, Eugene, 228
Boito, Arrigo, 174
Bolm, Adolf, 195
Bolsena, Girolamo da, 32
Bolsi (artist), 32
Bond, William, 9
Booth, Edwin, 172, 226, 236
Boquet, Louis-René, 84, 87
Borodin, Alexander, 191, 195
Borsato, Giuseppe, 147–48, *147*, 149
Bosch, Hieronymus, 36
Botticelli, Sandro, 27
Boucher, François, 84, 86, 88
Boucicault, Dion, 172
Boulée, Etienne Louis, 158
Bracciola, Mauro, 112, 140
Brady, William A., 233
Bragdon, Claude, 224–25, *225*
Brahm, Otto, 187, 214
Bramante (Donato d'Agnolo), 23, 24, 25, 30
Brancusi, Constantin, 244
Brandegee, Mrs. Edward, 10
Brandt, Fritz, 180
Brangwyn, Frank, 244

Braque, Georges, 183, 202, 213, 244
Breughel, Pieter the Younger, 36
Britten, Benjamin, 244, *245*
Bronson, William, 170
Brook, Peter, 87–88
Brown, John Mason, 198, 236
Brückner, Gotthold, 180
Brückner, Max, 180–82, *182*
Bruguiére, Francis, 233
Brühl, Graf, 156
Buffalo Bill, 226
Buontalenti, Bernardo, 36–37, 40, *41*, 46, 47
Burnacini, Giovanni, 50
Burnacini, Ludovico, 47, 50–51, *50*, *51*, 55, 58, 84, 87
Buti, Francesco, 44

Cadman, Charles, 232
Caesar, Julius, 19
Calderon de la Barca, Pedro, 47, 204, *204*
Callot, Jacques, 9, 36, 37, 84, 89
Cambon, Charles-Antoine, 159, 160, 162, 179
Campbell, Frank, 9
Canale, Bernardo, 92
Canaletto (Giovanni Antonio Canale), 92, 116, 121, 124, 237
Canaletto, Il. *See* Belotto, Bernardo
Canna, Pasquale, 121, 149, 152
Canova, Antonio, 116
Cantagallina (engraver), 38
Carboni, Angelo, 90–91
Carl Theodore (Elector of Bavaria), 94–95
Carpaccio, Vittore, 237
Carpezat (scenic artist), 159, 176, 179–80, *180*
Carracci brothers, 37, 57
Cassandre [Adolphe Mouron], 213
Castiglione, Baldassare, 23, 25
Catherine II, Empress (Russia), 114
Catherwood, Frederick, 172
Cato, 18
Cellini, Benvenuto, 30
Certani, Professor, 10
Cesti, Marc'Antonio, 51
Cézanne, Paul, 229
Chagall, Marc, 98, 244, 248
Chaliapin, Feodor, 192, 194
Challe, Charles Michel-Ange, 86–88, *86*
Chaperon, Philippe-Marie, 178, 179
Charell, Eric, 214, 220
Charles V, Emperor, 30
Charles VI, Emperor, 67
Charles III, King (Naples), 73, 81, 96
Charles IV, King (Naples), 80
Chase, Lucia, 252

Chauveau, F., *45*, 46
Chekhov, Anton, 111
Chekhov, Mikhail, 203, 204
Cheney, Sheldon, 224
Cheret, Jules, 167
Cherubini, Maria Luigi, 130, 160
Chiarini, Marcantonio, 61
Chiaruttini, Francesco, 116, *117*
Chirico, Giorgio de, 237
Christian VI, King (Denmark), 78
Church, Frederick, 173
Cicéri, Pierre-Luc-Charles, 74, 75, *75*, 158–60, *159*, *166*, 178
Cicero, 18
Cicognini, Bruno, 47
Cimarosa, Domenico, 104
Clare, Joseph, 170–73, *172*
Claudel, Paul Louis, 185, 234
Cocchi, Francesco, 140
Cochin, Charles Nicolas, 89, 156
Cochran, Charles B., 220, 241
Cohen, Gustave, 22
Cole, John. 172
Coleman, Basil, 244
Coleridge, Samuel Taylor, 75
Colomba, Giovan Battista, 84
Colonna (artist), 42, 116
Connelly, Marc, 235
Constantine, Emperor, 20
Conti, Metrodoro (Aretino), 75, *75*
Cook, Ansel, 224, *224*, 225, 226
Copeau, Jacques, 185, 200, 234
Copland, Aaron, 252
Corneille, Pierre, 44, *45*, 46
Cornell, Katharine, 245
Cossa, Francesco, 23
Cowl, Jane, 236, *237*
Coypel, Noel, 44
Craig, Edward, 190
Craig, [Edward] Gordon, 9, 12, 124, 160, 183, 185, 187–91, *188*, *190*, *191*, 195, 202, 208, 211, 214, 215–16, 217, 220, 224, 233, 234, 244, 251
Cranko, John, 244
Crosato, Giovan Battista, 96, 97
Cuevas, Georges, 213
Currier and Ives, 172
Cuvilliés, François de, 113, 240–41
Cybulski, Zbigniew, 211

Daguerre, Louis Jacques, 158
Dalberg, Wolfgang von, 216
Dalcroze. *See* Jacques-Dalcroze, Émile
Dali, Salvador, 238
Daly, Augustin, 172
Dante, 36, 233
Danti, Egnazio, 28, 33
Darius, 13
Daszewski, Wladyslaw, 211

Davenant, William, 40–41
Da Verona, Bartolomeo. *See* Verona, Bartolomeo da
David, Jacques Louis, 157, 159
Dean, Basil, 220
De Basil, Colonel W. (Vassili Voskrensky), 238
De Gaspari. *See* Gaspari, Pietro de
De Koven, Reginald, 173
Delfau, André, 212–14, *213*
De Mille, Agnes, 252
De Mille, Cecil B., 234
Democritus, 16
De Pian. *See* Pian, Antonio de
Despléchin, Edouard-Désiré, 159, 176, 179
De Vries, Jan Vredeman, 30, *30*
Diaghilev, Sergei, 10, 87, 184, 185, 192–93, 194–95, 197, 198, 200, 202, 213, 224, 229, 238
Dickens, Charles, 160
Diderot, Denis, 85, 86, 89
Dillingham, Charles, 170
Disney, Walt, 163
Doboujinsky, Mstislav, 198–200, *199*
Döll, Heinrich, 163
Domenichino, Il, 57
Donizetti, Gaetano, 151
Drabik, Wincenty, 211
Duflocq (director), 176
Dumas, Alexandre, 158, 167
Dumont (architect), 156
Duncan, Isadora, 183, 187, 188
Dunlap, William, 158
Dunoyer de Segonzac, André, 244
Durand, Asher, 172
Durazzo, Count, 92
Dürer, Albrecht, 223
Duveen, Joseph, 241
Dvorak, Dominik, 133

Eames, Marian, 109
Ebert, Carl, 244
Edison, Thomas A., 186, 224
Edward VIII, King (England), 220
Eigtved, Nicolas, 78
Eisenstein, Sergei, 209
Elizabeth I, Empress (Russia), 89–90, *90*, 91
Elizabeth II, Queen (England), 244
Ellis, Havelock, 249
Emerson, Ralph Waldo, 11
Engelbrecht, Martin, 74
Errard, Charles, 44, *45*
Erté (Romain de Tirtoff), 226–28, *227*
Este, Ercole d' I, 23
Este, Isabella d', 25
Este family (Ferrara), 23, 24
Eugen, Herzog Karl, 84

Euripides, 13, 14, 15, 16, 17, 24
Evans (scene painter), 226
Evreinov, Nikolai, 209
Exter, Aleksandra, 199, 202–204, *203, 204*, 238, 248

Fabris, Jacopo, 78–79, *78*
Fajt, Marianne, 10
Falconet, Étienne Maurice, 89
Fancelli (artist), 140
Farnese, Cardinal Alessandro, 28
Farnese, Duke Francesco, 74
Farnese, Pierluigi, 28
Fatio, Edmond, 10, *61*
Feigay, Paul, 252
Felsenstein, Walter, 210
Ferdinand, Grand Duke, 40
Ferrario, Carlo, 173–76, *174, 175*
Ferrario, Giulio, 9
Filosofov, Dima, 194
Fiocco, Giuseppe, 151–52
Fletcher, Ifan Kyrle, 180
Fokine, Michel, 87, 195
Fontaine, Pierre François, 156–58
Fontanesi, Francesco, 114
Fontanne, Lynn, 245
Fontebasso (artist), 116
Fossati [di Morcate], Domenico, 10, 116–17, *119*, 124
Fouquet, Jean, 22
Fouquet, Nicolas, 44
Fragonard, Jean Honoré, 86
France, Anatole, 234
Francesca, Piero della, 23, 27
Francesco I, King (Lombardy-Venice), 150
Francini, Tomaso, 52, *52*
Francis I, Emperor (Austria-Hungary), 124
François I, King (France), 30
Franconi, Adolphe, 179
Fraser, Lovat, 244
Frederick the Great, King (Prussia), 74, 78, 97, 98, 107, 117–20
Freedley, George, 9, 64
Freedman, Gerald, 254
Frederick Wilhelm III, King (Prussia), 120, 155
Fries, Count, 130
Fritsche, H. A., 92
Frost, Robert, 251
Frugoni, Carlo Innocenzo, 74
Fryz (designer), 211
Fueger (artist), 130
Fuentes, Giorgio, 113, 121, 149, 152–53, *152*, 154, 156
Fuller, Loie, 183

Fuller, Ronald, 244

Gabriel, Jacques Anges, 85
Gail, Matthias, 130
Galli, Giovanni Maria. *See* Bibiena, Giovanni Maria Galli da. *See also* Bibiena family
Galliari, Bernardino, 96, 97, *97*, 98, *99*, 117
Galliari, Fabrizio, 96, 98, *99*, 100, *100*
Galliari, I Fratelli, *101*
Galliari, Gaspare, 96, 100–105, *104, 106*, 130
Galliari, Giovanni, 98–100
Galliari, Giovanni Antonio, 96, 98, *101*
Galliari, Giuseppino, 100
Galliari family, 10, 57, 96–105, 114, 115, 117–20, 121, 146, 149
Garrick, David, 146
Gaspari, Giovanni Paolo, 112–13
Gaspari, Pietro de, 112–13, *112*
Gatti-Casazza, Giulio, 228
Geddes, Norman Bel, 215, 232–34, *233*
Genga, Girolamo, 25
Geoffreys, Susanna, 78
George II, Duke (of Meiningen), 180
George VI, King (England), 220, 244
Gérôme, Jean Léon, 172
Gershwin, George, 201, *210*, 228
Gest, Morris, 233, 234
Gibbs, Wolcott, 20
Gibelli, Giuseppe, *66*
Gielgud, John, 245
Gilberti, O., *204*
Gillot, Claude, 52, 88
Gilly, Friedrich, 155
Giraudoux, Jean, 238, *240*
Glaspell, Susan, 229
Gluck, Christoph Willibald, 92–94, 136, 156, 185, 238
Godwin, Edward William, 190
Goethe, Johann Wolfgang von, 120, 130, 152, 153–54, 156, 208, *216*, 218, 220
Gogol, Nikolai, 191
Goldoni, Carlo, 18, 104, 116, 202
Golovine (artist), 192, 194, 195
Goncourt, Edmond de, 158
Gontcharova, Natalia, 199, 201–202, *201*
Gonzaga, Pietro, 100, 113–16, *115*, 121, 152, 169, 173, 191
Gonzaga family (Mantua), 23
Gould, Morton, 252
Gounod, Charles François, 165, 169, 178
Gozzi, Carlo, 116, *218*, 220
Graf, Herbert, 217–18, 250
Grahn, Mary, 10
Granovsky, Aleksey, 198
Granville Barker, H. G., 185, 234

Grapheus, Cornelius, 30
Graun, Karl Heinrich, 78, 98
Gray, Camilla, 198
Gregor, Hans, 214
Gregor, Josef, 9, 64
Grieve family, 146
Griffith, D. W., 234
Gropius, Wilhelm, 156, 162
Grosse, Helmut, 9
Guarini, Giovanni Battista, 23, 24–25, 36
Guercino, Giovanni Francesco, 57
Guitti, Francesco, 37, 43
Guthrie, Tyrone, 220

Hadamowsky, Franz, 60, 67
Hamilton, Edith, 14
Hampden, Walter, 225
Handel, George Frederick, 77
Hardy, Alexandre, 36
Harker, Joseph, 190
Harris, John, 9
Hartson (scene painter), 226
Hasenclever, Walter, 220
Hasse, Johann Adolf, 98, 117
Hauptmann, Gerhart, 111
Hayes, Helen, 244
Hearst, William Randolph, 228
Hervieu, Paul Ernest, 167
Hilmera, Jiri, 133
Hindemith, Paul, 220, 222, *222*, 238
Hitler, Adolf, 92, 220
Hobin, Franz, *166*
Hoepli, Ulrico, 174
Hofer, Philip, 9
Hoffman, Gertrude, 234
Hoffmann, Joseph, 180
Hoffmannsthal, Hugo von, 217, 223
Hogarth, William, 146
Holdberg, Ludwig, 79
Hopkins, Arthur Melancthon, 234, 236
Hopper, De Wolfe, 233
Hopper, Edward, 33
Horace, 18
Housman, Laurence, *241*
Howard, Sidney, 245
Hugo, Jean, 213
Hugo, Victor, 111, 159
Hume, Sam, 224
Humphrey, Doris, 231, 236

Ibsen, Henrik, 111
Iffland, August Wilhelm, 120, 130
Iktinos, 15
Institoris, N., 130, 134–36, *135, 136, 137*
Ionesco, Eugène, 212
Irving, Henry, 187, 188
Isaacs, Edith J. R., 233
Isabey, Jean Baptiste, 158, 180

Isocrates, 15
Ivanovitch, Andrea. *See* Roller, Andreas Leonhard

Jacques-Dalcroze, Émile, 184–85, 234
Jank, Christian, 163
Jankus, Yozac, 209–10, *210*
Jeudwine, Wynne, 98
Johnson, Philip, 11
Jomelli, Niccolò, 84
Jones, Inigo, 40–41, *41*, 155, 170, 233, 240
Jones, Robert Edmond, 12, 185, 215, 234–36, *235, 237*, 244, 249
Joseph I, Archduke (Austria-Hungary), 56
Joseph II, Emperor (Austria-Hungary), 130
Jouvet, Louis, 238
Jung, Otto, 155
Jürgens, Helmut, 222–23, *223*
Juvara, Filippo, 11, 12, 72, 75–77, *76*, 79, 80, 89, 90, 95, 96, 130, 133

Kahn, Otto, 228, 232–33
Kaiser, Georg, 220
Karl August, Duke (Weimar), 152, 153
Karl Wilhelm, Prince (Prussia), 156
Karsavina, Tamara, 195
Kean, Charles, 160
Keene, Laura, 170
Keith, Benjamin Franklin, 234
Kelder, Diane, 9, 64
Kent, William, 240
Kern, Jerome, 228
Kerr, Jean, 252
Kessler, Harry, 187
Kidd, Michael, 252
Kinderman, Heinz, 9
Kinsky, Count, 130
Kleist, Heinrich von, 214
Klimt, Gustav, 216–17
Klingemann, Ernst August, 154
Knobelsdorff, Georg Wenzeslaus, 78
Kokoschka, Oskar, 222, *222*
Komisarjevski, Theodore, 198, 200
Knopleva, M., 91
Kook, Edward, 254
Koonen, Alice, 202
Kopit, Arthur, 252
Köpp, Jean George, 109, *110*
Korenyev, 199
Korovine, Konstantin, 192–93, *193*, 194, 198, 200
Kosinski, Jan, 211
Kotzebue, August von, 130
Kozakiewicz, Stefan, 92
Kramer, Hilton, 203
Krogh, Torben, 79

Laetus, Pomponius, 24
Lajoue, Jacques de, 88–89, *89*
Laloue, Ferdinand, *166*, 167, 179
Lambert, Mrs. Phyllis, *69*
Lancret, Nicolas, 88
Landi, Antonio, 28
Landriani, Paolo, 121–24, *122, 123*, 146, 149, 173
Langner, Lawrence, 230, 231
Larionov, Mikhail, 199, 202
Laurana, Luciano da, 27
Laurencin, Marie, 213
Laurent, Michel, 36
Lautenschlager, Karl, 165
Lavastre, Antoine, 176
Lavastre, Jean-Baptiste, 159, 176–78, *176*, 179
Laver, James, 240
Le Brun, Charles, 52
Le Corbusier, 183
Ledoux, Claude-Nicolas, 158
Lee, Ming Cho, *252*, 254
Le Gallienne, Eva, 248
Léger, Fernand, 184, 204, 213
Lenin, Nikolai, 198
Lenôtre, André, 52
Leo X, Pope, 25
Leonardo. *See* Vinci, Leonardo da
Leopold I, Emperor, 50–51, 55–56, 67
Lequeu, Jean-Jacques, *157*, 158
Lert, Ernst, 222
Lessing, Gotthold Ephraim, 107, 130, 180
Levinson, André, 198
Levy, Julien, 237–38
Lewisohn, Irene, 249
Lichine, David, 238, 252
Liechtenstein, Prince, 130
Lifar, Serge, 202
Limon, José, 254
Lind, Jakov, *252*
Linnabach (designer), 215
Lippi, Filippino, 23
Liszt, Franz, 184, 228
Longhi, Pietri, 116
Lorrain, Claude, 84, 89
Lotti, Cosimo, 47–50, *47*
Louis XIII, King (France), 52
Louis XIV, King (France), 44, 52, 84, 163
Louis XV, King (France), 84, 85, 86, 89
Louis XVI, King (France), 57, 158
Loutherbourg, Philip de, 146
Lubitsch, Ernst, 220
Ludwig II, King (Bavaria), 163, 170, 180
Lulli, Giovanni Battista, 52
Lunacharsky, Anatoli, 198

Lunt, Alfred, 245

McCaull, John, 173
McClintic, Guthrie, 245, 248
Macgowan, Kenneth, 222, 249
Machiavelli, Niccolò, 24, 28
McKendry, John, 9
Maclés, Jean Denis, 213
Macready, William Charles, 160
Maffei, Scipione, 77
Maeterlinck, Maurice, 200
Mahelot, Laurent, 36
Mahler, Gustav, 217, 228
Majewski, Andrej, 211–12, *212*
Mamontov, Savva, 192
Mamoulian, Rouben, 235, 236
Mancini, Enrico, 9
Mancini, Francesco, 81
Mansart, Jules Hardouin-, 52
Mantegna, Andrea, 23, 27, 237
Marcellus, 19, 20
Mare, Walter de la, 241
Marieschi (artist), 116
Maria Casamira, Queen (Poland), 77
Mariani, Valerio, 9
Maria Theresa, Empress (Austria), 107
Marie Antoinette, Queen (France), 107
Marinetti, Emilio Filippo, 202
Marivaux, Carlet de Chamblain de, 213
Marot, Daniel, 52
Martin, J. B., 88
Martinelli (artist), 140
Martiny, Suzanne, 10
Massenet, Jules Émile, 178
Massimo family (Rome), 23
Materelli, Niccolò, *165*
Matisse, Henri, 183, 213, 229, 248
Maximilian I, Emperor (Austria), 51
Mayor, A. Hyatt, 9, 57
Mayr, Michael, 10, 124, 130, 134, 136, *140*
Mazarin, Jules, 44, 50
Mazza (artist), 140
Mazzi, Vincenzo, 95, 112, 113
Medici (artist), 96
Medici, Cosimo I de', 23, 24, 28, 32
Medici, Cosimo II de', 47
Medici, Cardinal Gian Carlo de', 46
Medici, Lorenzo de', 28
Medici, Marie de', 52
Medici family (Florence), 23, 36–37, 40, 41, 46–48
Meierhold, Vsevolod, 198, 199, 200, 204, 208, 209
Meissonier, Just Aurèle, 88
Mendelssohn, Felix, 238, *239*
Menotti, Gian-Carlo, 238
Metastasio, Antonio Domenico, 78, 80, 104

Meyerbeer, Giacomo, 165, 178
Michaels, Sidney, 252
Michelangelo, 24, 30, 79
Mielziner, Jo, 244–48, *247*, 254
Mielziner, Leo, 244
Mikhailov, L., 210
Milizia (critic), 100
Miller, Arthur, 245
Miller, Gilbert, 244
Milton, John, 241
Mitelli, Agostino, 42, 50
Mitelli, Giuseppe Maria, 50
Molière, 18, 44, 52, *194*, 196, 212, *230*, 231, *231*, 232
Molnar, Ferenc, 245
Monet, Claude, 228
Mongan, Agnes, 9
Moniglia (librettist), 46
Montemezzi, Italo, 233
Monteverdi, Claudio, 25, 37, 89
Monticelli (artist), 149
Moore, Douglas, 250
Mooser, R.-Aloys, 109
Moreau le Jeune, Louis Gabriel, 85, 89
Morelli (architect), 156
Moretti (artist), 114
Moses, Thomas G., 225–26, *227*
Moxon, Edward, 146
Moynet, Jean-Pierre, 180
Mozart, Wolfgang Amadeus, 95, 130, 134, 152, 153, 154, 156, 160–62, 165, 220, 238, 239, 250
Muellers, B., 74, *75*
Müller, Wenzel, 156
Munch, Edvard, 214
Muraro, Maria Teresa, 9, 64
Murillo, Bartolomé Esteban, 49, 169
Musorgski, Modest, 191, 195, *211*
Myers, Mary, 80
Myers, Paul, 9

Nabokov, Nicholas, 238
Nagy, Elemer, 251
Napoleon I, Emperor (France), 121, 147–48, *148*, 152, 156–58, 191
Nash, George, 9
Nathan, George Jean, 20
Naumann, Johann Gottlieb, 95
Neefe, Herman, 130, 168
Nemirovich-Dantchenko, Vladimir, 200
Nero, Emperor, 20
Neroni, Bartolomeo, 32–36, *33*
Newlin, Jeanne T., 9
Nicholas I, Czar (Russia), 114
Nicoll, Allardyce, 9
Niessen, Carl, 9
Nijinski, Waslaw, 195
Nolde, Emil, 214, 223
Noverre, Jean Georges, 84, 87, 92, 107

Nutzhorn, William, 226

Oberbeck, Arthur, 226
Obizzi, Pio Enea II, 34
Odets, Clifford, 248
Oenslager, Donald, 249–52, *250*
Olivier, Laurence Kerr, 17
O'Neill, Eugene, 224, 245, 249
Orgel, Stephen, 41
Orlandi, Francesco, 105–107, *108*
Orlandi, Stefano, 105, 112, 113
Orlik, Emil, 214, 215–16, *215*, 234
Orme, Philibert de l', 30
Orsini family (Rome), 23
Ostrovski, Aleksandr, 191
Oswald, Genevieve, 9
Ottoboni, Cardinal Pietro, 75

Pacini, Giovanni, 151, 167
Page, Ruth, 213
Paisiello, Giovanni, 104, 109
Palladio, Andrea, 23, 24, 29, 58, 115, 146, 188, 237
Panfili, Pio, 112, *112*, 113
Pannini, Giovanni Paolo, 84, 85, 116, 237
Papp, Joseph, 254
Pappini, Giovanni, 202
Parigi, Alfonso, 37, 41, 46
Parigi, Giulio, 36–40, *37*, 46, 47
Parker, H. T., 233
Parks, Melvyn, 9
Parmigianino, Mazzuoli, *29*
Parrish, Maxfield, 229
Pastor, Tony, 170
Pater, Walter, 24
Paul I, Czar (Russia), 114
Pavlova, Anna, 195, 200
Pechstein, Max, 214
Pedroni, Giovanni, 121, 149, 152
Pelagi, Pelagio, 140
Pelegrino (artist), 25
Pellandi (designer), 149
Pellegrino (artist), 77
Percier, Charles, 146, *155*, 156–58
Perecinatti (artist), 90
Perego, Giovanni, 121, 148–49, *149*, 150
Perelman, S. J., 248
Pergolesi, Giovanni Battista, 212, *212*
Peri, Jacopo, 25
Pericles, 14, 15, 23
Peroni, Filippo, 173, 175
Perugino, Il (Pietro Vannucci), 27
Peruzzi, Baldassare, 19, 23, 25, 30, 237
Peruzzi, Sallustio, 29, *29*
Peter the Great, Czar (Russia), 90
Phidias, 15, 23
Philastre, Humanité-René, 159, 160, 179
Philip II, King (Spain), 30, 220

Philip IV, King (Spain), 47
Pian, Antonio de, 134, *134*, 135, 136, 168
Piancastelli, Cavaliere Giovanni, 10, *70*
Picard, Louis Benoît, 167
Picasso, Pablo, 183, 202, 213, 229, 237, 244, 248
Piccolomini, Alessandro, 32
Pico della Mirandola, 23
Piermarini, Giuseppe, 96
Pineau (artist), 89
Pinski, David, 248
Piper, John, 244, *245*
Piranesi, Giovanni Battista, 85, 86–87, 89, 116, 121, 133, 237
Pirchan, Emil, 215
Pius VI, Pope, 116
Planché, J. R., 167, 170
Plato, 15, 24
Platzer, Josef, *94*, 124, 130-36, *131*, *132*, 146
Plautus, 18, 19, 24, 25, 232
Pliny, 19, 24
Poccetti, Bernardino, 47
Poe, Edgar Allan, 213, 241
Poelzig, Hans, 220
Poetzl (artist), 130
Poiret, Paul, 226–27
Politian, (Angelo Ambrogini), 25
Pollux, Julius, 16, 17
Polyclitus, 14
Pompadour, Madame de, 88
Pompey, 18, 19
Ponchielli, Amilcare, 174
Pope, Arthur, 9
Popoff, Alexandre, *115*
Popora (composer), 74
Post, Chandler R., 9
Poulenc, Francis, 227
Povoledo, Elena, 9, 64
Pozzo, Andrea dal, 42, 55–57, *57*, 188
Price, Vincent, 244
Primaticcio, Francesco, 30
Pronaszko, Andrzej, 211
Prosperi, Bernardino, 25
Prud'hon, Pierre-Paul, 130
Purcell, Henry, *250*, 251
Pushkin, Aleksandr, 191

Quaglio, Angelo I, 160
Quaglio, Angelo II, 160, 162–67, *165*
Quaglio, Angelo III, 92
Quaglio, Domenico II, 160
Quaglio, Eugen, 92
Quaglio, Giovanni Maria I (Giulio III), 92–94, *94*, 95
Quaglio, Giulio I, 92
Quaglio, Giulio IV, 92
Quaglio, Giuseppe, 160

Quaglio, Lorenzo I, 94–96, *94*, 106, 160
Quaglio, Simon, 160–62, 163, *163*, *165*
Quaglio family, 57, 92–96, 160–67
Quarenghi (architect), 156

Racine, Jean Baptiste, 52
Rameau, Jean Philippe, 88
Raphael, 25, 30
Rapp, Franz, 9, 57, 58, 64, 153
Rastrelli, Carlo Bartolomeo, 90
Rava, Carlo Enrico, 9
Re, Vincenzo, 74, *80*, 81–84
Reiner, Fritz, 250
Reinhardt, Max, 185, 187, 188, 195, 214, 215–16, 217, 218–20, 224, 229, 234, 248
Rembrandt, 23
Reni, Guido, 57
Repin, Ilya, 226
Ricci, Corrado, 9, 48, 66, 95, 112
"Riccio, Il." *See* Neroni, Bartolomeo
Richelieu, Cardinal, 44, 52
Righini, Pietro, 72–75, *72*, *73*, *74*, 81, 96
Rimsky-Korsakov, Nikolai, 195, 202
Ringling brothers, 234
Robert, Hubert, 86
Roberts, David, 160
Robbins, Jerome, 252
Roccaforte (composer), 98
Rodgers, Richard, 228
Roerich, Nicholas, 194, 195
Roller, Alfred, 185, 214, 215, 216–18, *216*, 228
Roller, Andreas Leonhard, 161, 168–69, *169*, *170*
Romberg, Sigmund, 228
Ronchi, Giuseppe, 175, *176*
Rosenfeld, Sybil, 147
Ross, Denman, 9
Rossi, Giuseppe, 84
Rossi, Salomone, 44
Rossini, Gioacchino Antonio, 122, 151, 165
Rosso, Il, 30
Roszkowska, Teresa, 211
Rotrou, Jean de, 36
Roubo (architect), 156
Rouché, Jacques, 185
Rousseau, Jacques, 52
Rubé, Auguste-Alfred, 178–79, *179*
Rubinstein, Ida, 195, 197

Sabbatini, Nicolo, 43, 44, 56
Sacchetti, Lorenzo, 92, 113, 116, 124, *125*, *126*, *127*, *128*, *129*, 130, 146
Sacchi, Filippo, 116
Sachs, Paul, 9
St. Denis, Ruth, 234
Saint-Saëns, Camille, 178, 179

Salieri, Antonio, 96, 130, 152
Sangallo, Aristotile da, 8, 28–29, *28*
Sanquirico, Alessandro, 113, 121, 140, 149–52, *150*, *151*, 158, 173, 175
Santayana, George, 229
Santurini, Francesco, 34, 37, 84
Saracino, Francesco, 74
Sarro, Domenico, 73
Sartre, Jean-Paul, 252
Saxon, Arthur, 179
Scamozzi, Vincenzo, 29, 58, 237
Scarlatti, Alessandro, 77
Scaurus, Aemelius, 19
Scharhan, Johann, 130
Schenk, Otto, 248
Schiffman, Byron, 213
Schiller, Johann von, 120, 152, 153, 156, *215*, 216, *217*, 220
Schinkel, Karl Friedrich, 154, 155–56, *154*, 161, *162*
Schiskov, M. A., 191–92, *192*
Schnitzler, Arthur, 228
Scholz, Janos, 10, 57, 64, 67, 68, 92, 95, 124, 133, 134
Schönberg, Arnold, *235*, 236
Schöne, Günter, 9
Schutz, Carl, 107–108, *110*
Schwarz, Maurice, 248
Scolari (composer), 98
Scopas, 14
Scribe, Augustin Eugène, 167
Scribo, Scribonius, 19
Séchan (artist), 159, 179
Selva, Antonio, 148
Serlio, Sebastiano, 19, 23, 25, 28, 30–32, *32*, 56, 58, 188, 216, 237
Serov, Aleksandr, 200
Servandoni, Giovanni Niccolò, 10, 68, 84–85, *85*, 156
Seurat, Georges, 228
Sève, Gilbert de, 44
Sforza family (Milan), 23
Shakespeare, William, 18, 36, 156, 188, *190*, *191*, 208, 214, *214*, 220, *225*, *237*, 254
Shaw, Byam, 91
Shaw, George Bernard, 111, 188, *188*, 200, 229
Shaw, Irwin, 248
Shelley, Percy Bysshe, 235
Sherwood, Robert, 245
Sievert, Ludwig, 215, 220–22, *221*, *222*
Simonson, Lee, 23, 215, 229–32, *230*, *231*, 234, 244
Sitwell, Edith, 238
Smith, Oliver, *251*, 252–54
Soby, James Thrall, 237
Socrates, 16, 17
Sodoma, Il, 32

Sokolova (critic), 210
Somov (artist), 194
Sophocles, 13, 14, 15, 17, 24
Soudeikine, Serge, 200–201, *200*
Soufflot, Jacques Germain, 158
Spender, Stephen, 244
Stalin, Joseph, 199
Stampfle, Felice, 9
Stanfield, William Clarkson, 160, *161*
Stanislavski, Constantin, 187, 188, 195, 196, 198, 200
Stein, Gertrude, 238
Stern, Ernst, 214, 215, *217*, 218–20, *218*, 234
Stokowski, Leopold, 236
Stoll, Oswald, 198
Stopka (designer), 211
Strada (antiquarian), 30
Strauss, Richard, 183, 217, 218, 220, 223, *223*
Stravinsky, Igor, 202, 212, *212*, 235, 238
Strindberg, August, 111, 218
Strnad, Oskar, 215
Strong, Roy, 41
Strong (scene painter), 226
Strozzi, Roberto, 28
Strzelecki, Zenobiusz, 211, 212
Stucchi, Stanislao, 149, 151
Suratt, Valesca, 234
Symonds, John Addington, 35

Tacca, Ferdinando, 46–47, *47*
Tacca, Pietro, 37, 46
Taglioni, Filippo, 150
Tairov, Alexandre, 200, 202–203, 204, 208
Talea, Ermalinda, 75
Talma, François Joseph, 159
Tanguy, Yves, 238
Tasso, Torquato, 24–25, 36
Tatlin, Vladimir, 199
Taylor, Baron, 159
Tchaikovsky, Pëtr Ilich, 191, *192*, *193*, *197*, 213
Tchelitchew, Pavel, 236, 238–40, *240*, *241*, *241*
Terence, 18, 19, 24, 25, 232
Terry, Ellen, 190
Tesi, Mauro, 112
Themistocles, 15
Thespis, 14
Thieme-Becker (historian), 109
Thomas, Earl of Arundel, 40

Thorvaldsen, Bertel, 141
Tiepolo, Giovanni Battista, 97
Tiepolo [Giovanni] Domenico, 116, 237
Tirtoff, Romain de (Erté), 226–28, *227*
Tolstoi, Leo, 111, 191
Torelli, Giacomo, 43–46, *43*, 48, 50, 52, 169
Toscanini, Arturo, 185
Turgenev, Ivan, *199*
Tree, Herbert Beerbohm, 190
Trubetzkoy, Prince Paul, 202
Tyler, George, 233

Unruh, Fritz von, 220
Urban, Joseph, 9, 228–29, *229*

Vacconi (artist), 149
Vakhtangov, Yevgeny, 159, 204, 208
Valentino, Rudolph, 54
Valeriani, Giuseppe, 89–91, *90*, 191
Valois, Ninette de, 244
Van Alst, Pieter Coecke, 30
Vanvitelli, Luigi, *78*, 79–81
Van Wittel, Gaspar, 79
Varro, Marcus Terentius, 24
Vasari, Giorgio, 27
Vasnetzov (artist), 192
Veinstein, André, 9
Vega, Lope de, 47, 49
Velázquez, Diego Rodriguez de Silva y, 49
Venturi, Lionello, 30
Verdi, Giuseppe, 174–75, 250
Verona, Bartolomeo da, 117–20, *121*
Veronese, Paolo, 56, 172
Vesnin (artist), 199
Vestris, Mme. (Lucia Elizabeth Mathews), 167
Viale-Ferrero, Mercedes, 9, 96, 98
Vigano, Salvatore, 124, 150
Vigarani, Gaspare, 44, 52, 84, 87, 157
Vigarani family, 157
Vignola, Giacomo da, 28, 33, 49, 56, 58, 115, 188, 237
Vimarcati (designer), 173
Vinci, Leonardo da, 23, 24, 29
Viollet-le-Duc, Eugène Emmanuel, 178
Visentini (artist), 114
Vitruvius Pollio, Marcus, 16, 19, 23–24, 25, 28, 29, 30
Vollmoeller, Karl, *218*, 220
Voltaire, 89, 157
Voskrensky, Vassili (Colonel W. De

Basil), 238
Vries, Baron de, 107
Vroubel (artist), 192

Wagner, Cosima, 184
Wagner, Richard, 8, 153, 162–63, 165, 180–82, 184, *184*, 185-87, *185*, *187*, 220, 221, 229, *229*
Wagner, Wieland, 180–81
Wakhevitch, George, 213
Wallack, Lester, 170
Walpurgis, Maria Antonia, 74
Walser, Karl, 214–15, *214*
Walter, Bruno, 220
Watteau, Jean Antoine, 88
Weber, Karl von, 165
Wedekind, Frank, 214
Weichert, Richard, 220
Weidman, Charles, 231, 236
Whistler, Laurence, 241, 244
Whistler, Rex, 240–44, *241*
White, George, 227
Wilde, Oscar, 203
Wilder, Thornton, 248
Wilfred, Thomas, 249
Willbrandt, H., 167–68, *168*
Williams, Tennessee, 245
Wilson, Francis, 233
Winckelmann, Johann Joachim, 15, 155
Witham, Charles, 172
Wittich, L. W., 156
Wolf-Ferrari, Ermanno, 95
Wolkonsky, Prince, 197
Wood, Thor, 9
Willard, Helen, 9
Wright, Frank Lloyd, 183
Wunder, Richard, 9, 57, 64, 106
Wyspianski, Stanislaw, 211

Xerxes, 13

Yates, Francis, 40
Yeats, William Butler, 188
Youmans, Vincent, 228
Yousupoff, Prince, 114

Zarra (artist), *166*, 167
Ziegfield, Florenz, 170, 226, 227, *227*, 228
Zolotaryov, N. N., 210, *211*
Zurbarán, Francisco de, 49